Steel Trails to Santa Fe

Steel Trails
to
Santa
Fe

by

L. L. Waters

UNIVERSITY OF KANSAS PRESS, LAWRENCE, KANSAS - - 1950

PRINTED IN THE U.S.A. BY
THE UNIVERSITY OF KANSAS PRESS
LAWRENCE, KANSAS

Foreword

Steel Trails to Santa Fe represents a unique and exciting undertaking for the University of Kansas. The study is the first of what we hope will be many investigations of business enterprises which have shaped the destiny of Kansas and the great Empire of the Southwest of which it is a part.

In the early spring of 1941, M. L. Lyles, assistant to the president of the Atchison, Topeka and Santa Fe Railway System, and the late Bruce Hurd, solicitor for the Santa Fe in Kansas, on behalf of the president of the Company, asked the University of Kansas to undertake a study of the Company. A comprehensive yet searching record was desired. Officials wanted a university professor to do this because they sought an authoritative work. The University of Kansas was selected as the sponsor because, among other reasons, the Santa Fe and Kansas had so much in common, in history and development. 812523

Arrangements were made with the proviso that absolute freedom be given the author to probe into every aspect of the Company, and to prepare the manuscript with complete independence. We selected L. L. Waters, of the Faculty of the School of Business, who was granted a leave of absence during the academic year 1942-1943 to gather the material. The first draft of the book was completed in the fall of 1943. The manuscript slumbered during World War II; the Santa Fe moved such an amazing volume of persons and tonnage that the book was necessarily delayed until a logical stopping place had been reached in the economic and business history of the road.

I congratulate the Santa Fe on the splendid coöperation which made the book possible, and the author for the excellence of his study. The University of Kansas welcomes the opportunity to present an important chronicle of the taming of the West.

DEANE W. MALOTT,
Chancellor,
University of Kansas.

Preface

Steel trails to Santa Fe are being used more efficiently and extensively than ever before. Research on the far-flung operations of the growing railroad had to be halted arbitrarily to prevent the gap between writing and facts from widening to unbridgeable proportions.

This book, like the Santa Fe, is the work of many. Most of the virtues and none of the vices are attributable to the late Edward J. Engel, president; Fred G. Gurley, the present chief executive of the Santa Fe; Lee Lyles, assistant to the president; F. B. Baldwin, valuation engineer; W. M. Donaldson, general accountant; the late Joseph Weidel, retired valuation engineer; H. B. Fink, treasurer; and J. R. Hubbard, Ralph Ater, and Herbert Deeming of the Department of Public Relations. Glenn D. Bradley's *Story of the Santa Fe* facilitated research on the early history. Manuscripts of the late J. F. Jarrell were especially helpful.

A thousand and one sources provided the material. All the libraries of state historical societies in the Santa Fe territory were mined. Additional work was done in the Baker Library of the Harvard Graduate School of Business Administration, the Palace of Governors in Santa Fe, the Rosenberg Library in Galveston, the Huntington Library in San Marino, the Hopkins Transportation Library at Stanford University, the Library of Congress, and the facilities of the Interstate Commerce Commission and the Association of American Railroads.

A tour of the entire system and an examination of industries served by the Company preceded the writing. A dozen part-time secretaries, mostly students at the University of Kansas, were casualties. All were efficient and loyal but graduated too soon. Shirley Snyder, Everton Doom, Frances Richert, Katherine Davis, Myrta Anderson, Joyce Seever, and Jean Murray deserve special thanks. Chancellor Deane W. Malott, Dean Frank T. Stockton, and Dean John H. Nelson were indispensable to the project. Professor C. K. Hyder of the Department of English made me happy that the manuscript was published after, rather than before, it had the advantage of his editing. Last, and most important of all, only my wife, Mary Louise, could have provided the encouragement and evidence of faith necessary for such an undertaking. This is "our" book, not "my" book.

So much effort went into its preparation that I am reminded of the economic fallacy of the labor theory of value and of the ancient comment, "The mountains will be in labor and a ridiculous mouse will be born."

L. L. WATERS

Indiana University,
August, 1950

Contents

Illustrations

PLATES

MAPS AND GRAPHS

Steel Trails to Santa Fe

Introduction

THE HISTORY OF AMERICA is a heroic story of unparalleled achievement. The passing of two centuries has recorded the greatest rags-to-riches tale of the world. Two hundred years ago the present area of the United States supported less than half a million Indians on a level precariously close to starvation. Colonists along the eastern seaboard numbered about one million. They prospered only in a relative sense while enduring innumerable privations. The ensuing years brought a degree of economic development surpassing the wildest dreams of those who sought their fortunes in the New World. Where red men had eked out a bare existence, millions of people soon resided in opulence. The gratuitous income of incompetents eventually came to represent a higher standard of living than that enjoyed by the most affluent and industrious of days gone by. The good things in life became commonplace as the Nation skyrocketed to the top in agriculture, mining, commerce, industry, and wealth. Great cities were built which surpassed the grandeur of the fabulous capitals of old. These magnificent cities were erected by men who had increasing time and money for week ends in the mountains or at the seashore. In rural areas farmers became specialists in the crop best adapted to the local physiography. Each year they added new contrivances to facilitate their work, and lush harvests from fertile soils caused many to worry lest production overwhelm consumption.

The key to the emergence of this mammoth cornucopia has been the development of a great transportation system which conquered space, time, and weather. Vast distances over the continent made progress dependent on efficient, year-around economical movement of people and products. The richest resources of the area were valueless without access to markets. Without some effective solution to the vexing problem little more than a series of neighborhood self-sufficing economic units could have emerged. Transportation was absolutely essential to division of labor and exchange. To the railroads must go the credit for making possible the transition from Robinson Crusoe methods to regional and international differentiation of production and trade. But the railroads coincidentally did more. No greater social and political influence operated to weld diverse peoples and areas together into a united nation. Railroads solved the Indian question; brought pioneers who broke the sod; hastened the Civil War; then healed its wounds; killed the buffaloes; and took the major contract for the building of the United States. To speculate on the service of the railroads to the national development, especially in areas removed from navigable water, yields imprecise results, yet the direction of the evidence is apparent. Consider for a moment the retardation of the section west of the Mississippi if railroads had never enabled the pioneers to ship more than men could carry on their backs at rates of speed faster than they could walk. Admittedly the Nation as we know it today represents the influence of many indispensable factors, none of which are any more essential than the network of steel and iron which serves every garden, farm, hamlet, and city.

THE STRUGGLE FOR IMPROVED TRANSPORTATION

The struggle of the colonists for improved means of transportation was valiant but relatively unsuccessful. The abundance of fine harbors and short but navigable rivers was of inestimable aid, yet facilities for travel and traffic by water were woefully inadequate. Prior to the Revolution, Indian and game trails provided the majority of land routes. Labor and money were too scarce to permit much road construction. By 1776 there were only three roads north and east of New York, and only one leading west from Philadelphia. They were little better than trails and were rendered utterly impassable with every rain. Streams had to be forded. Wheeled vehicles were seldom seen except in the larger cities. Travel was usually on foot or horseback. When the rivers froze in the north, goods were conveyed on sleds drawn by hand or animal power. Pack horses were frequently used. Only costly items of small bulk and light weight could stand the imposts. The cost of transporting general merchandise from Philadelphia to Lake Erie was $349 per ton and the time in transit might be weeks. Forty miles a day was excellent time in the crack coaches of the era. The blight on progress can be readily appreciated.

Men of foresight who surveyed the profusion of natural resources were determined to improve the means of transportation. Diverse solutions were attempted with favorable results, to be sure, but the improvement was insufficient. Turnpikes were decidedly better than game trails, permitting a heavy volume of traffic, yet operations could not be conducted for less than $10 a ton for every hundred miles. Grains and flour, for example, obviously could not bear the charges.

The invention of the steamboat enabled greater use of waterways and was a stimulus to trade. Rates and time were whittled along the east coast and on the Ohio and Mississippi rivers. But steamboats, remarkable as they were, could not take a crow's route along the natural channels of commerce. The eastern states sought the products of the rapidly populating Ohio Valley, but commerce was balked by the isolation of the West. Yankee ingenuity sought a panacea in canals, constructing them for hundreds of miles. The most notable of these projects was the Erie Canal, opened in 1825. The boon to commerce was enormous. Rates tumbled and volumes multiplied as hundreds of boats plied the new waterways. This development stimulated large movements of population to the United States and especially to the areas over the Appalachians. A vicious circle of cause and effect was established. Slight improvement in transportation and communication caused a disproportionately large increase in the movement of people to the West. The benefits of canal construction were significant, but traffic requirements expanded far beyond the capacity of man-made waterways. Furthermore, canals could be built only where topography acquiesced. Trade was strait-jacketed into circuitous routes. Those in the North were subject to freezing. Transportation facilities were of the fair-weather type and trade demanded, among other things, all-weather service.

EARLY RAILROADS

The need and the hope in America, as well as in Europe, was a challenge to the inventive. Men began to experiment. Embryonic railroads evolved at widely scattered points—crude but promising. Steam power quickly supplanted horses and sails. Moral prejudice against the new-fangled contraptions was brushed aside and in 1830 a new era in transportation began. Companies were quickly organized and lines projected in all directions. By 1849 New York and Chicago were linked. The effect on the economy east of the Mississippi was enormous. New England manufacturing waxed rich. The states of Ohio, Indiana, and Illinois became the larder of the Nation. The greater the prosperity, the more railroads could be built, and, in turn, the greater the prosperity. At last the major obstacle of the continent had met its master. As decades passed, substantial improvements were made in railroad technology and by 1860 relatively dependable service was offered in the East.

The history of the early railroads reveals an astounding display of fortitude, ingenuity, and tenacity. The accomplishments were many. But the later western lines were even more significant to their territory. Impediments to financing, construction, and operation elude complete revelation. Eastern railroads were built where considerable settlement had taken place. The prospects of the locale were evident. Appreciable development had taken place by utilizing the simpler means of transportation. Sources of capital were at hand even though there was difficulty in securing adequate quantities. But western lines, contemplated about the time of the Civil War, were projected in an area believed by many to be a desert. Rivers were few and unsuited for handling traffic in the manner of the East. Beyond lay rugged mountains visited only by wandering trappers and traders.

Men who linked their chances with the West were convinced that the country had potentialities worthy of development. The fertile soil was limitless in breadth, and mineral deposits were widespread. Railroads to conquer the great distances were all that seemed lacking. Given transportation, the other constituents of an empire would follow—people, houses, barns, machinery, industry and commerce. Railroads became the pioneers of the West, paving the way for the sodbusters who built great states.

The story of the first transcontinental railroad has often been told. This book records the development of the second great continental bridge of steel. The Atchison, Topeka and Santa Fe pioneered in the southwest quadrant of the Nation. The new line was derisively said "to start nowhere and go nowhere." It left the vigorous little towns in eastern Kansas and stretched westward toward historic Santa Fe. Only nomadic Indians and buffaloes were on hand to dispute the right of way. The difficulties of financing would have balked any less resolute than the indomitable men who guided the venture. Somehow each problem was met and solved. Eventually the line touched the Pacific, the Gulf of Mexico, and Lake Michigan. Towns were organized, settlers were brought from as far as Russia, and the economy was given a healthy start. The population multiplied into millions and the Southwest moved to the fore as an influence in the affairs of the Nation.

Three-fourths of a century ago heavy wagons wormed over the old Santa Fe Trail. The oxen failed to share the anxiety of the bullwhackers, and the mules were by nature oblivious of the muleskinners. Rates were high and delivery was problematical. Today, freight moves over new trails of steel for a penny a ton mile. Delivery can be made in Santa Fe before the wagons could have advanced a dozen miles out of old Independence. Passengers leaving Kansas City at the same time as a wagon train of old could go to California and return to meet their forerunners at a point about forty miles from the beginning.

This great Southwest, as we know it today, is in large measure the natural result of the spectacular developments in western transportation. The story of the Santa Fe became the story of the Southwest.

I

Preparing the Seedbed

"Open the Atlas, conned by the rule
To the olden days in the district school,
Point to this rich and beauteous land
That yields such fruit to the toiler's hand.
Treeless desert they called it then,
Haunted by beasts and forsook by men."
—Kansas City *Star,* October 27, 1912.

Long before Cyrus K. Holliday planted the seed of the Santa Fe the Nation was preparing the soil for the Company. The tools were varied, but in the course of many years the spadework was thoroughly done. Incorporation in 1859 came after much history which had fundamentally influenced the conception and destiny of the enterprise. The roots of Atchison, Topeka and Santa Fe lay deep in the slavery controversy; gold rushes to California and Colorado; national clamor for a transcontinental railroad; struggles in Kansas for statehood; commerce over the Santa Fe Trail; rivalry of the United States with Mexico; subjugation of warring Indians; and the omnipotent desire to develop the resources of the country.

The "Forty-niners"

With discovery of gold in California in 1848 thousands of "forty-niners" began their famous rush. Some went overland across the continent; others sailed to Panama, crossed the Isthmus, and journeyed up the Coast; and still others rounded the Horn. The most magnetic of riches demanded better access. Californians began to lobby in Washington for action and rail results. Uncle Sam was warned that the Pacific Coastal area might fall into the hands of some enemy or be an independent country unless a transcontinental railroad was built. Financial support by the Government was essential. But members of Congress were more concerned with another aspect of the situation. The North and South stew was just short of the boiling point, and political implications of the proposed line were one more cause for controversy. If built from the South to California, the railroad would make more slave states; if built from a northern point, more free. Both sides were diehards. The organization of Kansas and the eventual emergence of the Santa Fe were profoundly conditioned by the ensuing political struggle over the route to the Pacific.

SLAVERY AND WESTERN RAILROADS

When Missouri was admitted to statehood, slavery was prohibited forever in the remainder of the Louisiana Purchase north of parallel 36° 30'. The present area of Kansas and Nebraska was therefore aligned with the North. Attempts of Iowa and Illinois leaders to further the cause of a centrally located transcontinental railroad quickly led to an impasse. The proposed route obviously would be north of the line drawn in the Compromise. No Southerner would ever support a project which would aggrandize free states and swing the balance of power more in favor of the North. Missourians, out to protect local interests, were exceptions and supported a central road originating in Missouri. Some plan had to be worked out to secure the approval of the South before a line west of Missouri or Iowa could materialize. Stephen A. Douglas, the great compromiser of Illinois, reasoned that southern leaders would assent to a central route if the rigid language of the Missouri Compromise were not applied. He professed no intent to repeal the Compromise but merely desired to make an exception and apply the rule of popular sovereignty which had been adopted for New Mexico and Utah in the Compromise of 1850. Douglas proposed to split the controversial area into two parts, Kansas and Nebraska, thus establishing the possibility of a Pacific route through each one. The bait for the Southerners lay in prospects for making Kansas a slave state. In the course of the Congressional

battle the Missouri Compromise was repealed, to the joy of the
Southerners, and popular or squatter sovereignty established for
statehood in the two newly created territories. Debate in Congress
tended to lose sight of the motive which had influenced the initi-
ating group. The whole effect was to intensify the bitterness over
the slavery issue. But Kansas, as such, was born for railroads.

The Kansas-Nebraska Act (1854), as the measure was called,
was hoped by its proponents to be unprovocative. As everyone
knows, the opposite was true. The Act was a signal for a free-for-
all. The real Civil War began immediately. For several years the
struggle raged within the confines of Kansas, which the South
expected to win, though it had no illusions about winning Nebraska. Antislavery organizations in the North were horrified at the
easy access of Missourians to the new territory. Abolitionist groups,
largely in New England, hastily began to form emigrant aid societies to facilitate the settlement of Kansas by free-state people.
Kansas Jayhawkers made raids in Missouri in retaliation for the
murder and pillage by the guerrillas from Missouri, or was it vice
versa? Both factions engaged in reciprocal bloodletting in "bleed-
ing Kansas." Thousands of dollars' worth of property was destroyed, and many were killed. Finally the free-state group gained
political ascendancy, and on January 29, 1861, the United States
Senate passed the bill admitting Kansas on a free basis as provided
in the Wyandotte Constitution. On the same day Jefferson Davis
and others resigned from the Senate, thereby removing the political impediments to transcontinental lines. The Pacific Railroad
had become an important factor in the influx of people into Kansas. Many of the early leaders of both sides took an active part in
the formation of the Santa Fe Railroad.

POLITICAL FACTORS

Apart from sectionalism there had been constitutional objections to any federal role in a transcontinental line. Many thought
that government participation was contrary to the Constitution,
yet all agreed that private enterprise could not carry out the ven-

ture unaided. Prospects for profits seemed too remote to draw capital. Some public men believed that the project was not economically sound even in the long run, because of the many mountains and deserts, involving heavy construction and maintenance costs, with no hope for traffic originating between the eastern and western extremities. Despite the many differences of opinion some important steps were taken. In 1853 the United States made the Gadsden purchase, thereby acquiring land deemed essential to an extreme southern route. During the same year Congress appropriated $150,000 "to ascertain the most practical and economical route for a railroad from the Missouri River to the Pacific Ocean." Five surveys were made of routes along the forty-fifth, forty-second, thirty-seventh, thirty-fifth, and thirty-second parallels. On the whole the exhausting reports were favorable but the battle raged unabated. Partisanship was as pronounced as ever. Senator Thomas H. Benton, an exponent of a central route, described the territory between El Paso and California as so sandy, sterile, and desolate that a "wolf could not make his living." Hon. Z. Kidwell in a dissenting opinion of the Select Committee appointed on February 21, 1856, to investigate the practicability of one or more western roads branded the route eventually taken by the Union Pacific as the limit in folly:

> So with a train of cars running up the plain from Iowa or Missouri to the foot of the Rocky Mountains, a distance of some 800 miles, how, in a storm, is shelter or wood, or water or food to be gained? Arrested 800 miles from Iowa in November, how is a train of cars to be relieved before May? By what means could it even be visited? In such a case the sheltering skill would be useless. To talk of doing business in the winter season on a road through such a region, though every conductor was a Kit Carson and every traveller a Fremont, would seem to be idle and preposterous.[1]

Kidwell spoke of conditions in winter. If he had spoken of conditions in summer, the intervening 800 miles would have been described as desert. The belief was widespread that Kansas, Nebraska, and points west were uninhabitable notwithstanding the fact that people were already settling in those areas.

Pressure for the road grew during the 'fifties. Many spoke of the benefits which would accrue from trade with the Orient. The United States would soon match knots with England as a maritime and commercial power. Thomas H. Benton used to point dramatically to the West and exclaim, "There is the East; there is India."

Numerous local influences pressed increasingly for the transcontinental line or any other lines. The West and Middle West needed transportation just as the East had needed it a few years before. In 1857 the Atchison and California Stage Coach Line offered one-way tickets between the Missouri River and California for $200. Time, thirty-five days not including optional stopovers. If a passenger took advantage of the privilege he had to wait until there was a vacant seat before reboarding. Twenty-five pounds of baggage was carried free and any surplus at fifty cents per pound. The Company advertised good meals at three dollars each. It assumed no responsibility for anything done to passengers by Indians or desperadoes. With the spreading of settlers on the prairies and the trek of migrants across the land, another cogent argument appeared for the Pacific Road. Indian depredations were frequent and never underpublicized. The tribesmen were a menace that should be liquidated. A limited number of soldiers had been unable to safeguard the palefaces from the redskins (and the redskins from the palefaces). The way to solve the Indian question, other than to kill the varmints, was to build railroads. This would bring settlers who would kill off the game and leave the Indians without sustenance. If the Indians objected and elected to fight, the railroads would enable the Government to rush strong forces to the vicinity to eliminate the difficulties in what a contemporary pun called "attackful" manner.

The Santa Fe Trail and Its Commerce

Not everyone in Kansas and Missouri busied himself fighting in preliminaries to the Civil War. Thousands carried on farming and trade, as unmindful as possible of the doings of their neighbors. A large number of the latter were engaged in the lucrative and dangerous commerce with New Mexico over the famous Santa Fe Trail. Kansas had long been a part of a great highway to riches, adventure, and hardship.

As early as 1540-1541 Francisco Vasquez de Coronado traversed a portion of the route eventually followed by the caravans of the Santa Fe Trail and the rails of later days. The great conquistador came from Mexico searching for the fabulous Seven Cities of Cibola with their golden streets and jewel-studded houses. Poignantly disappointed, Coronado returned to Mexico to face the wrath of the Viceroy. The passing of years brought a reversal of the verdict on the outcome of the exploration. A great territory had been claimed for Spain—a territory which in the end yielded much wealth even though some of it was in other forms than gold. In 1598 Don Juan de Onate established La Ciudad de la Santa Fe de San Francisco (City of the Holy Faith of St. Francis). The outpost, generally known as Santa Fe, became the seat of government and trade in the Spanish Territory of New Mexico. Here missionaries labored zealously among recalcitrant Indians. Adventurers came who sought fortunes in the rich mineral resources which were soon uncovered. Development of the area was halted about 1680, when the Indians scourged the Spanish settlements and laid waste to Santa Fe. Thirteen years later Don Diego de Vargas triumphantly re-entered Santa Fe and restored Spanish domination. During the ensuing century infiltration from Spain and Mexico continued steadily. Commerce expanded. Military control was made more secure but not so secure that the period could be described as anything other than hectic and turbulent.[2] Provisioning New Mexico was at best extremely costly and unsatisfactory. The economy about Santa Fe was largely pastoral and extractive. The Spanish relied wholly on the outside world for many of those things which differentiated civilized life from Indian life. All the niceties and essentials had to come over long and tenuous routes from seaports far to the south. Likewise the means of payment had to be transported over the same routes. Difficulties were such that the cheapest calicoes commanded prices of several dollars a yard. What a market if only it were not so remote!

Knowledge of prices in the Spanish territory was not long spreading to Yankee merchants. One glance at any crude map of 1800 which showed the Mississippi Valley and Santa Fe was enough to make a profit-seeker murmur, "I wonder."* William Morrison of Kaskaskia was one of the first to act. He outfitted Baptiste La Lande, supplied him with a stock of goods, and requested a report on marketing conditions in New Mexico. La Lande blithely forgot Morrison and set out for Santa Fe, arriving in the late summer or early fall of 1804. The market was good and the señoritas were most attractive. Besides, the Indians might cause trouble on the way back. La Lande's decision to stay obviated action on the part of Spanish traders whose interests were inimical to overland commerce with outposts of the United States. During the following summer another trader arrived in Santa Fe. He was James Pursley, an itinerant trader, trapper, and, later, carpenter. Like La Lande, Pursley happily decided to stay.

Captain Zebulon M. Pike gave the first authentic reports of conditions and trade opportunities with the Southwest. On July 15, 1806, Pike left the vicinity of St. Louis, striking westward.† He was to promote peace among some of the Indian tribes whose roaming grounds were in the Louisiana Purchase of 1803. He was also to make a report on the direction, extent, and navigability of the Arkansas and Red rivers. Historians believe, too, that Pike had an "off-the-record" order to meander into Spanish territory. While in winter encampment near the present site of Alamosa, Colorado, Pike was visited by a contingent of Spanish Dragoons under Lieutenant Salcedo. Being outnumbered six to one, Pike

---

*As early as 1739 a small party led by the Mollet brothers journeyed from the French settlements on the Mississippi to Santa Fe. A trading expedition to the vicinity north of Santa Fe was carried out in 1763 by some Frenchmen. They were imprisoned for a time until a decision was reached that trading operations were within the territory of Louisiana. No more trade stemmed from either pioneering journey.

†About the same time five hundred members of the Spanish militia and one hundred Dragoons under the command of Don Facundo Meigares left Santa Fe to explore territory to the northeast, just as Pike left to survey the Southwest—a little poaching on each side.

and his men agreed to accompany Salcedo to Santa Fe under friendly duress. General Alencaster, the Governor, ordered the invaders marched to Chihuahua in Mexico. En route Pike was greatly impressed with the immensity of the caravans that journeyed from the remote southern provinces to Santa Fe. Shortly after reaching Chihuahua, Pike and his followers were examined by the military commandant and released. The party was given an escort back to the United States, entering at Natchitoches, Louisiana, July 1, 1807. In a report to Henry Dearborn, Secretary of War, Pike declared that Mexico (including New Mexico) surpassed all other countries of the world "for riches in gold and silver, producing all the necessaries of life and most of the luxuries." Further in the report was contradictory evidence to the effect that good cloth sold for twenty-five dollars a yard and linen at four, indicating a lack of some necessities but a booming market.

News of Pike's report percolated slowly to the West notwithstanding the magic speed of the grapevine. In 1812 Robert McKnight, Samuel Chambers, James Baird, and others traversed the route laid out by Pike. They were arrested on arrival, their goods were confiscated, and they were then given an indefinite number of years for meditation in the prisons of Chihuahua and Durango. Liberation came in 1821 with the independence of Mexico. Other attempts were made to carry on the overland trade between 1812 and 1821, but the Spanish reception of them was hardly more cordial than the one given McKnight, Chambers, and Baird. Trade apparently was impossible as long as New Mexico was subject to the despised Spanish authorities. But with Mexican independence in 1821, the door was at least capable of being opened. First to take advantage of the change was Captain William Becknell of Missouri. Accompanied by a few friends, Becknell converted an Indian trading expedition of 1821 into the first successful commerce with Santa Fe. A small stock of goods was very advantageously traded. The route taken passed the present site of Kansas City and veered southwest by Council Grove to the

Arkansas River. The latter was followed around the great bend along the north bank to the present site of La Junta. The trail proceeded southward to the Purgatoire River, over the Raton and Glorieta Mountains, and entered Santa Fe from the southeast. Becknell was well aware in 1821 that he had taken two legs of a triangle. The next year he decided on the hypotenuse. The point of deviation from the old route was about five miles west of the future Dodge City. The new course held horrible suffering for the intrepid band. At the end of two days all canteens were dry and the arid land stretched on and on without a sign of relief. The scorching sun bore down relentlessly. In desperation the men killed their dogs and cut off the ears of their mules to slack their unbearable thirst. Mirages, curses of the desert, goaded the sufferers incessantly. Just as the frantic party was about to attempt to retrace their steps from the Arkansas River, one of them came upon a buffalo.

The hapless intruder was immediately dispatched and an invigorating draught procured from its stomach. I have since heard one of the parties to that expedition declare that nothing ever passed his lips which gave him such exquisite delight as his first draught of that filthy beverage.[3]

Reasoning that the buffalo would not have had so much water unless a river were nearby, the leaders ordered a reconnaissance. The men soon found water, but only in the nick of time. The expedition was able to continue and, if Becknell's word can be taken against Gregg's, reached Santa Fe by way of San Miguel. The course taken by Becknell became known as the "Cimarron" or "dry route." Most of its horrors were eliminated with the knowledge Becknell furnished of what lay in store. Successors, divided mainly between the bold and the less bold (not timid), used both ways.

Commerce over the trail developed rapidly. Franklin, a river town in central Missouri, became the outfitting point. From Franklin proceeded Marmaduke, St. Vrain, the Bents, Kit Carson, and many other stalwarts of the prairies and mountains. As trade expanded and navigation on the Missouri extended, the outfitting

point moved west. Blue Mills, Wayne City, Fort Osage, and Independence, especially the latter, became the eastern termini. Still
later Westport (now part of Kansas City) captured the business.
By 1850 the "Town of Kansas," Kansas City, was the leader. The
vast amount of commerce in these mushroom frontier towns and
the thousands of migrants presented a scene of wild confusion—
especially during the trading season. Little commerce was carried
on in the winter even after F. X. Aubrey had made the first successful midwinter journey in 1848-1849. Peaceful and temporarily
peaceful Indians mingled freely with the whites. Francis Parkman, the noted author, wrote in 1846:

> Westport was full of Indians, whose little, shaggy ponies were tied by
> dozens along the houses and fences. Sacs and Foxes, with shaved heads and
> painted faces; Shawnees and Delawares fluttering in calico frocks and tur-
> bans; Wyandots dressed like white men, and a few wretched Kanzas wrapped
> in old blankets, were strolling about the streets, or lounging in and out of
> the shops and houses. . . . Whiskey, by the way, circulates more freely in
> Westport than is altogether safe in a place where every man carries a loaded
> pistol in his pocket.[4]

The surrounding country was largely devoted to the production of provisions for the traders. Oxen and mules were raised for
the caravans. As time went on, oxen were favored more and more.
Breeders of riding mules and horses found an excellent market.
Requirements of flour, beans, corn, and bacon were heavy. The
merchants found coffee, salt, and sugar much in demand by the
traders. These same merchants ordinarily sold all the merchandise
for the trade in Santa Fe.

Once the bold entrepreneur had acquired provisions and goods,
loaded them on his prairie schooner, and hitched up his teams or
yokes, he was ready to "hit the trail." Little effort was made to
travel in caravans during the first part of the journey. The Indians
in this area during the 'thirties contemplated nothing worse than
the theft of anything available. Beyond Council Grove there was
safety in numbers. Council Grove consequently became a rendezvous for those on the great route to Santa Fe. Also this was the

last point where good wood for repairs and spare parts could be obtained. Here the quasi-military organization of the prairie train was established. As the caravan proceeded from the Grove, those in command took every precaution for security from Indians. In spite of this, members of the party often strayed, never to return. Small prairie trains were frequently objects of attack. Indians lifted many scalps and destroyed or stole much goods. Santa Fe was usually triumphantly reached in eighty or ninety days.

> The arrival produced a great deal of bustle and excitement among the natives. *"Los Americanos!"*—*"Los carros!"*—*"La entrada de caravana!"* were to be heard in every direction, and crowds of women and boys flocked around to see the newcomers while crowds of *"leperos"* hung about, as usual, to see what they could pilfer. The wagoners were by no means free from excitement on this occasion. Informed of the "ordeal" they had to pass, they had spent the previous night in "rubbing up"; and now they were prepared with clean faces, sleek-combed hair, and their choicest Sunday suit to meet the "fair eyes" of glistening black that were sure to stare at them as they passed. There was yet another preparation made to show off to advantage. Each wagoner must tie a brand new cracker to the lash of his whip; for on driving through the streets and the *"plaza publica"* everyone strives to outvie his comrades in the dexterity with which he flourishes this favorite badge of his authority.[5]

The goods, largely cottons, were then deposited in the ware-rooms of the custom house and negotiations were begun to circumvent the onerous tariffs by bribery. Evasion by smuggling and other sharp practices prevailed. In the course of time many residents of New Mexico entered in the trade and waxed equally rich. A venture that netted only ten per cent was disappointing. Commerce tended to be one way. Many of the wagons and teams were sold in Santa Fe or returned without a cargo. Eastbound traffic consisted of gold, silver, wool, blankets, and furs.

From small-scale commerce, the Santa Fe Trail swelled to great proportions owing to the advent of the railroads. Indicative of the trend is an extract from the table prepared by Dr. Josiah Gregg,[6] showing the value of merchandise traded in Santa Fe and Chihuahua and carried over the trail.

Year	Santa Fe	Wagons	Men	Traders	Chihuahua
1825	$ 65,000	37	130	90	$ 5,000
1830	120,000	70	140	60	20,000
1835	140,000	75	140	40	70,000
1840*	50,000	30	60	5	10,000
1843	450,000	230	350	30	300,000

From 1843 to 1846, during the controversy between the United States and Mexico, President Santa Anna enforced an embargo on trade with the Territory. Commerce was resumed after General Stephen W. Kearney led the Army of the West into Santa Fe, August 16, 1846. The volume of traffic in the same year was the greatest to that date. Dr. David Waldo made the following estimate: cost of goods, $937,500; cost of outfits and operating expenses, $414,750; profit, $400,000; wagons, 375; mules, 1700; oxen, 2000; and men, 500.[7] Over 500 wagons started from Kansas City in 1850. Goods valued at $5,000,000 were transported in 1855. In 1860, 16,439,000 pounds of merchandise required 9,084 men, 147 mules, 27,920 oxen, and 3,033 wagons. By 1866 the physical requirements had almost doubled over those of 1860. Between 5,000 and 6,000 wagons swept over the plains.[8]

The continued increase in commerce with Santa Fe gave hope of success to those who contemplated railroads in 1850 and 1860. What a plum to pluck! In the meantime other fruit had ripened and awaited the picker. Thousands of people were going to California and a considerable proportion went by way of Santa Fe. One and all would no doubt have gone by rail with their possessions had a railroad been in existence. A heavy stream of people and supplies flowed west over Kansas, as well as Nebraska, following the significant discovery of gold in Colorado in 1858. It was "Pike's Peak or Bust" and more potential traffic for railroads.

WESTERN NEEDS

After 1857 cattle drivers from Texas to Kansas City and beyond gave more encouragement to railroad enthusiasts. Migration

*Trade in 1839 amounted to $250,000 with Santa Fe and $100,000 in Chihuahua.

to Kansas from 1855 to 1861 had converted eastern Kansas into a settled area. The population had increased from 8,600 to 143,000. Kansas needed railroads at home. Most of the settlers were sodbusters and soon had produce that needed access to markets. Nature had not endowed Kansas with navigable waterways, hence the greater urgency of rails. The Territorial Legislature was cooperative. Perhaps the reason was that most of the members were financially interested in the railroads. Oddly enough, there was not the political conflict which characterized railroad matters in Washington. In Kansas abolitionists and proslavery advocates shelved differences in order to incorporate railroads. The seed of the Santa Fe, for example, was sown by leaders of both groups. Railroads were incorporated as early as 1855. In 1857 fifteen were created by the Legislature. They went in all directions. Each road was the pet project of an ambitious town. Atchison, Leavenworth, Lawrence, and Topeka were alternately working for or against one another and for or against Kansas City and St. Joseph. One of the prospective lines was the St. Joseph and Topeka Railroad. Included among its directors was Cyrus K. Holliday, who was to be the progenitor of the Atchison, Topeka and Santa Fe. According to a circular the future held great promise for the St. Joseph and Topeka.

The greater part of the route is over an ordinarily level country, unsurpassed in fertility, and much resembling the interior part of Missouri, through which the Hannibal and St. Joseph is located. The supply of timber is about equal and that of stone much better. There is ground for anticipating that such a road would yield a large percentage on the money invested in its construction, and that it can be built at less than the average cost.

But the greatest object to be secured at present by this enterprise, is the trade to Santa Fe and New Mexico, which is annually very considerable, and will richly reward the earliest railroad communication that may be extended in that direction. This trade is increasing yearly, and is composed mainly of the manufactures of the Middle and Eastern states; all of which, in the event of railroad communication west and south of St. Joseph, must pass over roads leading from the East to that place, affording them, in itself, a source of revenue by no means inconsiderable.[9]

Residents of Topeka and St. Joseph were not the only ones appraising the traffic possibilities of Kansas and the route to Santa Fe. Kansas Citians were in self-defense contemplating substantially the same route. They were bolstered by Captain J. W. Gunnison's highly favorable report on construction west to Colorado as well as by the accounts of western notables such as Bridger, Carson, Frémont, and Gilpin. More than a dozen railroads to Santa Fe were considered seriously enough to be discussed by the early newspapers. The seedbed had been prepared for the sprouting of the Atchison, Topeka and Santa Fe Railroad.

II

Trials and Tribulations of An Acorn

"It is true, as yet, we have only charters, but there never was a railroad built without a charter—so we have at least taken the first step."*

PROMOTERS ARE A SPECIAL BREED OF MEN. Their minds work differently from the minds of others. Promoters have more imagination and, like a great composer, they have an unstemmable urge to put ideas into something tangible. Establishing a business is a "must." Economists have long recognized the existence of the promotional type. Such a person is able to perceive opportunities for profit before his associates. Possessed of no stick-in-the-mud characteristics, he burns with zeal to establish ventures. Persistence, enthusiasm, and persuasive personality usually enable the promoter to interest a "favored few." The enterprise often dies before birth, but sometimes the promoter overcomes the inertia of conservatives and succeeds in launching the business for better or for worse. Regardless of what develops after the business is established, the promoter commonly withdraws. The normal operations of the going concern are much too prosaic to hold his attention. So many other situations await a challenger.

Cyrus K. Holliday, father of the Santa Fe, typified the promotional bent in its most productive form. Early in life he attained a degree of success in the East, yet he elected for inexplicable rea-

---

*Address of R. T. Van Horn, editor of the Kansas City *Journal,* December 24, 1857, "Railroads and the Press—Twin Brothers in American Progress and Development."

sons to pull up stakes and go west.* Arriving in Kansas in 1854, Holliday tarried in the free-state stronghold of Lawrence. There he laid plans with recent acquaintances to establish a new town. On December 5, 1854, a desirable site was found on the banks of the Kaw twenty-five or thirty miles west of Lawrence. A cabin had already been built in the vicinity by four of the nine organizers. The initial meetings of the town fathers proceeded with as much dignity as the speaker's chair, a sack of flour, permitted. Holliday rallied to the cause while temporary articles of association were drawn. Most of the members took up residence on the premises. A few days later the whole town was destroyed when

---

*Cyrus Kurtz Holliday was born at Kidderminster, Pennsylvania, April 3, 1826. He was educated in the common schools at Carlisle and was graduated from Allegheny College at Meadville in 1852. Alumni records show that Holliday also received a master's degree in 1855 from Allegheny, although it is known that he went to Kansas in 1854. Concerning his business career in Pennsylvania, Mrs. Louise K. Smithies, a granddaughter, wrote in a letter dated November 2, 1942: ". . . after finishing his law course, he expected it would be some time before he could make much money in his practice, so was agreeably surprised when the men who were planning to build a small railroad through Meadville called upon him and asked him to draw up the necessary legal papers. They had gone to Holliday as they thought he would not charge them as much as an older man. He readily undertook the commission but after the men had left and he studied the proposed route for the road, he realized the tremendous possibilities of the short line, for it would almost connect with a much more important system and would therefore be of great value. He therefore asked for a partnership in the venture, in lieu of the regular fee, and this was agreed upon. It all worked out as Holliday had foreseen and in a very short time, the small road had been purchased by the larger one. When the proceeds of the sale had been divided, Holliday was the proud possessor of $20,000 as his share, and it was this money which made it possible for him to migrate to Kansas.

"It has been difficult to find accurate information as to the names of the two roads but to the best of my knowledge the smaller one was the Pittsburgh & Erie, sometimes known as the Meadville line and the larger one was almost certainly the Atlantic & Great Western, of New York, Pennsylvania, and Ohio."

Holliday, notwithstanding this successful transaction, felt that opportunities were too limited in Pennsylvania to provide an outlet for his ambitions. In the autumn of 1854 at the age of 28, he migrated to Kansas, leaving his wife to follow. Almost immediately his natural ability to lead asserted itself in elections to innumerable posts of responsibility in the Territory. Holliday was elated with the land and his success. On Christmas Eve of 1854 he wrote his wife of his exploits, observing that ". . . it proves what I have often said to you—that I could do nothing at Meadville but let me go off and try my hand among a new people and under different influences and I could pursue a different course of action."

Holliday not only took the leading part in the founding of Topeka but was its first mayor. He held numerous local and state positions.

Association with the Santa Fe extended more than forty years. He was a director from September 17, 1860, to July 27, 1865, and again from September 24, 1868, to March 27, 1900. He was president from September 17, 1860, to January 13, 1864, and then secretary to August 19, 1865.

Colonel Holliday was for a long time president of the Excelsior Gas and Coke Company and the Merchants' National Bank. His scholarship was recognized by election to the presidency of the Kansas State Historical Society.

sparks from the chimney ignited the thatch on the roof and leveled the cabin. Topeka seemed already to possess great recupera-
tive powers, and soon people were attracted to the magnificent
site close to the great trails of the West. Within fifteen months the
first three-story skyscraper was begun. By 1859 Topeka was a
bustling western town of 1200.

Although Holliday was impressed with Kansas at first sight,
he made a complete survey of the West before settling permanently. He was able to report that "after having traveled over Illinois, Indiana, Michigan, Iowa, Wisconsin, Minnesota, and Nebraska and Missouri, I am prepared to say that Kansas exceeds
them all in point of true excellence." Political affairs of the young
Republican party and the slavery struggle occupied much of Holliday's attention. Although he speculated in real estate and did
some farming, 1854 to 1859 was a period of deficit financing. The
original nest egg of Leghorn proportions began to resemble more
and more a Bantam's creation which had been placed in cold
storage. Holliday's wealth, in short, was in frozen assets of little
current value but with great potentialities. A mere lack of money,
however, did not deter him from planning to establish the most
costly business of the time.

From the date of his migration to the land of uncertainty,
Holliday was actively interested in promoting railroads. Nor did
they all go in the direction of Santa Fe; some did. Although for
several reasons the time was propitious for railroads, the obstacles
were of the sort that daunted all but the bravest and most visionary. Holliday, bold among the bold, proceeded unflinchingly. He
would sponsor a railroad himself. Of course the railroad would
serve Topeka and would connect with some logical city to the east.
Holliday had already been a lesser light in a road to St. Joseph
which was not faring well. Kansas City and Independence gave
some promise as did Leavenworth, but Atchison gave the most
hope. From the very first Holliday contemplated Santa Fe as an
objective to the west. Subsequent steps are best told by him:

I wrote the charter, every word, line, paragraph and section, near the close of the legislative session of 1859, at Lawrence, and had the whole thing complete except filling in the names of the incorporators, in the first section, before any person was aware that such a charter was being prepared. I then advised Mr. Challis as to the names to be selected from the Atchison end of the line, I suggesting the names of General Pomeroy and Mr. Challis as two of the incorporators from Atchison, and he, in turn, suggesting my name as one of the incorporators from Topeka.

The charter was not written until nearly three-fourths of the time allotted for the session had expired. It was then written and introduced by myself into the council on Tuesday, the first day of February, 1859 (the session began on Monday, January 3). The next day, Wednesday, February 2, all rules were suspended and the Bill passed the council and was sent to the house of representatives. And on the last day of the session, February 11, the bill was returned to the council by Governor Medary with his approval.*

General incorporation laws had not been established at the time, hence the necessity for a special act of legislature. Among other things the charter provided:

That S. C. Pomeroy, C. K. Holliday, Luther C. Challis, Peter T. Abell, Milton C. Dickey, Asaph Allen, Samuel Dickson, Nelson L. Gordon, Geo. S. Hillyer, Lorenzo D. Bird, Jeremiah Murphy, Geo. H. Fairchild and F. L. Crane, with such other persons as may associate with them for that purpose, are hereby incorporated a body politic and corporate, by the name of the 'Atchison and Topeka Railroad Company'. . . .

The said company is hereby authorized and empowered to survey, locate, construct, complete, alter, maintain and operate a railroad, with one or more tracks, from or near Atchison, on the Missouri River, in Kansas Territory, to the town of Topeka, in Kansas Territory, and to such point on the southern or western boundary of the said Territory, in the direction of Santa Fe, in the Territory of New Mexico, as may be convenient and suitable, for the construction of such railroad; and, also to construct a branch of said railroad to any points on the southern boundary of said Territory of Kansas in the direction of the Gulf of Mexico.

Other provisions of the unusually lucid and interesting charter are reproduced in Appendix A. Although the capitalization was

---

*From a letter of Holliday to the Atchison *Globe,* July 23, 1891, refuting a newspaper article which credited Luther Challis with siring the Santa Fe. As time passed, dozens of fathers of the Santa Fe put in appearances. If they had not openly organized the Company, then they were the power behind the throne. There is no doubt that Holliday was the author of the charter and the early moving force. There were others, however, whose contributions were essential to the successful establishment of the Company.

set at $1,500,000, a payment of $5,000 on $50,000 in stock subscriptions was all that was necessary for organization of the Company. Since many of the names of the incorporators were included for qualifying purposes, several of the men took no further roles in the affairs of the Company. Asaph Allen, Samuel Dickson, Nelson L. Gordon, George S. Hillyer, and Jeremiah Murphy were among the temporary prestige-lenders. New names representing keen interests were attracted to the enterprise: E. G. Ross, publisher of the *Kansas Tribune,* a free-state paper, and later senator from Kansas and governor of New Mexico; Joel Huntoon, already a leader in Kansas; Jacob Safford, a new district judge; R. H. Weightman, ex-attorney general of Missouri; and J. H. Stringfellow, an Atchison leader with great influence and editor of *Squatter Sovereignty.* Those who carried through with Holliday from the start were: L. C. Challis, Atchison leader who later bulled his way to ephemeral riches in Wall Street; P. T. Abell, president of the Atchison Town Company; S. C. Pomeroy, ex-agent of the New England Emigrant Aid Society, political figure and future senator from Kansas; L. D. Bird, Yale law graduate and prominent Atchison lawyer; Dr. F. L. Crane of Topeka, financial contributor to countless railroads and industrial enterprises in Kansas; and M. C. Dickey, already a well-known leader in affairs of the Territory. All these men were well educated and were recognized as makers of history. It is remarkable that men of such diametrically opposing political views should coöperate in any venture. Challis and Stringfellow were especially active in support of slavery in Kansas, while others were allied with the abolitionists. Business makes strange bedfellows.

Holliday achieved no more progress with his brain child during 1859 in Kansas. A drought of virtually unequaled proportions prevailed over the Territory beginning in June, 1859, and lasted until November of 1860. Records show that the heaviest shower during the period did not penetrate two inches below the surface. "During the whole period there the roads were never muddy, and in the summer the ground would break open in great cracks, making it difficult for wagons to pass for fear the thin wheels would drop into them, while the winds blew with a burning parching sirocco blast from the south, and with hot beams from an unclouded sun, parched the soil and burned up vegetation."' It was another of those recurrent periods in Kansas history when most people believed the climate had undergone a permanent change. Crops were complete failures. Wheat in Shawnee County was not so bad—one-eighth of a bushel to the acre! Thousands of settlers were without any backlog of supplies or money and were soon in desperate straits. Those that still had the means abandoned their farms and fled eastward, their wagons bearing signs "In God we trusted and in Kansas we busted" or "We trusted, by God!"

Deferment of organization was in order while the question was determined whether Kansas was anything other than a periodic oasis. Besides many of the men identified with Holliday were busy administering the relief which had been so generously given by the East. Pomeroy was especially active. Holliday's confidence in the future of the state was unshaken. In September of 1860 when local business morale had ebbed to the greatest depths, he resumed work on his favorite project. An informal meeting of interested Topekans was held in the office of E. G. Ross. A decision was reached to undertake formal organization in Atchison as soon as possible. Holliday, Ross, Huntoon, and Dickey made up the Topeka contingent. Daniel Horne and one other person may have been in the party. A team and carriage were reported to have been borrowed from a liveryman for the trip. The rendezvous was the little one-story brick office of Challis. There on September 15 and 17 the Company was organized. C. K. Holliday rightfully received the honor of the first presidency. P. T. Abell was made secretary and M. C. Dickey, treasurer. Directors were L. C. Challis, George F. Fairchild, P. T. Abell, S. C. Pomeroy, L. D. Bird, C. K. Holliday, F. L. Crane, E. G. Ross, Joel Huntoon, M. C. Dickey, Jacob Safford, R. H. Weightman, and J. H. Stringfellow. Each of the thirteen subscribed for $4,000 in stock, thereby complying with the Territory's requirement of a total of $50,000 in subscriptions. Only $400 had to be paid on subscriptions, but, needless to say, some borrowing by these elite of Kansas was necessary. The directors agreed that if the venture were to succeed a land grant had to be secured; plans were laid accordingly. Business being completed, the men went to the Massasoit House, where they were the guests of ex-Governor Blick, B. F. Stringfellow, W. R. Peabody, and Peter Abell. A youngster, Jack Brown, undertook to drive the Topeka group to their home city. Near the present site of Valley Falls, a welcome storm delayed the trip overnight. "All slept in one room in the home of old man Coffee and all wore nightgowns—a new item of apparel to Brown. They reached Topeka the next day and were 'royally entertained at the old Capitol House . . .' Mr. Brown was given $10 and a new suit of clothes plus a promise of a job if the road ever was built."

During the preceding summer, E. G. Ross had suggested a state convention as a means of aiding in the acquisition of railroads for Kansas. Holliday coöperated with Ross to organize the meeting, knowing it would help the new company. On October 17, 1860, the convention assembled at Topeka. Representatives were present from all the settled parts of the Territory, but the men from Leavenworth and Wyandotte withdrew when local interests began to conflict. A resolution was unanimously adopted to memorialize Congress, asking for an appropriation of lands to aid four railroad projects in Kansas—one of the routes described was congruent to that contemplated by the Atchison and Topeka Railroad Company. As a matter of fact, B. F. Stringfellow displayed a map of the route of the new company, showing a line to Santa Fe by way of the Cimarron fork of the Trail. At Holliday's suggestion, a committee was appointed to draft a memorial. Congress was accordingly petitioned.

Although progress was being made, it hardly justified the optimistic item which appeared in the Topeka *Record,* November 24, 1860:

It is with a good deal of gratification that we are able to announce that the Atchison and Topeka Railroad, which has been a source of so much levity with many of our contemporaries and a prolific theme for prosy disquisitions by the score, the drouth, benevolence, railroads, etc., etc., is in a fair way to realize the expectations of its projectors. An active campaign is being made in the East for the desired subscriptions, by a gentleman, entirely competent for the business, and among capitalists who are shrewd enough to perceive that no better investment of their money can be made, and no better time could have been selected in which to make it, than is now offered and in the manner proposed.

In the first place, the building of this road is an independent enterprise, and although inaugurated as one means of affording relief to those who look only to labor of their hands for a subsistence, it is yet separate and distinct from all measures of relief which have yet or may hereafter be adopted . . . .

It is not proposed to appropriate to it one dollar which has or shall have been contributed to the general charity fund, but to rely solely upon funds appropriated to that especial object.

The author of the article stretched the truth a trifle when he asserted that there were shrewd men of means who looked upon Kansas as a source of "ten per cent for sure." Kansas seemed to be synonymous with certainty all right—certainty of loss.

Kansas had the good fortune about this time to lose its ray of sunshine. The rains came and hopes were revived, and the editor of the *Record* no doubt wrote, "I told you so." Congressional pressure while Kansas was a Territory was weak and success remote. With admission to the Union came berths in Congress. James H. Lane and Samuel C. Pomeroy, as the newly elected senators, immediately pressed for action. Their activities if viewed in the light of the present might cause more eyebrow-lifting, but at the time they blended well with contemporary procedures. At any rate they got results and that is what Kansas wanted. There was a state to be developed. Both men worked for the Pacific railroad bill. With its passage in 1862 the way was clear for consideration of other railroad projects.

Holliday and his associates had been able to do little since organization. Financiers were unapproachable, especially after the outbreak of the Civil War outside of Kansas. A great stride forward was taken early in 1863 when Congressional aid was secured.

Holliday drafted a land-grant instrument and sent it to Pomeroy for sponsorship. It passed both houses in substantially the original form and was signed by President Lincoln, March 3, 1863. The Act provided:

> That there be and is hereby, granted to the state of Kansas, for the purpose of aiding in the construction: . . . of a railroad from the City of Atchison via Topeka, the capital of said state, to the western line of the state, in the direction of Fort Union and Santa Fe, New Mexico, with a branch from where this last-named road crosses the Neosho, down said Neosho Valley . . . every alternate section of land, designated by odd numbers, for ten sections in width on each side of said roads and each of its branches.[2]

The grant, like most others, did not go directly to the Company but went to the state of Kansas. The state legislature then (February 8, 1864) had to pass an act to accept the land. The latter was to be doled to the Company as twenty-mile sections were completed in "good and substantial and workmanlike manner as a first-class railroad." The Federal Act also required that the line, from Atchison to the Kansas-Colorado state line, should be completed and in operation on or before March 3, 1873, i. e., in ten years. The usual in-lieu clause was included. The Company had the right to select an area of land equal to that already held by preëmption or any other legal rights. The substitution had to be made within twenty miles of the tracks. The in-lieu clause was especially important to the Company, since all of the land in the eastern part of the grant was already held.

Meanwhile Holliday and his friends busied themselves with other problems of the Company. In an effort to make the name of the railroad more inclusive and descriptive, "Santa Fe" was added. This was done at a stockholders' meeting in the Chase Hotel in Topeka, November 24, 1863.*

A couple of months later, January 13, 1864, for political reasons, a decision was made to change officials. Senator Pomeroy

---

*At a directors' meeting in New York on January 8, 1869, it was voted to change the name from the Atchison, Topeka and Santa Fe Railroad to the National Pacific Railway Company but this action was rescinded, February 17, 1869.

succeeded Holliday as president and the latter became secretary.
S. N. Wood became vice-president and D. L. Lakin, treasurer. A
committee of Pomeroy, Wood, Safford, and Holliday was formed
to push the sale of stock. It was to be offered locally first and then
in the East. Safford, Lakin, and Holliday lobbied for an enabling
act in the Kansas legislature to permit counties to vote bonds up
to $200,000 as subsidies. Success climaxed their efforts on March
1, 1864. Holliday left soon for New York to secure support. He
reported progress but no money.

President Pomeroy's strategic connections with men of affairs
were to serve the Company well, but even Pomeroy had his troubles. On April 18, 1864, his unpredictable colleague, General Lane,
pressed a bill to dismember the Santa Fe. Pomeroy resolutely de-
fended his company. In the interest of a more harmonious front,
he did delete Holliday's extension to the Gulf of Mexico from
maps showing the course of the AT&SF.

Pomeroy's next step was to enlist for a second time his brother-
in-law, Willis Gaylord, and Henry Cummins. Both of these men
had helped push the land grant and knew financial channels like
no other skippers.* Through the efforts of these men some stock
was reputed to have been placed. At least they were able to interest
capitalists in the venture sufficiently to make moves toward construction. A contract was signed in August, 1865, for 30,000 tons
of 56-pound English iron rail at $100 per ton, but the agreement
was later voided. Major O. B. Gunn was appointed chief engineer
and on November 27, 1865, he began surveys for the railroad,
proceeding from Atchison. By January 13, 1866, he had reached
Emporia. Early in March, Gunn submitted maps, profiles, estimates, and plans for the line, which was to be built immediately.

Although Holliday did not hold any official position with the
Company for three years following August, 1865, this period was
one of great personal effort in the interests of the Santa Fe. One
month he was in Kansas and the next in New York or Washing-

*Henry Cummins was identified with several promotions: the Northern Pacific, vari-
ous Jay Cooke mining enterprises, Postal Telegraph Company, and the Typewriter Trust.

ton, soliciting financial support. Mr. Challis had become a million-aire stock trader in New York and was able to give Holliday valuable leads. For a time Holliday contemplated taking the con-tract for construction of the railroad. He even submitted a bid.*

Busy as Pomeroy and Holliday were, they resembled squirrels on a treadmill, accomplishing little that was tangible. Pomeroy must have despaired of ever raising the necessary money, for in June of 1866, he backed a measure in the Senate to permit the AT&SF to build a road without rails.[3] As a concession the land grant would be reduced to three sections per mile instead of ten. The Company would construct a roadway as if it were to provide a railroad but would omit the ties and rails. Steam-driven tractors and cars (with flat-tired wheels, no doubt) were "to move not less than fifty tons, or two hundred passengers, in one train, at a rate of six miles an hour."

Holliday tapped local financial founts more successfully than those in the East. In July, 1867, Shawnee County reversed a pre-vious verdict at the polls and voted $250,000 in 7 per cent bonds to subscribe for a similar amount in stock of the railroad. Company officials carried out a house-to-house campaign to achieve the victory. Atchison, Jefferson, Osage, and Lyon counties authorized

*On March 1, 1866, Chief Engineer Gunn sent Holliday the following letter:

"Your favor just at hand. I have completed my Report and shall forward it to Wash-ington tomorrow with map and profiles and everything complete. I received a long letter from Mr. Pomeroy since I wrote you. He seems bound to put the road through to Topeka. I wrote to him about taking the contract in connection with you and he expressed himself very favorably and says, 'I shall like you to take the whole contract except track laying.' I think you and I had better pull together in this matter as we talked. Mr. Pomeroy writes that for the present he sees only the Road from Atchison to Topeka and I think is bound to get it started thus far this year. Your proposition to build the Road at $10,000 per mile is low enough. My estimates foot up as follows; To To-peka East Bank River without Kansas River Bridge average per mile without ties $10,128; average per mile with ties $11,794; and Kansas River Bridge per mile $13,690. Little Muddy Route as follows including ties and Kansas River Bridge average per mile $12,-667, but this would be about a mile longer up to your place where the depot would naturally be.

"I have made my estimates on a basis of labor at $2 per day and whoever takes the contract this spring will probably get the benefit of a considerable discount on these prices. I have put the average of Earth @ 40c Rock no. 2 2d Qual Bridge Masonry $12 1st Qual @ $15 Culvert $8 Short Truss Bridge $45 per lineal ft. Kansas River Bridge $55 per foot. Ties 75 cts. Something could be made on a decrease of quantities as well as price on careful location. You need not trouble yourself to send me any of the docu-ments I wrote for as I now have my report made up. I thought there may be something in them I might wish to embody in my report."

bonds-in-aid in amounts from $150,000 to $200,000. Jefferson County did not make payment.

By the fall of 1867 the project had gained sufficient momentum to warrant contracting for construction. An agreement was made with George Washington Beach of New York on October 12 for building from Parnell Junction (six and a half miles from Atchison) to the western boundary of the state.* Work was to begin in ninety days. Since nothing was done within the deadline, a new contract gave an extension until March 10. Beach was apparently unable or unwilling to carry out his half of the bargain and a replacement was sought. Holliday, Safford, and Lakin were working harder than ever. On June 20, 1868, T. J. Peter of the Cincinnati firm of Dodge, Lord and Company, entered into agreements with Willis Gaylord, Lakin, Holliday, and Safford to build the line with their entrepreneurial coöperation.† Five days later Peter secured the Beach contract by assignment at a cost of $19,330. Why Peter had to pay Beach anything is not clear. The Beach contract should have been voided by the failure of Beach to act.

Neither Peter nor the firm he represented contemplated assuming full charge of arrangements for construction. Rather, they were to be part of a larger group. Accordingly a construction company called the Atchison Associates was organized. The leadership passed into the hands of H. C. Lord of Cincinnati, General A. E. Burnside of Rhode Island, and Henry Keyes of Boston.

---

*Beach agreed to acquire the necessary right of way on private lands, locate, build, and equip the road with depots, machine shops, rolling stock, telegraph lines, etc., from Parnell in Atchison County to the west boundary of the state via Topeka. The line was to go through the counties giving aid. The Congressional Land Grant and all the county bonds were to go to Beach as well as all subsidies and mortgage bonds of the railroad. The Company agreed to place all the capital stock in escrow, except sixty-five shares held by directors and that held by counties to be delivered to Beach as the line was put into service. Any stock increases went to Beach. Company officials were to help Beach in every way as building progressed toward San Francisco. All maps and profiles were to be turned over to Beach at cost or $10,000, whichever was lower. Provision was made for assignment.

There is evidence that Beach had some backing from A. B. Balch of Hanover, New Hampshire, and Dodge, Lord and Company of Cincinnati.

†Peter visited Kansas before assuming any risk and, like many others, decided that land which would nourish so many buffaloes would support an agricultural empire. Beach had previously assigned Gaylord the right to build from Atchison to Topeka. The latter did nothing.

BIRTHPLACE OF THE SANTA FE, ATCHISON, KANSAS

CYRUS K. HOLLIDAY
founder and
president 1863-1864

THOMAS NICKERSON
president 1874-1880

WILLIAM B. STRONG
president 1881-1889

FRED HARVEY

William F. Nast succeeded Pomeroy as president of the Railroad but remained in office only three weeks.* H. C. Lord was then elected to the presidency of the Santa Fe.† For a time control rested in Cincinnati. Henry Keyes, also of the Associates and president of the Passumpsic Railroad, followed Lord and accounted for the shift in control to Boston. By 1870 the Santa Fe was guided almost wholly by Massachusetts interests. The Pierce brothers, Charles and Carlos, and the Nickerson family had established contacts which were to endure over many crucial years in the growing period of the Company.

Prospects for the foetal railroad improved fortuitously in '68 with the acquisition of some choice land. Just west of Topeka, in a well-settled area, lay the fertile Pottawatomie Indian Reservation. The Leavenworth, Pawnee and Western Railroad had held a six-year option to buy a certain portion, but had failed to exercise the right. In the course of treaty-making and revising between the tribe and the Government, the Santa Fe acquired rights similar to those previously held by LP&W. By Congressional action of July 25, 1868, "the Atchison, Topeka and Santa Fe Railroad Company might within thirty days after the promulgation of the treaty, purchase of the said Pottawatomies, their remaining unallotted lands, except as hereinafter provided, at the price of one dollar per acre of lawful money of the United States . . . ." The Company had six years to pay, with a carrying charge of six per cent on the unpaid balance. Low interest in those times, when a charge of twenty per cent was far from usurious!

The Indian lands, which consisted of approximately 340,000

*William F. Nast was born in Cincinnati, Ohio, on June 16, 1840. He was engaged in consular service in Germany from 1861 to 1865 and upon returning to the United States entered the brokerage business in New York. Incidental operations led to an interest in the Santa Fe. Nast served as president from September 2 to September 24, 1868.

†Henry C. Lord was the son of the president of Dartmouth. He was born in Amherst, Massachusetts, on October 2, 1824. His family moved to Hanover, New Hampshire, in a few months. Lord entered Dartmouth at thirteen, graduated, and began a tutoring career in Virginia. He took up the study of law and was admitted to the Suffolk bar in Boston. Upon marriage to Eliza Burret Wright of Cincinnati, he moved there in the early 1850's. He was identified as the promoter and rehabilitator of many local lines and assumed leadership of the Santa Fe September 24, 1868. His term of office lasted only five months.

acres, gave some basis for financing. The original grant, while large, was poor collateral. The lands were remote and lacked, among other things, a railroad. The Santa Fe quickly (August 7, 1868) contracted to exercise its right and to make the most of the acquisition. The Company now had some land of value and the assurance of county bonds as soon as parts of the line were prepared for service. Confidence of the Associates rose and the initial meeting was called for September 23, 1868. The Associates had to finance construction pending payment from the Railroad. Although simultaneous financing was virtually possible, the Associates needed some money. The interest in the Associates was to be represented by forty-eight shares of $10,000 par, and forty were to be subscribed for immediately. Payments to General Burnside, the treasurer, were as tardy as in the early subscription to the stock of the Railroad. Keyes and Emmons Raymond, a later president of the Passumpsic Railroad, borrowed money on personal notes from Boston banks to make up the recurring deficiencies.

Holliday, his spirit undaunted by the trials and tribulations of nine years, triumphantly sent word to Topekans from the Associates' meeting in New York:

> The child is born and his name is "Success," let the capital city rejoice. The AT&SF Railroad will be built beyond peradventure. Work will commence immediately. Please inform the good people of Topeka and Shawnee County of the brilliant future waiting them.[4]

For the nth time, the newspapers acted as sounding boards. The Topeka *State Record* editorialized:

> It is fitting that Col. Holliday should be the final successful negotiator in this enterprise. To no one man in Kansas can the praise be awarded more surely for fostering and encouraging the various railroad schemes now making every farmer in the state richer than he was than to Col. Holliday.
>
> While others have abandoned the project as chimerical, the Colonel has never faltered, but has steadfastly kept winning his way until his enterprising schemes became the people's, and success came of it. The Colonel is soon to return and will merit the approbation of every property holder in the city.[5]

This time the paper was right. The Santa Fe was to be built and soon. What a struggle it had been from incorporation to the

first spadeful! Little did the promoters realize that new and greater problems lay in store. Exit frying-pan, enter the fire.

III

Branching Out

The history of Western railroad construction for the past
quarter of a century has demonstrated that successful results
can be obtained only by occupying territory promptly, and
often in advance of actual business necessity. This was the
policy of the Atchison Company from the first . . . . It built,
not upon assured returns of profits, but upon a faith which
time has abundantly vindicated . . . that the great Western
and Southwestern regions of the country were rich in possibilities . . . . —Directors' Report of 1888.

As if to make up for lost time, work on the Santa Fe was begun
soon after the meeting of the Atchison Associates. T. J. Peter was
in charge as chief engineer.

Peter had had considerable experience as an engineer. He had
been city engineer of Cincinnati. Glenn D. Bradley, narrator of
the ancient and medieval history of the Company, wrote of Peter:

It seems he was strictly temperate in his habits, and would neither
smoke, chew, nor drink; but his profanity when once aroused was fearfully
sublime. He had an extraordinary memory and contrary to the usual
methods of civil engineers he made but little use of office records. It was his
policy not to issue written orders, and the subordinate who failed to remember his instructions three months after they were verbally given was
likely to arouse Peter's profane wrath.

Peter served also as superintendent from October 1, 1869, to
October 10, 1870, when he became general manager.

Captain Ellinwood, assistant chief engineer, was another dynamic man of strong personality and extraordinary competency.
He surveyed and located the line from Atchison to Larned and
was one of those in charge of construction on the scene until 1873.

GROUND-BREAKING

On September 30, 1868, Peter's assistant chief engineer, Captain John R. Ellinwood, and the latter's assistant, Fred Lord, began

surveys on the route south of Topeka. Each day the newspapers
waxed more eloquent over the prospects. On October 28 an ad-
vertisement in the Topeka *Weekly Record* called for five hundred
laborers to work on the new line at $1.75 per day. The contractor
was Dan Blush. Two days later came the real beginning of the
Santa Fe. Between Fourth and Fifth on Washington Street in Topeka, Dan threw the first spade of dirt. A small gathering of
townspeople and Company officials was present. Holliday took
this occasion to forecast again that the time would come when the
line would extend to Santa Fe and the Gulf. The consensus
termed him a "damned fool"; twenty years later he was to be
credited with powers of clairvoyance and an "uncommon amount
of common sense." Senator E. G. Ross of Kansas sketched the
hectic career of the Company but assured the crowd that the
pluck already shown would lead to bigger things.

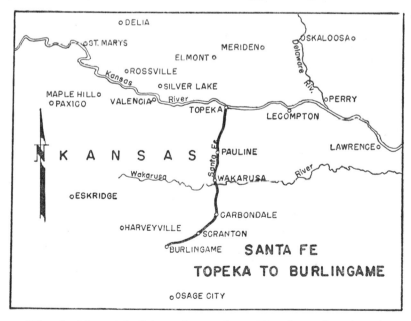

SANTA FE
TOPEKA TO BURLINGAME

The decision to build southwest from Topeka rather than from
Atchison was prompted by excellent coal deposits near the former.
The Kansas Pacific had already built from Kansas City to Topeka

on the north side of the Kaw (Kansas River). This necessitated construction of a bridge in order to secure supplies for the line. They were hauled to Topeka over the KP. In the course of the winter both bridge and ten miles of grading were completed. Tracklaying began early in the spring. Late in April seven miles had been laid with 50-pound iron rail. A secondhand locomotive was purchased from the Ohio and Mississippi Railroad and some other used equipment was acquired elsewhere. A celebration was in order. An excursion train consisting of the "new" secondhand locomotive and two coaches (one borrowed) steamed out of Topeka with almost a hundred passengers. The end of the line was reached at the hell-bent speed of fifteen miles per hour over a roadbed that was pronounced the best in the prairie country. The party proceeded on foot and in carriages a few miles to Wakarusa, where a picnic was held. There were numerous speeches. Oratory flowed to great heights as liberal quantities of firewater were imbibed. The climax came with Holliday's address. As a rule the Colonel limited likely extension at Santa Fe to the west and the Missouri River to the east. On this occasion he loosed all shackles, asserting that the Santa Fe would be built to Chicago, St. Louis, Galveston, The City of Mexico, and San Francisco. The crowd, although synthetically hyper-receptive, was unable to swallow such fantasy. Loudest to guffaw was Major Tom J. Anderson of the Kansas Pacific.

Anderson later became general passenger agent of the Santa Fe and stayed with the Company until 1881, when prospects for eventual accomplishment of Holliday's assertions at Wakarusa were well on the road to fulfillment.

But everybody had a good time and returned unable to detect any difference between the new line and the New York Central. Two months later the completed mileage had more than doubled on reaching Carbondale; therefore twice as big a celebration was held. By this time the rails had crossed the Shawnee County line, qualifying the Company for a portion of the subsidy bonds that had been voted.

Construction methods were based on brawn plus picks and shovels. Teams, of course, were put to good use. Most of the work was subcontracted, especially the grading.

Among the early contractors who took portions of the work were Craik Bros., Warner and Carpenter, Blackstone and Tolle, George Plumb, and J. D. Criley.

The number of men required was large even though the topography presented few difficulties. Thousands of man hours were necessary for the most unimposing cuts and fills, without the use of power shovels and dump trucks. Common labor built the railroad. Even the foremen were unskilled if the stories concerning the first tracklaying are true. One Leonard Blood, an inexperienced pint of recent vintage, went to Ashcraft, the boss, and boldly asked for the job of tracklaying foreman.

"Can you do it?" asked the mighty Ashcraft.

"If I can't, fire me," came the reply.

Somehow Blood could until he reached the first curve. There he was stumped.

"I didn't know whether the rails should be sawed or chiseled, so I resorted to diplomacy. There was a big, raw-boned Irishman in the gang, whose good nature had appealed to me, so I took a chance on him.

" 'Full time, Boss, full time it is, Sir,' Mike responded.

" 'Well, Mike, you go ahead and cut them. I have to make a trip up to see the timekeeper.'

"Mike was flattered by the responsibility reposed in him and went right at the job, while I went up the track a little way and hid behind the pile of ties and watched the proceedings. And the next time we hit a curve I knew how to cut a rail." Although the story has been in the above form for decades, the "curve" was probably a "turnout" or "switch."

Somehow the line advanced, preceded by a substantial boom in real estate. An Emporian wrote to a Topeka paper, June 15, 1869:

Things are lively here. Lots that went begging at $500.00 three months
ago are readily gobbled at $1000.00 now. About one hundred men are in
town awaiting the result of the railroad vote. Had it been adverse they
would have skedaddled tomorrow. As it is, they remain and go to work
tomorrow.

The goose was reported "never more loftily suspended."

FINANCIAL TROUBLES

All was not well backstage. The Associates were having a desperate time with the problem of finance. Although the workers
were paid with regularity, there was even betting on default. Officials had to accept bonds in lieu of cash for their salaries, and
the bonds were always of doubtful value. Shawnee County bonds
with their 7 per cent rate were selling at great discounts. The Associates complained that ". . . instead of finding a large proportion
of the Land subsidy, granted by the State to aid in constructing
the Road, . . . we find ourselves entitled only to about four thousand acres, on that portion of the Road now completed, thereby
cutting us off from one of our most valuable assets." After com-
pleting only twenty-eight miles to Burlingame in 1869, the Associates withdrew, and construction from there was by the Atchison, Topeka and Santa Fe Railroad itself. The Associates were
paid slightly in excess of $2,000,000 in par value of securities of
doubtful worth in return for the railroad assets. Henry C. Lord
relinquished the presidency and the woes it entailed to Henry
Keyes, whose rescue of the Connecticut and Passumpsic Rivers
Railroad had attracted much attention.*

---

*Henry Keyes was born January 3, 1810. Little is known of his early life, but in
1825 he moved to Newberry, Vermont, where he subsequently entered the mercantile
business. Keyes prospered and developed many outside interests. He served as state
senator and as chairman of the Vermont delegation at the Democratic convention of
1860 and was a candidate for governor on three occasions. The Connecticut and Passumpsic Rivers Railroad was revitalized as a result of his early efforts. He invested heavily in farming, and in stage and steamboat lines. Keyes refused the leadership of many
companies because the work might require too much time away from Newberry. His
service for the Santa Fe from February 17, 1869, to September 24, 1870, was cut short
by a fever which took his life after an illness of ten days. His kindness and integrity
were the subject of much praise.

T. J. Peter continued in charge of building operations and pushed ahead to Emporia by July 20, 1870. Grading had been completed well beyond that point, and a sizable stock of iron rail was on hand. The Directors proudly, and perhaps wishfully, asserted, "Few Western roads are so thoroughly built as this . . . . Stone is freely used in building the road. Equipment . . . is all of the best character. The passenger cars are handsome and commodious; and all pains have been taken to have none but good and serviceable cars and engines on the road." Actually construction was very poor, although less faulty if viewed in the light of the times. There was no ballast. The rails were light and of iron. Made in diverse countries, they were unstandardized. The ties, although untreated, were good, having been sawed or hewn from walnut or white oak. Buildings were of the cheapest wooden construction.

Work beyond Emporia to Florence was soon made possible by the placement of a large block of securities with Kidder, Peabody & Company.

Guiding the fortunes of the Santa Fe at this time was Ginery Twichell. He had accepted the presidency in 1870 and remained in office until May, 1873. Twichell was a self-made man of old American stock. He was born August 22, 1811, at Athol, Massachusetts. He left school at sixteen in favor of a job in a mill. He shifted to a livestock firm and later a store. At nineteen Twichell took charge of a stage line from Barre to Worcester. Soon he became the owner and rapidly outdistanced strong competition. At twenty-nine he controlled many lines through New England. Oddly enough, the secret of his remarkable success was not two-fisted aggressiveness but kindness and generosity. His unusual regard for fair play won many friends. On July 1, 1835, the Boston and Worcester Road was opened. Twichell competed with the new railroad and complemented it until June 1, 1848, when he became assistant superintendent of the line. Again Twichell went to the top and in 1857 the presidency was his. Although he had no penchant for politics, he served three terms as a representative in Congress. The utmost modesty and gentleness characterized his meritorious work.

After leaving the Santa Fe, Twichell headed the Boston, Barre and Garden Road and the Hoosac Tunnel and Western. His great philanthropy was always inconspicuous. He had a phobia about publicity, but his virtues were so many that his friends would not permit him to remain out of the limelight. Twichell was stricken with typhoid fever and died July 23, 1883, in Brookline, Massachusetts.

Across Kansas into Colorado

Not only was the line completed to Florence during 1871 but it was extended to Newton, coming town of cattle, gunplay, sin and eventual respectability.

Most of the towns of the line now west of Emporia were not in existence prior to the advent of the Railroad. The Company laid out and named many of them. As a matter of fact, the whole area was virtually uninhabited except by roving bands of Indians. R. R. Coleman, who assisted in early surveying, recalled:

> These operations were slow and more or less dangerous. The weather was hot and travel through the sandhills was tiresome. Much of the journey lay through great herds of buffalo. Stampedes were frequent, and, though the men suffered no injury from this unusual danger, the onrushing beasts occasionally crossed the line of survey. One buffalo was killed each day to supply the camp with fresh meat.
>
> Another menace to work of this nature in southwestern Kansas that summer was Indians. Only two years previously they raided the entire western half of Kansas and had been cowed into a sullen peace by Custer in the battle of Washita eighteen months before. The redskins were nominally quiet and a peace conference was then being held with the Cheyennes and Arapahoes. But these tribes were proverbially treacherous. Even in times of peace they were not indisposed to take advantage of any small detachment that might fall into their power. Consequently the surveyors had an escort of fifteen soldiers, and each civilian was well armed.

Arrival at Newton marked completion of 137 miles of road, scarcely one-fourth of the amount necessary to earn the original land grant. Disaster threatened, for the deadline was March 3,

1873. The Annual Report for the year ending March 3, 1873, tersely presented the problem and its solution:

The western boundary (Kansas-Colorado line) not having been established we estimated the remainder to be built at about three hundred and forty-three miles. The time for the completion of the road and telegraph was limited, and only one year remained. The consequence if it should not be completed within the time would be the loss of a large part of our Land Grant. The advancing cost of raw materials, and rates for money and the fact that five million dollars would have to be raised, presented serious difficulties and embarrassments.

The Report indicated that an attempt was made to get Congress to extend the time limit but "Congress was preoccupied with a presidential election and the risk of inaction too great." The Board on March 22, 1872, voted to complete the road by the deadline of March 3, 1873. The tight money market and the necessity of haste raised costs somewhat. On December 28, 1872, cars went over the whole, more than two months within the deadline.

. . . Thus about three hundred and sixty miles were constructed in less than nine months. Moreover the road is remarkably well built, much better than the majority of Western roads, and, in general construction, will bear comparison with the best roads either East or West.

Part of the mileage finished during the year was the long-awaited section between Atchison and Topeka. Faith had been kept with the citizens of Atchison and strategic rail connections were made with the East. Simultaneously a branch was built to Wichita from Newton under the charter of the Wichita and South Western Railway Company. This line was reputed to have been built as an independent venture by T. J. Peter, who had been unable to get fellow directors of the Santa Fe to undertake construction. At any rate, the line was leased to the Santa Fe on completion (for 35 per cent of gross earnings) and eventually consolidated into the system.

The extension west to Colorado followed a route marked out by Captain Ellinwood and A. A. Robinson.

Albert Alonzo Robinson was one of the outstanding men in Santa Fe history. He was born near South Reading, Vermont,

October 21, 1844. After the death of his father, Mrs. Robinson re-
married and moved to Wisconsin. Albert clerked in his stepfather's store three years until he was seventeen. Illness caused the
stepfather to give up the store and Albert undertook to support
the family by farming. In the four years which followed Albert
established a reputation as a tobacco grower. Reduction was made
on the farm mortgage and some capital accumulated. Albert found
time to attend a local academy and resolved to attend college. He
entered the University of Michigan in 1865, with a backlog of $175
to finance his college career. Income from part-time jobs and loans
from an older brother who was on the Michigan faculty enabled
Albert to meet his expenses and he was graduated in the class of
1869. Among the classmates of Robinson were George B. Lake,
Thomas J. Seely, and Daniel H. Rhodes. All three of these men
were later employed by Robinson in the service of the Santa Fe.
A degree of Master of Science was awarded Robinson in 1871, and
in 1900 the University honored him with a degree of Doctor of
Laws. His first railroad job was with the St. Joseph and Denver
City Railroad in 1869 and was interrupted by leaves of absence for
graduate study in Ann Arbor. T. J. Peter added Robinson to the
Santa Fe staff on April 1, 1871. Heavy responsibilities were thrust
upon his young shoulders but he carried the burden like a veteran.
Promotions followed rapidly and he became chief engineer and
later vice president and general manager. Under his supervision
five thousand miles of the present system were built.

Robinson was not only a man of unimpeachable integrity but
one who had the rare ability to impart his virtues to others. Good
men were attracted by his magnetic personality and made better
by association with him. Only Edward P. Ripley, the great president following the reorganization, compared with Robinson as a
molder of men. Robinson more than any other person was responsible for the scandal-free construction history of the Company.

Robinson left the Company when control of the Santa Fe
passed temporarily into the hands of financiers whose interests

and methods were at variance with the established Santa Fe ways. Offers were legion and he accepted the presidency of the Mexican Central. Between 1893 and 1906, the date of his retirement, mileage was increased and financial solidarity assured.

Twenty-one years after he had severed connections with the Santa Fe (1914), old associates held a banquet in Topeka in his honor. Men came from all parts of the country and messages from far corners of the globe. What better testimony of a man's greatness could be given than an honorary celebration more than two decades after leaving a post!

For a time the Company planned to build west from Wichita, taking a short cut where the Arkansas River veered to the north. The plan was abandoned, and the river was followed on the opposite bank. Although the route was longer, construction was easier. The Santa Fe has been accused of selecting the longer route in order to secure a large grant of land. In all fairness the judgment should be "not guilty." At the time the grant was acquired, the river route was contemplated. Besides, the value of the difference in the grant in 1872 was very little and not to be compared with the difference in the costs of construction. Beyond Dodge City the routes were identical.

Construction of the extension to Colorado was rather simple. The contractors were Wiley and Cutler, James Preston, Cunning and McIntosh, D. Coleman, and John D. Criley. The latter had helped to build the Kansas Pacific.

The land was relatively flat and there were few curves, cuts, fills, or bridges. In the interests of speed and economy, a minimum of grading was done. Miles of ties and rails were laid right on the prairie. Few station buildings had to be erected, for there were no towns in existence and not many were planned. Notwithstanding the crudity of the line, the limitations in building tools and the absence of machinery necessitated the use of hundreds of laborers. The men were boarded by the Company and bedded wherever the grass was thick and soft. Families were left behind, and the camp was moved five or ten miles at a time as the line progressed. Naturally the camp attracted numerous parasites who supplied such things as were currently desired. Even though the men earned only $2 per day, pickings were good.

On Saturday nights the construction gang backtracked to the nearest town, where they imbibed heavily and fought with the cowboys who were blowing wages at the end of the great cattle trails. Gambling and women of a less genteel sort were the other attractions. Only a half of a mile of track could be laid on Mondays and at least a mile on any other day.

The Indians caused little trouble. Santa Fe men bore charmed scalps throughout the period of construction. Local Indians either were temporarily peaceful or were engaged in distant wars. Tools were frequently stolen, bridges burned, and small groups of employees chased, but there was no trouble of the sort encountered by the Union Pacific. A rigid guard was maintained around camps and every train was a mobile arsenal. More than once the construction camp was a haven of refuge for hard-pressed traders who chanced along. Shortly after the line was extended twelve miles to Granada, Colorado, in the summer of '73, members of a train crew discovered the bodies of four prospectors along the right of way. They had been robbed and their bodies mutilated.

Building ceased for a couple of years while the Company attempted to assimilate what had already been provided. Other circumstances rendered cessation imperative. Funds of the Company were low, and the time was not propitious for raising capital. The period prior to 1873 had been one of unbridled expansion and speculation of the sort that characterized the decade following World War I. In September of 1873 the bubble was pricked by the failure of Jay Cooke and Company, backers of the Northern Pacific. Securities and brokers plunged into nose dives. Before the year ended, over five thousand businesses had collapsed. Among these were many railroads and financial houses. The Santa Fe was fortunate to stay afloat, let alone expand.

Another factor which deterred expansion was the terrible grasshopper horde which jumped on Kansas in 1874. Millions of voracious jaws came suddenly out of the west during midsummer. F. W. Giles, Topeka newspaper editor, wrote:

> It would tax the powers of an abler writer than this to clearly portray the changes that ensued. The tree yesterday laden with its heavy drapery of green, today denuded. The peach, and pear and apple trees, with luscious fruitage, rejoicing the beholder, today leafless, fruitless, withered as the fig tree accursed. Gardens with lawns and shrubbery and flowers, now lifeless, seared, and fallen to decay. The cottage, embowered, now exposed and blistered by the burning heat of the summer sun. The farmer's fields of ripening grain—his only promise, his only hope—now blackened by the countless myriads of the all-devouring plague—Egypt's dread. A summer scene, in an hour, as it were, transformed to one of winter.[1]

The hoppers were so bad that the driving wheels of the locomotives slipped on starts and on inclines. Sanding the rails did not help. One of the Santa Fe employees, H. V. Faries, master mechanic, finally contrived a brush which was put in front of the wheels to sweep the hoppers off.[2]

News of the visitation to Kansas spread and brought much-needed money for relief but no money for investment. Physical facilities of the Company required what free capital could be scraped up. During 1874, maintenance had cost only $172.51 per mile. Consequently the line had deteriorated. Superintendent C. F. Morse reported that the rail from Topeka to Emporia was already in need of replacement, that ballasting of cuts was essential, and that both bridges and buildings were in acute disrepair.

In Kansas hope is perennial in the spring, and 1875 brought the renewal of railroad activities. Negotiations had been under way during 1873 and 1874 between the Santa Fe and those interested in the Maxwell Land Grant of New Mexico to route the southwest extension of the line from some point in extreme eastern Colorado or southwestern Kansas.

At the helm of the Company during the negotiations was Henry Strong. He was the seventh president of the Santa Fe. Henry Strong was born in Helensburg, Scotland. His father was the Con-

sul General at Glasgow and the family remained abroad until
Henry was four. He matured in America and eventually began a
legal career at Keokuk and Burlington, Iowa. Like many other
Santa Fe officials, Strong spent several years in the service of the
Burlington Railroad. His term as president of the Santa Fe lasted
from May 22, 1873, to May 28, 1874.

Surveys were made by A. A. Robinson, but the project was
abandoned on account of the Panic. Later the Santa Fe was to
build into New Mexico but follow a more indirect route.

From Dodge City west to Granada the Santa Fe owned a dead
limb. Traffic was light and without immediate prospects of becoming better. Terminating in Granada was literally terminating,
and a further extension might turn a liability into an asset. Extensive coal deposits existed in the vicinity of Trinidad and Canon
City. Forest resources on the mountain slopes offered lumber traffic to woodless parts of Kansas and materials for the railroad.
Mining operations in southern Colorado required transportation
for ore, machinery, and supplies. Already Colorado was becoming
a mecca for vacationists and was being advertised as the "Switzerland of America." The decision to build had to be made.

Construction west was under the control of the Pueblo and
Arkansas Valley Railroad Company. The firm was dominated by
Santa Fe backers and was wholly integrated with the policy of the
latter.

Affiliated or subsidiary companies are established for diverse
reasons. In some cases foreign corporations (those incorporated
outside the state of operations) may not hold title to property in
certain lines of business. This necessitates incorporation of a local
company controlled by the larger concern if operations are to be
conducted in the state. Difficulties in financing arising out of the
circumscriptions of "after acquired property clauses" in the mort-
gages of bond issues cause resort to subsidiaries in an effort to expand. There are many other reasons for such corporate complications, but the two mentioned are among the more important.

KANSAS

AND SOUTH WEST

SOUTH CENTRAL

"OUT OF THE WOODS" INTO KANSAS

"IN THE WOODS"

Copyrighted by A.S. Johnson in 1881.

2,000,000 ACRES OF LAND. $5 TO $8 PER ACRE

A PEEP "OUT OF THE WOODS" INTO KANSAS ON THE LINE OF THE ATCHISON TOPEKA AND SANTA FE R.R.

LAND EXPLORING TICKETS TO DODGE CITY AND RETURN on sale at all the PRINCIPAL R.R. TICKET OFFICES WEST OF AND INCLUDING ROCHESTER, BUFFALO, SALAMANCA, PITTSBURG AND WHEELING. for FURTHER PARTICULARS ADDRESS A.S. JOHNSON LAND COM'M'R TOPEKA KANSAS.

THE RESOURCES OF KANSAS WITH FINE MAP MAILED FREE ADDRESS A.S. JOHNSON TOPEKA KAN.

Top: Paycar, 1884. Center: Streamlining began in 1911. Bottom: Payload on the Santa
Cajon Pass, California

Las Animas was reached September 13, 1875, La Junta February 16, and Pueblo February 29, 1876.

At Las Animas the Santa Fe encountered bitter opposition from the Kansas Pacific. The Santa Fe, being south of the Kansas Pacific, had wrested the Texas cattle trade from the KP. The latter threatened to parallel the SF to Pueblo and did build to La Junta. The lines were only ten feet apart in places. Later an amicable agreement was made and the KP took up its tracks from Kit Carson to La Junta.

The date for celebrating the completion to Pueblo was set for March 7, and the *Chieftain* announced, "The biggest drunk of the present century will occur here on the 7th of March." An excursion train bringing Santa Fe notables encountered a blizzard near Larned and was unable to get through. After the first round they were never missed.

To Kansas City

As if to balance the teeter-totter, the Company expanded to the east during 1875. An entrance to Kansas City was secured by the leasing of the Kansas City, Topeka and Western. This added sixty-seven important miles which had gone through a hectic career. The tenuous history of all the additions to the System cannot be traced within reasonable limit. A sketch of the background of the KCT&W will indicate how complex was the corporate history of the lines that comprised the Santa Fe as it came of age. On December 2, 1868, the ubiquitous Holliday and his business associate, Joel Huntoon, secured a charter for the Lawrence and Topeka Railway. Holliday, as president, directed Huntoon to locate the line. A contract was let, but no construction took place until 1872. Between May and September rapid progress in construction and in diminution of funds was reported. The L&T was unable to proceed and entered into an agreement on July 14, 1873, with a company known as the Kansas Midland (incorporated May 29, 1873) to complete the work. Lawrence was reached with 50-pound iron rail on June 2, 1874. In the meantime other interests developed the line between Lawrence and Kansas City. On July 20, 1865, the St. Louis, Lawrence and Denver Railroad Company was incorporated. This was part of a scheme to build a line from St. Louis to Denver via Lawrence, the great advantage of which was that it saved ten miles by missing Kansas City! All of the corporate relationships are not worth worrying about; it is sufficient to say that on December 2, 1871, track had been laid between Lawrence and Pleasant Hill, Missouri, via De Soto Junction. The despised Kansas City had been left off the line.

KANSAS CITY— TOPEKA
AND VICINITY

On August 12, 1874, the Kansas Midland began the use of the new line from Lawrence through De Soto to Olathe, where it had trackage rights into Kansas City over the Missouri River, Ft. Scott and Gulf Railroad. This was a rather devious route to Kansas City, but already steps had been taken to provide a line directly east from De Soto. On June 11, 1874, a contract was entered into with the Kansas City, Lawrence and Topeka Railroad (incorporated September 14, 1872, with the right to build from Kansas City, Missouri, to the Kansas state line, a distance of two miles) to build from De Soto to Kansas City. Work was begun shortly and some difficulties with the initial contractor forced changes.

The Santa Fe was reported in June, 1875, to be about to acquire control of the segments to Kansas City, and before the month ended Santa Fe engineers were in charge. The following month the Kansas Midland was amalgamated with the Lawrence and Topeka Railway to form the Kansas City, Topeka and Western Railroad Company. The latter was owned by the Santa Fe and leased its facilities to the Santa Fe for a period of thirty years.* The Company now controlled all except a few miles between Lawrence and De Soto. This was acquired by purchase in 1877 by the KCT&W from the St. Louis, Lawrence and Western, successor to the St. Louis, Lawrence and Denver. Finally, in 1899, the KCT&W was merged with the Atchison, Topeka and Santa Fe Railway.†

Not all of the mileage of the Santa Fe was as hectically developed, but the case chosen is by no means extreme. Important phases as well as details of other acquisitions will of necessity be passed over.

The program of maintenance was greatly accelerated in 1875 and succeeding years. Substantial additions were made to the roll-

---

*The newly acquired line was in wretched condition, for the Kansas Midland had had an overflowing measure of woe. The town fathers of Lawrence had hamstrung the Company on one occasion by refusing to permit the line to be built within the town limits, thereby preventing the Midland from qualifying for subsidies voted by Topeka and Shawnee County. After the line was completed, it was rendered incomplete with every heavy shower. The quality of operations was no better than the construction. Wm. S. Hinchley, an early Santa Fe agent, described some of the difficulties that confronted his friend, Hiram W. Diggins, composite conductor, superintendent, and roadmaster of the Midland: "Conductor Diggins had many things to contend with, and it was a common occurrence that constables and sheriffs along the line made an attachment on his train for an old material bill due some farmer along the line. Mr. Diggins would compromise by giving them a box, coal or flat car, which would be chained or locked to the rails on the side track. As soon as cash fares were collected Mr. Diggins would settle the bill and get ready for more trouble."[3]

†At the same time the line from De Soto to Pleasant Hill, known as the De Soto and Pleasant Hill Railroad Company, was acquired by the Santa Fe. It was operated as a branch until 1884 and merited the appropriate nickname of "Calamity Branch."

ing stock. It was still cheaper to pay the cattle claims than to build fences to keep herds off the tracks. Sixteen miles of track were relaid with steel rails in 1877 and fourteen miles had rerolled iron.

TOWARD SANTA FE

For a while the Santa Fe was relatively inactive. The year of 1877 witnessed the completion of only thirty-one miles, a branch down the Walnut Creek from Florence. But already the fuse was lit for a tremendous burst of expansion, for during that year William B. Strong came to the Santa Fe.* He was as his name suggests—strong, a mighty man of vision, a righteous doer of things, and an empire-builder. Strong teamed with A. A. Robinson to push a building program of almost unparalleled magnitude.

First to be undertaken was the long-awaited projection into the Territory of New Mexico. Although the Company from its inception had contemplated building to Santa Fe for a long time, the line was not feasible. Beginning late in 1872 with extension of the line to Colorado, officials began to take preliminary steps. Robinson examined several possible routes to the "City of the Holy Faith" as far as Cimarron, New Mexico. In 1874 he examined a route between Trinidad, Colorado, and the country south of the Raton Mountains via Raton Pass. In 1877 just before Strong shifted to the Santa Fe, Robinson surveyed the line through the Pass with the help of W. R. Morley. The latter had recently begun a career with the Santa Fe which was to be brilliant but short-lived. The preliminary studies convinced Robinson that the best route from an engineering point of view was to branch from the mainline in the vicinity of Dodge City and proceed southwest to Wagon

---

*William Barstow Strong was born in Brownington, Vermont, on May 16, 1837. His parents moved to Beloit, Wisconsin, while Strong was quite young. He attended the local public schools and the Chicago Business College, graduating in 1855. Starting his career as a station agent and telegraph operator, Strong worked successively for the Chicago, Milwaukee and St. Paul, the McGregor Western Railway, the Chicago and Northwestern, the Chicago, Burlington and Quincy, the Michigan Central, and then the CB&Q again. Each change meant a step upward. Strong came to the Santa Fe as general manager and in a month and a half was also named vice-president. On July 12, 1881, he was elected president and held office until circumstances forced resignation in 1889. Retirement followed in Beloit and later removal to Los Angeles, where his death, though long expected, still came with startling finality August 3, 1914.

Mound, skirting most of the mountains. But the Company did not follow this course, at least not then. The Raton route was selected for good economic reasons, as Engineer Robinson explained:

The line having been built to Pueblo, when the question of building to New Mexico came up in 1877, there could be no hesitation as to what route to take; no scheme for extensive construction had been developed nor could be with the then financial condition of the country. Local interests had to be considered; the coal fields at Trinidad being an important one. At the time and even now it is in my judgment a serious question, had the direct line from Dodge City been available, whether it should have been chosen or not.[4]

Strong was quick to act, for the Denver and Rio Grande was operating in the same vicinity and was believed to be on the verge of appropriating the Raton Pass for its own use.* Aided by Governor Pitkin of Colorado, Colonel H. C. Nutt, western railroad leader, and Miguel Otero of the distinguished New Mexican family, Strong succeeded in securing a charter to build south from Colorado in New Mexico. The victory was important because other railroad interests in the Territory had tried to prevent the entrance of a rival company. (Strong had more trouble in adjusting himself to the local bill of fare than he had in getting the charter. Tortillas and chili were too hot to handle. Strong jokingly said that he almost committed highway robbery when he saw a man with some fresh eggs. The only thing that prevented a crime was that the possessor was willing to accept a handsome payment.) The charter was granted February 6, 1878, in the name of the New Mexico and Southern Pacific Railroad Company. Construction south from the mainline to New Mexico was to be by the Pueblo and Arkansas Valley Railroad. In order to establish possession grading was started in the Pass on February 27, but the major work was not commenced until a little later.

The mountainous country made construction difficult, but the work went ahead relentlessly. Trinidad on the Purgatoire (Picket

*The account of the spectacular struggle between the Santa Fe and the Denver and Rio Grande for control of Raton Pass will be traced in Chapter IV, "Wars of the Santa Fe."

Wire) River was reached by September. Notwithstanding the excellence of the Pass, a decision was made to tunnel through near the summit in order to obtain long-run economies of operation. The Pass had an elevation of 7,807 feet and the Company burrowed about 200 feet under the highest point. The solid rock was exceedingly difficult to penetrate. Alive to the danger of delay, the engineers built a temporary switchback over the hump, and train service began almost a year before the tunnel was finished. Early in July of 1879 the first train into Las Vegas astonished a throng of curious Indians and Mexicans. The occasion was momentous, for it meant more than a celebration: it meant a fundamental change in the way of life. Las Vegas soon was to become a modern city and attract from all over the world notables who sought its hitherto inaccessible waters. Trade was to change from a simple barter economy to a highly productive commercial economy.

On and on went the line. Some days a mile and a half of track was laid. To the keen disappointment of Company officials as well as the people of Santa Fe the mainline could not be projected through that city. There was no way that the line could extend beyond. *The New Mexican* was temporarily chagrined, but, after studying the situation more carefully, saw no alternative.* The Company even paid for an independent survey and report in order to give an impartial opinion on the decision. The mainline swung south to Albuquerque. The public-spirited people of Santa Fe were not to be left off the line for which they had yearned so long. They determined to coöperate with the Company for a branch. A bond issue to aid in building was presented, and "An election never took place in Santa Fe which was so one-sided." February 14, 1880, dated the driving of the last spike and two days later the first train puffed into Santa Fe.

What a feeling of triumph and of vindication must have entered the heart of C. K. Holliday! His brain child was to be built to many other cities which would contribute more ton miles of

---

*Even the early Palmer survey indicated that no route to the Pacific could pass through Santa Fe.

traffic but none of which would symbolize quite so much. The other early objectives—the Gulf, the Pacific Coast, and Chicago— were not ridiculous after all. Time and William B. Strong would prove it.

The first train into Santa Fe was more than a personal or a Company triumph. A milestone in the history of the West had been reached, marking the end of one era and the beginning of another. The dust had settled on the old Santa Fe Trail for the last time. Great as had been the volume of trade and the benefits of the old commerce of the prairies, the new trail was to accommodate infinitely more. The shackles on development had been loosed. No longer would calico sell for fantastic amounts. Time, space, and expense between Santa Fe and the East had shrunk. There were homes for newcomers, lands to be plowed, and mines for those who preferred to dig deeper. A new and greater Trail had been blazed.

EXTENSIONS IN COLORADO AND KANSAS

Traffic possibilities west in Colorado took a sharp turn for the better about the same time that the Company began to move toward Santa Fe. Pay dirt had been discovered in the vicinity of Leadville far up in the mountain area. Soon dozens of mines were producing almost fabulous quantities of silver. A rush was on and there seemed to be silver for all. Every miner represented demand for transportation of food, mining supplies, and ore. The Santa Fe was out to satisfy that demand.* Again the Denver and Rio

---

*Holliday was quick to apprise President Nickerson of the opportunities: "Dear Sir and Friend:

"I have just returned from a three weeks trip to Del Norte, Lake City and the adjoining mineral districts: and I have thought it might be worth while to tell you briefly what I saw and learned in that remarkable country.

"First: I think there can be no question as to the *extent* and the *richness* of the San Juan mines. Unlike California, Nevada, 'Deadwood,' &.c.&.c. the universal judgment is that the San Juan mines are rich and numerous beyond any other known mineral district anywhere. Miners from Australia, Mexico, California, all concur in this. Then one's personal observations among the mines soon confirm this seemingly extravagant statement. Around Lake City, Silverton, Ouray, Mt. Sneffles [sic], San Majuil [sic], Burrous Park, Henson Creek, Leadville, &.c.&.c. there are hundreds of mines—many hundreds—now opened sufficiently to produce their tons each of rich paying mineral every day and hundreds of others are under continual process of development. As a rule

Grande loomed as a rival, and one of the most unusual wars in the history of the country was waged as these competitors struggled in and out of court for control of the only route up the narrow Royal Gorge of the Arkansas.* The Annual Report for 1878 included this laconic comment:

The extension of the P & A V Road to Leadville being decided on, and the Grand Canyon of the Arkansas River presenting the only feasible

---

none of these mines 'pinch out'; but grow richer and better the farther they are developed. I was at several of these mines which are taking out from one to ten tons of ore per day; and I saw scores of others capable of doing the same thing as soon as circumstances will justify—notably the Ute, the Ouray, the Belle of the West, the Mountain Queen, the Americco, the Copper Hill Mines &.&.

"The 'circumstances' to 'justify' are *simply* the *question of transportation.* If they can have *cheap* and *quick* modes of shipping their ores and bullion *out* and their supplies *in* to that country, the business of that country will immediately assume such enormous proportions as to startle both you and me.

"Mr. Hill—with whom I traveled—a large operator in the Lake Superior Copper Mines—a most intelligent and observing gentleman, and also is about to transfer his large mining interests to Lake City—informed me that the production of Leadville was over 300 tons per week; he believes far beyond that.

"One of the Mepus Crooke's told me that their *Bullion* product was *now* 40 tons per day. This was all they could handle with their present means of transportation. With a Railroad to Lake or conveniently accessible, they would increase their productions to *300 tons per day*—or two trains of fifteen cars each. I have no doubt but that Mr. Crooke means precisely what he says and knows what he is talking about. Now please, multiply this one district—Leadville—and this one Mill—Crookes—by the scores *now*, and soon by the hundreds of others and you can see the enormous proportions to which this business must attain. Especially when another thing is considered: and that is: that you must soon either carry the fuel to the mines, and mills, or else carry the raw ores instead of bullion out. In either case the business would be largely increased.

"The fuel around the mills and mines must rapidly disappear and its place must be supplied with coal, or coke from Trinidad, or the Gunnison, or some other, as yet, undiscovered source. The Crooke's now use a large amount of Trinidad coke, hauled that long distance by wagon. It costs them $30 per ton. The Lexiciating [*sic*] works consume large quantities of salt—140 to 160 lbs. per ton of ore—5 or 6 lbs. to a 10 ton mile—All of them—with the general increase of ordinary trade and travel, ought to give a large and variable business for a Railroad to the celebrated San Juan. The people of Lake City—and they all pleasantly recollect your visit among them with Eng. Robinson—think you should build the Road from the South Arkansas via Limichi Creek and Lake Fork of Gunnison to Lake City. I think myself it is an excellent Railroad project: as at Lake City the Road would really control the business of Ouray, Silverton, and the districts above named, as well as its own.

"Or a road by Marshall Pass and the San Luis Valley to Del Norte, Wagon Wheel Gap, and Antelope Park, would probably largely control the same trade. Should you build the latter, however, there would be great dangers that sooner or later, the Denver Road to Fairplay would be extended via the Lake Fork of Gunnison to Lake City: thus cutting off the Eastern and Northern portion of the San Juan country proper. I incline, therefore, to the view: that with a Road Completed to Leadville, the next best move would be to extend an arm up the Lake Fork to Lake City. Begging pardon for troubling you so much longer than I expected when I began tonite. I remain as ever.

"Very truly yours
C. K. HOLLIDAY"

*Recounted in Chapter IV, "Wars of the Santa Fe."

route, possession was taken of the Canyon the 19th of April. The right to the Canyon has been vigorously contested by the D & R G Railway Company, both by force and in the United States Courts, where it is still undetermined; but work has steadily continued, and we shall be laying track through the Canyon in March, and hope to reach Leadville by the 1st October, 1879.

The line to Leadville was never finished by the Santa Fe, but some parts were completed during the struggle. By this time activities of the Company were like a three-ring circus. Lines were being built in many parts of Kansas to act as feeders or branches to the trunk. Some of the projects of 1879 were:

Kansas City, Emporia and Southern Railroad, 63 miles from Emporia through Eureka. The last 12 miles to Howard were being built by the Elk and Chatauqua Railroad.

Marion & McPherson Railroad from Florence to McPherson, 47 miles. Lyons was to be reached June 1, 1880.

Cowley, Sumner and Fort Smith Railroad, an extension of the Wichita and Southwestern. The line went south from Wichita to Mulvane and branched to Wellington and Arkansas City via Winfield. Arkansas City was on the fringe of the Indian Territory and the line to "Ark" City was to become of great importance. At Wellington construction proceeded toward Caldwell to the south.

A line from Burlingame to Manhattan, 59 miles, owned jointly with the Union Pacific, was being constructed by the Manhattan, Alma and Burlingame Railroad.

Improvements were being made in the older part of the system. Almost one hundred miles of track were relaid in 1879 with steel. Telegraph line construction kept abreast of rail-laying. Lack of fences still plagued train service, causing two derailments and a $33,000 bill for cattle claims. At the beginning of 1880 the "Jerk Water Railroad," as it was called in its early days, was a $31,000,000 organization with almost 1,300 miles of track. The first dividend was paid on the common stock May 1, 1880, and the Santa Fe was only beginning.

A Second Transcontinental Line

Albuquerque was entered in April of 1880. Not much of a celebration was possible. The old settlement was two miles distant

from the site of the new terminal. Henry A. Tice, an early employee, described the appearance of "new" Albuquerque as it was
when he arrived in the spring of 1880:

> The depot was an aggregation of old boxcars . . . . Not a building was
> on the townsite. The first merchant was on the ground, however, with
> a stock of goods. He had no tent or other covering to protect his merchan-
> dise in event of sandstorm or rain. In fact, the only effect that water could
> have had on his stock would have been to dilute it, and I assume he had
> already seen to it that none of the practices incident to his business had
> been neglected where possible to be performed. He had preëmpted six feet
> square of ground; had dug a hole in the sand about a foot deep for his
> cellar, which he filled from the barrel in which the bulk of his goods had
> arrived; had secured a few broken boards from the vicinity of the boxcar
> depot, placed them over his cache, and turned the barrel end up for his bar.
> With his ten-rod stuff in a suit case and his beer under his feet he was
> ready for business and ballyhooed his delectables at two bits a drink—take
> your choice.
>
> There were numerous small signs scattered over the sandy waste where
> now is Albuquerque, and these signs conveyed the information that lots
> were for sale at ten dollars each, make your own selections. No lots had
> yet been sold . . . . Talk about acres of diamonds! They were right there
> in the sand and we didn't see them.[5]

Albuquerque was merely on the way. Before the line was complete to that point, grading had been started toward San Marcial.
Six months later more than a hundred miles had been completed
into San Marcial without a sign of stopping. Not only was the
building program continued but an agreement was reached with
the Southern Pacific to connect with the latter at Deming, New
Mexico. The Santa Fe could now offer a through route to California, and the Nation had its second transcontinental railroad! To
keep faith with the Southern Pacific, Robinson and his assistants
worked south to Rincon, and southwest to Deming, where union
was officially made March 8, 1881.* A silver spike was driven by
R. R. Coleman of the AT&SF, A. Longstreet, J. H. Bates, and
J. F. Kilalea of the Southern Pacific. Three and one-half months
later operations into El Paso from Rincon were possible. Comple-

---

*Work south of San Marcial was in the name of the Rio Grande, Mexico and Pacific
Railroad. From the Texas line to El Paso construction was under the Rio Grande and
El Paso Railroad.

tion of the Mexican Central soon enabled travel to Mexico City from Atchison.

A connection to the Pacific, while desirable, was not all that the Santa Fe sought. More independence to develop traffic and territory was required than the connection at Deming could provide. The Company wanted its own outlet to the Coast. Steps had already been taken to provide controlled mileage beyond Deming. As early as 1878, when the line was just entering New Mexico, W. R. Morley had been instructed to find the most available route in the direction of Fort Yuma, Arizona, as far west as Florence and Tucson, and learn the resources and probable traffic of the country. This was substantially the much-discussed 32nd-parallel route. Morley, who had some familiarity with the 35th-parallel route, pronounced the 32nd preferable owing to the superiority of the hinterland. The mineral resources were richer, and the area was not limited. The Grand Canyon narrowed the sources of traffic for the northern line. A large business from "Old Mexico" could be acquired. "This would bring Adventurers, who will persistently work for, and finally succeed in obtaining another 'Texas' from the Territory of Old Mexico." Morley's incidental imperialism did not strike a responsive chord, but the remainder of his report did.[6] The following year Lewis Kingman directed a survey toward Tucson. Field operations were hampered greatly by the scarcity of water and lack of grass for the horses. Kingman on one occasion was fortunate enough at a critical time to buy corn in the middle of nowhere. The cost was eight cents a pound.

Instead of extending the mainline to the Coast, officials decided to start at the Coast and work back. A separate company, the Sonora Railway Company Limited, was organized to proceed from Guaymas far to the south on the Gulf of California.* A subsidy of

---

*The limitations and rights of the Company were unique. Freight and passenger rates were prescribed in the original agreement. In order to obviate international complications, Article II of Chapter II of the contract between the Government and the Company prescribed: "The enterprise shall always be Mexican, even when all or any of its members are foreigners." The Company had to pay the $400 per month salary of a Government supervisor for each surveying corps.

$7,000 per kilometer was granted. Work began in 1880 and by 1881 some ninety miles had been completed to Hermosillo. The Southern Pacific was aware that the Santa Fe planned to fill the gap between the northern end of the Sonora near Nogales and the western extension of the mainline. Collis P. Huntington of the Southern Pacific therefore suggested that the Santa Fe use the intervening SP line as far as possible. A joint trackage agreement would eliminate unnecessary and wasteful paralleling of lines. The Santa Fe agreed and secured rights from Deming to Benson, 174 miles west. The gap was now cut to ninety-five miles. It was bridged by the formation of the New Mexico & Arizona Railroad, authorized to build from Benson to Nogales. Work began during 1881. In March, 1882, the Sonora Railway was acquired by the Santa Fe through a two-for-one exchange of stock and a guarantee by the Santa Fe of the Sonora's 7 per cent bonds ($4,107,000). The buyer was to be the beneficiary of the earned subsidy ($2,570,530 at the close of 1881). The two railroads added about 350 miles. Work continued on the Sonora, and on October 25, 1882, the line was completed. Another silver spike was produced for the occasion and this time driven into a polished mahogany tie. The site was Guaymas.

What did this mean to the Santa Fe? Not so much as appeared at the time. True, salt water had now been reached over an independent route (joint trackage, Deming to Benson). Guaymas, to be sure, was closer to Australia than any Southern Pacific outlet in California. Great potential mineral wealth was adjacent in Mexico. The mainline was now 1,700 miles in length and longer than any other railroad in the World. What of it? The mineral wealth persisted in being potential. No great overseas traffic was to make Guaymas another San Francisco. At best the line developed into a thorn in the soft side of the Southern Pacific, and in the course of time when the Santa Fe was developing a better Pacific outlet, the Sonora Railway was to be an excellent bargaining agent in securing concessions from the Southern Pacific.

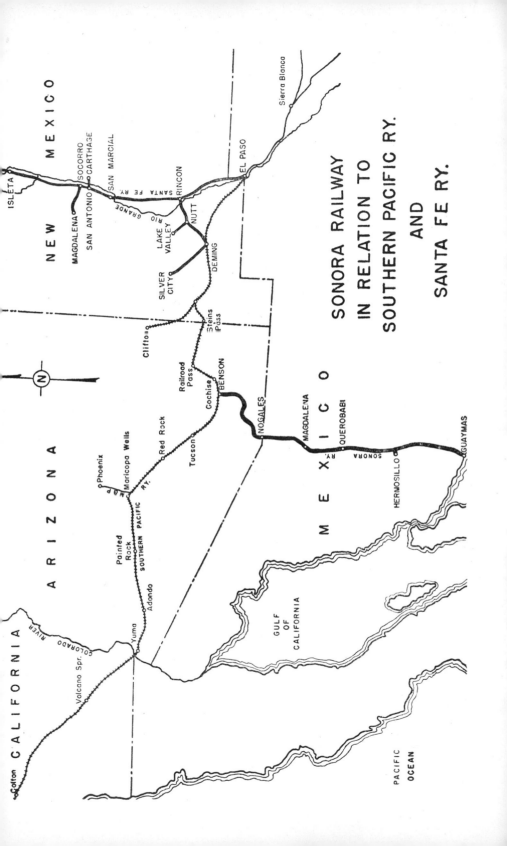

SONORA RAILWAY
IN RELATION TO
SOUTHERN PACIFIC RY.
AND
SANTA FE RY.

THE 35TH-PARALLEL ROUTE OF THE A&P

About the same time that plans crystallized for the southern
course to the Pacific, measures were taken to provide a route along
the 35th parallel on the north. This was to play an important role
in the history of the Company and to emerge as the mainline to
California. The project was to be undertaken with the coöperation
of the St. Louis and San Francisco. The principals were to operate
through the historic Atlantic and Pacific Railroad. The latter was
one of the oldest railroad enterprises of the West. In 1849 Thomas
Allen, at a St. Louis Convention, had sponsored a resolution to
build a railroad across Missouri. He applied to the Legislature for
a charter and "on the 12th of March, 1849, a charter was granted
providing for a capital of $10,000,000 and with power to survey,
mark, locate and construct a railroad from the city of St. Louis to
the city of Jefferson; and thence to some point on the western line
of Van Buren County, in this state, with a view that the same may
be hereafter continued westwardly to the Pacific Ocean."[7] In 1851
Missouri authorized an issue of $2,000,000 of 6 per cent bonds to
aid the new firm. A lien was taken by the state. The following
year 1,200,000 acres of land were given as bounty. Little was done
by the Company, and early in 1866 the state took steps to foreclose.
On May 12, 1866, John C. Frémont, Western hero and son-in-law
of Thomas H. Benton, offered the state $1,300,000 in installments
for the Southwest Pacific. The bid was promptly accepted. Frémont's next move was to secure another charter and form a new
company into which he fused the old.* The newcomer was the
Atlantic and Pacific Railroad, established by an Act of Congress,
July 27, 1866. The Company had the right to build a railroad and
telegraph line beginning at Springfield, Missouri, to the Canadian
River, Albuquerque to the headwaters of the Colorado Chiquito,
and via the 35th parallel to the Colorado River from where the
best route to the Pacific might be taken. Authorized capital stock

---

*Actually the South Pacific Railroad Company succeeded the Southwest Pacific and
in 1870 the South Pacific joined the Atlantic and Pacific.

was set at $100,000,000. An empire in wasteland was granted—
12,800 acres per mile in states and 25,600 acres per mile in territories. The line was to be completed by July 4, 1878. The charter
had one qualifying clause which was unique. "That the Southern
Pacific Railroad, a company incorporated under the laws of the
State of California, is hereby authorized to connect with the said
Atlantic and Pacific railroad formed under this act, at such point,
near the boundary line of the State of California, as they shall
deem most suitable for a railroad line to San Francisco, and shall
have a uniform gauge and rate of freight or fare with said road."
Already the influence of Collis P. Huntington was active in the
maintenance of a monopoly in California.

The A&P, as it was called, was unable to make much headway.
By 1872 service was offered from Pacific, Missouri, near St. Louis,
to Vinita in Indian Territory, a distance of 361 miles. The forty-
seven mile Pacific Railroad of Missouri was leased. An unsuccessful attempt was made to get San Francisco capitalists to aid in completion of the A&P. Financial distress of the panic of 1873 proved
too much to withstand and in '75 receivership was inescapable.
The following year brought substantial changes. The line from
Pacific to Seneca emerged under the control of the new St. Louis
and San Francisco Railway Company (Frisco). The remainder
(thirty-four miles to Vinita) was held by the A&P but the stock of
the A&P was wholly owned by the Frisco. No other mileage had
been built in the central division toward Albuquerque, and nothing had been done on the western division except some token grading at Soledad Pass in California. The situation was rather ludicrous. The Frisco was in straitened circumstances and could not
possibly finance the venture. Besides the Central Division offered
no justification for continuance. Being in the Indian Territory,
for the most part, it was not open to colonization and held poor
prospects for tonnage. The Frisco was ambitious and resourceful
and announced plans to build to California or bust. The Santa Fe
was disturbed not a little. The Southern Pacific had apparently

preëmpted the best southern route on the 32nd parallel and the A&P had valuable rights over the most eligible route near the 35th. What should be done? The "Big Four" (Huntington, Stanford, Crocker, and Hopkins) were known to be toying with the idea of attempting to make a deal with the Frisco.* If no agreement could be reached, the "Big Four" might build from the West. Canny Nickerson, alert to the threat to the Santa Fe's development, opened negotiations with the St. Louis and San Francisco to provide a transcontinental route from St. Louis to the Coast. Part and parcel of this was a line from Albuquerque to California. Thomas Nickerson and James D. Fish of the Frisco reached a preliminary agreement on November 14, 1879. The latter was to build from Pacific, Missouri, into St. Louis and from the mainline in Missouri to Wichita.† The Santa Fe would provide the connection from Wichita to Albuquerque and both companies would promptly finance building west to the Coast under the charter of the A&P. Final contracts were entered on January 31, 1880. Under the two agreements of that date the Santa Fe acquired a half interest in the A&P. Both major participants were to coöperate fully. The A&P was to issue $25,000 per mile in mortgage bonds and $18,750 per mile in income bonds to finance construction of the Western Division, and both the Santa Fe and Frisco were liable for half of any unpaid interest up to a certain amount. Eastbound traffic was to be routed from the A&P to Wichita via the Santa Fe, where a division would be made. The Frisco was to have the St. Louis business and the Santa Fe goods bound for Chicago and points north. The Central Division was to be undertaken jointly.

The A&P was now firmly backed. Thomas Nickerson, the newly elected president, offered $10,000,000 in mortgage bonds and $500,000 in income bonds to stockholders of the sponsors, and each group promptly supplied half. A. A. Robinson was ordered three weeks later to hold Quirino Canon, 180 miles west of Al-

---

*Mark Hopkins died in 1878 but negotiations continued.
†Costs between Wichita and Kingman were to be shared by the Frisco and the Santa Fe.

buquerque. The purpose was to check any designs of the Southern Pacific for this strategic route.

Construction was to follow a general course which had been examined several times. The famous trader, F. X. Aubrey, had inspected the route and later Lieutenant Whipple followed in Aubrey's steps. General William J. Palmer made the next survey in the interest of the Union Pacific Railway in 1867-8. A line almost congruent to the current one of the Santa Fe was advised, passing through such common points as Fort Lyon, Las Vegas, Isleta, Needles, Tehachapi, to San Diego and to San Francisco via the San Joaquin Valley.*

During the youthful and optimistic days of the A&P in 1870, a survey was ordered by F. B. Hayes, president. Chief Engineer J. Blickensderfer directed E. Godfrey Rehrer, F. S. Hodges, and R. J. Lawrence in the operations west from Albuquerque. The Palmer survey was heavily relied upon, the only major deviation from it being in California. A route through Chalania or Pollinia Pass from San Joaquin to the Salinas Valley was suggested.

Late in 1879 Lewis Kingman and W. A. Drake journeyed west from Albuquerque over most of the A&P route, the trip having been ordered by the Santa Fe. The following spring the last of the many A&P surveys was made. Robinson recalled Holbrook from the east to supervise field parties operating under Kingman and J. E. Early. Notes of the earlier studies were available, but even then the task was difficult. Much of the route was over trackless wastes. The only inhabitants were a few ranchers, Mexican herders, Indians, Mormons, and those attached to the military post at Fort Wingate. Navajo Indians were a serious threat. Although actually there was little trouble, the surveying parties were kept on edge. Wandering groups of Navajos followed the camps and interfered greatly with the work. Ostensibly the redskins were peaceable. The only sure means to keep them feeling so was to dig

---

*Much of the field work was done by W. R. Holbrook, later chief engineer of the A&P, and William G. Smyser and John D. Criley, both of whom spent many years with the Santa Fe.

deep into the larder. Memoirs of all the men in the surveying party testify that the nomads' stomachs were bottomless pits. Little work could be done during the week, or more than a week, required to execute a "dodge." There was too much danger to supplies if only a couple of men were left to guard the camp while forty Indians speculated on what they would like to "lift."

Operations were seriously restricted by the lack of water. Kingman's party was able to continue east from the Colorado River under the most trying circumstances. Each member had only a pint a day for washing plus a minimum for cooking and drinking. Often the haul was over forty miles. On one occasion when all water was gone and the men wanted coffee, they used canned beef soup for the brew.

The course, as finally laid out, crossed "the divide from the Rio Grande to the Rio Puerco, thence up the last-named stream for about six miles to the mouth of the Rio El Rito to its source in Campbell's Pass in the Continental Divide, thence down the Rio Puerco of the West to its junction with the Little Colorado to Sunset Crossing, thence crossing to the south side and following the Colorado Plateau, the high divide between the drainage of the Rio Colorado and the tributary water of the Rio Gila and descending on the west slope of this plateau by a series of washes or ravines to the Colorado River." A decision was reached to make the point of departure from the Santa Fe at Isleta rather than at Albuquerque.* Engineering problems west of Isleta were substantially less.

Contracts for grading were let early in the spring. Several Mormons of northern Arizona secured some of the work. Among them was John W. Young, son of Brigham Young. The income was much needed at the time for bread, and the means of buying it were scarce among the Mormons in the Little Colorado country. By fall fifty miles of track had been laid and the A&P was ready to face a critical test. The old charter had specified

---

*Construction from Albuquerque to Isleta and beyond had been greatly hampered by the local Indians, who undid at night about as much as the tracklaying crews did in the day. Largely through the influence of Father Dourchee, missionary at Isleta, the redskins were induced to cease nightly destruction of the line.

that the line must be finished by July 4, 1878, to merit the land grant. The deadline had not been met. Application was fearfully made for inspection and acceptance of the line and donation of the land. The legal question was submitted to the Attorney General, who ruled that, since Congress did not expressly provide for forfeiture, only a special act of Congress would cause withholding. No special act having been passed, the A&P was entitled to the land.

On February 2, 1881, the *Daily New Mexican* announced that Wingate had been reached, about 150 miles from Albuquerque. Most of the rail used was 52-pound. Iron was laid on the sidings and steel on the mainline. The A&P work involved many difficulties which were not encountered in construction elsewhere. The country was different. Although rainfall over the years was scanty, flash floods were frequent and precautionary measures relatively impossible. The location and volume of rivers were fickle. Lessons had to be learned that dry creek beds today might be raging torrents tomorrow. Where to build bridges was problematical. The river might be five miles west next week. Divided responsibility made for some personnel trouble. Holbrook and Kingman, successor to Robinson and chief engineer of the A&P, both resigned. Each would have been happy to have been a part of an exclusive Santa Fe team or a Frisco team but not a part of a combination. Replacements were made with a minimum of disruption.

Building troubles were minor as compared with the unexpected impediments placed by the Frisco in 1882. Tycoons Huntington and Gould of the Southern Pacific and Texas and Pacific secured control of the Frisco and stalemated plans to extend the A&P to the Coast.* The best arrangement the Santa Fe could press through the A&P was to get the Southern Pacific to connect at the Colorado-California line. Provision had been made for a connection in the original charter. The Southern Pacific subsequently built from its mainline at Mojave to Needles.†

---

*Chapter IV, "Wars of the Santa Fe," traces these events in detail.
†The work was done by the Pacific Improvement Company owned by Huntington and Stanford.

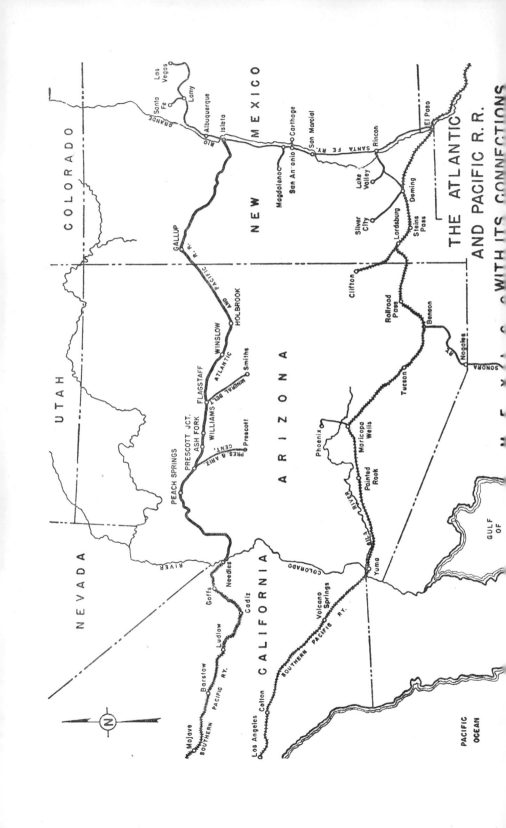

THE ATLANTIC AND PACIFIC R.R. WITH ITS CONNECTIONS

Despite backstage wrangling the A&P pushed ahead. Canyon Diablo was reached in May of 1882 and spanned two months later. Between Williams and Ash Fork the short, but hard, Johnson Canyon Tunnel was bored. The distance between the approaching lines narrowed quickly. Supplies were rushed by rail over completed portions of the A&P and SP and up the Colorado to Needles by Huntington's steamship line. On August 3, 1883, contact was made with the completion of a pile bridge over the river. Another route to the Coast had been finished, yet the Santa Fe was far from satisfied. Independent lines in California were absolutely essential to satisfactory and profitable operations. The barrier thrown up at the Colorado River had to be hurdled and soon.

Management of the Santa Fe during the period of expansion was so far-sighted as to be almost intuitive. Long before problems appeared to the general public, they were perceived by those in control. The common sponsorship of the Sonora Railway and the purchase of the half-interest in the A&P anticipated moves of competitors. Likewise provision had been made for possible blocking of the A&P at Needles long before Huntington ever took steps to apply pressure.

Union in Southern California

Before the Santa Fe had entered into an agreement to coöperate in building the A&P, the possibilities of Santa Fe-owned California lines were carefully studied. Representatives of the Company, G. G. Wilbur and L. G. Pratt, were sent to San Diego to confer with civic leaders. The people of San Diego were extremely eager for a connection with the East, having been balked once when early Texas and Pacific plans collapsed. The city offered 6,000 acres plus a mile of water front, and the public-spirited Kimball brothers offered 10,000 acres and another mile of water front. Leaders of San Bernardino, who were still piqued because the Southern Pacific by-passed them and built to Colton, hurriedly organized a delegation on October 20, 1879, to go to San Diego to induce the Santa Fe men to build north.[8] Forty dollars was raised to finance the expedition. It was headed by Fred T. Perris, who afterwards took a leading part in affairs of the Railroad. Time for the journey was three days one way. The Santa Fe men were interested and later inspected the suggested route. Morley examined the supposedly insurmountable Cajon Pass and remarked, "This is nothing; we can go through here easily enough."

Negotiations continued and finally an agreement was reached on July 10, 1880, to build a line to a junction with the A&P. Parties to the contract were Frank Kimball (representing three groups— Kimball Brothers, the Chamber of Commerce, and the Board of City Trustees of San Diego) and the California Southern (organized by Kidder, Peabody and Company, Cheney, Wilbur, Pratt and Nickerson). The California Southern Railroad Company was established by the same capitalists who led the Santa Fe. Junction was to be made with the A&P north of San Bernardino by January 1, 1884, but the deadline and point of contact were altered when the A&P stopped at Needles.*

Construction began soon and by August 21, 1882, Colton was reached where the line intersected the Southern Pacific. The latter did nothing to facilitate work on the California Southern.† The route was from National City, south of San Diego, north to Oceanside, Fallbrook, Temecula, Elsinore Junction, and Colton. Rough country made work difficult and costly. Kimball had estimated the cost at $10,000 per mile and Morley at $15,000. Nickerson cautiously described the cost at $18,000 in a circular, but, to be safe, provided for a possible issue of $25,000 in 6 per cent bonds per mile. He was horrified when Chief Engineer Joseph O. Osgood's costs came between $25,000 and $26,000. Osgood had spared no expense. The road was good—too good. He had been honest but lavish. Nickerson pleaded for economy to no avail.

---

*Originally the California Southern was to build to San Bernardino and the California Extension Railroad Company was to complete the sixty miles to the A&P. The two were merged in 1881.

†Discussed in Chapter IV, "Wars of the Santa Fe." The California Southern organized by the Santa Fe should not be confused with the company of the same name which Huntington brought into temporary being a decade before.

Finally, he detailed D. B. Robinson to report and to draw the reins. On August 5, 1882, Robinson sent his survey. The line was in excellent condition but promised inadequate traffic to support the investment. Additional mileage was without frills and Mr. Osgood. On September 13, 1883, the first train whistled into San Bernardino.

Elation over the extension of the line to San Bernardino was greatly dampened during the succeeding winter. Rain fell almost continuously during four weeks. The line through Temecula Canyon was inundated and washed out February 16, 17, and 18. Little could be done immediately because the storms persisted. After a brief subsidence, the floods rose to new heights and destruction extended over the whole line. The minor repairs that were made during the interim were wrecked. When the heavens and the waters had spent their fury, damage was estimated at $319,879.90 above a salvage figure of $11,000.[9] The California backers of the line were downhearted and Santa Fe men none too happy. An estimated $1,700 was needed to make repairs and build the line north of San Bernardino. New construction was out of the question, and independent financing of repairs was too formidable for the little line. The earnings dried up to a trickle, with various parts out of service, and interest on $2,784,000 of first-mortgage bonds was defaulted in July of 1884.

President Strong of the Santa Fe had an eye on developments and so did leaders of the Southern Pacific. The latter knew that the half-drowned California Southern was not going to be allowed to sink. No doubt the Santa Fe would enter at the last moment, rescue the line, and make a connection with the A&P at Needles. If this were done, the new work of the Southern Pacific from Mojave to Needles would be unused, since traffic would move over the new part of the California Southern. The Southern Pacific was on the spot, but so was the Santa Fe if costly construction was to be held to a minimum. Happily the two were able to get together, and the A&P leased the Mojave-Needles line in August of

1884.* The next step was formal union with the California Southern. On January 5, 1885, the Santa Fe acquired 50 per cent of the
stock as well as the right to sell $10,000 per mile in first-mortgage
bonds ahead of the old issue. The latter were relegated to income
bonds. The Santa Fe agreed to repair the damage and to build a
good 61-pound line to a junction with the A&P. The distance was
seventy miles and the point of contact, Waterman, now Barstow.
Strong acted with characteristic dispatch and soon had gangs at
work. On November 9, 1885, the gap had been spanned and another milestone had been passed. In the course of all this the
Southern Pacific leased joint trackage rights to the Santa Fe from
Colton to Los Angeles. Strong's determination to build if no lease
were forthcoming again had served the Company well. He was
no man to procrastinate, as the Southern Pacific leaders knew.

While the Santa Fe battled for suitable outlets to the Pacific,
another struggle was fought to retain supremacy in older parts
of the system. Other companies were preëmpting areas near by.
Branch lines had to be developed to preserve and to expand traffic
if economic extinction were to be averted. Needless to say, the
lusty Santa Fe was not to die.

New Branches

In 1880 the Santa Fe became embroiled in a rate war with the
Kansas City, Lawrence and Southern Railroad in the vicinity of
Wichita and Wellington, Kansas. Both companies had connections into Kansas City and fought bitterly for traffic. Rates were
cut to ruinous levels. Directors of each saw the folly of cutthroat
tactics and on December 16, 1880, the Santa Fe acquired control

---

*The Southern Pacific agreed to handle A&P business north of Mojave on a coördi-
nated basis with monthly settlements on the usual foreign car basis. The A&P could
solicit freight and passengers in San Francisco but was not to build terminal facilities.
The Southern Pacific would furnish the necessary traffic accommodations. In the final
analysis the agreement was much more than a lease. It resembled a deferred-purchase
plan. Since the original lien on the property could not be lifted until 1905, a purchase
price was agreed upon to be met in 1905; and in the meanwhile the line was to be
rented for 6 per cent of the purchase price.

over the smaller company by an exchange of securities.* The
newly acquired lines were excellent complements to the relatively
branchless Santa Fe and added 365 miles to the system. Most significant of all was the fact that no other large company had secured the mileage.

During 1881 and 1882 extensive building operations were
sponsored under various corporate names. They were:

Road	Place	Length
Marion and McPherson	Lyons to Ellinwood	20
Florence, El Dorado and		
Walnut Valley	El Dorado to Douglas	24
Harvey County	Sedgwick to Halstead	9
Kansas City & Olathe	Olathe to Waseca (Holliday)†	14
Leavenworth, Topeka and		
Southwestern (joint		
with the Union Pa-		
cific)	Leavenworth to Meriden Junction	47

Three short branches were built in New Mexico during the same
year.

---

*The new mileage had followed a devious corporate route. On February 12, 1858,
the Territorial Legislature of Kansas granted a charter to the Leavenworth, Lawrence
and Fort Gibson Railroad Company. Two grants of land were secured (125,000 and
62,000 acres). In 1866 the name was changed by substituting "Galveston" in place of
"Fort Gibson." Ground was broken for construction August 1, 1866. Garnett was
reached January 1, 1870, and by July 20, 1871, the line extended to the edge of the
Indian Territory at Coffeyville. Financial woes forced reorganization in 1878 and the
Company emerged as the Lawrence and Galveston Railroad. It was amalgamated with
the Kansas City and Santa Fe (Ottawa to Olathe) and Southern Kansas Railroad (Cher-
ryvale to Independence) and came out of this as the Kansas City, Lawrence and Southern Railroad March 29, 1879. Construction was pushed from Independence to Harper
with a branch to Hunnewell. The line was sold to Santa Fe interests, although purchase was made through the Kansas City, Topeka and Western. The Kansas City,
Lawrence and Southern was changed to the Kansas City, Lawrence and Southern Kansas. In 1883 the latter became the Southern Kansas Railway Company and in 1885
"the" was capitalized in the corporate title.

†There is an interesting sidelight on early personnel and construction methods in a
letter of one of the old-timers who worked on this line: "I was at that time working
loading dirt on wagons pulled by mules to make a level roadbed. We were from 28 to
35 men in one gang of different nationalities and our foreman used to put so many
Irish on one wagon, same amount of Dutch or Swedes or Americans on separate wagons
and then called on us to see who could load their wagons the fastest. If anyone thinks
the dirt was not flying he is mistaken. It was a good way to get us all to work fast and
as we were nearly all young and willing workers it was more or less sport or fun."
From a letter to M. L. Lyles by Andrew Nelson, Redondo Beach, California, July 29,
1937.

By the end of 1882 the Santa Fe had a well-developed network in Kansas. The mainline was now laid with steel and the newly acquired and run-down lines were rapidly being raised to Santa Fe standards.

Little completed branch mileage was added in 1883, although almost two hundred miles was begun. The year of 1884 brought completion of many of the projects and added the following:

Road	Place	Length
Wichita and Western (50 per cent by Frisco)	Wichita to Kingman	45
Kansas Southern	Chanute to Girard	40
Harper & Western	Harper to Attica	12
Kansas City & Emporia	Ottawa to Emporia	56
New Mexican	Nutt to Lake Valley	13
New Mexican	Socorro to Magdalena	31
Silver City, Deming, and Pacific	Deming to Silver City	48

Two of these developed into important parts of the mainline of the System. The investment of the Santa Fe in the Kansas City Belt Line Railway through the KCT&W was quintupled by $265,000 to $325,000. The Belt Line owned terminal tracks and facilities in greater Kansas City.

Salt Water in the Gulf

The rapid building pace set by the Santa Fe showed no signs of abatement; in fact, the rate quickened and three major programs were launched in a short period of time. William B. Strong remarked, "When a railroad ceases to grow, it begins to decay." The Company under his leadership as president was not to atrophy and disintegrate. Strong had realized Holliday's ambitions of a road to Santa Fe and the Pacific; now Strong was to vindicate Holliday again. The second portion of the dream of the "father of the Santa Fe" was to come true. The line would reach the shores of the Gulf of Mexico. The Company would do even more than that. Rails would extend over the sea to the great island city of Galveston. Since the Indian Territory intervened, Congressional assent had to be secured to build toward Texas from Kansas. A. A. Robinson detailed H. L. Marvin to examine three routes through the Territory from Coffeyville and Arkansas City. On May 20, 1884, Marvin reported that the most feasible line was from Arkansas City to Gainesville. Congress was approached for permission to build between the two points. The Southern Kansas Railway Company made the request. On July 4, 1884, permission was given, although near-by Denison was mentioned instead of Gainesville. At the same time authority was secured to construct a branch from the mainline at or near where the mainline entered the Indian Territory. The branch was to extend west to Medicine Lodge Creek and then southwest to the point where Wolf Creek crossed the west boundary of the Territory. No land grant was given but a right of way a hundred feet wide was obtained, together with modest amounts for stations. The Indians were to be indemnified for land required by the railroad.

Strong as usual had more irons in the fire than those pointing south. Long before, he had sounded out leaders of a struggling railroad which proceeded north from Galveston.* Why duplicate existing facilities? Why not unite? The Texas railroad lacked finances, while the Santa Fe was a tower of strength. Each line desired outlets in the vicinity of the other. An understanding was natural and informal coöperation began early in 1884, although no formal agreements were made for two years.

On the same day that Congressional blessings were bestowed on projection of the Southern Kansas to the south, the Gulf, Colorado and Santa Fe was given similar rights across the Indian Territory to the north. Preliminary surveys were soon made, and on November 25, 1884, M. L. Lynch, locating engineer, submitted a plan to Chief Engineer W. Snyder for a line north from Fort

---

*Implicit in H. L. Marvin's report of May 20, 1884, was a connection with the Gulf, Colorado and Santa Fe (Texas company). Marvin also observed that a connection with Mexican lines at Presidio might be desirable. The latter was made many years later.

Worth. For the greater part of the Territorial crossing, the route
was identical with Marvin's but deviated in the northern portion
and connected at Hunnewell, Kansas.

The years of 1884 and 1885 brought great financial distress to
the long-suffering Gulf, Colorado and Santa Fe. Trade stagnated,

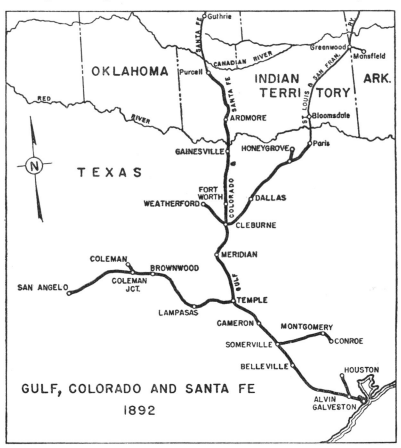

crops failed, rate-cutting and rebating staunched the flow of
revenues. The situation of the Company, which had never been
any too good, was critical. Lack of an outlet to the north promised
to be an even greater handicap in the future in competing with
the systems which offered through service. Something had to be
done. When George Sealy, president of the GC&SF, broached the

question of sale to the AT&SF, he found that Strong's interest in the Texas line had not diminished. A generous offer was made at a price which neither betrayed AT&SF stockholders nor took unfair advantage of the plight of the GC&SF. The AT&SF agreed to the $8,000 per mile in Santa Fe stock for the outstanding stock of the GC&SF.

Three months prior to the sale, the GC&SF had 625 completed miles and had 70 under construction. The mainline was from Galveston to Brownwood, 345 miles, via Somerville and Temple. The course lay northwest in the direction of Santa Fe, New Mexico, and Colorado. In addition there were the following branches:

Alvin to Houston	24 miles
Somerville to Montgomery and Conroe	74 "
Temple to Fort Worth	128 "
Cleburne to Dallas	54 "

Under way were extensions from Lampasas west and from Montgomery to the International and Great Northern Railway.

The contract between the two companies had a unique requirement. The GC&SF was required to convey, not 695 miles of line, but 1,000. The Santa Fe was to pay for the unbuilt part at the same rate. A further contractual qualification was a limitation of one year for completion to Purcell, where union would be made with the line sponsored by the Santa Fe. The branch which extended from Cleburne to Dallas was to be extended to Paris, Texas, to tie to the Santa Fe's ally, the Frisco. Another shorter branch was to run from Cleburne to Weatherford (see map). What a large order for a company that had been on the verge of financial prostration since inception!

The new member of the Santa Fe's growing family had been a community undertaking. Business men of Galveston who desired to improve the transportation facilities of the city's trading had conceived and financed the line. Houston had been invading the territory served by Galveston, and the commercial rivalry of the two was an important factor.*

The Gulf, Colorado and Santa Fe Railway Company was created by an Act of the Legislature of Texas on May 28, 1873. Business organization followed shortly, and the first set of officers was elected November 26. Albert Somerville was made president; M. Kopperl, vice-president; C. R. Hughes, secretary; and George Sealy, treasurer. All of these officers were men of importance, and they were supported by other influential men of Galveston, including W. L. Moody, Henry Rosenberg, John Sealy, R. S. Willis, A. C. Crawford, J. H. Hutchings, A. Ball, N. B. Yard, and many others no less worthy of mention. Galveston business men favored the project, although stock subscriptions were slow. Galveston County voted $500,000 in bonds for stock purchases, and the state of Texas granted over three and one-half million acres of land. This last was of the dime-an-acre quality. The Company disposed of the certificates or rights to the sections rather than located land.

By midsummer of 1874 sufficient support had been gained to warrant definite steps toward building. General Braxton Bragg, famed in the Civil War, was secured to act as chief engineer.† On September 18, 1874, Bragg appointed Col. J. P. Fresenius as chief of a field party to run the first 150 miles of the line. Fresenius had previously been warned that "it is expected you will preserve good discipline and subordination in your party—as far as your authority goes, prevent straggling and marauding. Discharge

---

*Details are given in Chapter IV, "Wars of the Santa Fe."

†Many military leaders became construction engineers. The best explanation was that few men knew anything about construction and that military men at least had experience in organizing and handling large numbers of men. General Bragg confided in a letter to his wife that he shuddered at the thought of the responsibility of construction. He later wrote that he would put on a bold front and make believe that he was competent.

Bragg plunged wholeheartedly into the venture and repeatedly urged the officials to proceed with dispatch in order to maximize the benefits of the line. On October 29, 1874, he wrote to the president and directors as follows:

". . . we must reach out our arms and gather the fruits with which a bountiful nature has surrounded us or others will soon do it, and we shall repeat the history of many of our Southern marts where the daily hum of business has ceased and decay is doing its work."

anyone who does not conform to your rules, or who fails in his duties. The excessive or habitual use of ardent spirits is prohibited by the Company's regulations."[10]

Bids were solicited in the spring of 1875 and the offer of the well-known firm of Burnett and Kilpatrick was accepted. On May 1, 1875, Henry Rosenberg, the president, turned the first shovelful. A small but distinguished audience was present. Guy M. Bryan declared that construction would give "a highway for the grain of the West, the wealth of the Pacific, and the mineral resources of the far-off mountains of Colorado to reach a European market through the chief port of the Gulf of Mexico." Several others made equally optimistic statements. Notwithstanding the presence of Bragg, all rules were suspended and the contractors satisfied the currently large demand for champagne, cheese, and crackers.

Work in earnest began on the mainline the following month. Fresenius replaced Bragg. The Company sustained a severe setback when a storm from the tropics wrecked much of the early construction. Progress was hampered by lack of money. Three years were required to complete a trifle over sixty miles. Galveston County harried the enterprise with attempts to withdraw the aid that had been voted. The Company was unable to buy adequate rolling stock and the limited operations were a brilliant shade of red in the books of account. Various emergency loans were secured but these were merely stays of execution. On April 15, 1879, the Company was offered at public sale and bought for $200,000 by George Sealy (a stockholder and a creditor to the extent of $250,000).

Many of the men who were early identified with the project joined Sealy in the rejuvenation which followed. Construction was actively pushed by Major B. M. Temple, chief engineer. Brenham, 126 miles distant, was reached August 1, 1880. On the same day trackage rights were secured into Houston. By the following March the mainline of 60-pound steel had been extended to Belton, 226 miles from Galveston. Near Belton a branch projected north toward the town of Fort Worth. This offshoot was opened for freight traffic at the start of 1882. Later in the year the Chicago, Texas and Mexican Central was purchased. This acquisition extended northeast from Cleburne, skirting Dallas. The pineries of east Texas gained the attention of Sealy, and he took steps to buy the Central and Montgomery Railway. It was really an exchange of securities to finance access to a source of ties as well as traffic for timberless areas on the rest of the system. With minor exceptions there was little additional expansion until 1885.

The GC&SF had a formidable task ahead when it entered the contract with the Santa Fe. Building 300 miles in one year was no small undertaking for a line that had required over a decade to build 700. Financing was made easy by the alliance and backing of the AT&SF. Chief Engineer Sherman spent a third of the allotted time organizing his crews and acquiring materials. A force of 100 engineers and 5,000 men was required. About 2,000 teams had to be rounded up. During the hot summer months when the pace was fast, Sherman substituted whiskey for water for the last rounds.

The Southern Kansas Railway was building south to Purcell at the same time that the GC&SF approached Purcell from Fort Worth. Progress reports were exchanged and a race developed to see which gang would be first. Sherman made rapid progress by an ingenious method. Each day he spotted enough track materials for a "superhuman" performance. The men were told that when they finished the work laid out, they could have the rest of the day off. Everybody worked with zest and determination. Sherman gauged the amount so that the men always finished a few minutes early, yet in doing it, they accomplished the normal result of a day and a half of labor. Gradually the objectives were raised and the pace was quickened. But Sherman was pitted against the smoothest building organization in the country. Anything under the tutelage of A. A. Robinson was done thoroughly and with speed. Nearer and nearer came the two crews. It looked like a dead heat. At the very last Sherman's men mustered new power and reached the rendezvous only four hours ahead of their rivals. Or did they? Sherman said they did, but members of the other crew to a man declared that GC&SF men lost by a few minutes. At any rate the connection was made on April 26, 1887. Other construction called for by the contract was completed and the mainline extended from Coleman Junction to Ballinger.

No country could have been much wilder than the Indian Territory was at the time the building race was on. There were no towns, nor even legal settlers. Curious Indians frequently put in appearances. Col. J. W. F. Hughes, who had charge of track work from Ponca to Purcell, built the first houses at the present location of Guthrie, Edmond, and Oklahoma City. The structures were temporary shelters for the trackmen and were made of ties. Two years later mushroom towns were to spring into being with the Oklahoma rush of April 22, 1889.

The second line of the Southern Kansas Railway which was authorized by the Congressional Act of 1884 was laid out simultaneously with the projection to the south. Grading from Kiowa, Kansas, to Waynoka in the Territory began in the fall of 1886 and tracklaying was finished the following spring. On September 12, 1887, the Texas limit was touched and construction on to Panhandle City was continued by the Southern Kansas Railway Company of Texas. The new line was said "to start nowhere and go nowhere." In time it was to become an extremely important link in the transcontinental route of the Santa Fe.

More Branches

Various small undertakings throughout the system had added branches here and there to improve the whole. Under the charter of the Harper and Western a short section was built in 1885 from Attica to Kiowa. The Florence, El Dorado and Walnut Valley was extended in 1886 from Douglas to Winfield and the Kansas City, Emporia and Southern built between Howard and Moline.

The majority of small additions in 1886 were brought into the Santa Fe fold by a new subsidiary, the Chicago, Kansas and Western Railroad Company. The CK&W amalgamated several small railroads and soon let contracts for over 400 miles of construction. Some of the lines were:

Location	Mileage
Great Bend to Scott City	120
Hutchinson to Kinsley	84
Larned to Jetmore	46
Benedict Junction to Madison Junction	41
Havana, Independence to Cedar Vale	55

The line from Hutchinson to Kinsley took a short cut across the "great bend" of the Arkansas River and effected a substantial saving in miles for cross-country trains. Many of the branches undertaken by the CK&W were not completed until 1887. During 1886 the Leavenworth, Northern and Southern Railway was finished forty-six miles between Cummings on the line from Topeka to Atchison and Wilder on the line from Topeka to Kansas City. Kansas was not the only state in which branches were being developed. Numerous corporations were bought or established by Santa Fe interests between 1885 and 1887 to secure the branches in California. The chief results were to provide independent contact into Los Angeles and to furnish a system of feeders for the promising orchards and gardens of southern California. On May 20, 1887, the California Central Railway Company was established, and the various small companies which had built the branches disappeared into the California Central much as chicks hide under a hen.

ANOTHER GOAL

While the Santa Fe crisscrossed Kansas with feeders during the 'eighties other railroads did the same thing. The period was one of great expansion throughout the industry. From the east came the Burlington, the Frisco, the Rock Island, and the Missouri Pacific. These lines had connections with Chicago and as they moved west, Kansas City no longer was a dividing point for exchanging traffic. The invaders picked up tonnage in Kansas and hauled to Chicago. The Santa Fe perceived the handwriting on the wall and as early as 1883 located two lines from Kansas City to Chicago. Little more was done until 1886. By this time the invasion of Kansas had reached alarming proportions. Norris L. Gage wrote A. A. Robinson a cogent letter stressing the desirability of immediate action. He contended:

1—A line could now be selected which would likely support itself and pay a fair interest in the investment not counting its value to the present system. Every year's delay makes such selection more difficult as the territory between Kansas City and Chicago becomes occupied by other roads.

2—It would place your traffic Department in a more independent position in dealing with Colorado, Trans-continental, and all other competitive business.

3—The line would be shorter and with better grades than any other now in existence or likely to be built hereafter.

4—The present and prospective enormous mileage of your road, and its concentration upon natural and easy lines at Kansas City, as the most important gateway to the State will make both your system west of the Missouri River and the proposed extension of special value as auxiliaries to each other.

5—By at once placing your entire patronage in direct rapid and unobstructed communication with Chicago, you deprive other roads of inducements which now exist to build in this direction, and thus, in a large measure, you protect your entire system.[11]

Robinson did not need any urging. At President Strong's request he had begun in the spring of 1886 a system of surveys intended to establish the best route to Chicago. Santa Fe officials, although convinced that something had to be done, were not certain that an entirely new line would have to be built. At the time of the surveys, they were sure that a long-term traffic agreement with their rivals was inadvisable, being "always uncertain and unsatisfactory, and generally neglected or odious." There was feverish excitement over the possible purchase of the Alton until a quotation was given for Alton stock.

If the Santa Fe were to enter Chicago, new tracks would have to lead the way. Strong hoped that the "two streaks of rust" of the Chicago and St. Louis Railway could be purchased on favorable terms to provide an excellent right of way into Chicago from the vicinity of Streator.* The C&SL extended from Chicago to Pekin, Illinois, hopefully en route to St. Louis. The venture had been launched in 1859 but did not float well. F. E. Hinckley, its most successful president, fought a hard but losing battle against creditors and competitors. The odds were too great, and the line deteriorated. When makeshift repairs rendered one part passable another section went bad. Hinckley was more than willing to talk terms with the Santa Fe. As early as October of 1886 a "meeting of minds" had been reached, and actual sale occurred on December 15.

The Santa Fe acted as quietly as possible. The right of way had to be acquired, and widespread publicity would have made the price of portions prohibitive rather than a modest amount in excess of the current price for other uses. Virtually no effort was made to induce towns to assist in the venture. The Company was determined to have the best line possible from an engineering viewpoint and had no intention to meander into every community in a twenty-mile swath. The new extension was too important to the remainder of the Santa Fe to permit anything but the best.

The secrecy of the surveying parties played on the imagination of every newspaper man in the area. One and all turned sleuth, saw little, and concluded much. Keokuk and Fort Madison on the Mississippi waged a seesaw journalistic struggle for the new railroad long after the Santa Fe had ruled out a Keokuk crossing as impractical. When the location was announced the Ft. Madison *Democrat* consoled Keokuk and expressed the hope that a branch could be built to the latter. "Tee hee" was gleefully added to the barb.

---

*The Chicago and St. Louis Railway was the last in a series of companies. They were: the Chicago, Pekin and Southwestern Railroad; the Chicago and Plainfield Railroad; and the Chicago, St. Louis and Western Railroad.

Early in November, 1886, parties were put in the field to establish the final location. Robinson's only instruction was to "be sure not to have any curves that could not be satisfactorily accounted for."

On December 3, 1886, the Chicago, Santa Fe and California Railway Company was chartered in Illinois to carry out the pro-

KANSAS CITY TO CHICAGO

ject. A separate Iowa charter was obtained for the portion from Fort Madison, Iowa, to the vicinity of Kansas City, Missouri. Grading began in March and progressed rapidly in succeeding months. By this time construction of railroads by the Santa Fe was like the manufacture of a modern car on a great assembly line. Experienced engineers had perfected an organization which seemed to anticipate every difficulty. There was never any delay while supplies were restocked. Materials to meet all needs were on hand. Construction laborers were not green hands where old hands were needed. Seasoned gangs whose business was to build were brought from all parts of the Santa Fe. Largest obstacles were the bridges over the Mississippi and Missouri. Octave Chanute, world-renowned bridge builder and mechanical sage, was retained in a consulting capacity. Spanning of the treacherous channel of the Big Muddy was the more difficult, but Chanute and those under his direction were equal to the task. Tracklaying with 72-pound steel rail came on the heels of grading. On December 5, 1887, the last rail between Chicago and Fort Madison was put in place. On December 31 twin ribbons of steel were complete to the Missouri River. Thus in a single year the whole line had been finished. Special thanks were due the various intersecting railroads which hauled materials to many points, making possible the use of several crews.

Completion of the bridge over the Missouri at Sibley was checked by inclement weather. Late in January of 1888 train service was begun before finishing touches had been applied. Regular operations began on May 1.

Terminal facilities in Chicago were acquired by the newly organized Atchison, Topeka and Santa Fe Railroad Company in Chicago. Various short lines were bought or leased and when pieced together they provided an excellent crow's route to the leased Dearborn Station. Several parcels of real estate were purchased to meet the terminal requirements.

In the course of construction to Chicago the Santa Fe encountered one of the very few lawsuits which were ever directed against it by a contractor. Neither party had been at fault. The case was "one of those things" and developed into spectacular proportions. Payment for grading varied with the nature of the material graded, such as common, loose rock, shale, solid rock. Williams, McRitchie and Company encountered some clay in Missouri which had been hardened by sustained dry weather. The substance was described as yellow clay, as hard clay, and by a dozen other terms. Before grading had been started, Santa Fe engineers warned the contractors that the material was regarded as common clay. After the work was finished the graders wanted $188,000 extra for work in "loose rock." Loose rock included "hard-pan which could not be loosened by a 10-inch plow and a six mule or horse team." The Santa Fe balked. For six years the legal battle was waged to the Supreme Court of Missouri and down again. Experts were consulted by the dozens. One man was summoned from the Holy Land, where he was building a railroad to Jerusalem. Others were brought from equally distant points. When the testimony of B. F. Booker, a former Santa Fe engineer who had assisted in surveys in the disputed area, was needed, all the participants in the case went to Mexico City to hear the evidence. Booker's health not permitting a journey to Hannibal, the referee and the lawyers went to Booker. Booker's condition improved at the pleasant reunion he had with his old co-workers. The hearings of 1894 lasted seventy-five days and filled 14,000 pages. The Santa Fe had made an out-of-court offer, and when the decision was announced the contractors regretted their obstinacy. The award of $30,000 was only a fraction of the voluntary offer. Seven years had elapsed since the grading. The suit had been costly to both and the reputation of Missouri soil had been impugned.

Various enterprises were auxiliary to the line to Chicago. The Company investigated opportunities to develop new connections. In April and May of 1887 surveys were made of several routes from the Pekin branch to St. Louis. G. W. Vaughan directed field work under Fred Mack, E. Treadwell, and C. S. Carpenter. Surveys were made the following month for a branch to Monmouth, Illinois. A rumor was circulated that the line would be extended to St. Paul, Minnesota.

In the summer of 1887 the Santa Fe bought the old St. Louis County Railroad. The line was only five miles long but possessed valuable terminal rights in St. Louis. The intention was to join the mainline to Chicago in central Missouri and provide Kansas City-St. Louis service. Under the new corporate name, St. Louis, Kansas City and Colorado Railroad Company, an extension was made to Union, Missouri, but short of independent connection. No more work was ever done on this by the Santa Fe.

NEW ADDITIONS

Purchase was made in August, 1887, of the St. Joseph and St. Louis Railroad from St. Joseph to a junction with the new mainline at Henrietta, Missouri. The Santa Fe made this move while entering St. Joseph from the southwest over the tracks of the wholly owned St. Joseph and Santa Fe Railroad.

One other project was begun and completed in 1887. The Santa Fe built from Pueblo to Denver a long-desired line, which marked the end of an unsatisfactory armistice with the Denver and Rio Grande. The work was under the charter of the Denver and Santa Fe Railway Company. Entrance to the city was simplified by the purchase of the local Denver Circle Railroad.

The year of 1887 marked the end of a great period of construction. For the most part all immediate needs had been met. A variety of adverse factors was soon to impair revenues and render additional work financially inexpedient. The Santa Fe did make two other additions to the System which fall into the era of expansion. On May 23, 1890, the purchase of the Frisco (St. Louis and San Francisco) was announced. This was not an unexpected move and was designed among other things to "obviate all the cumbersomeness and expenses incidental to the joint operation of so much rail." The transaction was not a cash purchase but an exchange of stock. The Santa Fe paid $22,511,687.50 of par in common stock for the Frisco equity. There were 1,329 miles of mainline and branches, 188 of sidings, and 980 miles which had been owned jointly with the Santa Fe (see map). Entrance to St. Louis was considered one of the brighter spots.

The Santa Fe made a second important purchase in 1890. On September 5, title to the Colorado Midland Railway was acquired at a cost of $1,900,000 in cash and $4,400,200 plus in par value of Santa Fe stock. The property was subject to a debt of $11,000,000. The objective of this purchase was to bolster traffic on the new line out of Denver.

Both the Frisco and the Midland were on financial rocks, but profitable operations were expected under the new relations.

In 1892, twenty-four years after ground was broken in Topeka, the Santa Fe had grown to a system of 9,300 miles. It linked Lake Michigan, the Gulf of Mexico, and the Pacific and served the growing cities of Chicago, Kansas City, Fort Worth, Dallas, Galveston, Denver, San Diego, Los Angeles, and San Francisco. Agriculture and mines of the great Southwest had their livelihood indissolubly integrated with the railroad.

In Retrospect

Several factors had been noteworthy during expansion. First, the Santa Fe, unlike most railroads, did not resort to construction companies. The Santa Fe did not only its own work but also that of its subsidiaries. There was no nest-feathering, and a dollar of real assets was produced for each dollar invested. The men who headed the Company were railroad men who wanted to build and run a railroad. They were not financiers who played checkers with railroad stocks and bonds. Second, much of the Santa Fe was built in advance of traffic, and paved the way for the sodbuster, the miner, and the cattleman. Lines were built where trade had the best prospects of flourishing. Third, construction was of the best quality which techniques and materials of the times afforded. No effort was spared in the attempt to build a substantial railroad. Fourth, keen competition among railroads occasioned construction of many lines long before traffic warranted. Territories had to be tapped or they were permanently lost. Those companies which hesitated were doomed. Traffic was to go to the first on the scene. Fifth, as the population increased, a necessity developed for dozens of branch lines and small railroads to fill the gaps between mainlines. The Santa Fe, for its own sake and the sake of the people of its hinterland, built dozens of feeders. Sixth, many lines which were financial failures as small independent companies could be highly profitable segments of a larger company. The Santa Fe wove dozens of bankrupt lines into a prosperous whole. Seventh, rapid expansion in undeveloped areas was fraught with the danger of adding lines which would prove undesirable. A few of the additions turned out to be unwise. These will be considered later. Eighth, a railroad network was logically developed which spread in ideal fashion from Chicago over the southwest quarter of the nation. The system served the two states, Texas and California, which were to develop most in the years to come and provided long hauls over the natural routes of commerce to and from Chicago. Ninth and last, there was nothing that Holliday had envisioned which had not come true. The good Colonel had been unduly conservative. Was it not generally known that the Santa Fe was on the verge of absorbing the Baltimore and Ohio or the New York Central?

IV

Wars of the Santa Fe

"Truth is stranger than fiction."

USINESS CONDUCT like general human conduct has been greatly modified in the course of time. The two are actually inseparable, for businesses are managed by individuals. A corporation is not without a conscience. There was a time in the West when justice was determined by speed on the draw. If ammunition failed, brute savagery was held to be the next barometer of right and wrong. There was no corner policeman or riot squads to stop the "normal processes." The slogan was "Give 'em room." When persons violated the "Code of the West" individuals stepped forward to conduct impromptu court sessions. Horse-stealing was the most frequent cause for spur-of-the-moment judiciaries. The percentage of convictions was extraordinarily high and the sentence invariably severe. Perhaps the lack of jailing facilities accounted for the extensive use of limbs. Murdering a man was not such a heinous crime as stealing a horse and seldom merited any outside interference. Many years had to pass before the rudiments of modern law enforcement agencies were organized.

In the business world there was no I.C.C. or S.E.C. to stand guard over companies. Each company could preëmpt like a person and was never asked "to show cause why it should or should not."

The Santa Fe in the course of rapid expansion collided with other companies which sought the same objectives. Since "possession was nine points of the law," there was nine times more effort to secure possession than there was legal backing. At least three large-scale military campaigns were fought, along with numerous minor ones. The conflicts did not end with the period of construction. Clean-cut victories were infrequently the case and both companies might build into the same territory. The battle then shifted to one for traffic. In the days before regulation, rate wars were waged repeatedly. On one occasion when the Southern Pacific and the Santa Fe were embroiled, the former sold tickets from the Coast to the Missouri River for a dollar. The rate was soon raised lest the Santa Fe bankrupt the Southern Pacific by paying the dollar for people to ride on the competitor's line. Dozens of town rivalries in which the Santa Fe was the prize grew up. Where would the county seat be located? Was not Guthrie the logical capital of Oklahoma?

THE GULF, COLORADO AND SANTA FE IS BORN

If a railroad passed through a town, it would expand, becoming the county seat, the center of commerce, and all its citizens would amass great fortunes. A town rivalry accounted in large measure for the birth of the Gulf, Colorado and Santa Fe. The municipal strife which was responsible arose many years before the Atchison, Topeka and Santa Fe looked into Texas. The fuse which set off organization of the GC&SF was a quarantine applied by Harris County (Houston) on Galveston's commerce.

Galveston was once the port of entry and exit for the entire state. Commerce flourished. Great merchant ships disgorged the needs of an empire at the wharves and in return swallowed thousands of bales of cotton. Even New Orleans' supremacy as the mouth of the South was threatened. But all the trading which was handled so expeditiously within Galveston had to overcome great handicaps in the hinterland. Transportation to the interior was primitive. Efforts were made to secure improved means but not much was accomplished. A railroad was built to Houston, the Galveston, Houston and Henderson, and another line, the Houston and Texas Central, was extended beyond. The Houston Direct Navigation Company had boats and barges plying between Houston and Galveston. The effect of these enterprises was the opposite of what Galvestonians had hoped. Houston began to grow commercially at the expense of the Island City. If shallow-draught vessels could be floated up the Buffalo Bayou from Galveston, then there was little reason why ocean-going vessels should stop at the great port. Goods could be loaded and unloaded from large vessels to barges without the aid of middlemen of Galveston. Houston businessmen aggressively fought for a larger volume. Railroad projects fanned out in all directions from Houston, but Galveston held tenaciously to its supremacy.

In 1867 fate dealt Galveston a cruel blow. Yellow fever had long ravaged the Galveston populace during the summer months. Ships from ports to the south seemed to be the carriers. Some years brought more severe attacks than others; periodically there were horrible epidemics. The year of 1867 was especially bad. An estimated 1,150 out of a population of 18,000 succumbed to the scourge. Panicky fears were expressed by people to the north that goods from Galveston might spread the disease. Texas, at the time, permitted counties to place a quarantine on goods from infected sources. Harris County (Houston) promptly placed an embargo on trade with Galveston. Since the bulk of Galveston's business was routed through Houston, normal trade was paralyzed. Houston merchants obligingly stepped into the breach and offered to accommodate the cotton growers and businessmen to the north as well as all the ship companies. The businessmen are said to have been so happily impressed with the quarantine of 1867 that they concocted "scares" in succeeding years when the number of yellow fever cases was below normal. The only fever that Galvestonians admitted was a fever of rage over the strangulation of their business. Civic leaders had long contemplated a railroad to the north, and the quarantines put an end to procrastination. Soon the GC&SF began to take form. Needless to say, the new railroad by-passed Harris County and the quarantines stopped. Though the GC&SF was to serve Galveston well, the centralization of commerce at Houston could not be arrested. Eventually even the Gulf was imported and Houston's growth outstripped

GALVESTON — HOUSTON
AND
VICINITY

that of all other southern cities. Galveston did not slip back; she simply did not go forward as fast.

D&RG War I

The most sensational of all the Company's wars were fought with the Denver and Rio Grande, commonly called "The D&RG Wars" by Santa Fe men. The prizes were control over the most feasible route into New Mexico and the route west to the great silver mines in and near Leadville. William B. Strong had joined the Santa Fe in the fall of 1877 and was determined to carry out the long-deferred plans to build into New Mexico. But the Santa Fe was not the only railroad that aspired to entry into the untapped riches toward the south. The Denver and Rio Grande had the same ambition, only in a more intensified form. This company had been organized in 1870 to build north and south along the eastern slopes of the Rockies. A rich traffic was expected, supporters believing that the new line would handle an excellent exchange with the various transcontinental east-west roads. General William J. Palmer, late of the Kansas Pacific, was the moving force of the D&RG. He was a capable administrator and a real match for any adversary. Organization was quickly accomplished without benefit of land grant and about January 1, 1871, construction began between Denver and Colorado Springs. The gauge was narrow, three feet, and prompted the nickname "Baby Railroad." Late in October, 1871, the first segment was completed, and by the following midsummer Pueblo had been reached. A branch toward Canon City was begun and finished as far as Labran, seven or eight miles short of Canon City. There the line languished for two years while finances were bolstered.

General Palmer was keenly disappointed over the failure of the D&RG to obtain a lion's share of the commerce with Santa Fe, New Mexico. The wagon trains continued to haul to and from the Santa Fe Railroad and Kansas Pacific to the east. Palmer reasoned that the D&RG had not been extended far enough to the south to divert traffic. Steps were taken to secure the benefits at the earliest moment. In June of 1873 work toward Trinidad was begun. The source of funds was cut off because of the Panic, and the terminus was not reached until April 20, 1876. To the dismay of Trinidad the railroad veered to the east and stopped five miles distant. Palmer's associate, Governor A. C. Hunt, laid out the new town of El Moro. El Moro developed quickly, but its founding was a tactical blunder. Residents of Trinidad were alienated and were ready to lend active support to any prospective, competing road.

Palmer intended the D&RG to build into New Mexico from El Moro, and there is no doubt that he intended the line to go through Raton Pass. Long before construction of the Santa Fe was begun in Topeka, Palmer had investigated possible routes for the Kansas Pacific from Fort Wallace to Albuquerque. By far the best one was through the Purgatoire and Chequaco valleys toward Las Vegas via the famous Raton Pass.* When Palmer established the D&RG he contemplated following the same course into New Mexico and expressed this intention on many occasions. With Governor Hunt, Palmer reëxamined the Territory in 1874 and concluded that construction should be undertaken immediately.

---

*Raton Pass had a great influence in shaping the channels of trade and development. The breach was undoubtedly the best way over the Raton Mountains. Other passes were so inferior that the barrier for all practical purposes had only one break. Early commerce over the Santa Fe Trail sought passage to the south over this long-used Indian thoroughfare. Traders who took the Cimarron Route veered south of the mountains and had no need to cross. When the railroads were built into eastern Colorado, traffic north and south became much heavier. Points on the Kansas Pacific and later the Santa Fe became the eastern termini of the abbreviated trail.

Although Raton Pass was the best route to the south, it was none too good in an unimproved state. Uncle Dick Wootton, an illustrious Indian fighter, scout, and trader, decided to cease his rovings and do something to help commerce over the barrier. In 1865 he secured charters from the legislature of Colorado and New Mexico to authorize a toll road from Trinidad to Red River, New Mexico, via Raton Pass. The highway was cut and filled during the following spring and was a boon to travel and to Uncle Dick. Business was good, but it took all of Uncle Dick's fighting qualities to cope with some of the customers. An inn was built near the Pass where lodging, food, drink, and supplies were available. The tolls were tailor-made. Dogs, cats, horses, mules, cattle, etc., bore various imposts. Indians and posses after horse thieves were free. Uncle Dick regretted that he had not put Mexicans in the free category. No end of trouble developed with them.

Wootton coöperated wholeheartedly with the Santa Fe and was on hand to ward off the D&RG men when a clash threatened. In return for his services the Santa Fe gave him a life grant of $50 per month in credit in a supply store at Trinidad. Payment was shifted to Mrs. Wootton when Uncle Dick died in 1892 and later to a daughter.

Financial difficulties checked action. When the line was finished to El Moro, Palmer assumed that everyone knew that construction would proceed through Raton Pass. It was the only worth-while route south, and the D&RG was within a few miles of the opening. There was no apparent need to file a plat and profile for the line, because no rival was near to dispute the right through the bottleneck. The D&RG was to pay heavily for its smugness. Santa Fe men had quietly formulated plans for a *coup d'état*. The plot was difficult to keep secret because certain public acts were necessary. General Palmer learned that Strong had secured a charter for New Mexico lines and promptly took steps to establish a supremacy in Raton Pass. On February 26, 1878, Nickerson authorized Strong to proceed with construction south from the mainline of the Santa Fe. This was not interpreted to mean that work should begin at the mainline—work was to begin where Strong thought best and that was in the Pass. Accounts of the race to seize control vary in detail but agree in substance.

Strong immediately ordered A. A. Robinson to go from Pueblo and begin grading in the critical area at the earliest possible moment. He took the next D&RG train to El Moro. On the same train was Chief Engineer J. A. McMurtrie of the rival company. The latter had identical instructions and, of course, neither man confided in the other. The train reached El Moro shortly before midnight, and McMurtrie retired for much-needed sleep. Robinson did not seem to care about rest; all he wanted was the earlier start. He had already made some arrangements for a working crew before leaving Pueblo and desired to be on the scene to supervise. Securing a horse, Robinson hurried to Uncle Dick's home on the north slope. There with the help of Uncle Dick he mustered a semblance of a force among the transients. Morley and Kingman were busy recruiting men near by, and in early morning hours reinforcements arrived from Trinidad. At 5:00 a.m. Robinson, Uncle Dick, and their sleepy-eyed men walked up the north slope of the Pass and began to shovel by lantern light.

Meanwhile McMurtrie had not been idle. How early he arose is not known, but most accounts indicate that he and his men arrived on the controverted scene less than thirty minutes after Robinson and his graders. There was not much the D&RG men could do. Only one railroad could go through and the Santa Fe was in possession. Since each side had about the same number of men doubt existed whether Robinson's party could be ousted. Threats were made but nothing developed. The D&RG men withdrew and began work in near-by Chicken Creek. The impracticability of the alternative was soon evident and the project abandoned.

By the narrow margin of a few minutes, development of the Santa Fe had been fundamentally affected. Loss to the D&RG would have meant indefinite postponement of construction to the west. Later development of the Company in New Mexico and Arizona was conditioned so much by the circumstances of the moment that a shift in early timing would have made for radical changes in the course of its history. The Santa Fe would have entered New Mexico and extended on to the Coast, but the route, time, and methods would probably have been different.

D&RG WAR II

Rivalry between the companies had not ended; in fact it had just begun. Soon the two were to wage a battle in which nothing was conceded without a struggle. During the 'seventies rich silver deposits were discovered in many parts of Colorado, especially near Silverton and Leadville. Thousands of miners were attracted to the areas from all parts of the world, and an exceptionally choice plum ripened before the eyes of the traffic-hungry Santa Fe and D&RG. The Maker in his inscrutable wisdom had not deposited the silver where it was readily accessible. As is true of many good things in life, hardship had to be endured in order to reap the harvest. Leadville was located in a mountain fastness that seemed to defy any attempt to conquer its isolation. Brave men were not lacking, and both the D&RG and the Santa Fe resolved

to make available the riches to the Nation and the traffic to themselves. The only feasible route to the treasures of the Rockies was
along the Arkansas River. Leadville could not be approached from
the east. The line had to begin far to the southeast at Canon City
and intertwine with the river. Immediately west of Canon City
all semblance of a flood plain vanished where the river coursed
through a spectacular defile. Sheer rugged walls rising one thousand feet compressed the channel to thirty feet. Construction of a
railroad posed great engineering difficulties. Two railroads
through the Gorge were impossible. Control of the Royal Gorge,
or Grand Cañon, as it was called, carried a monopoly of the cov-

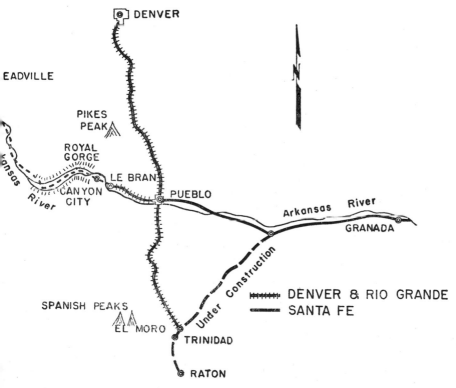

eted traffic. Accounts of the war of occupation not only vary in
details but are full of contradictions. Courts had great difficulty
sifting the truth. The passing of time has eliminated the bias of

fact-finders, but time itself has taken a toll. Newspaper reporters in quest of a raise in pay and publishers anxious for circulation accounted for gross distortion of events which needed no exaggeration.

The background of this, the greatest of the wars of the Santa Fe, was similar to the setting at Raton Pass. There was room for only one line, and substitute routes for the loser were so inferior as to be worth nothing. As in the earlier skirmish the D&RG had alienated local residents. The disadvantage of a hostile populace did much to offset an obviously superior location of the narrow-gauge line. The people of Canon City had suffered long from the high-handed policy of General Palmer. Their city seemed too insignificant to be recognized.

In the spring of 1872 the D&RG was completed from Denver to Pueblo. A thirty-six-mile branch was promptly undertaken west from Pueblo. The objective was the coal fields at Labran, about seven or eight miles short of Canon City. Rails were laid into Labran on October of 1872 and grading was soon finished to Canon City.[1] Then work was discontinued, to the dismay of the people of Canon City. Residents contended that the Railroad was blackmailing the city into voting bonds, and the officials of the Company claimed that national financial collapse had weakened the D&RG too much to complete the work. For two years inaction of General Palmer goaded Canonites. The D&RG told the citizens that all Canon City business was secured at Labran and that they would have to finance much of the cost of completion if they desired more convenience. One bond issue was voted and then invalidated, but in 1874 Canon City voted $50,000 in city bonds and a like amount in real estate in return for completion to a point within three-fourths of a mile from the center of business. The track was laid promptly. Town boosters assumed that the D&RG would do more than meet the bare requirements of the agreement and would build to the heart of the community. They were enraged when tracklaying was stopped precisely three-fourths of a mile away. The ill will generated by Palmer and his men was to backfire on the D&RG when signs pointed to the arrival of the Santa Fe.

In the contest for control of Raton Pass the D&RG had the advantage of lines much closer to the coveted area than the Santa Fe. The same situation existed in the Cañon War. The Santa Fe had been extended west only as far as Pueblo by the Pueblo and Arkansas Valley Railway. The D&RG with its branch of forty-three miles to Canon City was within a couple of miles of the narrows.

The surveys through the Royal Gorge duplicated the history of examinations in Raton Pass. General Palmer had long envisaged construction west from Cañon City. George L. Anderson in his study of Palmer wrote:

He [Palmer] had called attention to the route in his surveys for the Kansas Pacific; he had included it in the main line of the Denver and Rio Grande when the certificate of incorporation was prepared; he had caused it to be surveyed in 1871 and 1872; in 1873 in company with Governor Hunt he had personally surveyed the entire route to Leadville, or California Gulch as it was then called, with a view to building a railroad; and he had ordered the grading and masonry work to be done on a short section of the route in the Royal Gorge as early as 1871. The only thing he had neglected to do was to file a plat of the route with the General Land Office as he was required to do by the act of March 3, 1875, if he wished to hold a prior claim against any subsequent railway organizations. There isn't anything more certain in the early history of the Denver and Rio Grande company than the fact that its promoters looked forward at all times to the completion of a railroad west from Canon City through the Big Cañon of the Arkansas.[2]

For the second time the negligence of the D&RG in filing a plat was to prove costly.

The D&RG viewed extension of the Santa Fe into southern Colorado with apprehension. The Santa Fe seemed too concerned with local traffic and appeared as a threat to the traffic prizes. During the time that the D&RG rails extended to Labran, the people of Canon City tried to induce the Santa Fe to parallel the narrow-gauge railroad and build into their city. But the Santa Fe was busy assimilating hundreds of miles of new line and did not have the wherewithal to continue west. After the Santa Fe reached Pueblo in 1876, leading men in Canon City thought again of means to improve local transportation. The interior of Colorado was steadily showing more treasures and Canon City wanted to open the vault. Coöperation with the "Baby Railroad" was unthinkable, but the citizens believed that if a start could be made Santa Fe officials could be induced to lend a hand or to take over. The plan was to build west of Canon City and depend upon the Santa Fe to extend its line from Pueblo. Accordingly the Canon City and San Juan Railway was incorporated on February 19, 1877. Santa Fe officials already were working behind the scenes and before the end of the month, H. R. Holbrook of the Santa Fe began a crude survey through the Cañon for the new company. The line was staked and a plat prepared and filed with the General Land Office. On June 22, 1877, formal acceptance of the first twenty miles was made by the Secretary of Interior. Beyond twenty miles there was believed to be room for two railroads. Holbrook had secured the critical part while the D&RG napped.

The boom hit Leadville about a month after the Canon City line had been located. Thousands of fortune hunters swarmed into the area. Of silver and lead there was an abundance. Of provisions and transportation there was practically nothing. Stages and pack trains carried passengers and freight at fabulous operating costs, but the rates were so high that profits were fantastic. The first railroad was sure to make a rich strike too. When the alarm sounded General Palmer renewed his interest in the Cañon. About September 1, 1877, he joined Chief Engineer J. A. McMurtrie in an eight-day survey of the route to Leadville.[3] Palmer reported potential traffic in glowing terms and argued that no other route to Leadville compared with the one from Canon City. Not only would the proposed line control the traffic of southern and western Colorado but it would be a springboard to California by way of Salt Lake City or by a southwest course north of the Colorado River. During October the D&RG decided to build through the Cañon at the first opportunity—this being whenever a buyer could be found for more bonds.

Friction had already developed during 1877 between the Santa Fe and the D&RG over existing traffic in southern Colorado. The common territory made for a pool or sharp competition. A pool was more logical because the supplementary aspect of the two, as well as the competitive, showed the way to profits for both. No agreement was reached and the D&RG entered into traffic arrangements with the Union Pacific and Kansas Pacific. All east-west shipments to and from points served by the D&RG were routed north of the Santa Fe. Feeling was strong on each side. Interchange between the rivals was kept at an absolute minimum. Relations became even more hostile when Robinson beat McMurtrie to Raton Pass in February of 1878. Neither company would exchange passes with the other.

After the Santa Fe had seized Raton Pass, the Cañon struggle loomed more ominous than ever. The fight obviously was to be a knockdown, dragout affair with no holds barred. Each side spied on the other. William B. Strong attempted to exchange information and opinions by wire with officials of the Canon City and San Juan Railway. Since the telegrams traveled over the wires from Pueblo to Canon City, Strong took the precaution of using code messages. The telegraph line served the D&RG as well as the public, and the telegraphers of the railroad copied the messages and apparently succeeded in deciphering the code. General Palmer was aware of every step taken by his rival. Furthermore, Palmer asserted that the Santa Fe did its share of wire tapping and decoding.

By the middle of April the companies were eyeing each other carefully. A break for the Cañon was imminent. On April 16 the D&RG began to withdraw its men and materials working in Chicken Creek, the alternate to Raton Pass. A. A. Robinson suspected more than a discontinuance of work and wired Strong in

El Moro that men and supplies were being loaded on a work train bound, perhaps, for Canon City. Strong answered with instructions to continue on the alert and "to see to it that we do not 'get left' in occupying the Grand Canyon." Robinson gave the following version of the next move: "Feeling certain of the intentions of the D&RG I selected Mr. Morley, my assistant engineer, as advance agent—as the man most likely not 'to get left'—to go to Canon City and look out for the AT&SF interests." McMurtrie concentrated about one hundred men at El Moro and made ready to move west. Strong saw all the preparations and boldly asked the D&RG for a special train to take him to Canon City. The answer was a flat refusal. Robinson tried the same thing and also failed. The Santa Fe seemed cornered. The D&RG would stop all telegrams to Canon City. The train of workmen of the D&RG could take a crow's route to Pueblo and then proceed west, while Strong and Robinson would have to take a circuitous route back through La Junta. If the Cañon were to be seized some time-saver had to be utilized. The wires to La Junta were controlled by the Santa Fe, and La Junta and El Moro were equidistant from Pueblo. Robinson hastily dispatched a message to his lieutenant, William R. Morley, in La Junta and ordered him to head off the force of the D&RG at any cost. There was nothing "poky" about the resourceful Morley. He commandeered a Santa Fe work train and soon was speeding west toward Pueblo while the D&RG forces steamed north from El Moro. Morley arrived in Pueblo about three o'clock in the afternoon of April 19. Some accounts state that he asked the D&RG for a special train from Pueblo to Canon City. If the request was made it was refused, because Morley had to reënact Paul Revere's ride in order to reach his destination. He secured a horse at a local stable and headed for Canon City. The forty-three-mile journey speaks amply of Morley's courage and stamina. Dramatic accounts of the thrilling ride indicate that from time to time Morley and his steed could hear the wheezy whistle of the locomotive pulling the hated rivals. Mountain lions and all the varmints of the night are here supposed to have crossed the trail as the mad dash continued. Much of this is pure fiction. Morley had a substantial head start on the D&RG and maintained a lead of several hours. But he did not need a whistle in the background to exhaust the last ounce of endurance from his valiant steed. The D&RG had a working crew all ready to start and Morley had to organize and equip a force.

Morley neared his destination shortly before midnight. The horse was spent. All efforts at encouragement were of no avail. The horse stumbled, then fell. Morley dismounted as the animal went down. It was already dead from exhaustion. No time was wasted, not even to remove the saddle. Morley hurried forward on foot. Local officers of the Canon City and San Juan Railway had just retired after appointing Strong and Robinson as general manager and chief engineer of their company when Morley routed them out of bed. In the middle of a chilly night a working force was recruited. Men were secured by a house-to-house process. Happily one of the officials ran a hardware store and tools were available for the impromptu crew.

At dawn the town migrated to the Cañon and began shoveling. Morley had not waited but had gone ahead and was busy digging when his friends from Canon City arrived. About a half hour later the D&RG crew neared the opening to the Gorge. They were shocked at what they saw, but this time there was no intention of giving up without a fight in spite of the presence of Morley and his friends. The D&RG men began work on final location of the line into the Gorge. What followed in the struggle for control is almost unparalleled in the history of American business. Both companies were diehards and resolved to hold the Cañon at all costs.* Reinforcements were mustered on each side. Strong or-

---

*William R. Morley proved to the D&RG for the second time that one had to rise early to beat the Santa Fe—in fact it was necessary to stay up all night. Morley was on familiar grounds in the Gorge. He had taken part in McMurtrie's survey for the D&RG in 1873.

William B. Strong gave Morley a splendid gold-mounted Winchester in recognition of his fearless action. About five years later when Morley was serving as chief engineer

dered work on the line between Pueblo and Canon City. Two days later (April 22) grading was under way. A pony express was organized to handle Santa Fe communications. Full control was assumed over the Canon City and San Juan. Materials were ordered for most of the work to Leadville. On April 21 Strong had 300 men in the Gorge and more on the way. A third of the force had been secured among the D&RG men. Palmer had hired almost as many from the Santa Fe camp. Each side attempted to seize control of the narrowest points. Claims were about equally divided.

Strong sent one of his lieutenants, W. H. Pettibone, with instructions to find one hundred men who were well armed and quick on the draw. He went only as far as Dodge City. There he met men who fought for fun, and when they were told that the Santa Fe would pay from a dollar and a half to three dollars a day for their toughness Pettibone feared that he would have to take too many. Bat Masterson, one of the most fearless and daring sheriffs who ever plugged a man, agreed to command the army. Only Bat could have taken over. D&RG trigger men were recruited among those who follow miners and get rich without mining. Men who in modern times would be gunmen in the slums of big cities swelled the ranks of both sides. Temporary facilities for boarding the men were erected, the rival camps being a mile apart. Pettibone brought camping equipment for the army of Kansas. Many men elected to sleep in the open. Both sides had a considerable number present who were not expected to work. No end of devilment developed as these bad men tried to stir up excitement. A local crime wave is generally reported to have begun in Canon City.

Since neither side would hesitate to seize strategic points from the other, some system of defense had to be arranged. Trenches

---

of the Mexican Central he started to pick up the rifle and it was accidentally discharged. The tragedy ended a career which had been short but productive. A handsome monument of stone was erected to his memory in Las Vegas. Although there is no specific marker, the Santa Fe is another memorial to Morley and other men of his fiber.

were dug, but the main reliance was placed on stone forts. These were so substantial that a few still remain. Although most of the fighting was in courtrooms the stand-by role of the forts was important.

How much local justice was influenced by the general antipathy to the D&RG cannot be ascertained. The Santa Fe had a marked advantage. D&RG officials claimed that their men were arrested by the sheriff and his deputies on the slighest pretexts and released provided they entered the employ of the Santa Fe. Earnings of local law enforcers were said to have soared from "unknown" sources.

Meanwhile the legal arm of the Santa Fe had been as alert as the engineering branch. A writ of injunction was secured in the name of the Canon City Company. County Judge N. A. Pain, acting in the absence of Judge John W. Henry of the Third Judicial District of Colorado, issued the order restraining the D&RG from continuing work or occupying the Cañon. At three o'clock on the afternoon of the first day of the War, work ceased but the men refused to vacate the strongholds. Chief Engineer McMurtrie and R. F. Weitbree, treasurer of the narrow gauge, were arrested. The Santa Fe had taken round one by a wide margin.

On Judge Henry's return, hearings were held on the original injunction case and both companies were enjoined to halt operations until the issues could be seen more clearly. Later in the same day, April 26, Judge Henry dissolved the injunction against the Canon City Company. Attempts of the Santa Fe to continue work were balked by the threats of superior forces in numbers and arms. Gilbert B. Reed, lawyer for the Santa Fe, had taken round two in the courtroom but was unable to follow up his advantage outside.[4]

The legal counsellors of the D&RG were anxious to get proceedings into the federal court. They contended, and rightly, that the local units were biased. A company could not pursue Palmer's high-handed course of ignoring local interests without alienating everyone from judge to petty thief. H. A. Risley of the

D&RG asked for an injunction in the Circuit Court of the United States presided over by Judge Moses Hallett, but the case was remanded back to Judge Henry's court. Judge Henry refused to transfer the case and tartly remarked that the D&RG was already in contempt of court, since the Company had not vacated the Cañon. The Santa Fe continued to hold its advantage in round three.

A second attempt was made to get the case into the federal court, and this time the D&RG was successful. Judge Hallett agreed that in view of the public temper justice could be served better outside of Fremont County. A petition was filed to set aside the injunction against the D&RG. Meanwhile, the Santa Fe attempted to proceed with construction through the Cañon in spite of every conceivable kind of sabotage. Accusations were made that D&RG men rolled stones from the top, stole tools and pitched them in the river, kidnapped employees, shifted stakes, and harried the builders in innumerable other ways.

In the arguments before Judge Hallett the D&RG was represented by Wells, Smith and Macon of Denver and H. A. Risley of Colorado Springs. Gilbert B. Reed of the Santa Fe was buttressed by William Teller and Charles E. Gast. While the arguments and deliberation continued, the Santa Fe asked Governor Routt to send the militia to maintain order, having in mind curtailing activities of the D&RG. The latter made the same request in reverse application. On May 9, 1878, Judge Hallett ordered a cooling-off period pending final sifting of the facts. He issued an order restraining both parties from working in the disputed area until a determination of their respective rights could be reached. He granted an injunction by the Rio Grande against the Santa Fe, and permitted the writ already in existence to stand against the narrow gauge. He ordered both parties to withdraw from the field and to give bonds of $20,000.

The decree was accepted in good faith, and the contestants withdrew their laborers and soldiers. Prospects for peace were good, although some of the gunmen shot up things on their own before departing. Round four had evened the battle. Hallett called upon a colleague, Judge Dillon of St. Louis, to assist in reaching a final decision. The concurrent judgment was given June 1 and was a great triumph for the Santa Fe (acting as usual through the Canon City and San Juan Railway Company). The injunction against the Rio Grande remained unchanged, but the one on the Canon City Company was modified. Grading could be resumed through the Gorge, but no rails could be laid on the grade. The judges contemplated eventual construction to Leadville by both concerns and the joint use of right of way where space was limited. The orders were to operate until the case could be scrutinized more carefully at the regular term of the United States Circuit Court beginning in July. Round five was carried handily by the Santa Fe.

The legal struggle was renewed July 9 with Judge Dillon presiding. Lengthy arguments were presented. The D&RG sought a perpetual injunction to restrain the Canon City Company. Attorneys Usher and Macon of the D&RG launched a bitter but irrelevant attack. Macon contended that the Santa Fe and not the Canon City and San Juan was the real aggressor; that the latter if it possessed any rights at all under the general act of 1875 had forfeited them not only by acquiescing in the action of the Santa Fe in taking forcible possession of the line but also by aiding it to carry out its illegal purposes; and that the Santa Fe, having no corporate existence in the state, could have no rights. Macon further contended that the capital stock of the Canon City Company was only $100,000 and was therefore ridiculously inadequate to build the line. In short, the purpose of the subsidiary was to serve as a cloak for the Santa Fe, a foreign corporation which had no rights under the law. How a lawyer representing a corporation could seriously advance such an argument is difficult to understand. Was not the Canon City Company a legal entity? Ownership by the Santa Fe could not impair the rights of the subsidiary.

Dillon and Hallett were unimpressed. Numerous witnesses were called to testify on both sides regarding the dates of surveys.

Not until August 23 did Judge Hallett announce the decision. The Canon City and San Juan was granted the right to construct the line as surveyed. Priority through the twenty miles of the Gorge was established by the filing of the plat in 1877. The Denver and Rio Grande was restrained from any interference with the Canon City Company but could construct a separate line. Provision was made for the D&RG to use the track of the Canon City Company at points where only one line was possible. The original track was not to be built in such a manner as to make joint use intentionally and unreasonably expensive or difficult for the narrow gauge.

Palmer and his men were keenly disappointed over the outcome. They preferred it to be a "whole hog or none" proposition. The traffic would not support independent lines, even though it was ample for one. A compromise of a single line all the way with joint use was partially corrective. The variance in gauges would necessitate three rails. D&RG men conceded round six to their adversary but continued to fight.

The Santa Fe did little or no work on the line during the early summer while awaiting the final decision. A contract was let by the Canon City Company for construction of the first fifty-seven miles to the mouth of the South Arkansas by the Pueblo and Arkansas Valley, another Santa Fe subsidiary. Subcontracts were signed with graders but no work was done. The D&RG went ahead with grading beyond the twenty-mile mark outside of the constricted zone.

New conflicts began in the area beyond the end of the twenty-mile mark. Previously it had been assumed that beyond twenty miles from Canon City there was room for two railroads. This was substantially true, but one of the roads was certain to have a decidedly superior line. The north bank was much better than the south. Canon City and Santa Fe men had not filed for right of way beyond the twenty-mile mark, and this time the D&RG men were not caught napping. They located on the north side and authorized the Union Contract Company, a constructing affiliate, to take the necessary steps to complete the line. The P&AV attempted to proceed on the same side. On August 15, the D&RG instituted suit in the Circuit Court in Denver to enjoin the P&AV from interfering with construction.[5]

The armies were called out once more and were located west of the earlier troubles. Additional forts were erected, guards patrolled the intertwining rights of way, and bloodshed was feared. Meanwhile on September 12, the Canon City and San Juan was absorbed by the Pueblo and Arkansas Valley. Headquarters continued in Pueblo and the capital stock was raised to $6,000,000. Plans were announced for building from Pueblo to Canon City through the Grand Cañon to Leadville, through Gunnison Pass, and to Park and Summit counties, with a number of branches covering all the Rio Grande territory, including Colorado Springs and Denver. Virtually every mile of the D&RG was to be paralleled. The fight was to go to the finish. The P&AV filed a cross bill against the D&RG, charging that the latter was guilty of malicious acts of interference. The narrow gauge had appealed to the Supreme Court for reversal of Judge Hallett's pronouncement regarding the first twenty miles.

Both sides let the grading contracts and had crews busy preparing conflicting lines to Leadville. Some graders had contracts with each side and shuttled employees back and forth. The rank and file of men in the area did not know friend from foe and so most of them became friends. Meredith Jones, an engineer of the Santa Fe, recalled friendly visits from De Reemer, a leader of the D&RG.

By October the struggle had taken a paradoxical turn. The workers on the scene were apparently peaceable. The legal departments were fighting with tooth and nail while the heads of the two companies were talking peace.

William B. Strong was in favor of crushing the opposition. He was a man of direct action and preferred to accomplish things by actual battle rather than diplomacy. Thomas Nickerson, the president of the Santa Fe, was by no means a timid man but he preferred to utilize diplomacy where it would accomplish fighting objectives.* The D&RG was tottering financially. Strong concluded that the kill was imminent; Nickerson reasoned that the D&RG could be leased on favorable terms. There was the difference in temperament between the two men. Nickerson held the superior position. Rumors of a lease of the narrow gauge to the Santa Fe reached incredulous observers on October 8, 1878. By October 11 hearsay seemed reality. The fight was called off, or at least an armistice declared, in the middle of the seventh round.

As early as September senior security holders of the heavily bonded D&RG had been getting in touch with the Santa Fe and exerting pressure on Palmer to lease the narrow gauge. News escaped and people speculated whether a lease, a sale, or a pool was in the offing. Palmer went to Boston and by October 19 a lease had been arranged which was relatively satisfactory at the time. All of the "heretofore constructed and operated" mileage consisting of 337 miles together with equipment, grounds, and buildings was to be turned over to the Santa Fe on December 2. The lessee agreed to the following important provisions: not to build, operate, or encourage any road, directly or indirectly, not already constructed, that is parallel to, or competing with, the Denver and Rio Grande's then constructed lines; not to change the gauge nor lay a third rail without widening the gauge or laying an additional rail over all the lines, except between Pueblo and the coal mines east of Canon City; not to discriminate in freight or other charges in any manner to the injury of the D&RG;

---

*Thomas Nickerson had few equals in business ability in the history of the Santa Fe. He seemed to be a forerunner of E. P. Ripley, whose leadership was so renowned. While William B. Strong was occasionally irked by Nickerson's apparent hesitancy, the latter usually had excellent business reasons.

Nickerson was born at Brewster, Massachusetts, September 19, 1810. His ancestors had sailed the seas for many generations. After thirty years in ocean shipping Nickerson turned to overland transportation and about 1870 invested heavily in the Santa Fe. He served on numerous committees of the Company and in May, 1873, became the vice-president. He was advanced to the presidency a year later and remained in office for six years. Nickerson began when the Company was financially hard-pressed. His judicious leadership established solidarity. He was also a leader in the Atlantic and Pacific, the Sonora Railway, the California Southern, and the Mexican Central. He administered construction of 12,000 miles of the latter. Nickerson was a member of the Massachusetts legislature and well known as a philanthropist and church leader. He died in Newton Centre, Massachusetts, July 24, 1892.

to carry out D&RG contracts; to rent the facilities for thirty years at a rate varying from 43 per cent of gross earnings during the first year to 36 per cent during the last fifteen years, payable monthly; to pay all bills (except interest on the bonded debt and the debt, which were to come out of the rent) and maintain the property in good condition; and to pay for all materials on hand. Dozens of other features were included in the original instrument, but two supplemental agreements were necessary to cover other factors. Provision was made to exchange D&RG stock for P&AV at a rate of five to one. Oddly enough, no complete meeting of minds was reached regarding the extension from Canon City to Leadville. Nickerson later claimed that he had assumed that the D&RG rights had been secured and Palmer vehemently denied the contention.[6] The Santa Fe called a halt to work on its own line from Pueblo to Canon City, and D&RG contracts beyond the twentieth mile were cancelled. Palmer asserted that the narrow-gauge cancellations were in error and the orders were rescinded.

Stockholders of the Rio Grande met at Colorado Springs November 29 to consider ratification of the lease. There was much dissension but little choice. On the motion of Dr. W. A. Bell the stockholders adopted a resolution permitting the property to be turned over after Palmer was satisfied that payment would be made for various material and supplies. Formal transfer took place at midnight of December 13, 1878.

Hopes that the lease would establish an enduring peace were quickly dashed. D&RG men felt that the Santa Fe had taken unfair advantage of the financial plight of the little company and were resentful. Strong had opposed the lease during negotiations, but once it was in effect he made the most of his dominant position. The Santa Fe had long been at a disadvantage in handling Colorado traffic. The D&RG was linked with the Kansas Pacific and the Union Pacific. All Denver business went to the northern lines and the D&RG transferred goods south. When Strong assumed control he ordered rates on the D&RG south from Denver increased. In some cases they were quadrupled. Charges from Denver south were prohibitory and business wasted away. Consumers naturally secured their goods by the next cheapest method, which was to ship over the Santa Fe from Kansas City to Pueblo for transfer on D&RG branches. Pueblo became the wholesale center instead of Denver. Not only had a body blow been directed against the Kansas Pacific but the rental paid to the D&RG was reduced by the decline in gross revenues. The Santa Fe secured the prize of long hauls on much traffic. Strong rubbed additional salt on old wounds by using the D&RG line to transport building materials into the Cañon area.

The D&RG men were far from dormant lessors. The appeal to the Supreme Court was still pending and assumed increased significance when the Court in an analogous case ruled in a manner which seemed to support the claim of the narrow gauge. Efforts of the Santa Fe to halt the proceedings were of no avail. Construction was stepped up by the P&AV and the army hired for the third time. D&RG forces were bolstered. Bat Masterson forsook the quieter Dodge City to lead a division. Some blood was shed. Whether the men were fighting over the railroad issue or simply fought because they ordinarily became embroiled in scrapes is not known.

Palmer and his friends were still directors of the D&RG even though the Santa Fe was acquiring most of the stock under the exchange plan which had been agreed upon. The annual meeting was not to be held for many months, and the only way to block the Supreme Court appeal was to override the uncontrollable directors. A sleeper was attached to a bill in the Colorado legislature. The measure ostensibly affected religious corporations, but an amendment enabled the majority of stockholders of a corporation to set aside decisions of the directors at any time. Palmer discovered the ruse after the bill had been enacted. T. Jefferson Coolidge, trustee of the D&RG stock held by the Santa Fe, notified Palmer to call a meeting of the stockholders to withdraw the appeal. Palmer refused, and before further action could be taken the Supreme Court issued its ruling, April 21, 1879.[7]

While attention was centered on the attempts of the D&RG and the Santa Fe to build to Leadville, another railroad took steps to steal the prize from both of them. The Denver, South Park and Pacific completed two-thirds of a line from Denver to Leadville. The Santa Fe viewed the project with alarm and at the close of 1878 took steps to purchase the line. The deal was never consummated, partly because the assent of the D&RG bond-holders could not be secured as required in the lease.

On the eve of the Supreme Court decision both sides were heavily armed and resolved to have the Cañon line regardless of who won in court. There was common talk that the D&RG wished to break the lease and that the Santa Fe had already done so but would not admit the fact. The P&AV was laying track in the Cañon. Several hundred heavily armed men of the standard gauge matched the firing strength of the enemy. The situation was more explosive than ever.

Santa Fe good will in the state capital had reached a record low when Pueblo began to encroach on Denver business as a result of the rate policy pursued by Strong. Actually Denver was not being victimized any more than Pueblo had been in earlier years. Strong entered the lion's den in Denver on April 10. He was prepared to fight the battle in all quarters. Fearful of an attack and seizure of D&RG trains, Strong directed W. W. Borst, superintendent of the Santa Fe interests, to issue a circular to all employees to be on guard. Events leading to the lease were outlined, and the circular stated that it had been learned from trustworthy sources that Palmer would attempt "by arresting employees on trumped up charges, and by forcible means, to obtain possession of their property." Disorder broke out at Colorado Springs and a few shots were fired.

Early in April the sharp competition between the Santa Fe and the Kansas Pacific and Union Pacific was ended by a pooling agreement which split Colorado traffic and territory. Palmer charged this was another violation of the lease.

The momentous decision of the Supreme Court was delivered by Justice Harlan on April 21, 1879, Chief Justice Waite dissenting. Both roads were held to be entitled to joint occupancy of the Gorge but this time the D&RG was given the prior right. The reasoning was that the D&RG had the right to the Cañon after occupation under the Act of Congress of June 8, 1872, which gave the narrow gauge its right of way. The survey of 1877 and the occupancy of April 19, 1878, established the claim. The injunction against the Rio Grande was dissolved and construction was to proceed without obstruction. Both companies were to have joint use of the right of way where space was inadequate for two. The D&RG was to share expenses with the P&AV at points where the latter had done work in the Cañon and room was available for a single line only.

The D&RG had to all appearances won a great victory in the second campaign. Once again the war did not cease when all signs pointed to mopping-up operations or cessation of hostilities. Everything that had gone before turned out to be preliminary forays to major clashes soon to follow.

Palmer now charged the Santa Fe with violation of the lease on a dozen counts and began steps to recover the property. Attorney General C. W. Wright was induced to begin *quo warranto* proceedings to oust the Santa Fe from the state. Officials of the Santa Fe were required to appear before Judge Thomas M. Bowen of the State District Court at Colorado Springs to account for the Santa Fe's authority to operate as a Kansas corporation in Colorado. Public censorship of Wright's interference was widespread. Judge Bowen upheld the D&RG side on the grounds that the Santa Fe had not filed a copy of its charter with the Secretary of State.* The Santa Fe on April 27 lost its right to do business in

---

*The arguments were heard by Judge Bowen at San Luis and Alamosa. The Santa Fe Attorney, William Teller, asked for a change of venue but it was denied. Teller assumed that Bowen was biased and that there was no chance for impartial consideration. He minced no words about his views and his withering blasts at Bowen removed any possibility of a favorable decision. Judge Bowen struck back and popular excitement was further heightened by the sensational accusations.

Colorado but before any move could be taken to oust the Company, the Supreme Court of Colorado froze the order until additional evidence could be considered. Months later Judge Bowen's action was reversed.

The controversial lease which was turned over by Palmer to S. E. Schlessinger, the escrow officer, had never been delivered to the Santa Fe. On April 16 suit was instituted in the United States Court in Boston to stop delivery on the grounds that the lease had already been broken by the Santa Fe. A compromise was worked out to keep matters in suspense for a time.

Shortly after the decision of the Supreme Court was announced, Rio Grande lawyers appeared before Judge Hallett and asked for execution of the pronouncement. The P&AV simultaneously filed a supplemental bill purporting to show that the lease assigned all D&RG rights to the P&AV and that therefore working crews need not be withdrawn by the latter. Hallett reaffirmed the ruling that in event one company took over the roadbed of the other, reimbursement should be made.[8] A final ruling was not made until further consideration could be given by Hallett and a colleague or two. Both sides were ordered to withdraw until the decision had been reached.

A contemporary gave the following description of the battleground after Hallett's preliminary announcement:

I arrived in Pueblo from Denver yesterday and found the eating station surrounded on three sides with a motley crowd of men. Some of them bore the appearance of rough usage. Some were drunk and sleeping off their intoxication in out-of-the-way corners on the platform, while the majority were staggering about heavily laden with blankets and traps, swearing, yelling, and making themselves felt as forceful masters of the situation. They had been paid off immediately upon the announcement of Judge Hallett's order directing both parties to withdraw from the disputed ground in the Grand Canon of the Arkansas, and had spent the night in boisterous carousal. The people in households near the center of the town slept through the night. Gangs of men who paraded the streets occupied the saloons, gambled, guzzled and made the metropolis literally a howling wilderness. Though but little damage was done, various articles of movable property were carried off, chicken roosts seriously decimated, clothes lines robbed, and the police kept busier looking after the peace of the town than at any former time since its organization.

At three o'clock Saturday afternoon the AT&SF train for the east pulled out laden with a large force of laborers, brought to the canyon for use in the conflict there from different points along its line. Two Rio Grande trains, one headed for the north, the other south, were crowded with laboring men, who shrieked, yelled and hooted at the broad gauge as they left, and continued the salute till they were out of sight. Shortly afterward, the D&RG processions moved to their respective destinations leaving Pueblo pretty thoroughly emptied of its late unwelcome visitors. Nearly three carloads of the worst elements of this dreaded crew were unloaded at Denver Saturday night. I tried to get a press dispatch to you warning the public of their coming, but the office at the depot was packed to suffocation, and it was impossible to reach the operators until too late for your afternoon edition.

Proceeding to Canon City the same afternoon, I had opportunity for measuring the state of public sentiment there. Every resident of the place was outspokenly partial to the cause of the AT&SF Co., and during the stormy scenes enacted in the canyon threw all the sympathy and influence they had against the Rio Grande. Inquiring into the causes I discovered they were based upon a grievance and a hope. The complaints of injustice at the hands of the Rio Grande in multifarious ways were widespread and very bitter. That Company is charged with all the offenses in the calendar and credited with no virtues or benefits conferred. Hence when the road came to peril not a hand was raised to save or shield it. On the contrary, the hope consisted in the advantage to be derived by a directly competitive broad-gauge line. Col. Strong and his agents had filled the public mind with glittering promises of what should be done when this great work was completed. It was understood and made abundantly manifest by deeds that the AT&SF had plenty of money and could promptly execute any contract that might be undertaken, while it seemed to be the generally accepted belief that the Rio Grande had no means, did not intend to build through the canyon to Leadville, but were making the contest simply to hold exclusive possession of the ground until such time as they could get the means to grade and iron the line up the Arkansas. . . . Both the Rio Grande and the AT&SF Cos. have groups of graders in the canyon above the point in dispute, both making for Leadville with all possible speed. I heard last evening there had been a slight but bloodless collision between the opposing forces during the day.

Canon City has been under great excitement for two weeks past and has been filled with rowdies, gamblers and wild rioting. . . . Coming to Pueblo this morning it was my ill-fortune to be in a car full of sharks, gamblers, and thieves who had been preying upon the railroad hands, beating them out of every dollar they could get. These were landed in Pueblo so that the town is not yet rid of its evils. . . .

The majority of the armed forces went on furlough for about two weeks, but they returned to active duty when events moved toward a climax. Attorney General Wright applied to Judge Bowen for a writ of injunction to prohibit the Santa Fe from operating the D&RG. The proceedings took a spectacular turn when newspapermen pointed out that Wright was a member of the private law firm of Butler, Wright and King who represented the D&RG. Impeachment was demanded. Colorado newspapers took sides in the controversy and mighty battles were fought with the pen. Both wild rumors and true reports circulated concerning the activities of each side. Rio Grande forces were said to have routed P&AV employees at the stations in Colorado Springs and Labran. Train crews were armed. Judge Bowen was marked for kidnapping. Sheriffs were bribed. Telegraph wires were cut. Officials of each company had great difficulty traveling, because the strangest things could go wrong with the locomotives if the views of the engineer were at variance with those of his passengers. Governor Pitkin remained as neutral as possible and ordered sheriffs to call for troops if the occasion warranted.

Construction of the line continued. The P&AV gauge was narrow and suitable for D&RG rolling stock. The Santa Fe completed tracklaying in the Cañon and reached the twenty-third milepost on June 16. The point was known as "De Reemer's Deadline." A fort of the D&RG was a little beyond, and the first Santa Fe man to cross the line was promised an efficient and effective ventilation. Beyond the deadline to the thirty-seventh mile in the fortified area of the D&RG eight miles of grading was completed by the Rio Grande. The Sante Fe had graded the right of way from the west end of the D&RG zone to the South Arkansas and had supplies on hand or ordered for completion of the entire line to Leadville. Robinson asserted that, in the absence of Rio Grande sabotage, operations to Leadville could begin October 1, 1879.

General Palmer broadcast a circular in which he charged perversion and violation of the lease by the Santa Fe. He asserted *sub rosa* aid by Santa Fe officials to the Denver and South Park in its effort to build to Leadville. This action followed after the trustees of the D&RG bondholders had exercised their prerogative of refusing to sanction Santa Fe aid to the new line. Palmer contended that Rio Grande line and rolling stock were permitted to deteriorate. Rental payments were in arrears. No auditor's office had been provided in Pueblo. Goods were hauled by circuitous routes over Santa Fe lines to avoid use of the D&RG. Countless other accusations were made to the effect that the Rio Grande was discriminated against in matters of rates and shipments.

Most of the accusations were debatable. The securities market can be a coldly calculating judge at times and it preferred to discount Palmer rather heavily. D&RG bonds rose from less than 50 per cent of par before the lease to 90 per cent. Apparently the Santa Fe was not such a cruel foster father as Palmer asserted. The rise in the value of the stock was even more impressive.

Judge Bowen on June 10 issued the injunction sought by Wright and Palmer. The properties were to be returned to the D&RG immediately. Some delay ensued in affixing the seal, because the deputy clerk went on a vacation on the spur of the moment and took the seal along. Before Bowen had announced his findings Palmer had already arranged the machinery for serving the writs on officers and agents along the line. Sheriffs began to take over. In the early hours of the morning of June 11 an organized posse broke open the door of the general office in East Denver, and Rio Grande men were put in charge. Next, the roundhouse was seized and trains were held up while crews were replaced. Alarming conditions prevailed and the postmaster withheld the mails pending developments. Writs were served all along the line and apparently the sheriffs had considerable backing by Palmer and his men. Members of train crews were outnumbered, treated roughly, and replaced. Stations, roundhouses, and other facilities were seized. Santa Fe men refused to vacate the train dispatcher's office in Pueblo and an exchange of bullets followed. No one was struck. The Santa Fe retreated. The roundhouse was held by Bat Masterson and his followers. Ex-Governor Hunt arrived late in the day with additional support, and capitulation followed. Several were reported injured, kidnapped, or killed. Careful sifting of accounts indicates that any reported deaths were figments of reporters' imaginations. The station at Colorado Springs was taken without resistance. The speed with which the D&RG captured control of the telegraph lines did much to disorganize the Santa Fe and to curb further conflict. The garrisons lost contact with each other and quickly yielded. Governor Pitkin was swamped with requests to intervene, but pursued a policy of strictly hands off. No attempt was made by the D&RG to take over at Canon City and in the Gorge. Blood would have flowed freely at the first move.

On the same day that the D&RG regained control Teller, the Santa Fe attorney, asked Judge Hallett to transfer injunctive matters to the Federal Court. This was done, and on June 12 Hallett nullified Bowen's writs and ordered the property returned to the Santa Fe. A manuscript in the possession of the Santa Fe indicated that "Hallett was recklessly assailed by certain of the public journals, upon the ground of his prejudice against the Rio Grande; accused of ruling steadily against it in favor of its rival. But in the heated condition of the public mind, the magnitude of the contest, the violence employed, the sheddings of blood, the marching and turbulence of armed men, the thousand wild rumors floating about, and the intense hostilities of the contending factions, the adherents of each party made unscrupulous use of every pretext, real or imaginary, that offered in support of its own cause, and in condemnation of the other, and the court did not escape."[9]

Before further steps for recovery of the property from the Santa Fe were taken, the D&RG made another unexpected move. L. H. Meyer, trustee for the bondholders, requested that Judge Bowen place the narrow gauge in receivership. Three days later H. A. Risley, a D&RG attorney, was named receiver. The Santa Fe contended this move was solely to obstruct justice rather than to protect interests of the bondholders. On June 23 Judges Hallett and Miller called for immediate restoration of the property to the D&RG stockholders but suggested that proper steps might be taken for the cancellation of the lease. The question of receivership was to be determined later. The application for a receiver was then transferred to the United States Circuit Court. Judge Miller ruled July 3 that the receiver had been appointed in a proper manner. After additional arguments, Receiver Risley was discharged on the fourteenth. New evidence had indicated collusion in his appointment, the sole purpose of which was to negate Hallett's order. Risley was given two days to restore the property. This was done on July 16, when Dodge and Palmer accepted the road and promptly turned it over to the Santa Fe.

What happened in the sacred halls of justice was of little concern to men in the Cañon area. Fighting broke out daily. Blood flowed. Threats of death intimidated some and caused others to fight back. A riotous situation prevailed and authorities lost any semblance of control. Building was at a standstill.

The Santa Fe did not have the D&RG long. Eight days after regaining control Judge Hallett appointed L. C. Ellsworth of Denver receiver while all the pending litigation was settled. The Santa Fe turned the property over to Ellsworth. A lull followed, to the great relief of all.

During the following September rumors circulated that Jay Gould had purchased half of the D&RG stock from Palmer and his friends and had assumed the risk of adverse court results. Gould had recently acquired the Kansas Pacific. Word that the Santa Fe was going to build immediately from Pueblo to Denver was soon announced and made headlines but no rail lines.

Judge Hallett directed a three-man Board of Commissioners (one independent and one from each company) to ascertain the value of the work done by the contestants between Canon City and Leadville. Their report was filed October 20 and it had not only detailed cost records but also the flat statement that any joint arrangement was not feasible. One company should have the sole right to build and operate.

The annual meeting of the D&RG brought new men to the Board of Directors. Palmer and Bell were joined by Jay Gould, Russell Sage, and C. F. Woerishoffer. All the past actions of Palmer and his allies were lauded at the meeting and the Santa Fe was denounced. The Board was to sue for damages.

There was a sign of peace when the Union Pacific, the Kansas Pacific, and the Santa Fe entered into a new pooling arrangement December 20. The D&RG was to distribute southern traffic and litigation was to cease. But court controversies were to continue.

After much delay Judge McCrary, sitting for Judge Hallett, announced the basis for winding up the prolonged engagement. The Rio Grande was to have the prior right from the mouth of the Cañon to the South Arkansas River, but the P&AV was entitled to an amount set by the Board of Commissioners. The right from the South Arkansas to Leadville was ruled to belong to the P&AV by reason of prior location. If the D&RG was to have the second segment, payment must be made within sixty days in the amount specified by A. N. Rogers of the Board. The report of Commissioner Rogers was not quite complete, and Judge Usher, representing the D&RG, asked for immediate possession so that his client could proceed. McCrary insisted that no action could be taken until the estimates were finished.

The legal offensive was continued by the D&RG in Washington on January 5, when application to the Supreme Court was made for a writ of mandamus to compel Judge Hallett to carry out "properly" the mandate of the original Supreme Court decree of April, 1879. Supposedly this would give the D&RG the disputed territory and would not require payment for work done by the P&AV. The writ was denied and Hallett's action sustained. The remedy for the D&RG was held to lie in appeal, not mandamus action. The decision was released February 2, 1880.

During January Gould and Palmer attempted a bluff. They announced formation of a new company, the Pueblo and St.

Louis, whose main function was to parallel the Santa Fe from Pueblo to Great Bend, Kansas. Eastern connections were to be made at Salina and Wichita. Funds were reported to be available from stock subscription. The project was designed as a scare to make the Santa Fe more conciliatory.

On the same day that the Supreme Court rebuffed the D&RG in the application for a writ of mandamus, both parties came to an out-of-court agreement. The litigation stopped and the lease was canceled. The receiver was to be discharged and the D&RG and P&AV stock reexchanged so that the original holdings prevailed. The Rio Grande was to have all rights from Canon City to Leadville. Santa Fe expenditures for construction totaling $1,-400,000 were to be paid by the D&RG subject to certain adjustments. A bonus of $400,000 to the Santa Fe was also provided. Plans for the Pueblo and St. Louis were to be dropped as well as continuance of the D&RG into Santa Fe, New Mexico. The Santa Fe was to build into the Canon City coal fields but not to invade other territory designated as belonging to the narrow gauge. This provision included Leadville and Denver. Other phases of the gentlemen's agreement covered division of Denver and southern Colorado traffic.

The end had finally come to one of the most spectacular competitive struggles in the history of American business. A state had been ripped apart and a nation distracted as the adversaries fought with every legal and military weapon available. A new war veterans' organization came into being—veterans of the Grand Cañon War. When the sound of gunshots had faded and the accusations of enraged officials had been tempered, both sides had paid heavily. Wars are commonly won by inflicting more damage on the enemy than he inflicts. This was no exception. Any advantage gained in the peace by either side had been paid for several times.

When the Santa Fe clashed with the D&RG the route to Leadville seemed much more important than the disputed Raton Pass. With the passing of years it was evident that the initial victory at

Raton was much more important than any success in the Cañon could have been. Raton was the key to the riches of an empire; the Cañon opened the treasures of a province.

THE SOUTHERN PACIFIC, A LARGER FOE

One could have expected the Santa Fe to pursue a peaceful policy after the ordeal with the D&RG, but it discovered another opponent. The new enemy was much larger than the previous one and had more weapons at its disposal. The Santa Fe was to be the underdog in a long-drawn-out scrap. Subsidiaries, affiliates, and future parts of the Santa Fe were to face the Southern Pacific led by Collis P. Huntington. No more potent adversary could have been met. Huntington had considerable financial backing at his command and, what was more important, he had almost complete control over the right people. Moreover, Huntington and his associates, Leland Stanford, Mark Hopkins, and Charles Crocker, had an airtight monopoly of transportation in California. Coping with the Southern Pacific was difficult enough on neutral ground, if there was such an area; invading Huntington's private territory appeared to be prompted by infantile optimism. But the Santa Fe was case-hardened by its recent wars, and its leaders felt that they were a match even for Huntington.

When the Santa Fe was linked with the Southern Pacific at Deming, New Mexico, on March 8, 1881, it was hoped that much traffic would be handled over the new transcontinental line. Santa Fe officials believed that most of the volume of southern California and all of the shipments to Arizona would be hauled southwest by the Santa Fe. A rude awakening was in store. Huntington flatly refused to establish any rates which would enable goods to move over the new route. He insisted on exorbitant charges for shipments destined for points west of Deming. He demanded equally high rates if the Southern Pacific moved freight to eastern points. The strategy was to maintain the monopoly of the Union Pacific and the Central Pacific over transcontinental shipping. San Francisco would remain the distributional point for Southern

California and Arizona. Huntington's lines in the Southwest would not have to share with the Santa Fe. One week after the coveted junction had been made, the Santa Fe announced that it would not receive shipments for the Pacific Coast. The Southern Pacific would have taken virtually all of any reasonable charge that would be expected from shippers notwithstanding the longer haul of the Santa Fe. Inability to secure a volume of business was especially embarrassing. The Company had recently authorized an issue of stock rights. The purpose was to assist in raising $6,-000,000 to put roadbed, rolling stock, and shops in condition to handle the expected increase in business—part of which was to flow over the transcontinental union.

The Santa Fe extended its lines to Guaymas in an attempt to loosen the strangle hold of Huntington. The move forced Huntington to give the Santa Fe joint trackage from Deming, New Mexico, to Benson, Arizona. The Sonora Railway reached the Pacific all right, but the outlet was remote from a market for transportation. The extension in Mexico was a mistake and failed to achieve Santa Fe objectives. A corrective was sought and took the form of another wrong. In 1884 the Santa Fe bought a seveneighths interest in a steamship, "The City of Topeka." The purpose was to gather eastbound shipments up and down the Pacific Coast and bring them to Guaymas to send over the Santa Fe. Westbound merchandise could be distributed on the same cruise. Service was interminably slow and uncertain. The story circulated that the steamer was too big for the harbor and the dock facilities. Earnings of the Sonora improved somewhat, but "The City of Topeka" was a financial fiasco. Huntington lost no sleep and Strong gained none.

Huntington was equally troublesome when the Santa Fe sought entrance to California by means of the Atlantic and Pacific. A clause in the A&P charter of Southern Pacific origin read: "And be it further provided, that the Southern Pacific Railroad, a company incorporated under the laws of the State of California, is hereby authorized to connect with the said Atlantic and Pacific

Railroad, formed under this act, at such point near the boundary line of the State of California, as they shall deem most suitable for a railroad line to San Francisco." Did the clause mean that the A&P could not be built to San Francisco? Apparently Santa Fe officials believed that the line could be extended. The co-owner of the A&P, the Frisco, felt the same way. About $16,500,000 in bonds was offered in January of 1882 to complete the railroad to the Golden Gate. The amount was cut before all were sold, but $2,-000,000 in bonds was issued on the proposed line from Needles to San Francisco. Meanwhile Huntington and Jay Gould hurriedly began to accumulate Frisco stock and before the end of January had a controlling interest. The motive was apparent; the A&P was to be blocked lest it interfere with Gould's Texas and Pacific and Huntington's Southern Pacific. Control of the Frisco meant equal power with the Santa Fe over the A&P. No action could be taken without the consent of both. The Santa Fe was stopped. To add insult to injury, there was the very embarrassing problem of $2,000,000 outstanding in bonds on the California lines which Huntington would not permit to be built. Huntington's conscience bothered him not. He had little money in the Frisco, and more was to be gained by the failure of the A&P than by its success. The Santa Fe, on the other hand, relied heavily on the A&P and could not afford failure. Finally, the A&P guaranteed construction or reduction in the amount of bonds.

The Santa Fe was extremely disconcerted by the presence of an enemy on the board of directors of the A&P. Strong realistically accepted the situation and sought the best way out. He reached an agreement with the Southern Pacific to halt construction of the A&P at Needles. The Southern Pacific built from Mojave to Needles and supposedly the Santa Fe had an outlet to San Francisco. Whatever legal rights the A&P had to build in California were to be unimpaired. Since a clause provided for the interchange of business there would never seem to be any occasion for the Santa Fe to parallel the Southern Pacific to the north in California.

Southern California was something else. Already the sponsored California Southern was moving toward the A&P.

Junction with the Southern Pacific at Needles was made in August of 1883. Once again linking lines with the Southern Pacific meant substantially nothing. The Southern Pacific consistently routed traffic over other lines. When California shippers specified use of the Southern Pacific, A&P, and Santa Fe, route service on the Southern Pacific mysteriously bogged down. The situation was intolerable, and the Santa Fe resolved to parallel the Mojave Division of the Southern Pacific or construct over a shorter route to union with the California Southern. In the face of this decision Huntington no longer held dominance. He had to come to terms or have the new Mojave Division reduced to scrap value. Negotiations were begun in April of 1884, and a deal was completed the following August. Huntington and Gould unloaded their Frisco stock, having no more need for ownership. The A&P bought the Mojave division at cost, although lease arrangements had to be made until existing bonds expired and a clear title could be given. The rental was six per cent of cost ($30,000 per mile for 242 miles). The Southern Pacific was to handle A&P through traffic beyond Mojave on a coördinated basis, and the usual foreign-car rules were to apply. The A&P could solicit freight and passengers in San Francisco but could not build terminal facilities. The Southern Pacific exacted terminal charges of fifty cents per passenger and five cents per hundred pounds of freight in addition to a proportionate allocation of revenue. After twelve months' notice the A&P had the option of joint use of tracks from Mojave to San Francisco at a rental of $1,200 per mile plus a percentage of maintenance costs.

The compromise had its good and bad points from the viewpoint of the Santa Fe. On the asset side, the Mojave Division was acquired at a reasonable cost and greatly aided in developing lines in southern California. On the liability side the elaborate agreements regarding traffic to San Francisco and intervening points on the Southern Pacific line north of Mojave were as meaningless as the agreement of 1882. Santa Fe cars were obstructed at every opportunity. Shipping service was unreliable. When pooling arrangements were made, the Southern Pacific continued to ignore agreements which the Santa Fe respected. As late as 1889 the Santa Fe had only 16 per cent of the California business south of San Francisco.

Building of the California Southern, the close relative of the Santa Fe, was interrupted repeatedly by the Southern Pacific. The new line was an interloper which dared to challenge the exclusive rights of Huntington, Crocker, and associates to the railroad business of California. San Diego aided the California Southern out of righteous indignation over the exorbitant rates. In other communities aid was not possible. Well-placed money on the day for voting bond subsidies curtailed assistance. When the bonds carried in spite of vote-buying, the election was frequently ruled illegal on specious grounds. The Southern Pacific also made frequent use of injunctions to harry the work of construction. Invariably there was no basis for the writs but somehow they were secured.

The Southern Pacific was especially obnoxious when the California Southern began to build from Colton to San Bernardino. A crossing of the Southern Pacific tracks had to be made at Colton. Engineer Fred T. Perris directed B. F. Levet to design the crossing and arranged for its acquisition. Late in July the crossing was ready. It was in National City, at the south end of the line, awaiting shipment. Southern Pacific spies learned the location of the crossing and had Sheriff Bradt seize it on a spurious charge. Perris and his men were enraged but helpless. Bradt kept guards on a round-the-clock basis, and Perris watched the guards. Opportunity knocked while the sheriff himself was on duty. Things were so quiet that Bradt decided to take a nap. As soon as he seemed sound asleep, Perris's men silently seized the crossing, loaded it on a flat car, and were miles away before the sheriff awakened.

Perris had the crossing, but he still had to put it in place. Bradt notified the Southern Pacific officials, who telegraphed ahead. J. N. Victor, an engineer of the California Southern, was to lay the crossing. First, he secured a court order directing the Southern Pacific to permit him to go ahead. Work was about to begin when a Southern Pacific locomotive, tender, and gondola appeared and

began to move back and forth at the point of intersection. The general belief was that the gondola contained from twenty to thirty men with rifles. They crouched below the line of vision of onlookers. Events are best told in the words of Victor, who reported proceedings in a letter to Thomas Nickerson, the president of the California Southern and ex-president of the Santa Fe.

Early Thursday morning—9 a.m.—I telegraphed SP Asst. Supt. at Los Angeles that we were in readiness and wished to put in crossing that afternoon. As soon as their Overland mail had passed, we were on hand to begin when a ten-wheel SP engine came to point of crossing and stopped. The fire alarm at San Bernardino was sounded and people came from all quarters. Of course there was great excitement and the people wished to clear the track. It was only by the greatest caution riot was prevented, and there would certainly have been blood shed. Things finally quieted down and the crowd dispersed; but there was great excitement yet. I thought it advisable to have final order of court printed and each SP employee served. It was also asserted that headquarters at San Francisco had not received the final order.

The danger of a riot was so imminent, by legal advice I had the order telegraphed to the Sheriff at SF to serve on the President or Secy. It will probably cost us one to three hundred dollars; but I thought it the best thing to do. In the meantime the Sheriff had organized a posse, with arms and was waiting for order of court to clear the track, on our application. Of course they were in contempt of court and in bad shape, and they wired their atty. here to fix things up. In view of our condition here—using their turn-table and tracks, and being on their depot grounds; also that it was advisable to work here peaceably if possible—I thought it best to accept overtures. They have removed all obstructions and are to lend aid and assistance in getting crossing placed; it goes in this P.M. They also agree to release all material for the extension to San Bernardino. I go home tonight.

The Colton incident was only one of countless attempts of the Southern Pacific to harass a new line in every conceivable way. Breaking the monopoly in southern California was no easy undertaking. Fate contrived to make things worse by disastrous washouts. Completion of the line to Barstow ended the sole supremacy of the Southern Pacific in the Southland, but many years were to elapse before the invader could compete on an equal basis.

Cracking the monopoly of the Southern Pacific in the San Joaquin Valley and San Francisco was an even more formidable task. The Santa Fe cannot claim credit for the victory. The war was waged by a "people's railroad" built by shippers who refused to wear the yoke of the Southern Pacific any longer. The victor, like the California Southern, soon became a part of the Santa Fe system and now comprises the lines from Bakersfield to San Francisco. Early hostilities are sketched because the Santa Fe was to engage in later stages of the battle.

The objections to the Southern Pacific were almost exclusively based on the contention that the railroad was attempting to maximize monopoly gains. Actually the situation was not one of solely monopolistic greed: rather, it was an outgrowth of the rate structure which necessarily would attach to any locale similar to California. Rail rates quoted on transcontinental business had to match water rates to all cities accessible to ships. Competition was primarily on carload lots of nonperishables. The result was that cities located on navigable waters enjoyed transcontinental rates which were extremely low. Other cities located where there was no competitive service had to pay relatively higher rates on shipments from the east. Furthermore, J. C. Stubbs, the rate expert of the "Big Four," saw to it that inland points in California could not spoil the structure. High tariffs were made on local shipments from the cities on water. This had the desired effect of preventing supplies of the inland cities from moving by water to seaports and then by a short haul inland. Instead, the railroads had a long overland haul from the eastern states direct to the interior of California. Coastal cities were retarded because the high local rates nullified the low transcontinental level forced by ships. In vain San Francisco wholesalers protested vigorously.

The Union Pacific and the Central Pacific took steps during the 'seventies and 'eighties to lessen the effectiveness of water competition to California. A contract was signed with the Pacific Mail Steamship Company, which controlled shipping from the Atlantic Coast to Panama, and from Panama to San Francisco. The Pacific Mail also had exclusive rights over the Panama Railroad. Various guarantees and subsidies were given to the Pacific Mail and were intended to throttle clipper competition around the Horn and to maintain overland tariffs. The arrangement appears to have been successful.

San Francisco merchants hoped that the creation of a board of railroad commissioners would lead to the lowering of transcontinental rates as well as those to interior cities. "The results were disappointing. Three more men were corrupted."[10] Coastwise shipping was in complete control of the Transcontinental Association of which the Southern Pacific was a leader. San Francisco merchants had little choice but to pay the asking prices. Because of a prohibitory statute foreign ships could not be hired to handle coastwise shipping. California businessmen put their brains to work and in 1891 evolved an ingenious way to crack the controls. Merchandise was ordered in eastern cities. It was shipped to Antwerp or some other European city, then unloaded and reloaded on boats of foreign registry for movement around the Horn to San Francisco. No duties were paid, because the goods were made in the United States, even though they came direct from a foreign country. Great savings were possible if speed in shipping was not important. The use of roundabout shipping was ended in 1893 by statutory amendment.

Late in 1891 the Traffic Association of California took form in San Francisco "to organize a freight bureau and traffic association for the mutual benefit of merchants in the city." The organization hoped to secure rate adjustments which would enable San Francisco to develop as a point of distribution. Under the leadership of Joseph S. Leeds the Traffic Association pursued an aggressive program of competition. Money was raised and contributed to the friendly Merchants' Shipping Association to finance an agreement with J. W. Grace and Company calling for clipper service around Cape Horn. Great reductions in rates were secured—in fact shipping rates between the Coast and San Francisco sagged under costs.

The Transcontinental Railroad Association disintegrated in 1892, and the contract between the Pacific Mail and the Panama Railroad expired. The latter were unable to agree on terms and the monopolistic use of the Isthmian railroad ended. The Panama Railroad announced its intention to deal with all comers. The Johnson-Locke Mercantile Company of San Francisco undertook to handle freight on a competitive basis between Panama and San Francisco. Other means were available to get the goods from eastern cities to Panama. The business of Johnson-Locke was done under the name of the North American Navigation Company and was subsidized to the extent of $300,000 by the Traffic Association. Service lasted until the spring of 1894, when no more funds could be raised. The subsidy had been well spent. Estimates of the amounts saved on all shipments, including rail shipments at the reduced rates, ranged from two to ten million. The benefits were broadly distributed, but some of the donors were never fully compensated.

Most of the early activities of the Traffic Association were directed at transcontinental charges. Inland rates remained high. Many commodities were said to move from New York to San Francisco for less than from San Francisco to Bakersfield, California. Merchants in the San Joaquin Valley claimed that trains of pack animals were cheaper than the Southern Pacific. On a few occasions goods were transported on muleback between towns served by rail.[11] The Traffic Association had made a few early attempts to secure relief in the Valley, but no significant action followed. The corrective was to be a railroad down the Valley. In June, 1893, a committee was appointed to solicit subscriptions for the San Francisco and San Joaquin Valley Railroad. Actually the line was not to enter the Golden Gate City but was to begin at Stockton and proceed south. Passengers and freight could go by steamboats as far as Stockton. No land-office business was handled in subscriptions, and the enterprise languished until the following spring. A more descriptive name appeared which was intended to interest investors—the "San Francisco, Stockton and San Joaquin Valley Railroad Company." The venture made little headway for a time.

In October, 1894, the executive committee of the Traffic Association decided on a systematic drive for funds. Isaac Upham, president of the Association, asked for $350,000 of the estimated cost of $3,000,000. The campaign was again disappointing. Capitalists either feared the Southern Pacific too much or owned too many bonds of the enemy. Upham decided that the time had come to cast the die. Either the railroad would be built or it would not. A meeting of the Association was called for January 22, 1895, to decide once and for all. The showdown was attended by leading merchants, capitalists, and men of affairs including Claus Spreckels, the sugar king. All agreed that the railroad was sorely needed and was practical, but no action seemed to be generated from the various talks. Claus Spreckels arose for comments. He bluntly asserted that the amount initially sought ($350,000) was too little rather than too much. "Make it three millions and I will put my name down for fifty thousand dollars." The magnate's lead was all that was needed. Everyone was ready to sign on the dotted line. A few days later the capital was set at $6,000,000, and the men decided to raise $2,000,000 in cash. Subscriptions really began on January 29. Spreckels signed for $500,000 for himself, and his brother and son each pledged $100,000. One month later, February 25, papers for the incorporation of the San Francisco and San Joaquin Valley Railway were filed.

The campaign to complete the subscription to the stock generated unprecedented enthusiasm. Spreckels carefully observed that necessary money would be raised by many small investors. There were no other capitalists to tap, and he could not put any more into the project. The fact that Spreckels, who was always a winner, invested $500,000 bolstered the timid, and the idea of challenging the mighty Southern Pacific appealed to the sporting. The Traffic Association and the newspapers throughout the Valley declared that Californians had the patriotic duty of supporting the venture. Subscription blanks were printed in the newspapers. A gold watch was awarded by the San Francisco *Examiner* to the first one organizing a share club.[12] House-to-house canvasses were made in towns all along the line. The Southern Pacific was consigned to the eternal fires and the new company pictured as a redeemer. Right of way, grounds, and depots were secured on favorable terms. President Spreckels secured an area known as the China Basin in San Francisco for terminal purposes.

Work began soon after the organization of the Valley Road.* The line was completed from Stockton to Fresno early in October, 1896. A great celebration was held on October 5 to commemorate completion. The San Francisco *Call* made the following comments:

> Fresno, Cal., October 5, 1896.—This was a great day for Fresno and the San Joaquin Valley. It was the day of its liberation from a bondage of high tariffs. Just as the slave snaps his shackles and steps forth a free man, so Fresno broke the chains that have for years linked her to the Southern Pacific Railroad Company and cast them to the four winds.
>
> . . . beautiful day . . . 10,000 people . . . men in parade carried melons on long poles. . . procession over a mile long . . . while inspecting a fine bridge at Berneyville Ferry Director James D. Phelan tore a considerable rent in a pair of new trousers while crawling through a barbed wire fence. . . . . Claus Spreckels was the hero of the day.[13]

A mammoth barbecue was held and festivities lasted far into the night. The occasion was more like a great fair than anything else. There was a bicycle parade of two hundred and fifty, with prizes for the best decorated. Produce of the Valley was displayed and notables came from all over the state. Spreckels asserted that ten million people would eventually live in the Valley.

The celebration marking completion to Bakersfield took place on May 27, 1898. The scene duplicated the one at Fresno when the Valley Road reached that point. A special train with whistle blasting heralded the "new era."

---

*Its construction is traced in Chapter X.

The Valley Road was not a great financial success as far as
dividends were concerned, but it was never seriously expected to
be a direct "money maker." The real objective was to reduce rates,
and the Valley Road achieved this purpose, bringing about sub-

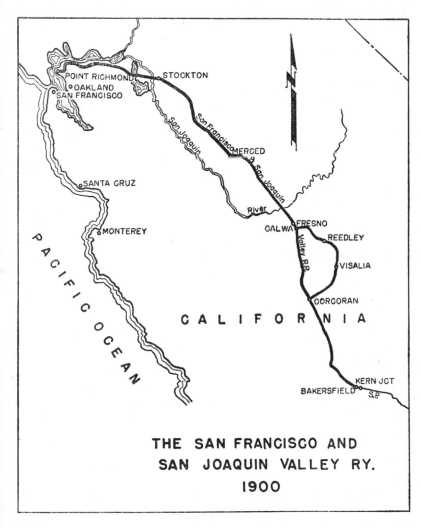

THE SAN FRANCISCO AND
SAN JOAQUIN VALLEY RY.
1900

stantial savings. After the Company had been established, steps
were taken to prevent it from being bought by Southern Pacific
interests by gradual accumulation of stocks. A ten-year voting

trust was established, and most of the issued stock was assigned in return for trust certificates. The trustees had to lower rates if earnings on common advanced beyond 6 per cent. The line could not be leased or sold to or affiliated with any competitive line. Coöperation or merger with the Southern Pacific was not to be permitted.

Merger of the Valley Road with the Santa Fe was not frowned upon—in fact the leaders looked forward to eventual sale. They were not railroad men, and, like Spreckels, wanted to return to their own chosen pursuits. When the Santa Fe gave assurance of preservation of a competing line, they were ready to dispose of the property. Another consideration was the expiration of the trust. There had been a sizable turnover in the trust certificates, and the danger lurked that control might pass to the Southern Pacific. Some stockholders were surprised and disappointed over the sale. On the whole, however, satisfaction was generally expressed when the deal was made in 1898.

The story is told that President Ripley of the Santa Fe visited the veteran leader of the Southern Pacific to tell him of the sale. Huntington is said to have remarked, "Yes, I knew you had bought it. This is a sad day for me. I had longed for the time when the leaders of the Valley Road would come and beg me to take it off their hands."

The Santa Fe promptly leased trackage rights over the Southern Pacific from Mojave through Tehachapi Pass into Bakersfield and completed the northern portion of the line to Point Richmond, across the Bay from San Francisco.

Another of the long-sought objectives of the Santa Fe had been reached. Terminal accommodations in the Bay area left much to be asked for, and the handicap has never been wholly overcome. The Southern Pacific was too well entrenched. Much progress has been made, so that one may say that the Santa Fe has never betrayed the trust of those who launched the "people's railroad." The Valley has been given a quality of service that belies the lowness of rates.

Rivalry between the Southern Pacific and the Santa Fe was not confined to California. Arizona was another bone of contention. Great efforts were made to resist extension of lines controlled by the A&P or the Santa Fe. In August, 1901, the Santa Fe bought the Santa Fe, Prescott and Phoenix, a road known as the "Pea Vine," running from the main transcontinental line at Ash Fork to Phoenix, Arizona. The little line had long been nurtured, and the move was expected. The next move was not. Plans were announced immediately for construction between Phoenix and Benson, Arizona. The Phoenix and Eastern was incorporated August 31, 1901. Its stock was held by the SFP&P. Southern Pacific officials regarded the move with consternation. The new line invaded private territory. Construction was spasmodic, but Winkelman was reached on September 28, 1904, after difficulties. By this time the project had assumed new proportions and was part of a plan to build a new low-grade line from Deming, New Mexico, to the West Coast via Winkelman, Phoenix, Wickenburg, and Cadiz, California. The Arizona and California Railway was the subsidiary to function between the SFP&P and Cadiz. Grading began in the spring of 1904.

Harriman, the new leader of the Southern Pacific, was determined to protect his territory. The Arizona Eastern Railroad Company was incorporated in February, 1904, to defeat the Santa Fe. The charter specified construction of a railroad from the Colorado River near Yuma in an easterly direction to a point at or near Clifton, Arizona, with branches to Jerome, Tucson, and Globe. Engineers began running lines which conflicted with the surveys of the Phoenix Company between Kelvin and Dudleyville. Numerous conflicts developed in the field and in court. At one point where the P&E was located in a canyon below the Arizona Eastern, the men of the latter blasted enormous quantities of stone on the lower right of way as fast as crews could clear the debris. Injunctive relief was secured in April, and the rivals moved off the P&E right of way. The court soon dissolved the injunction, with the understanding that the Arizona Company would refrain from its trespassing tactics and begin legitimate construction in other territory. But the following day the Arizona Company moved its men back on the right of way and resumed its work of obstruction. Finally a compromise was reached, and the P&E was able to build into Winkelman in peace, the opposition undertaking to build from Deming to Dudleyville. Three years later in March of 1907, the Santa Fe sold the line of the P&E to the Southern Pacific and ended what might have been a major battle.

The Santa Fe has had only one other clash of any great importance in the opening of lines, but it concerned bus lines. The competitors once again were the Southern Pacific plus its affiliates. When the issues were decided by the Railroad Commission of California in 1938, the Santa Fe received a favorable verdict.

The Santa Fe has waged a never-ending struggle for traffic. Usually it has been an effort to enlarge existing shipping rather than to deflect business from other lines. The competitive element should not be minimized. Notwithstanding the uniformities growing out of I.C.C. regulations there is a wealth of old-fashioned competition in the operation of the Atchison, Topeka and Santa Fe. This competitive spirit has encouraged the technological progress of the nation's railroads.

Perhaps the Wars of the Santa Fe should not have been fought. Economic waste clearly resulted. Yet there was merit in the crude selective process. The Santa Fe matured into a strong, well-knit organization, fearless of opposition and ready to haul man and his trappings from the shores of California and Texas to Lake Michigan.

V

All Aboard!

The time will come when people will travel in stages moved by steam engines, from one city to another, almost as fast as birds fly, fifteen or twenty miles an hour.—Oliver Evans, Patent Right Oppression Exposed (1813).

A RAILROAD ordinarily is built before timetables are issued. The Santa Fe was an exception. Promoters had waited so long for the beginning of operations that their patience gave out. Grading had scarcely begun when time cards of the service were posted. When the fifth timetable, effective May 1, 1869, was issued covering runs as far as Burlingame, the line was complete less than halfway.

Atchison, Topeka & Santa Fe Railroad
Time Table No. 5
In Effect May 1, 1869.

Read Down

No. 3	No. 1				No. 2	No. 4
P.M.	A.M.				P.M.	A.M.
3:00	7:30	Lv.	North Topeka	Arr.	1:25	8:35
3:05	7:35		Topeka		1:20	8:30
3:45	8:15		Pauline		12:40	7:50
4:10	8:40		Wakarusa		12:15	7:25
4:45	9:15		Carbondale		11:40	6:50
5:09	9:35		Scranton		11:20	6:30
5:35	10:05		Burlingame		10:50	6:00
P.M.	A.M.				A.M.	P.M.

Trains run daily except Sunday. Connect at North Topeka with Kansas Pacific, and at Burlingame with Barlow, Sanderson & Co.'s Overland Stage.
T. J. Peter, General Manager   W. W. Fagan, Superintendent

THE FIRST TRAIN

Patrons could buy tickets for travel over as much of the line as was finished. James Pratt of Wakarusa was the first paying passenger. The historic fare was collected during April, 1869. Pratt rode in the only passenger coach of the Santa Fe. The car was stubby and light. The better part of its running life had been spent in the service of the Indianapolis and Cincinnati road. All trains were mixed, and no doubt the passenger car carrying Pratt was behind flat cars "deadheading" to Topeka for company building supplies. The new railroad did not own any boxcars but had a dozen new flat cars to handle freight. Length was twenty feet and weight limit, 20,000 pounds. Like the passenger coach, the locomotive had seen previous use. The Niles Machine Works of Cincinnati had built it for the Ohio and Mississippi Railroad. The early owner operated on a gauge six feet wide, necessitating a change for the new purchaser. The engine arrived in Topeka, March 31, 1869. The man who delivered the locomotive, George Beach, was induced to join the Santa Fe and he piloted most of the early runs. Service was offered for two months before the Company hired W. W. Fagan to be its first conductor.

During 1869 imposing additions were made to the rolling stock. The first locomotive, the "C. K. Holliday," was joined by the "General Burnside." The newcomer was named in honor of the Civil War hero and treasurer of the company building the Santa Fe. Manufacture was by the Baldwin Locomotive Works. Wood was used for fuel. On December 31, 1869, the Company had two coaches, one baggage car, twelve box cars, and twenty-four coal cars. Two mixed trains made the daily round trip between Topeka and Burlingame. The "General Burnside" was a very small engine and often had great difficulty if the train was longer than four cars. When it reached Wakarusa, twelve miles out, it took water from the local creek. Beyond, there was a short rise to the prairie toward Burlingame. The little teapot was not equal to the hump and usually backed through Wakarusa part way up another slope and then went forward as fast as possible. As a rule the top was reached, but occasionally no amount of huffing and puffing would avail and a second attempt had to be made. Operating the "General" was no easy undertaking. The train crew had to load the tender a stick at a time. Later when the line was extended and difficulties were encountered, the supply of fuel might be exhausted in open country. The crew and obliging passengers would fan out to search for dry wood and cow or buffalo chips. Engine No. 1 was more dependable, but loading coal was a slow and arduous task. The engineer, brakeman, and conductor formed bucket brigades.

Although the early equipment of the Santa Fe was limited in quality and quantity, the service was immeasurably better than that afforded by any other means. Fourteen miles an hour is slow in comparison with modern travel, but actually swift in comparison with the plodding pace of oxen or the most elastic step of man—especially after fifteen or twenty miles. The breach filled by railroads in the West should not be underestimated. There were no rivers on which travelers floated to their destination in idyllic bliss. The choice was to walk, ride a mule, or go by ox or mule-drawn wagons. In a section where distances were great the best of such means of travel were woefully unsatisfactory.

Early Years

The needs which the new railroad served may be indicated by the patronage during the first full calendar year of operation, 1870. Service was offered as far as Emporia. The total number of passengers carried during the year was 33,598. Freight tonnage was 78,917 plus approximately 20,000 tons of Company matériel. Clearly the new line had justification for being. Car loadings were divided as follows: coal, 3,753; livestock, 593; lumber, 1,146; merchandise, 973; grain, 89; sand, 94; and road construction and supplies, 2,617. The rolling stock was more than doubled during the year to handle the swelling volume of business. Four locomotives were added. The annual report listed the total mileage of the engine fleet as 87,679. Coal consumption for all purposes was 70,-235 bushels. The measurement in bushels is mute testimony of the absence of mechanical weighing and loading devices. In 1870 the first accidents occurred. A tender axle broke and derailed two cars during the month of April. A second derailment happened in August when a train backed into a cow near Burlingame. The damage in both accidents was set at $225.

Receipts from operations in 1870 are not available for the whole year. Records show that gross revenues were $126,960 for the last five months. Expenses were estimated at 50 per cent, "which shows that the road has fairly earned during the last five months, more than double the interest on its mortgage." The building of the railroad heralded the coming of thousands of homemakers. Emporia buzzed with business activity. The annual report stated that "the firm of John Wayne & Co., now Charles F. Pierce and Co., lumber dealers of Emporia, were selling at a rate of $400,000 per annum while Baker and Co., grocers, were selling at $200,000. Almost 200,000 cattle were shipped to Kansas City by rail from the vicinity of Doyle Creek."

Cattle Drives, Buffaloes, and the West

Emporia marked the last of the settled communities into which the Santa Fe built. Beyond it were no towns of any size. A few pioneers had located on the better sites, but they were few and far between. Newton was laid out as the rails neared, and in the summer of 1871 service was begun. A tremendous volume of cattle traffic was secured. Newton was about sixty miles south of Abilene, the previous cattle capital of the West. Thousands and thousands of Texas longhorns moved north in the spring over historic trails through the Indian Territory. The destination was the plains of Kansas and Nebraska. The succulent buffalo grass of the North made for rapid gains in weight as well as noticeable improvement in the quality of the meat. Abilene early dominated the northern end of the business in Kansas. In 1871 an estimated 600,000 head grazed in the vicinity. Abilene was located on the Kansas Pacific and offered quick access to the markets of the east. Completion of the Santa Fe to Newton intercepted the moving herds. The weary drivers had little reason to go farther. Both objectives, grass and rails, were to be had in and around Newton.

Extensive pens and loading chutes were erected. Hotels and cow-men's camps went up overnight. The majority of the early busi-ness buildings housed a bar, a dance floor, and a gambling lay-out.

The cattle drives involved more hard work and less adventure than is commonly supposed. Grub en route was monotonous and coarse. The usual drink was black coffee strongly alkaline or un-adulterated alkaline water. The trip was lonely. The only associa-tions were with the other men in the outfit. Little contact was made with men with other herds. Each group kept at a distance from others lest the herds mix. Women became merely a poignant memory.

Arrival at the northern destination meant a celebration. All the pent-up feelings of the cowboy had opportunity for expression. His pockets bulged with money, not so much because his wages were high as because he had worked a long time without having a chance to spend anything. Off went the whiskers and dust ac-cumulated during the many weeks on the trail. His six-shooter was well oiled "just in case." Hungrily he contemplated a meal with all the trimmings, and he drooled at the thought of a change in thirst quenchers. Petty differences among the outfit which had grown into feuds as the drive dragged on and on disappeared near the end. The outfit usually set out to see the sights together.

Newton was taking form. Insufficient time had elapsed to pro-vide for anything in the way of town government. Local men were too busy building and doing business to bother with official organization. In the absence of law-enforcing agencies and in view of the circumstances preceding the cowmen's arrival, shootings were common. When every other man was a walking arsenal and had had a drink or two, scrapes were bound to occur. The drinks doubtless kept mortality down by spoiling the aim of cele-brants. The toll taken between June, 1871, and January, 1873, has been estimated as high as fifty, but probably twelve to twenty would be nearer the truth. About half of the fatalities resulted from one wild shooting spree in August, 1871.*

---

*The trouble began when a Santa Fe employee, Arthur Delaney alias Mike Mc-Cluskie, had words with a Texas gambler and gunman called Baylor. McCluskie was

T. J. Peter and M. L. Sargent of the Santa Fe visited Newton several times during the early fall of 1871. From observation at a distance on their first visit they reported that the leading saloons were "The Mint," "The Sidetrack," "Bull's Head," "Legal Tender," "Do Drop In," and "Gold Room." Peter and Sargent looked over the scene in the "Gold Room." Whiskey and gambling prevailed in the smoke-laden den. A minister was singing and preaching at one end, and painted women sought business at the other. After the religious service ended, the proprietor gave the preacher a five-dollar bill and offered him a sociable drink on the house (Peter afterwards was told that the preacher was a down-and-out confidence man). Sargent was afraid to stay in any of the lodging houses and sought refuge in the new station. He built a barricade of barrels next to the stove and was horrified the next morning to discover that he had used kegs of gunpowder.

The supremacy of Newton did not last long. When the line was built south and west, Wichita, Raymond, Great Bend, Larned, and Dodge City successively captured the business and its riotous accouterments. Still later Las Animas, Colorado, and Raton, New Mexico, became great loading points. Extension of the receiving points was not the only factor working to move the drives west. As the rails went west the Company brought thousands of settlers who located on the land, especially around water. After 1873 barbed wire was available at steadily declining costs, and the fencing of the frontier began. Quarantine and herd laws also helped to bring a cessation of that spectacular part of American development. While the drives lasted the Santa Fe played a major part.

---

the quicker on the draw and Baylor died with his boots on. Friends of the Texan vowed revenge, and McCluskie was warned to stay away from their hangout at the Tuttle Dance Hall. McCluskie rashly walked into the enemy stronghold and started talking to the opposition. Without warning, Hugh Anderson, the leader, shot McCluskie in the neck. A fusillade poured into the railroader, who was able to wound one assailant before dying.

An Irish friend of McCluskie by the name of Riley burst into the hall. His gun flashed repeatedly and with each shot a Texan went down. In all Riley killed outright or fatally wounded six. The hero escaped. It is said that Riley was tubercular and elected to fight for his pal partly because death was imminent. No one has recorded what became of Riley. The establishment of law and order began immediately.

Annual reports of the Santa Fe during the 'seventies placed the number of cattle shipped east over the railroad between 70,000 and 90,000 each year. These figures are much more conservative than those ordinarily reported, but there is no reason to doubt their accuracy. Not all cattle shipped east were of Texas origin, although the majority were.

When the Santa Fe was first built into Dodge City the cattle business was handled at eastern points. For a time buffalo trade dominated the scene. Dodge City was the outfitting point and home base of the hunters. By 1868 the slaughter of the monarch of the prairie had attained large-scale proportions. The hides were staked, dried out, and loaded on wagons for transportation to eastern rail points. When the Santa Fe reached the vicinity of Dodge City, individual gunshots could scarcely be heard as hundreds fired on the hapless beasts. Lt. Col. Richard I. Dodge wrote that in 1872 near Dodge City, "Where there were myriads of buffalo the year before, there were now myriads of carcasses. The air was foul with a sickening stench . . . ."[1] Brick Bond, one of the most famous hunters, boasted that he averaged 150 per day for four years. From five to fifteen skinners were required to keep pace with his deadly rifle. Very little meat was saved.* For every marketable skin, two buffaloes were slain. Hides brought from one to three dollars. Later the skeletons were collected for fertilizer and sold for about eight dollars a ton. One hundred skeletons made a ton of bones. More than $2,500,000 worth of bones was shipped east. Enormous mounds of skeletons and hides were piled high around the railroad yards. At one time Charles Rath and Robert Wright of Dodge City had 40,000 buffalo robes stacked and awaiting shipment. Statistics on the total volume of the buffalo trade between 1868 and 1881 are incomplete, but the following give a sample of the scale of operations.

The Santa Fe also annually transported about 19,000 Indian-tanned robes during the early 'seventies. Other railroads in Kansas

---

*Choice hindquarters of buffalo could be bought in Dodge City for as little as seventy cents.

Buffalo Shipments over the Santa Fe

	Hides	Meat (lbs.)	Bones (lbs.)
1872	165,721	none	1,135,300
1873	251,443	1,617,600	2,743,100
1874	42,289	632,800	6,914,950
1877	96,505		4,179,700

hauled about two-thirds of the total shipments. Although the buffalo herds were ruthlessly and wastefully decimated, their extermination was inevitable. The inexorable march of settlers to the plains ended the reign of the buffalo. The death knell of the antelope, the deer, the prairie chicken, and the Indian who attempted to remain a warring nomad was also sounded.

The career of Dodge City as cattle capital has often been described with embellishments. Although the tales were tall, there was much truth in them. Boot Hill was a reality, and vice and crime were once commonplace. Dodge City was Newton and Abilene moved west on an enlarged scale. The reputation of the toughest city in the world was well earned. Countless stories are told of the two-gun men who on the slightest provocation threw lead with unerring accuracy. Many of the bad men met up with Sheriff Bat Masterson, who consistently beat them to the draw.

Railroad operations around Dodge City were hazardous. Nothing delighted the cowboys any more than a shot at the oil headlight of a locomotive. Next best was a shot at the taillight. A. R. Glazier, an early employee, has given a vivid account of the trying circumstances under which train crews operated:

On December 31 [1872] my engine was ordered to Dodge City. When we arrived orders were received to put the engine in the roundhouse, with fire and steam up, and be ready to report at Camp Criley to be turned over to the operating department. I got my supper and went to the roundhouse and lay down in the engine cab to take a nap. About 9 o'clock the hostler called me and told me to go to the depot for orders. I told him to leave the engine in the house until I got back, as I wanted to oil around in the house, where it was warm. I lighted my lantern and got about half way down from the roundhouse to the depot when I heard a shot fired; then a bullet whistled very close to me. About that time Harry Campbell, who was braking for Joe Hanson, stuck his head out of the caboose window and said, 'You fool, put that light out; they are celebrating down there and they will kill you; they are shooting at your light.' The light was out before he finished the sentence.

I crossed over behind a string of box cars, got to the depot, got my orders, went back to the roundhouse behind the same string of cars and told the hostler to set the table. He wanted to light the headlight for me. I told him, 'No lights for me at all.' I got out of the house and turned on the table, had the fireman throw the main line switch for me, and, after we got out onto the main line, I thought he never would get that switch closed and get back onto the engine. His name was George Veach.

All this time they were celebrating the incoming new year down town, and it sounded like a battle royal. I got out about three miles from Dodge City when I stopped and lighted my head, tail and cab lights.

They made up a party that night in Dodge City, confiscated a negro drayman and a pair of mules, drove over to the fort, back to the west end of town, killed the negro, laid him across the main street, took off his boots, then drove to the east end of town, killed one of the mules, swung the mule across the street and turned the other mule loose.

About the same time that Glazier had his difficulties, John B. Bender, a conductor, had an experience which has been retold a thousand times. Bill Evans, a well-known gunman, boarded a train at Dodge City. When Bender asked for a ticket Evans pulled the larger of his two shooting irons and said, "This is my ticket; pass on." Bender passed on to the back of the car. There he picked up his indispensable sawed-off shotgun, and, having walked up the aisle behind Evans, rammed the gun in Evans's back. "I'll punch that ticket now."

Another oft-quoted story originated in the same area. Somewhere west of Dodge City a discouraged prospector boarded a train. The conductor asked where the old-timer was going.

He answered, "Hell."

"That will be sixty-five cents and get off at Dodge City."

Gunmen were not the only dangers to operations on the prairies. Buffalo and cattle wandered at will over the fenceless expanse. The middle of the railroad track was the ideal resting spot to tired bovines. Accidents were frequent. Several times trains were blocked by immense herds of buffalo. Peter Tellin related that he once encountered one of the main herds on a run east of

Lakin. Hours were required to ease through. The beasts were so packed that they could not clear the track quickly. Tellin kept the whistle blowing and the bell ringing. When the little train was in the middle, a solid mass of buffalo could be seen in all directions. The best plan was to wait and not attempt to go through a herd.

The passengers had great sport shooting from the trains. Antelope, coyotes, buffalo, and prairie dogs must have damned the Santa Fe, because every coach contained one or two men who fired at anything that moved. On a few occasions the line of fire was reversed by wandering Indian tribes. Near Cimarron, Kansas, Indians peppered the cab in which Engineer Tellin rode. The fire was returned. Every train crew was well armed for Indians or robbers.

Prairie fires were a serious threat to the line as well as the country. Many of the fires were started by sparks from the locomotive. During the late summer when the grass was dry it ignited easily and miles were laid waste. The Santa Fe tried many variations of smokestacks in an effort to lessen the danger. The boot stack which worked best on sparks caused the smoke to trail low and invade the coaches.

Operations in the winters were plagued with snows. The Company lacked the means to provide snow fences. Light locomotives were unable to cope with heavy drifts. A blizzard during the winter of 1874-5 held up service west of Dodge City twenty-four days.

EQUIPMENT IN 1881

Railroading in the early days of the Santa Fe was at the half-way stage in development between the Baltimore and Ohio of 1832 and the railroads as they are today. The first locomotives of the Santa Fe were of the 4-4-0 wheel arrangement, with traction power as low as 7,900 pounds. Few changes in type were made during the first twelve years. Virtually all of the engines were new and had been bought from a half a dozen different manufacturers. By 1877 the Santa Fe had sixty locomotives, and the number had quadrupled in 1881.* The standard type of 1881 had the same wheel arrangement as the first locomotives, but the tractive power had been increased to 14,000 plus. Electric headlights were yet to come. Reference to the tallow pot was literally correct. Mutton tallow seemed to be the best lubricant. The engines had to be overhauled frequently. The water for the boilers was hard, and the Company had no means of treating it. Boilers scaled rapidly, and in western Kansas the flues burned out every three months. The trains were short and moved slowly. Time Table No. 37 of February 1, 1874, admonished engineers about speeding. "The speed of passenger trains must not exceed 3 minutes per mile; freight, construction and work trains must not exceed four minutes per mile, unless by special order of the superintendent." Top speed permissible was fifteen miles for freight trains and twenty miles for passenger!

Rolling stock of freight trains during the first years of operation was light. As has been mentioned, the boxcars had a weight capacity of 20,000 pounds. Improved finances and better methods of construction enabled the Santa Fe to provide progressively larger and sturdier cars. Capacities of 26,000 to 40,000 pounds prevailed in 1881. Everything but the trucks on freight cars was wooden. The little locomotives could not have pulled steel cars had they been available. The costs were low. Boxcars bought in 1878 were priced at $433 and $459. Coal cars were only $200, $210, and $349.

Passenger coaches had a seating capacity scarcely half that of twentieth-century ones. There were no vestibules at the ends, and passengers remained on the car they boarded. Conductors risked

---

*In 1878 the Santa Fe ordered its most famous locomotive, "Uncle Dick." It was named after Uncle Dick Wootton and was bought to act as a helper in boosting trains up the switchback and the 6 per cent grade at Raton Pass. "Uncle Dick" was said to be the largest locomotive in existence when built. Delivery was made January 7, 1879, in a stripped condition lest the bridges would collapse under the great weight (118,000 pounds). The tractive force of this 2-8-0 was 23,200 pounds. Crowds congregated at all points to view the monster as it went west. "Uncle Dick" did yeoman work at Raton and had a long career in service.

life and limb negotiating the space between the coaches. There were no air brakes, and the hand brakes were said to be of "armstrong" design. Diners had not been introduced on the Santa Fe. Most passengers had enormous baskets of sandwiches and fried chicken. During the summer, swarms of flies buzzed about in spite of the efforts of conductors to sweep out the crumbs. Heating the coaches in the winter was a difficult problem. Coal stoves were used. Close to the stove the temperature might be 120° while ten feet away the passengers froze. Beginning about 1873 arrangements were made to provide eating stops for the convenience of passengers who did not want to take provisions. In the western part of Kansas the dining halls were dugouts or sod houses. The cuisine was substantial enough but in variety and quality left much to be desired.

The year of 1876 was notable in the history of passenger equipment. The first sleeping cars were secured from the Pullman Palace Car Company. They were "the newest and best coaches" to be had. An idea of the quality of the regular coaches may be gained from the costs. Cars bought in 1878 cost $2650 and $3250. Oil lamps provided feeble light for evening travel. The seats had low backs and little padding. Trips of two or three hundred miles were an ordeal, yet they were immeasurably easier by train than by any other means.

The roadbed was steadily improved during the 'seventies, especially in the last three years. Maintenance was understandably light in 1874. Very little ballast was used in the original construction. When heavy rains persisted the weight of the locomotives sometimes caused the tracks to sink into the mud. The Company regraded much of the right of way in the east and began ballasting the line. Steel rail was substituted for the malleable iron rails, ninety-five miles of rails being replaced during 1879. Bridges were strengthened and improved. Untreated wood continued to be the building material. All the ties were untreated and therefore required frequent replacement. Ties used in western Kansas and eastern Colorado were floated down the Arkansas River. Lack of fences was increasingly expensive. In 1879 a total of $33,523.50 was paid for killing livestock. Two trains were derailed as a result of striking bovine trespassers. Fencing was deferred until the 1880's.*

BUILDINGS AND OFFICES

Stations of the Santa Fe were always described in reports as "neat and capacious." The superintendents had other terms to use in their reports. C. F. Morse reported that all buildings were in "fair repair in 1874. Painting and carpentry work were badly needed if future costs were to be checked."

Early shop facilities were quickly outgrown. Initially a six-stall roundhouse was planned in Topeka. Two stalls were completed before the other four. Repairs were made under the most trying circumstances. There were no traveling cranes to lift the engines. Tools were limited in quality and quantity. Lighting was especially bad. Tallow candles and torches were the only means of illumination. Little regard was paid to ventilation or heating. As locomotives were added the roundhouse became progressively less satisfactory.

The first storehouse for all materials was only 20'x24'. Car repairs were made on a sidetrack. The costly construction program of 1872 across Kansas precluded any allocation of funds for improvement of the shops. In 1874 one large shed was erected to house the car, machine, and blacksmith departments, but it was used during the first winter as a dormitory for several hundred land-seeking Mennonites. During the first decade of operation the Santa Fe made no commitment regarding the permanent location of the mother shop. Topeka was apprehensive and voted a

---

*William Schultz, a veteran engineer, said that it was the fireman's duty to walk ahead of the engine with a poke pole to get wandering herds off the track. One night while running between Granada and Syracuse Schultz spied an obstruction in the middle of a bridge in the nick of time. A Texas bull had attempted to cross and had slipped so that its legs straddled the ties. The whole train crew had no end of trouble lifting the brute. Their aid was unappreciated and as soon as the bull scrambled to its feet a charge followed. Everyone escaped, but the locomotive had to resist one and only one rush.

$100,000 grant in 1872 contingent on the final decision. Lawrence eyed the Santa Fe hopefully and made overtures. The die was cast in 1878, when the Santa Fe purchased the extensive facilities of the defunct King Wrought Iron Bridge Manufacturing and Iron Works of Topeka. The acquisition was renovated for railroad use, and for the first time the Santa Fe had adequate shops. As the line grew, shops had to be provided outside of Topeka. Repairs were made at Newton until 1879, when the shops were moved to Nickerson.* In due time Dodge City, Coolidge, La Junta, Raton, Las Vegas, and Albuquerque were made repair centers.

The first general office of the Santa Fe was in a room over Costa and Hanley's butcher shop on Kansas Avenue. The building was of frame construction. At the outset there were only two employees, but additions were soon made and the room became congested. Enlarged quarters were available in 1872. The Santa Fe erected a multi-purpose frame structure. The lower floor was used as a freight and passenger station and the second floor for offices. Four years later a lunchroom was sandwiched into a portion of the second floor. The Company expanded rapidly and more space was required. Various departments were moved to the business district of Topeka. Space was rented in three office buildings. By 1880 two hundred were engaged in the white-collared work of keeping track of the Company's manifold activities.

The handling of wage payments during the early days was interesting. A special paycar with sleeping quarters was built. Once

---

*Nickerson was on the "great bend" of the Arkansas River. After the Kinsley cutoff was built in 1886, few trains went around the bend, most traffic being routed over the short cut. Nickerson no longer was a desirable point for repairs. Newton citizens eyed the situation hopefully for signs of a return of the shops. Santa Fe officials said that they were reluctant to return, because of the poor water supply. The Newton Commercial Club set out to prospect in 1896. Aid was sought of Erasmus Haworth, Professor of Geology at the University of Kansas. Haworth had made a study of underground streams in Kansas. He journeyed to Newton, studied his notes, viewed the lay of the land, and declared, "Dig here and within 200 feet you will strike excellent water in ample amount." At 130 feet the scientist's judgment was confirmed. The Commercial Club was charged $6 plus expenses of $7.50 for the work of location. An agreement was reached with the Company (March 22, 1897). Newton soon boasted a monthly railroad payroll of $40,000.

a month the paymaster, James Moore, raced over the line, his pay-car pulled by the fleetest engine. As he neared divisions, he wired ahead and on entering each town the engineer gave a few short blasts. Even at midnight the employees came on the run, half-clad, sleepy but ready for their pay. Between August, 1872, and January 1, 1873, the men were paid in cash, and no little danger was attached to the runs of the paycar. After January of 1873 checks were carried. The new plan was safer in many respects, but had one undesirable result, stimulating the cashing of checks in saloons.

Traffic in the 'Seventies

The best barometer of the rapid growth of the Santa Fe down to 1880 is the following statistics on freight and passenger volume. Regardless of adverse climatic conditions along the line or national financial straits the Santa Fe forged ahead each year.

Year	Gross Earnings	Tons of Freight Moved		Passengers Carried	
		East	West	East	West
1870	182,580	98,917 East&West		33,628 East&West	
1871*	498,278				
1872*	1,172,013				
1873	1,222,766				
1874	1,250,805	79,416	106,894	32,248	37,411
1875	1,520,358	104,897	147,486	32,877	40,065
1876	2,486,582	157,141	168,481	60,109	73,618
1877	2,679,106	176,122	195,961	76,667	88,651
1878	3,950,868	322,808	288,278	99,690	117,415
1879	6,381,442	305,235	496,886	144,796	169,505
1880	8,556,976	311,182	642,519	184,574	196,748

Completed mileage in 1880 was three times that of 1874; gross revenue was up 6.8 times; gross revenue per railroad mile had in-creased more than 2.25 times. Especially significant was the con-sistent excess of passenger traffic west over traffic east. During 1874-1880 inclusive the net was 92,000. Behind that figure of 92,000 is the story of the building of the West. Those 92,000 were the pio-

---

*Year ending the following March 31.

neers who broke and sowed the soil, planted the trees, and tended the livestock. They fashioned temporary sod houses, and when several crops had been harvested, substantial homes dotted the prairies. Schools and churches were provided unbelievably early. The 92,000 who came by rail plus those who migrated by other means were the basis of a great economy. Thousands of tillers of the soil meant a demand for enormous quantities of supplies. The "tons of freight moved west" were the tools of empire-builders. Emigrants from distant Russia brought their seeds, choice implements, and personal effects all of the way to Kansas. Young Illinois farmers brought what they thought they would need and then sent back east for more. "Tons west" were lumber, hammers, plows, harness, cloth, and everything else necessary to establish farmers and to supplement the partly self-sufficient western life. Also included were the needs of coal, gold, silver, and salt miners and the equipment for rapidly rising factories and mills. "Tons east" were the products of a new country in the extractive stage. They were cattle, sheep, hogs, coal, ores, grains, buffalo, and bones.

The business of the Santa Fe was not passively acquired during the 'seventies. In reality much was created by the Company as an outgrowth of a well-calculated program of development. Officials realized from the beginning that in order to secure the maximum profits the country had to be populated by men of industry. Pioneering had to be encouraged by every available means. The key to railroad riches was a large volume of traffic, and the latter could stem only from a healthy economy. The Santa Fe advertised Kansas in every state in the Union and every nation in Europe. Immigrants were subsidized, seeds were hauled without charge, shelter was provided, and relief was given in event of initial crop failures; in short, the Company did everything in its power to encourage settlement and industry. The Company worked and so did the settlers. The harvests were abundant for all concerned. The Santa Fe traversed river bottoms almost all the way across Kansas, and the land was rich and productive. The grant embraced much of the flood plains of the Arkansas and Cottonwood rivers. No more fertile line could have been followed east and west in Kansas. By the end of the 'seventies there was no doubt that the Santa Fe was on the way to transformation of the Southwest.*

TALES OF THE WEST

At the beginning of 1881 the Santa Fe was a $50,000,000 organization. During the previous span of twelve years much progress had been made. The mileage in operation had expanded from nothing to 1500. The critical early stages were behind. During the next fifteen years the Company was to quicken the various lines of progress which had been so well started. In 1893 the Santa Fe-controlled locomotives shuttled back and forth between such remote points as St. Louis, Galveston, San Diego, Denver, and Chicago. The Company neared its maximum in extensive development. After 1893 growth was almost wholly intensive.

At no time in the history of the Santa Fe has the process of refinement or improvement ceased. Between 1881 and 1896 every phase of operations changed. Men working during the 'eighties gasped at the wonderful innovations of the decade and recalled how primitive was the operation of the railroad in the 'seventies. From the hindsight of the twentieth century the 'eighties were days of crudities in transportation by rail. Kansas towns were more sedate during the 'eighties than they had been, but in that decade the Santa Fe entered new territories which were sparsely settled. Hair-raising incidents again occurred.

The bone business removed the last vestige of the great buffalo herds. Most of the Indians had been suppressed, although Apaches were still on the warpath. The cattle drives were almost at an end, but the cattle business was only beginning. Texas herds were to move north to Kansas but not on foot. Great cattle ranches were established, and the Texas longhorn began to follow the way of the buffalo. But the West was far from tamed. Kansas in the

---

*The role of the Santa Fe as an empire-builder is traced in detail in Chapter VII, "Peopling the Prairies."

'seventies was no wilder than Arizona, New Mexico, and Oklahoma in the next decade. Raton emulated the bloodiest brawls of Dodge City and Newton. Six men were killed on June 26, 1882, when a deputy attempted to hold a gambler. One of the slain was Harvey Moulton, engineer of the "Uncle Dick" and justice of the peace. The leading culprit was finally hanged and according to the custom his body given to a Mexican for burial. The next day the sportiest clothes in town did not fit too well.

Train robberies were much more frequent during the 1881-96 period. The increased popularity of holdups was due to perfected methods as well as the transportation of larger sums of money and gold by express. Many spectacular robberies took place as A&P trains crossed the deserts of New Mexico and Arizona. The usual procedure was for a couple of the gang to hide on the train and climb over the tender after leaving town. The engineer would then be ordered to proceed to a previously determined point and stop the train. The rest of the gang were there waiting to begin looting, with extra horses saddled for those who had ridden the train. The train was stopped in a desolate spot, and the brigands vanished into wild country, where they would be untrackable. Robbing a train was a sizable undertaking, and the best-laid plans went awry in fifty per cent of the attempts. The bandits were killers, and much shooting attended the holdups. Many a loyal employee lost his life when the robbers shot without provocation, but many a robber was outsmarted and slain by members of the train crew or employees of Wells Fargo.

The excitement which attended the early train robberies was dwarfed by the fervor generated in the settlement of Oklahoma. The Santa Fe had completed its bridge over the Indian Territory before the area was opened to settlement. When the gun was fired to start the rush, the Santa Fe was prepared to meet enormous demands for service. Dozens of boxcars were loaded with the belongings of the contestants. Coaches were accumulated at the borders to provide rolling stock as far as possible. Clerks, helpers, and agents were sent into Oklahoma ahead of time in order to handle the business. The Company was unable to provide adequate terminal facilities, having had only thirty days' notice.

When the gun was fired April 22, 1889, Santa Fe trains steamed forward to match speed with people on foot, on horseback or muleback, in buggies, wagons, sulkies, ox-carts, and every other means of conveyance. To the victor did not belong the spoils. In a measure everyone in the race won a prize, but the choicest lands and lots were gone long before the starting signal. Hundreds of people had gone ahead and had "soonered" the land. Frank J. Best, a Santa Fe employee at Guthrie, at the last hour decided to stake a lot before the contest began. All the attractive lots were gone and fighting prevailed over conflicting claims. Best decided to stick to railroading. The telegraph operator at Guthrie was much less scrupulous than Best. Thompson had taken the job for the sake of the land he might secure. A week before the race Thompson had decided on a particularly fine quarter of bottom land. He had induced his fiancee to go with him and claim the adjoining quarter. In addition the two had mentally claimed two lots. Bright and early on the eventful day Thompson forsook his job and went with his sweetheart to occupy the lands. A dozen well-armed "Sooners" had been equally impressed with the fertility of Thompson's choice. It seemed inadvisable to press any claim. Thompson still had the town lots, and he decided to continue as a telegrapher, since his farming career had been nipped in the bud. The loss of the farms and the critical remarks of his girl were disconcerting. A train order to sidetrack the southbound passenger train in favor of a northbound extra cattle freight was not given and the trains met head-on. Wreckage was strewn along the right of way and traffic interrupted at a critical time. Thompson lost his job, the town lots proved to be in the street, and the fiancee sought other company.

A "Sooner" who had equally bad luck was a Civil War veteran. A little while before the rush he rode up to Best and, pointing to a choice meadow, said, "That's mine and now Uncle Sam and I are even." The veteran explained that the Government had never given him a pension. On following days he visited Best and cautioned him to remember the entry. A little later the two met, and the "Sooner" passed without a sign of recognition. Best was dismayed and sought an explanation.

"What's the matter? How's that claim coming along?"

The veteran turned and spoke just three words:

"Damned school section."

During the first days the Santa Fe concentrated its efforts on bringing water and food to the settlers. Most of them had made the run without proper regard for their needs. Local water was unfit to drink and the abundant game was quickly dispatched. Serious suffering prevailed, in spite of mitigation afforded by the railroad, before supplies were gradually built up and chaos subsided into order.

The Santa Fe took part in another migration during the same period of operations. When the Government moved the Apaches from Arizona to Florida, the Indians were transported by rail. Some 900 were rounded up at Fort Apache and moved overland to Holbrook with a cavalry escort. The redskins took with them all their belongings, including 1,200 horses and about three mongrels per capita. Old Indian fighters were said to have trailed the motley crew at a distance hoping for one more shot at the enemy. The progress of the procession was slow. At last camp was made beside railroad tracks. Drums and chanting sounded all through the final night. Dogs howled, horses whinnied, and peace was maintained only with great difficulty. The next morning the soldiers began the formidable task of loading the Apaches. Most of them had not previously seen a train, and probably none of them had ridden on one. The Indians balked, and the soldiers had to pick up the squaws and children and hoist them into the cars. After a few had been launched without visible injury the remainder were herded into the eighteen coaches. Dogs and horses were left, as well as bulky paraphernalia. The train crew and army officials feared pandemonium when the train started, but the Indians seemed too awed to make havoc. As the train rolled out of Holbrook the yelping dogs tried to keep pace. The hardier ones followed for nearly twenty miles. Cowboys had new targets besides coyotes. Once a day the train stopped while the Indians were let out for rations. The condition of the cars became progressively worse. The situation was very much the same as if the passengers had been animals. Company officials debated whether to burn the cars at the end of the journey. An attempt was made to clean them with a fire hose. It is not clear whether the eighteen coaches were ever put back into general service.

Improvement in the 'Eighties

The Santa Fe was obligated to make substantial changes in the character of expenditures at the beginning of 1881. Funds had been spent for extension of the lines as fast as money could be obtained. Very little had been spent for maintenance. This was natural; few repairs had been necessary during the years immediately after installation. By 1881 the original rails and ties needed replacement. Meanwhile equipment had become much heavier and accentuated the need for a more substantial roadbed. Traffic was increasing as the West was settled and as feeders were built. More traffic flowed over the older parts of the mainline. This in turn necessitated larger terminal facilities, more roundhouses and stalls in existing roundhouses, bigger passenger stations and freight depots, newly equipped and expanded shops, and more office space. The Santa Fe had become of age and was then a great operating railroad, even though many miles of rail were yet to be built. Major problems in the future were to be concerned more and more with efficiencies in operation. The new order was apparent in the following excerpt from a circular issued by the president and directors on January 3, 1881:

But the road is not in a suitable condition to do the large business which has already come upon it. Our earnings for the past year, amounting to about $8,500,000, have been seriously interfered with by the condition of our track and the want of suitable rolling stock. And our best customers and friends on the line in Kansas and New Mexico, have not received the accommodation which we would have given them if we had been able to do so. The road has not been sufficiently ballasted, and a large part of it was laid with light iron, which is giving way rapidly both in Kansas and Colorado. In the latter State, we are in perpetual danger from cattle straying on our track, and a great deal of expensive fencing will have to be done before we can run at full speed. We require at the present time 25,000 tons of steel and 50,000 tons cross ties to lay down as rapidly as possible. The machine shops at Topeka are altogether insufficient in size, and we are without the necessary shops to repair rolling stock both in Colorado and New Mexico. In or near Kansas City we shall require at least 100 acres of land to make exchanges of cars, with the necessary roundhouses, coal chutes, etc. The renewal of bridges, which should be done at once, will require some $80,000, and the water service not less than $110,000. At Topeka we ought to erect the necessary buildings for the business of the company. Passenger depots should be put up at Lawrence and Emporia, and round houses should be either enlarged or built at Atchison, Emporia, Florence, Newton, Nickerson, Dodge City, Sargent and several places in Colorado and New Mexico. In the matter of rolling stock alone, we require engines and cars which will cost in the neighborhood of $2,500,000. Besides all this, some forty miles of side tracks should be laid at once. In short, although the road has been a successful one and the business has increased as much as the stockholders could hope, vast sums of money will have to be spent before we can work economically and profitably. The directors, after giving the whole matter a careful consideration, have decided that $6,000,000 should be spent on the road. And they consider it much more conservative to issue stock and sell it at par to the stockholders than to load down the road with a heavy debt in the shape of bonds. They therefore have decided to issue one share in four of new stock—which will be used as explained above, for construction and rolling stock.

The program to refurbish the Santa Fe was pushed aggressively in 1881 and in the years to follow. In 1881 and 1882 orders were placed for major additions to the motive power. A total of $4,712,700 in rolling stock was contracted for in 1881, delivery to be made during the next year. Most of the locomotives were Hinckleys, Manchesters, or Baldwins. The 4-4-0 wheel arrangement persisted. In an effort to secure equipment at a lower cost the Santa Fe went into the manufacturing business. A locomotive was built in the Santa Fe shops at Topeka in 1881. It was the second No. I and was also named "C. K. Holliday." Other engines were soon to follow. On March 13, 1882, the Topeka *Daily Capital* announced that the first completed train built west of the Mississippi had just been finished in the shops. The engine, the "William B. Strong," had cost only $8,587. The newspaper was lavish in its praise of the coach.

The passenger coach is covered on the outside with narrow plowed and grooved lumber, the ordinary wide panels splitting when exposed to the hot winds in more southerly latitudes. Inside, the polished walnut panels, sunk and raised, the grouping of artistic carvings, the painted and polished white oak ceilings, decorated with the brightest colors after East-lake designs, the elegantly-upholstered seats, the lamps, the hardware, both tasteful and in strict keeping with the general design form a panorama of art which exalts the beholder.

In 1886 and 1887 the Santa Fe again stepped up the rate of locomotive purchases. Although many 4-4-0s were bought the Company began the use of 2-6-0s and 4-6-0s. A period of limited additions followed, but in 1890 the expansion was resumed. An extensive fleet of 4-6-0s was obtained from the Brooks Works during the two succeeding years.[2] Great improvements had been made in the locomotive during the 'eighties and early 'nineties. Tractive power was in excess of 20,000 pounds, more than double the first locomotives used on the Santa Fe. Electric headlights were introduced. The "Uncle Dick," sensation of an earlier decade, was surpassed in size, power, and refinements by the standard engines.

Passenger equipment improved as much if not more than motive power. When the mainline was extended from Kansas City to Chicago the Santa Fe put trains in service which embodied all the latest innovations. The Kansas City *Times* of April 29, 1888, headlined its description "The Santa Fe's Vestibuled Trains on Exhibition Here." Vestibules were deemed even more newsworthy than electric lighting. Each car had a light switch. "Lamps are also in position, so that in case of failures of electrical appliances they can be used." Woodwork in the first class coaches was "of English antique oak in Moorish design and elaborately carved." The dining car was "a gem of comfort." The sleeping cars, "sixty-nine feet long, are furnished in Louis XV design with Mahogany and English antique oak. They are elaborately upholstered in peacock blue glace plush. . . ." Safety devices to prevent telescoping were embodied in construction of the cars. Automatic brakes assured control over the train. The "longest vestibuled train in the World" had most of the features which were to prevail for the next fifty years. The diners on the run to Chicago were the first ones used on the Santa Fe system. The practice in western operations had been to stop the train at Fred Harvey's fabulous oases. Because of the desire for speed and the lack of existing Harvey Houses the diners were put in service. Naturally the inimitable Fred

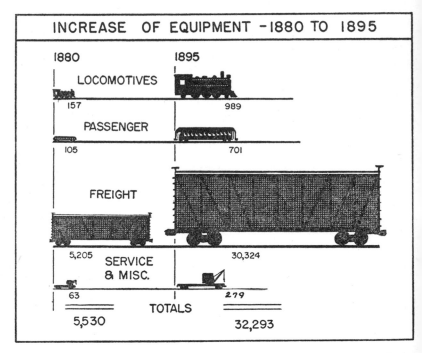

Harvey was in charge. The first menu card issued on a diner offered the typical Harvey cuisine. Prairie chicken could be had as the *pièce de résistance* of a multi-course dinner for seventy-five cents.

Improvements in rolling stock devoted to freight service were less obvious than those made in passenger cars, but the changes were no less significant. The evolutionary process of the boxcar continued. The progeny were consistently larger, sturdier, and more costly to buy but less costly to operate. Eight refrigerator cars were listed in the 1884 statement of rolling stock. These are believed to be the first ones on the Santa Fe. Automatic airbrakes on freight trains were introduced during the 1881-1896 period. The initial test run was May 23, 1885, between Topeka and Emporia. Although the results were gratifying, many years elapsed before the majority of cars in freight service were equipped.

An overall picture of the increase in equipment may be had by comparing the inventory at the end of 1880 with that of 1895.

The density of equipment per mile of track had almost doubled. The capacity of the locomotives and cars in 1895 was greater, so that the total given above does not fully represent the actual increase.

A railroad grows like an animal. Although certain parts may develop more or less rapidly at different stages, on the whole the growth is uniform. Heavier rolling stock inevitably means better roadbed for the same reason that an elephant cannot step in mouse tracks. Greater density of traffic forced improvements in rails, ties, ballast, grades, and bridges. Back in 1876 the Santa Fe had replaced six miles of iron rail with 56-pound steel. The superior durability of steel wholly justified the change. Steel laid in 1876 was not of present-day quality. There were no devices for detecting flaws. Imperfections were many, but they were fewer than in iron rails. Steel was put down on sixteen miles in 1877 and fifty miles in 1878. Throughout the 'eighties steel was laid as iron on the mainline wore out. Old rails were relegated to branch lines. Rerolling was often necessary. The period between 1881 and 1896 featured the substitution of steel for iron rather than any sizable increase in the weight of the rails. When track was laid to Chicago, the Company girded for heavy volumes by laying 71-pound steel. The distribution of weights on the main lines of the Santa Fe on January 1, 1896, is given on the following page.

DISTRIBUTION OF WEIGHT OF RAIL ON JANUARY 1, 1896

71——70 pounds	410 miles
67——65	389
62½—60	1,735
58——55	109
54——50	832
48——45	83
Under 45	1
Total	3,567

Light rails were used on all branches. Out of 6,481 operated miles in 1895, steel had been laid on 6,155. The transformation was virtually completed.

The problem of ties was given its share of attention. Tie plates to ease the cutting effect of the rails were yet to come. The Santa Fe was plagued by the rapid deterioration of its ties. Most of the supply was of soft woods and in spite of the dryness of the territory, the life of the rail support was short. Hardwoods were costly and distantly located. The corrective for the plight of the Company was to treat the ties with creosote or some other preservative. A plant was erected at Las Vegas, New Mexico, in 1885 and hundreds of thousands of ties of inferior wood were given long leases of life. When soft pine was treated, it became virtually as good as the finest white oak. Ties formerly had to be replaced as often as every four years, but with the new methods fifteen years of service were possible.

Ballasting the Santa Fe began in 1881, when a crusher was built near Strong City, Kansas, to provide rock. Other crushers were put in operation, and the line was ballasted from Atchison to Newton. Progress on the remainder of the lines was slow. Suitable materials were lacking on many divisions. Burnt clay was used on parts of the Missouri and Illinois divisions of the road between Kansas City and Chicago. On January 1, 1896, only 1,113 of 3,567 miles of mainline were ballasted. Crushed rock was used on 322; pit-run gravel on 587; engine cinders on 65; and burnt gumbo on 137. Branch lines and the A&P were unballasted. The latter was facetiously excused on the grounds that the whole country was nothing but ballast.

Bridgework in the 'eighties was relatively light as far as replacement work was concerned. Hundreds of new bridges were installed on new lines. Since the majority of all bridges were new, little work had to be done. Essentially the work was that of raising the load capacity of the older structures. The span at Topeka was bolstered in 1882 for the second time. Bridgework, however, was cumulative. Because most of the bridges were built at the same time, replacement could not be staggered. The Company was hard pressed for funds in the 'nineties, but a broad bridge program was pushed between 1892 and 1899. A total of 2,467 bridges aggregating over thirty-five miles was replaced. Steel and heavy masonry were substituted for untreated wood. The loading adopted for the program was sufficient to meet all requirements of heavier rolling stock. Trestles gave way to fills, and box culverts yielded to cast-iron pipe.

The gradual process of reducing grades here and straightening the line there was under way during the 'eighties. This work was to be of more concern to later generations of Santa Fe personnel. Control work on river channels began to receive increasing attention. Rivers in the Southwest were fickle and difficult to manage. When would the rivers flow where? The story is told that a sight-seeing preacher walked up to a Santa Fe engineer whose duty it was to do something about the periodic rampages of the Rio Grande and asked, "Where is the mighty Rio Grande that I have read about?" The engineer replied, "You're standing on it."

The problems of section crews in the early days were numerous and varied, but tools and techniques were few and simple. One old-timer on the Paris extension of the GC&SF recalled that the men had few shovels and no track jack, level board, or gauge. A long pole was used to pry the rail and the foreman had a tape to measure the gauge. Maintenance work on the A&P lagged far behind the times. Oscar Gabriel, who began as a section foreman in 1890, wrote:

When I first entered the service on the old A&P., it looked more like the old Santa Fe Trail than a railroad. So with 50 and 56 lb. rail, dirt and sand ballast and a lot of poor and rotten ties, I found it rather interesting. One day in early June of 1890 when I found eleven broken and rotten ties in a rail length of 30 feet, it had me guessing what to do for the safety of trains. At that time we had small untreated 6″ x 8″ x 8′ ties and we could only get a carload once in a while, and no switch ties. But we could get a few old bridge stringers once in a while to make repairs to our switches. Water was also at a premium at the time. Most of the section houses had old barrels set in the ground and the local freight trains had instructions to fill the barrels. However, this was often forgotten by engineers and trainmen, regardless of a red flag being set up by the section foreman's wife when out of water. All of our switches on the old A&P were stub switches and no switch lights, so all we could do was to trust in God and good luck.

Arizona and New Mexico posed so many railroad problems that the territories came to be the proving ground for countless men on their way to high official positions in the Santa Fe.

Brick and stone stations replaced many smaller wooden buildings on older parts of the system between 1881 and 1896. The most impressive addition to Santa Fe terminal facilities was the leasing of rights in the Dearborn Station in Chicago. It had been built between 1883 and 1885 and was considered to be one of the finest in the country.

Repair shops underwent modernization and expansion as the Santa Fe grew. During 1881 facilities were virtually doubled in Topeka. Old buildings were torn down, renovated, or put to other uses. The original roundhouse was used to shade unrefrigerated California fruit cars. Provision was made for major repairs at many new points. Topeka retained its supremacy in scale of operation, but Cleburne, Texas, San Bernardino, California, and Albuquerque, New Mexico, boasted extensive shops.* When the Chicago line was completed the Company erected repair facilities near Fort Madison, Iowa, and in Chicago. Provision was made for

---

*Bernalillo was originally chosen instead of Albuquerque as the site of the shop. A. A. Robinson went to José Leander Perea, owner of the required land, and asked for a favorable quotation. Perea was not interested. He had unsuccessfully subsidized trail building and was convinced that a railroad had no better chance for success. The more Robinson argued, the higher became Perea's price. Finally Perea demanded $1,000 per acre for the necessary plot of twenty acres. Robinson negotiated no longer. The shops were located in the wide open spaces near the "old town" of Albuquerque.

engine servicing at several other points on the Chicago line as well as at many towns on other parts of the system.

Office requirements of the maturing Santa Fe overtaxed the old frame general office building. In an effort to ease the strain, quarters had been rented in the early 'eighties in three office buildings of downtown Topeka. The cure was unsatisfactory, especially in handling inter-office business. The 325 general office employees outgrew even the scattered quarters of 1884. Steps were taken to provide adequate space and a four-story, red brick building was erected at Ninth and Jackson in Topeka.* Once again office space caught up with requirements. The new building was badly damaged by fire in 1889. It was more than rebuilt. A fifth story was added to keep abreast of the growth of the Company.

During the early history of the Santa Fe the executive offices were in Boston. In Allen Manvel's administration the directors recommended a shift to Chicago. Manvel's successor, J. W. Reinhart, persisted in maintaining headquarters in Boston.

Traffic to 'Ninety-six

Santa Fe freight traffic between 1881 and 1896 was closely correlated with the fortunes of agriculture, especially in Kansas. Proper distribution of sun and rain meant wheat and corn and ton miles for the agencies of transportation. Traffic revenues did not move exclusively in sympathy with crops but were conditioned by mileage in operation and by declining rate levels which emerged from struggles with other railroads and hostile legislatures. Below are the figures for the period.

The year of 1883 was the first which did not bring an increase in gross revenue. The decline, however, was not a function of crop

*The structure was completed during 1884. A rumor circulated that the Santa Fe contemplated moving the office to Kansas City. A. E. Touzalin was supposed to have attempted a change after construction was under way. Newspapers alleged that he had tried to buy off Contractor Charles A. McConigle, for $10,000. The records and office equipment were to be spirited out at night. Whether or not there was anything in the rumors cannot be ascertained. The governor of Kansas was sufficiently perturbed to intercede and to threaten to call out the militia. Touzalin was roundly assailed in the press, with or without justification.

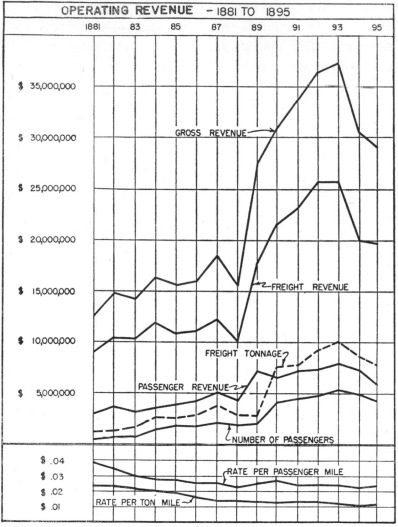

OPERATING REVENUE — 1881 TO 1895

Note: Figures subsequent to 1889 are system figures.

volume, for Kansas had record-breaking harvests of corn and wheat. The key was in the reduced rates. Following 1883 the Santa Fe encountered frequent crop failures and uninterrupted lowering of passenger and freight rates. Passenger rates between 1881 and 1895 were off more than one-third and freight tariffs were halved.

The period was one of continual struggle. The Annual Report for 1888 cursed the accumulation of woes which Fate had meted out. "Droughts, failure of crops, excessive competition, continually decreasing rates, unwise legislation, strikes, and other calamities have befallen us, as they have other Western roads. But your Directors could not know in advance that any of these unfavorable conditions would have to be met—much less that they would all have to be met, at one and the same time." The financial position of the Santa Fe was severely rocked in 1888, and the jolting reached earthquake proportions as misfortune followed misfortune. The Company was plagued not only by national economic prostration, competition, and adverse local crop conditions but also by the aftermath of much new construction. New mileage is seldom able to stand on its own legs for several years even in settled country. The Santa Fe had built hundreds of miles in undeveloped regions which had to be populated before traffic would flow. Such a high percentage of the system was new that a weakening influence prevailed when strength was needed most. The addition of the Colorado Midland and the Frisco was a heavy burden on previously strained financial resources. The A&P and Sonora Railway were consistently in the red. Errors of the Santa Fe seemed confined to some of the acquired lines rather than constructed lines. But under the circumstances the Company could hardly be indicted for overexpansion. From a standpoint of long-run development the expansion was essential to maintain territorial control. Other railroads would have preëmpted the same areas. They too would have met with financial troubles and probably would have collapsed. But with reorganization and time, the lines would have become profitable for the Santa Fe's rivals. The forces making for monopoly in railroad service obliged the Santa Fe to seize and preserve territory by extensive construction.

Lean years had little effect upon the quality of service and operating policy of the Santa Fe. Officials continued to sow the seeds of traffic. Hope is perennial in Kansas projects, and the confidence of the leaders of the Railroad was unshaken. Efforts to colonize the prairies were redoubled. Industry was encouraged. The Santa Fe advertised the great Southwest with every technique at its disposal.

The colonization program reached its peak in 1885.* Offices were maintained throughout the eastern part of the United States and in Europe to encourage the migration of farmers to Kansas and to other areas tributary to the line. The Santa Fe expended great sums to facilitate the movement. Economy was not to be gained by skimping on immigration projects.

Freight solicitation was aggressive. Agents all over the system ministered to the mutual interests of the Santa Fe and its clients. Off-line offices were established in eastern cities, where up-and-coming employees convincingly advised manufacturers to "ship Santa Fe."

Passenger travel was encouraged no less than freight traffic movement. The wonders of Colorado, "the Switzerland of America," were widely advertised. The fame of Fred Harvey's sumptuous meals lured thousands of travelers from competing lines. A resort hotel, the Montezuma, was built at Las Vegas to accommodate those who sought rest and the benefits of the local mineral waters. Las Vegas became "the Carlsbad of America." In 1884 the Montezuma was destroyed by fire but was replaced by a handsome stone structure at a cost of $165,000 in excess of the insurance collected. Wealthy people and nobility from far corners of the world thronged to the spa. Business was well under way in 1885 when fire leveled the Montezuma for the second time. The loss was fully covered by insurance and the Company provided an even more luxurious building. In an effort to break the spell the hotel was renamed "The Phoenix," but, since the clientele persisted in speaking of the Montezuma, the old name was restored. For the next decade the Montezuma was the rendezvous of the idle and busy rich from near and far.

---

*See Chapter VII, "Peopling the Prairies."

SPECIAL TRAINS

Outstanding in the annals of passenger service between 1881 and 1895 were the sensational runs of two special trains from the Coast to Chicago: the first was "the Nellie Bly Special," and the second was "the Cheney Special." Jules Verne's novel, *Around the World in Eighty Days,* was at the height of its popularity in 1889. A New York newspaper publisher conceived the stunt of having a reporter attempt to surpass the storybook hero. To heighten interest he selected for the race a woman, Nellie Bly. Scarcely any trip ever received as much notoriety unless it was the one of Death Valley Scotty, years later. Nellie's courage was lauded to the heights. In Paris she interviewed the creator of her rival, Monsieur Verne. Nellie reached San Francisco on the home stretch on January 21, 1890, and immediately boarded a special train for the run to Chicago. All trains were sidetracked for Nellie. Crack crews and engines were selected to obtain the maximum speed. Thousands congregated at every town to see the train go by at a breath-taking pace. The trip of 2,577 miles was made in sixty-nine hours at an average of slightly more than thirty-seven miles per hour. Speeds approaching ninety miles were attained on favorable portions of the line. Nellie more than maintained her round-the-world schedule and reached New York after a total elapsed time of seventy-two days, six hours, eleven minutes, and forty-two seconds. The Santa Fe had secured world-wide publicity, and each division superintendent received a quart bottle of Mumm's Extra Dry.

Scarcely less spectacular than the run of the "Nellie Bly" was the dash of "the Cheney Special," which carried the Boston capitalist, B. P. Cheney, Jr., from Colton, California, to the side of his ailing son in the East. The trip was made July 23-26, 1895. The newspaper accounts of it caused Rudyard Kipling to incorporate the episode in *Captains Courageous.* The running time of fifty-seven hours and forty-six minutes to Chicago surpassed the speed of "the Nellie Bly," but the total time (seventy-nine hours and two minutes) was slower, much delay being caused by washouts.

COMPETITION AND POOLS

During its trying years the Santa Fe placed little reliance on pools or rate-fixing to bolster its income. In the absence of governmental establishment of minimum rates, some agreements were necessary to prevent complete breakdowns of tariff structures. In the middle 'seventies the Santa Fe had participated with the D& RG and the Kansas Pacific in a Denver-east pool. The experience was relatively unsatisfactory, and working arrangements were intermittently discontinued. When the Santa Fe gained access to California, the Company entered into the Transcontinental Association for regulating rates and traffic distribution of business with the Pacific Coast. The Southern Pacific was successful in preventing the newcomer from benefiting appreciably. When junction was about to be made between the A&P and the California Southern at Waterman, the Santa Fe contemplated using steamers from San Diego up the Coast in order to secure a fair share of the business. The Southern Pacific offered a new traffic split, which was accepted. Again the results were disappointing, and in 1886 the Santa Fe broke off relations with the Transcontinental Association. Previously the Company was supposed to have 23 per cent of the business between the Pacific Coast and points east of the Missouri River. The amount actually handled was much less. President Strong in February of 1886 demanded 50 per cent of the business of southern California and 28 per cent of the remainder on the Coast or 30 per cent of all. The Southern Pacific proposed to allocate business on a basis of what had been done during earlier periods. This time the Santa Fe refused to compromise, and a severe rate war followed. Santa Fe passenger rates between Chicago and the Coast were cut from $115 to $70 for first class and $42 for second class. On February 24, 1886, tickets between Kansas City and San Francisco were $30 first class with a $5 rebate and $24 second class with a $3 rebate. The Southern Pacific countered with $16 to the Missouri River, $20 to Chicago, and $35 to New York. Tickets from California to Missouri River points were $1 for a few hours on March 8. The low of the Santa Fe was $5.[3] Hostilities persisted into 1887, when higher levels were restored by a new understanding. The disdain of the Santa Fe for pools was evident in the Annual Report for 1886. The Directors asserted, "A traffic agreement, at best, is always uncertain and unsatisfactory, and generally becomes neglected or odious. . . ." Management preferred competition for volume at reasonable rates to rate wars or traffic allocations. There seemed to be no tendency to exact exorbitant charges. The Company was committed to maximizing gains from the development of a volume of traffic rather than from securing the greatest return from the existing sources.

Although the period of 1881 to 1896 had led the Santa Fe to financial prostration, the basis had been laid for eventual solidarity. The Company had acquired or built thousands of miles of lines. Some of the additions proved undesirable and were discarded, leaving a well-integrated system capable of the maximum operating efficiency. The Railroad had brought countless settlers to its territory and had coöperated wholeheartedly in establishing agriculture, forestry, mining, and industry. The Southwest in 1896 was out of the stage of incubation and ready to take contemporaneous strides with the revitalized Santa Fe.

VI

Tremblingly Clipping Coupons

*Ad astra per aspera.**

THOSE WHO CYNICALLY damn the profit system are commonly blithely blind to its accomplishments and blissfully ignorant of the shortcomings of the program they would substitute. The economic system of the United States has had its imperfections, to be sure, but the accomplishments should not be underrated. Developing a nation requires more than a high degree of business acumen and the application of brute strength. Risk-takers must provide capital out of existing stocks to implement the ambitions of the industrious. There is a wise old saying that "it takes money to make money." Finances dedicated to the production of useful goods for profit fructify more than uninvested dollars.

The financing of American enterprise was fraught with risks and difficulties. Relatively new countries offer prospects for rich rewards and likewise possibilities of loss. Commitments are at best speculative. Local funds are usually inadequate to meet the needs of the most promising ventures of the captains of adolescent industry. Promoters have to reverse their field and return to old capital markets for support.

The Atchison, Topeka and Santa Fe is a typical case history in the development of American business. Financing was achieved under trying circumstances. Resort was made to many methods. Under more favorable circumstances different means would have been utilized. Other companies had similar woes and had to resort to improvisation. The Santa Fe boomed when the Nation boomed and collapsed once when the Nation collapsed. As the United

---

*"To the stars through difficulties," the motto of Kansas.

States grew in strength, the Santa Fe kept pace; in fact, it did more than that. The West was backward and undeveloped, yet before the race had run its course, the West had come abreast of the East. The time came to pass when a Westerner spoke of stock and meant securities.

The First Financing

Kansas could supply the brains and brawn for the Santa Fe but not the money to command them. Holliday, Pomeroy, and associates had to seek financial support in the money capitals of the East. Although much money was secured from eastern financiers, adequate amounts could not be raised in the United States and resort had to be made to the great creditor nations of the period— England, Holland, and Belgium. The problem was still difficult, because the purse strings abroad were tightly drawn when conversation dwelt on a "railroad for warring Indians." Only limited amounts could be obtained at any one time, and as a consequence the financial founts had to be tapped frequently.

Mystery shrouds the early issues of the Santa Fe. Sources of information which should be authentic vary as to the number and amount of bonds offered during the first years of construction, but there is enough similarity in the versions to make the deviations from the general account seem of minor importance.

The charter of the Santa Fe authorized the issuance of $1,500,-000 in capital stock of $100 par value. Provision was made for increasing the amount when circumstances required. At the first meeting of the incorporators on September 15, 1860, subscriptions were taken for $52,000 in common stock. For years the amount outstanding was limited to the initial pledge, which, incidentally, was not fully paid. Most of the stock was reacquired and in 1867 the Santa Fe had only sixty-five shares outstanding. They were owned by the directors. At the time of the building contract with George W. Beach, October 12, 1867, all stocks, land bonds, and municipal bonds were to go to Beach except the sixty-five shares owned by directors and the stocks destined for counties in return for the latter's bonds. T. J. Peter and the Atchison Associates succeeded to the rights of Beach. The new syndicate was able to raise the first sizable sums. A bootstrap technique was used. Few outsiders could be induced to put money into a paper railroad. Most of the money came from the wealthier members of the Associates and a small circle of friends.

The block method of offering was followed. Various issues were lumped together and units prepared which contained small parcels of each. The initial offering, dated 1869, including $960,000 in par value of common stock, $150,000 in Shawnee County, Kansas, bonds, $192,000 of first-mortgage bonds of the Santa Fe, and $768,500 of Pottawatomie land bonds. All of the fixed obligations carried nominal interest of 7 per cent. The first-mortgage bonds had thirty-year maturities, and the land bonds came due in ten years. The total amount offered in the block was $2,070,500 in face value, but only $955,700 was realized. This was as satisfactory a sale as could have been expected, but the shortcomings are obvious. Discounts on securities are obnoxious enough when the variance from par is slight, but serious problems are posed when only 50 per cent of par is obtained. Watered stock results.

The first financing venture of the Santa Fe throws light on an interesting aspect of watered stock which is generally not appreciated by friendly as well as caustic critics of corporations. More watering has grown out of the unwillingness of investors to pay par for securities than from misrepresentation of assets of issuers. The market, in effect, insisted on paper evidence of two dollars in rights for one dollar. The lone dollar expended with the greatest prudence should be represented by an accountant's recognition of one dollar in cash converted in another asset of one dollar. Substantial discounts were inevitable as new issues emerged. The task of servicing the interest charges in the inflated structure was made doubly hard, and, at the same time, prospects for dividends on common were remote. Rendering stock fully paid and nonassessable had complications.

Buyers of the various county bonds issued as subsidies to the Santa Fe could not look to the Railroad in event of default. These bonds were as lacking in quality as were those of the Company.

The Company apparently issued to the Associates a total of $128,700 in par value of stock in addition to the original block. During 1871, $21,300 in stock and $8,000 of the first-mortgage series were assigned to the Associates to extinguish debts. Since the Pottawatomie land bonds were linked with a self-liquidating venture the result of all the preceding financing was to yield the Company $955,700 in cash to represent $1,100,000 in common and $200,000 in bonds. Soon steps had to be taken to secure additional funds to build beyond Emporia. On September 6, 1870, an agreement was reached with Kidder, Peabody and Company of Boston to raise the money. Again substantial discounts had to be conceded. A block of $1,350,000 in par netted $880,000. The accounting breakdown was as follows:[1]

Security	Par	Discount	Commission	Bonus
Capital stock	$200,000			$200,000
First-Mortgage 7% bonds	600,000	$120,000		
Land-Grant Mortgage 7% bonds	500,000	100,000		
Land-Grant Mortgage 7% bonds	50,000		$50,000	
Total	$1,350,000	$220,000	$50,000	$200,000

About the time that the finishing touches were applied to the above transaction, the Associates withdrew and the Company no longer had an intermediary to handle financing. Completion of the line across Kansas to beat the deadline on the land grant necessitated the issuance of more securities. The accounting method was altered but not the fundamental block system. Common stock of $6,855,000 par was sold at face value. This was made possible by the subterfuge of bond bonuses for all stock subscribers. The bonds supported the value of the stock. Records reveal that $9,294,000 in par value of various bond issues of the Company and $483,000 in county and township bonds were donated. This method was technically superior at the time to the system of paying for bonds and receiving a bonus in stock, since the latter was nominally sold at par. The injection of water into the structure was retarded by the fact that many of the securities sold were not considered of railroad character. The subsidy bonds of local governmental units, the Pottawatomie land bonds, and the land-grant bonds were not to be retired out of operating revenues. For this reason, the securities dependent upon operating revenues were more reflective of the actual expenditures on assets. Although no capital deficit was shown, investors no doubt were cognizant of the deficiency in the consideration paid for the securities.*

The financial expansion of 1872 was fully as impressive as the spectacular extension of the tracks across the state. The investment in railroad facilities increased tenfold. The annual report for the year ending March 31, 1873, boasted 497 miles of main track and 31 of side track. The cost of construction, $22,015,836 was divided as follows: for roadway, $20,593,233; equipment, $1,214,307; and material and supplies, $208,296. A figure of $11,427,052 was arbitrarily assigned to the land grant. The demands of construction were so heavy on the treasury that the sprouting Santa Fe soon found itself in a quandary. The new mileage was understandably unproductive. Every available dollar was sequestered for running the line to Colorado to preserve the land grant. The small floating debt grew rapidly and threatened to sink the Company. During 1870 and 1871 no great concern was expressed, but current obligations soared to alarming heights in 1872. Dollars that were needed to clear the books had to be devoted to building. The primary trouble was not so much the lack of profitability of early operations as it was the lag between expenditures and sale of securities. The common sequence of securities, then construction, was of necessity reversed. When the lag increased, difficulties ensued. By March 31, 1873, the situation was critical. Default of the interest on the funded debt was inescapable. Compromise meas-

---

*Under an offer of March 22, 1872, each subscription of $1,000 entitled the investor to a first-mortgage bond of $800, a land-grant bond of $500, and $1,000 in stock.

ures were taken to alleviate the crisis. Bondholders were offered twice the value of their current interest coupons in new consolidated mortgage bonds. Bondholders were also asked to buy the new issue in order to fund the remainder of floating debt. The attempt was partially successful. Additional sales of first-mortgage bonds enabled the Company to pay equipment and construction bills.

The year 1873 was essentially one of borrowing from Peter to pay Paul. Obligations continued to mount and revenues were disappointing. By the end of 1873 the floating debt was $486,000, with an additional $50,000 in accruals. Besides, the land department had $350,000 in short-term obligations and nothing to serve as legal tender. Taxes, commissions, and advertising combined with the liberal credit policy brought little into the coffers of the department in early years.

A judicious mixture of threats and promises obviated a second crisis. Existing holders of securities were warned that unless they coöperated by subscribing for bonds to fund the current debt, bankruptcy was inevitable. On the other hand, if support were given, the impending increase in business would bring a handsome reward. Old values would be recovered and new investments solidified. The panacea was announced on December 20, 1873, in the *Commercial and Financial Chronicle*.[2]

To provide for the wants of the land department it is proposed to issue at par $700,000 of 12 per cent currency income bonds, running 5, 6, and 7 years, to be paid for ⅓ Jan. 1, '74, ⅓ July 1, '74, ⅓ Jan. 1, '75, in cash or in land mortgage coupons due three months later.

These bonds are abundantly secured and their interest provided for by the assignment by the railroad company and the land bond trustees of land contracts, amounting to $1,105,744, which are constantly increasing in value by the improvement of the lands.

And to provide for the other wants of the company it is proposed to issue at the price of 50 per cent in currency, $1,852,000 of the consolidated 7 per cent gold bonds, being a second mortgage on the road and the lands, the first coupon on same being due Oct. 1, '76, producing $926,000, and payable—⅓ Jan. 1, '74, in cash or coupon, due within three months thereafter; ⅓ July 1, '74, in cash or coupons, due within three months thereafter; ⅓ Jan. 1, '75, in cash or coupons, due within three months thereafter.

Each holder of twenty-five shares of stock has the right until Dec. 20 to take $500 of the consolidated bonds and $200 of the land income bonds.

MONEY AT TWELVE PER CENT

The rate of 12 per cent on the land bonds is symptomatic of the times and territory. The high rate was to enable sale at par and, in reality, was not out of line with the effective rate paid on other issues. The interest charges on the consolidated-mortgage bonds was the highest ever paid by the Santa Fe. The Company was to pay $7 in interest each year for every $50, or 14 per cent, and in addition was to return $2 in principal for every $1 invested. The usual consequence of distress financing of the type pursued by the Santa Fe is merely a stay of execution. This case was an exception. The improvement in business, which had been assured by management, materialized. The funding process was deemed a great success. At the beginning of 1875 the treasurer announced, "We take pleasure in informing you that the floating debt is paid, excepting the current liabilities in Kansas for which we have ample cash assets in hand."

The "ample cash" mentioned in the treasurer's report assumed more modest proportions as months passed. By midsummer the Santa Fe was again embarrassed. The circular was issued stating regretfully that the Company did not have the means to meet in full the coupons on notes due July 1, 1881. One-half of the interest was paid in cash and the remainder in 7 per cent scrip maturing with the notes. The scrip was convertible into consolidated bonds on a dollar-for-dollar basis of face value. Happily the vexing problem was solved without any drastic action by the bondholders, nor did the Company have to offer usurious rates to raise money.

After 1875 the fortunes of the Santa Fe began to vindicate the judgment of those who had backed the venture. Net revenue swelled, except in 1877, and finances of the Company were cautiously handled, with emphasis on guarding against a repetition of the earlier troubles. Discounts on offerings of securities narrowed as the Santa Fe demonstrated increasing signs of fundamental strength. By 1879 financial solidarity had been attained; bonds of the Company were widely sought, and even common loomed attractive to men who sought income. The crucial days of hand-to-mouth existence were behind. Officials could safely devote their time to developing a great railroad rather than worrying how one dollar or less could meet several dollars in pressing obligations.

THE RECORD OF THE 'SEVENTIES

Nutshell presentation of the financial record of the Santa Fe during the 'seventies is embodied in the following key statistics taken from annual reports and other official sources:

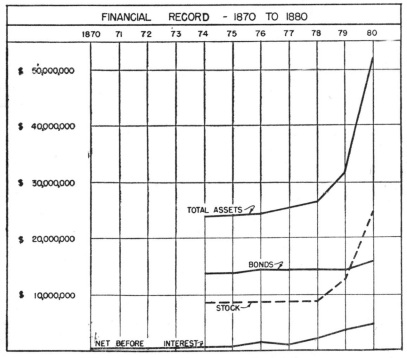

The graph does not reflect fully the strengthening of the Company's resources. While proper basis existed for the entries in 1874 under assets and bonds and stock, the evidence of the discounting process was obscure. Assets were swollen to offset the discrepancy between par and the net proceeds from the disposal of securities. Most of the discount was incurred in 1872. The total market penalty between January, 1869, and April, 1879, was more than 50 per cent of the par of the $21,783,700 offered in securities or $11,641,000. Ordinarily the process of wringing out the water would have been long and drawn-out. In the case of the Santa Fe the period was highly compressed. The proceeds of land sales and local bond subsidies were invested in the railroad as the money was realized. The growth of the territory matched the predictions of the most optimistic early clairvoyants. Consequently the value of the assets of the Company advanced far beyond initial costs. Facilities in a booming area were much more valuable than the identical equipment, roadbed, and right of way in a section that had only dubious prospects for success. By 1878 the Santa Fe capitalization was more than matched by real investments in road and equipment and other assets. Excellent earnings were realized in 1878, while in 1879 the ratio of earnings to capitalization was almost 13 per cent. At long last the day of dividends had arrived. On August 9, 1879, the directors declared a dividend of 3 per cent. Twenty years had elapsed since Holliday chartered the Santa Fe, and ten years had passed since the first dirt had been thrown. Operating profits, the driving force of the Santa Fe, had been slow in coming but had finally emerged.

SOLIDARITY IN THE EARLY 'EIGHTIES

The early 'eighties were the antithesis of the preceding decade as far as financing of the Santa Fe was concerned. In the early days leaders of the Company pleaded for money at reasonable rates and finally resigned themselves to paying exorbitant charges. There was no choice; the demands of capitalists had to be met or no money would have been forthcoming. The tide had turned in the 'eighties. The Santa Fe was conquering the "Great American Desert." Ability to sustain the heaviest financial burdens had been demonstrated under the most disadvantageous circumstances. Formerly officials sought support in the far corners of the globe; now the far corners of the globe sought the Santa Fe. Financing became easy, perhaps too easy. Moneyed men of England and Holland offered checks in any amount designated.

The great expansion of the 'eighties was financed in a variety of ways. Some mileage was built by the Santa Fe itself. Payment was made out of the proceeds from the sale of securities or from the retention of earnings. Most of the newly constructed mileage was paid for by indirect means. Subsidiary corporations were established and funds for construction were advanced by the parent company. Santa Fe construction crews were used. Stocks and bonds of the subsidiary were turned over in liquidation of the construction advances. The stocks were retained for purposes of control and ownership. The bonds of the subsidiary were offered for sale with or without parental guarantee but ordinarily with a guarantee of payments of interest and principal by the Santa Fe. Resort was made to collateral trust bonds in order to secure low interest rates or improved marketability. Subsidiary bonds were hypothecated for issues of the parent company.

Many small railroads were added to the Santa Fe family by purchase. As a rule corporate entities were not disturbed, and the ownership passed to the Santa Fe by an exchange of securities. The Company succeeded to the obligations of new subsidiaries. Cash purchases were the exception.

At the outset of the second decade of Santa Fe operation the finances of the Company were in good order.* The annual report

---

*President of the Santa Fe at the time was T. Jefferson Coolidge. He came from one of America's oldest and most distinguished families. His mother was a granddaughter of Thomas Jefferson. Other relatives held positions high in public service. Coolidge was born in Boston, August 26, 1831. His early school years were spent in Dresden, Germany, and Geneva, Switzerland. He returned to America to attend Harvard. He began his business career as a clerk. Later he engaged in the East India trade and amassed a fortune. The Amoskeag Manufacturing Company next claimed his attention and soon he was associated in numerous banking, manufacturing, and railroad enterprises. His service as leader of the Santa Fe lasted from May 13, 1880, to August 1, 1881. In later years Coolidge devoted his efforts in behalf of the diplomatic service and held many important posts, including that of Minister to France. He died November 17, 1920.

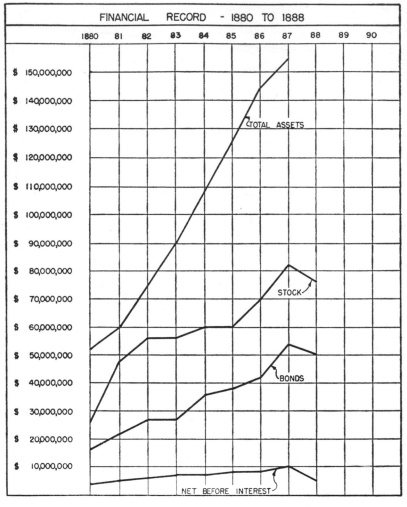

for the year ending December 31, 1880, disclosed total assets of $51,940,657, of which $18,604,126 represented securities of subsidiaries. Funded debt of $15,873,000 was less than two-thirds the capital stock account of $24,891,000. The ratio of debt to capital stock was extremely conservative and well within the limits laid down by rules of sound, conservative finance. Interest charges, carried over from leaner days, averaged about 7 per cent. The coverage of fixed charges was in excess of the widely recommended figure of two. After all obligatory payments had been made, a balance from earnings of $2,668,912 remained, equivalent to 10¾ per cent on the outstanding stock. The showing was all the more impressive when consideration was given to the fact that one-half of the stock had been issued during the year and did not reflect full earning power in such a short period.* Quarterly dividends aggregating 7 per cent were declared, and almost a million dollars added to surplus. The surge of prosperity persisted to 1887, when diverse factors led to a major recession culminating in a voluntary reorganization late in 1889.

The fortunes of the Santa Fe are revealed partly in a continuation of the statistical record presented earlier in the chapter. During the 'seventies statistics under the above items gave true perspective of the Company, but the figures for years between 1880 and 1888 were not fully reflective of actual conditions. Many subsidiary companies came under the umbrella of the Santa Fe. They were not conservatively financed like the parent company, and their funded debt approached, equaled, or exceeded the value of the properties. The balance sheet and profit-and-loss statements of the subsidiaries were not consolidated; hence the figures for the Santa Fe showed neither the operations nor the assets and liabilities of much of the system. The main evidence in the statistics of the parent company was the continuance of balance in the financial plan, although this equilibrium was upset if consideration were given to affiliates. Net earnings continued to increase, although not in proportion to the increase in capitalization. One substantial increase in stock brought no earning assets into the enterprise. A 50 per cent stock dividend in 1881 raised common $18,077,250. Securities sold during the period brought

---

*All of the new stock did not bring cash into the treasury, but the overall operations during the year were to increase the capitalization coincidentally by the amount of the stock. Of the increase in stock, $3,257,500 grew out of the conversion of consolidated mortgage bonds and $6,756,700 was issued in exchange for securities of newly acquired lines. The remainder of $2,242,400 was marketed to provide means of buying equipment. Two bond issues bearing only 5 per cent were floated to raise $4,916,000.

par in most cases, although some discounts were given on bonds. One of the largest discounts was allowed in 1887, when stockholders had the right to buy $1,000 par value of Santa Fe collateral trust, 5 per cent bonds, $1,000 par value of the Chicago, Kansas and Western Railroad Company first-mortgage, 5 per cent bonds, and $500 par value in income bonds of the same subsidiary for $2,000. The discount was assigned wholly to the income bonds. The procedure of offering stockholders the first chance to buy new bond issues was consistently followed and tended to assure protection of equities. The stockholders enjoyed the usual preemptive rights to subscribe to new issues of stock.*

The high level of the operating ratio in 1881 and 1882 arose in large measure out of the highest maintenance ratio in the history of the Company. In 1881, 34.85 per cent of gross revenues was spent on maintenance. The resurgence of the operating ratio in 1888 was caused by the sharp decline in traffic receipts.

Interest coverage between 1880 and 1888 began strong and ranged around five. As subsidiaries were added during the middle of the period, the coverage shown by the parent company became less important. In 1888, when coverage of the Santa Fe proper was two, nearly all of the subsidiaries suffered staggering losses.

As early as 1884 the vaunted strength of the Santa Fe began to be questioned. The wisdom of the extensions to the Pacific was challenged. Doubt was expressed about the fate of the Company in event of crop failures in Kansas. Disappointment was expressed, too, over the failure of earnings to keep pace with additions to mileage in the system. On April 18, 1885, the *Commercial and Financial Chronicle* reported:

> The managers of the Atchison, Topeka & Santa Fe, in their report submitted this week, give evidence that they appreciate the situation that confronts them, and know how to deal with it in an effective way. The net earnings of the property have lately fallen short of expectation; its future has been pictured in most gloomy colors; its policy condemned;

---

*Early in 1881, for example, one-for-four stock rights were given to buy at par.

the course of the managers criticised; always subject to more or less hostility from without, it has now been attacked in the house of its friends, and a Boston journal, hitherto famed for its advocacy of the enterprise, has turned into a severe unfriendly critic. At this juncture, too, some of the gentlemen who have been identified with the property almost since its inception, are to sever their active connection with it, and the new board of directors therefore contains neither the names of Thomas Nickerson, the former president of the company, nor that of A. E. Touzalin, the vice president of the road in recent years up till now. Well may the management be anxious to have the affairs of the road properly presented to its security holders, and the general public. They have done what under the circumstances was the best thing they could do to clear up doubt and misunderstanding, namely, issue a report clear, full and explicit on all the points involved.

And here we would say that the reader must not make the error of supposing that the Atchison is hereafter to be guided by new and inexperienced hands. Notwithstanding the recent changes, most of the old officers remain with the company, and Mr. W. B. Strong as president continues the active head of the enterprise as in other more recent years.[3]

ENCOUNTERS WITH BEARS

Affairs of the Company continued on an even tenor. Rumors of weakness still circulated, but no pronounced signs of distress were evident. The market's indecision provided the setting for a spectacular attempt by a few operators to profiteer in Santa Fe securities. The Company had assumed the interest payments of the bonds of its subsidiary, the Sonora Railway. The issue amounted to something over $5,200,000 in 7 per cent first-mortgage bonds. About December 11, 1885, a banker of Middletown, Connecticut, visited several banking houses in Boston. He asserted that he was prepared to sell $300,000 to $400,000 of Sonora bonds for a client and was willing to accept a quotation of 2 per cent off the existing market price. Supposedly delivery could not be made for thirty to forty days. Many firms made purchases and some sold currently held Sonora bonds so that their holdings would not be unduly large. The Connecticut banker acted quietly, and the buyers were unaware that they were not the only party to the transactions. As firms unloaded existing holdings to switch to the same issue at the preferred price, the quotation on Sonora bonds sagged. Simultaneously, one John W. Fletcher of Detroit brought suit to enjoin interest payment by the Santa Fe on Sonora bonds. He charged that Santa Fe stock had been illegally issued. Fletcher had purchased two hundred shares of Santa Fe stock two months previous to his charge. He hired two shyster lawyers and found in Wyandotte County, Kansas, an anti-railroad judge who was elated at the chance to harry the enemy. Fletcher demanded that dividends declared but unpaid on Santa Fe common be held up. The judge readily granted an injunction on the interest payments in spite of the utter lack of occasion for the action. The Santa Fe was innocently unaware of the action until the notification was given. Fletcher and his henchmen capped their plot with numerous bear stories to the effect that the Santa Fe was withdrawing from the Sonora. Hysteria struck the bonds and prices sagged. The plotters then rushed into the distressed market to cover their short sales. The Santa Fe hurriedly appealed to the Supreme Court of Kansas, and the injunction was thrown out.* The local judge was given a blistering reprimand for gross miscarriage of justice. Losses were widespread. The identity of all the conspirators was never discovered.

Storm clouds remained over the Santa Fe and steadily became larger and blacker. Agricultural production withered away after early lush years. The statistics of the two leading crops in Kansas, corn and wheat, give some idea of the general decline:

Year	Wheat bu.	Corn bu.
1884	48,050,000	190,870,000
1885	10,772,000	177,350,000
1886	14,571,000	139,569,000
1887	9,728,000	75,791,000
1888	16,724,000	168,754,000

The customary lag between corn production and traffic prevented the Company from enjoying immediate relief from the crop of 1888. Crop failures involved more than the loss of revenue

---

*The Atchison, Topeka & Santa Fe Railroad Company, Isaac T. Burr, *et al.,* v. John W. Fletcher, Kansas Supreme Court, January term, 1886.

on grain or cattle. If the farmers had no income they could not buy manufactured goods from the East. Bad crops had many repercussions, all discouraging.

Santa Fe supremacy in Kansas and the Indian Territory was seriously challenged by inroads of the Rock Island, the Missouri Pacific, and the Denver, Texas and Fort Worth. In 1886 came the rate war with the Southern Pacific, which destroyed the scant hopes for current profits out of the relative trickle of transcontinental business.

Meanwhile the pendulum of public opinion concerning the railroads swung to the opposite side. The attitude of encouragement to railroads yielded to discouragement.* Economic distress in rural areas arising largely from a period of currency deflation and adverse growing conditions was wholly attributed to the railroads, though what ailed the farmers was really not an overcharge of a half a cent a ton mile, but no tons. An anti-railroad platform became the basis for vote-getting. Railroad commissions whittled rate structures. The average rate per ton mile on the Santa Fe declined from 1.882 cents in 1884 to 1.258 cents in 1888. Passenger rates were also reduced.

OVEREXPANSION

The major threat to the economic welfare of the Company stemmed from the financing of the vast expansion program prosecuted from 1885 through 1887. In 1885 the Santa Fe had a funded debt of $36,334,000. Subsidiary lines other than the A&P had $11,819,000 outstanding in bonds on which interest was

---

*A schedule of aid given to the Santa Fe and its predecessors by Kansas counties and towns prior to 1886 reveals a total of approximately $4,637,000 in bonds. The rates ranged from 6 to 10 per cent. By June 23, 1893, the precise total was $7,245,400. All the bonds sold by the Company were discounted heavily, so that the money subsidy was much less than the face value of the local governmental bonds. Stock was exchanged in many cases for the bonds. Subsidies given by units in relatively unsettled areas were not gifts in the complete sense. The Santa Fe facilities and land holdings constituted as much as 50 per cent of the taxable properties. The Company, therefore, paid the subsidy in part in the form of taxes. When counties in Santa Fe territory voted subsidies to other railroads, the Company in reality made gifts to competitors. The same effect often benefited the Santa Fe when another railroad preceded the Santa Fe into a community.

payable by the Santa Fe. Thus the total debt was about $47,000,-
000. The amount of subsidiary stock was negligible, but the consolidated ratio of debt to net worth was still conservative. The
building program was financed almost exclusively with fixed
interest-bearing obligations of affiliated companies. At the beginning of 1888 two-thirds of the mileage was directly held by
top-heavy subsidiaries, and the total was distributed as follows:

	Miles
Atchison, Topeka and Santa Fe	2,080.85
Southern Kansas System	935.50
Sonora System	350.19
Owned jointly in Kansas	227.56
Owned through subsidiaries but not consolidated	2,974.83
Owned jointly in the A&P	918.86

Little mileage was built during the next two years. Projects under
way were finished and new ones deferred. On October 1, 1889,
the outstanding bonded indebtedness stood at the crushing total
of $158,891,820. The consolidated figures did not include the A&P.
Consolidated stock was $80,925,275. The debt was almost twice
the amount of the stock. The balance sheet of the parent company
was as reassuring as ever, with stock half again the amount of
bonds. The fixed charges had risen to $8,487,045, with contin-
gent charges on income bonds of $703,470.

Much of the new mileage was initially unproductive, and
the burden on the strained resources of the Santa Fe was made
heavier. Some of the older subsidiaries and jointly owned lines
also had operating difficulties. Staggering losses were sustained
by the A&P. In October, 1886, the 6 per cent bondholders of the
A&P accepted 4 per cent on a new issue in return for guarantees
by the Santa Fe and the Frisco. Not even temporary relief was
afforded to the stricken A&P, and the position of the co-owners
was rendered more acute. The GC&SF, the Sonora, the Manhattan, Alma and Burlingame, and the Leavenworth, Topeka
and Southwestern were all using red ink regularly. The year of
1888 brought the heaviest reverses. The Sonora Railway lost $355,-

915; the Chicago, Santa Fe and California (a new line between Kansas and Chicago) lost $441,555; the GC&SF recorded a loss of $1,328,791; and the A&P went $1,578,404 closer to receivership. Other smaller subsidiaries suffered setbacks in proportion.

The combination of costly expansion and operating deficits of subsidiaries was a severe strain to the cash position of the Santa Fe, but other aggravating factors were present. Costs of some of the new lines were underestimated and required additional funds. Maintenance and outlays for new equipment proved to be unavoidably large. Current liabilities went up and current assets down. At the end of 1888 the current ratio had sagged to 93 per cent. An attempt had been made during the years to ease the problem of the floating debt by intermediate financing. A guarantee fund of $7,000,000 was authorized and subscribed. The notes were to mature in three years and carried a rate of 6 per cent. The relief afforded was only temporary, and in a few months the current position of the treasury was worse than ever.*

The final straw of adversity heaped on the struggling Santa Fe in 1888 was the costly and protracted strike of the locomotive engineers which began in March. The labor difficulties were not confined to the Santa Fe but were encountered on most western lines.

Those who held the purse strings of the Santa Fe began to exercise power in 1889. The American group was headed by Kidder, Peabody and Company. This firm had underwritten many of the security issues. The leading foreign financial interests were led by Baring Brothers. The latter had conducted in the United States extensive activities which were locally handled by Kidder, Peabody and Company. At the annual meeting of May 9, 1889, the old order yielded, giving place to the new. Boston interests were replaced by New York and London financiers. Five new faces appeared on the board—Thomas Baring, Oliver

---

*Dividends on Santa Fe stock were maintained until November 15, 1888. Much censure was later heaped upon officials for not buttressing the current position by retaining money declared for dividends. The Company had paid 6 per cent from 1881 to 1887, 6¼ per cent in 1887, and 5¼ per cent in 1888.

W. Peabody, Edwin H. Abbott, William Libbey, and John J. McCook. George C. Magoun of Kidder, Peabody and Company had filled a vacancy during the previous October and he continued on the board. J. W. Reinhart was appointed general auditor in October, 1888. His role in Company affairs was to become more important. William B. Strong was retained at the meeting as president, more in name than in fact. A division of executive powers was adopted which in effect was in the nature of a shift. The chairman of the board, George C. Magoun, assumed complete control of financial affairs of the Company.* Strong presumably was to concern himself with actual operation of the railroad. While the press was given harmony statements, the breach between the old and the new widened. Strong was tied hand and foot and averted removal by resigning on September 6, 1889.† Fortunes of the Santa Fe were slipping fast. Stock which had been quoted around $140 dropped to $20. The new men diagnosed the ailments and applied their remedies.

The successor to Strong was Allen Manvel.‡ Kidder, Peabody and Company had been impressed earlier with his ability, and the appointment elicited favorable comment in most quarters. Old-time Santa Fe employees regretted the loss of Strong and

---

*George C. Magoun was born in Cambridge, Massachusetts, August 25, 1840. His father was a schoolmaster. He was educated locally through high school and began work at the age of seventeen with the old Boston firm of Stimson, Valentine and Company, manufacturers of paint and varnish. He stayed with this company and its successor, Valentine and Co., until March, 1867, when he resigned his job as a salesman to accept a clerkship in Kidder, Peabody and Company. Progress was rapid and in December, 1867, Magoun was sent to New York to open a branch there. Full partnership in the firm was accorded him in 1871. Labor on the financial affairs of the Santa Fe and on the wreckage that came in the wake of the collapse of the House of Baring led to physical complications. Death came December 20, 1893, at the age of 52. The news shocked the business world. At the time, his death was said to have been a great loss to the Santa Fe.

†Frank E. Peabody succeeded to Strong's position on the board.

‡Allen Manvel was born in Alexander, New York, September 26, 1837. He went to work in 1859 as a clerk in the purchasing agent's office of the Rock Island at a salary of forty dollars a month. Promotions were successively to paymaster, purchasing agent, assistant superintendent, and general superintendent. In 1881 he became assistant general manager of the St. Paul, Minneapolis and Manitoba. Later Manvel was advanced to general manager and finally first vice-president and general manager. The next move was the presidency of the Santa Fe. Manvel was an indefatigable worker, spending fourteen hours a day at his desk. His frugality was the subject of much comment.

would have preferred A. A. Robinson to an outsider, but Manvel had winning ways and the employees eventually were well pleased with his selection.

VOLUNTARY AND INVOLUNTARY REORGANIZATIONS

Under the tutelage of Kidder, Peabody and Company a plan for voluntary financial reorganization of the Santa Fe was prepared. Magoun and Reinhart were the chief exponents of the changes. On October 15, 1889, the board offered its program to the bondholders for consideration. The objectives sought were a reduction in fixed charges, a consolidation of various issues and simplification of the corporate structure, and funding of the floating debt. Prior to the reorganization the Santa Fe and its subsidiaries had thirty-seven bond issues, totaling $151,904,-870. In addition, the issue of $1,500,000 of the Chicago and St. Louis Railway Company first-mortgage, 6 per cent bonds and $7,000,000 in the guarantee fund notes of 1888 needed attention. The Company owed about $160,000,000 in principal of bonds on which an average of 5.84 per cent was paid for interest, or $9,190,-515. Taxes, insurance, rentals, and other fixed charges made the annual burden $11,157,770.

The new plan authorized two mammoth bond issues to replace the thirty-seven conglomerated in the Santa Fe family. A total of $150,000,000 in general-mortgage, 4 per cent bonds was provided. These bonds covered all of the assets held in the Santa Fe system and were to mature in 1989. The second issue was $80,000,000 in income bonds. Each series had multiple purposes. Refunding of outstanding issues was to be the use made of $131,-766,550 of general 4s;* cash was to be raised by the sale of $12,-500,000, and the remainder ($5,733,450) was to be held in reserve. Most of the income bonds ($73,602,160) were to be added to the general 4s to refund existing issues; par value of $1,250,000 was to be given as a discount or "sweetener" in the sale of $12,-

---

*Bonds bearing a rate of interest of 4 per cent are described in the market and printed as "4s."

500,000 of the senior issue; another block of $4,692,914.30 was to be exchanged for some outstanding income bonds; and the residual of $454,925.70 was to remain in reserve.

The basis of exchange of new for old was exceptionally well adjusted. The task was delicate and required a fine touch for security values. Preferred ratios of exchange were given those with prior claims on assets and earnings. The holder of an Atchison first-mortgage, 7 per cent bond of $1,000 denomination, for example, was given $1,100 of the new general 4s and $520 of the new income bonds. A holder of a GC&SF second-mortgage, 6 per cent issue received $300 in general 4s and $960 in income 5s. There was no change in the interest each issue could receive; for in the first case only $26 out of $70 was contingent, and in the second $48 out of $60 was dependent upon earnings.

The plan was an overwhelming success with bondholders of every class. The directors announced on November 23 that the exchange was to be made on or before December 15. The percentage of deposits was a revelation to all. A total of $148,446,000 of old bonds was exchanged for new by the deadline. The same terms of exchange were kept open, and in all the holders of $150,349,920 out of $151,904,870 acquiesced. Only the holders of $1,554,950 balked and the bonds held by them were scattered among fourteen of the thirty-seven issues. Twenty-three issues were entirely extinguished. The maximum of non-assenting bondholders in any one issue was 4 per cent. The refunding operation had been an astounding success.

The new securities offered for cash were subjected to a substantial discount. The block of $12,500,000 in general 4s and $1,250,000 in income 5s brought $10,000,000. The proceeds were allocated as follows: retirement of equipment obligations, $1,445,-660; completion of lines and purchase of new equipment, $5,-000,000; and application on floating debt, $3,554,340.

The cost of the reorganization was moderate to heavy and was recorded as $1,440,772. This included a commission of $125,-000 paid to Kidder, Peabody and Company for the cash sales.

The general effect of the shuffling was to raise the funded debt and reduce the fixed charges. The first was the compensation for the second. The outstanding bonds had been increased one-third.* The larger principal was partly offset by reduced rates of interest. The original bonds carried an average nominal rate of 5.84 per cent. The secured bonds were on a 5.82 per cent basis and the income bonds were 6.02 per cent. Under the new arrangement the secured obligations bore 4.16 and the unsecured 5 per cent. The average saving on both issues was 1.35 per cent. The portion which was contingent on earnings rose from a negligible amount to more than one-third of the interest claims. This, combined with the reduced rate on the new bonds, caused the fixed interest payments to decline about 45 per cent.

The reorganization had eased the position of the Santa Fe appreciably. Charges were lower and the current position was improved. Prosperous times seemed in store. Crops were better and traffic picked up. The Kansas wheat crop in 1889 was 35,-319,000 bushels as compared with 16,724,000 bushels in 1888. Corn production rose from 168,754,000 in 1888 to 273,888,000 the following year. Barring catastrophic acts of God and man the Santa Fe should have been able to carry on. Unfortunately, adverse acts of both were soon to follow.

On May 23, 1890, the Santa Fe announced the purchase of the St. Louis and San Francisco Railway Company by means of an exchange of stock. The move was taken for several inadequate reasons: first, access to St. Louis was secured; second, since much of the Frisco was in Santa Fe territory, a defensive purchase appeared in order lest some rival company intervene; and, lastly, the Santa Fe and Frisco used mileage together and the purchase "would obviate all the cumbersomeness and ex-

*Not all of the new bonds earmarked for the refunding operation had to be used. A statement of the Company indicated that only $111,075,777 of the general 4s was issued in exchange. The amount of income bonds added in the trading was $77,881,923. The funded debt in the end approximated $213,000,000. Some old bonds had been bought by the Company in the market and new bonds sold for cash. According to records of the I.C.C. the total amount of new bonds issued was $202,707,670 and the net increase was $52,357,780 par value (I.C.C. Valuation Reports, CXXVII, 364).

penses incidental to the joint operation of so much rail." There
were other reasons, such as the price, operating economies arising
out of the complementary location of the two systems, the need
of access to timberland for ties, and the idea of expansion for the
sake of sheer size.*

The Frisco had 1,329 miles of mainline and branches and
189 of sidings in addition to 50 per cent ownership (the Santa

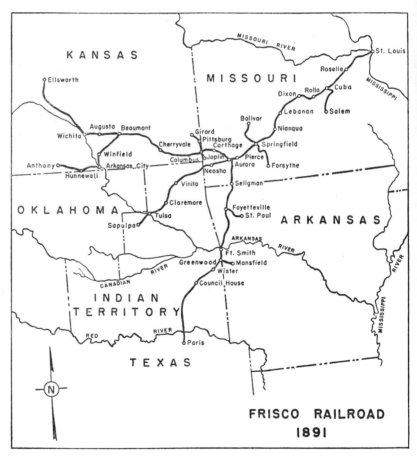

Fe had the other 50 per cent) in 919 miles of the A&P and 125
of the Wichita and Western.

---

*The two systems connected at such points as Paris, Texas, and Wichita, Burrton,
Augusta, and Girard, Kansas.

The Santa Fe did not acquire all the outstanding securities of the Frisco, but only the common and a secondary issue of preferred. The assets remained subject to a funded debt of $31,593,-500. Also undisturbed was $4,500,000 in par of first preferred. The Santa Fe later acquired the second preferred by trading eleven common for eight preferred. The outstanding Frisco common was secured by trading three shares of Santa Fe common for four shares in the other company. The cost to the Santa Fe was $22,511,688 in par of its own stock.

Purchase of the controlling interest in the Frisco was an invitation to trouble. The heavy funded debt made for large fixed charges. A deficit of $277,000 had been incurred in 1889. Officials of the Frisco had been worrying over $2,000,000 in current liabilities for which legal tender was not available. Why the convalescent Santa Fe acquired the headaches of the Frisco has confounded every succeeding generation of officials.

Acquisition of the financially impotent Colorado Midland was even less defensible than the purchase of the Frisco. The railroad comprised 327 miles. The mainline extended from Colorado Springs to Glenwood Springs, where junction was made with the D&RG to Salt Lake City. The purchase was supposed to be defensive and directed against the D&RG. The smartest defensive move would have been to permit the Midland to pass to the rival. The Midland was expected to continue its role of feeder to the Denver and Santa Fe (the new line between Pueblo and Denver) on a larger and more profitable scale. The exact cost of the Midland has been given at varying figures. Apparently all the Midland stock was obtained for $4,355,200 in par of Santa Fe common (market value $45 per $100 in par) and $1,955,424 in cash. The funded debt guaranteed by the purchaser amounted to $11,244,866. The Santa Fe also assumed the steadily growing floating debt.

Financial results of operations after the reorganization were mixed. The annual report, dated June 30, 1890, showed gross revenue of \$31,004,357.03 and net revenue of \$10,083,971.* These figures excluded the A&P, the Frisco, and the Midland. Gross had risen \$4,500,000 over the preceding year while costs had remained constant. Bumper crops in Kansas were the chief cause of improvement. Gross revenues improved slightly during the operating year of 1890-1891 in spite of agricultural adversity. Wheat in Kansas in

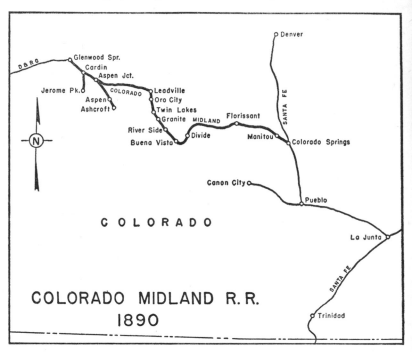

COLORADO MIDLAND R. R.
1890

1890 was off 20 per cent and corn more than 80 per cent. Higher operating expenses were incurred, and net before charges was \$9,620,546. The new additions continued in distress. The Frisco lost \$99,344 and the Midland, \$76,826. The A&P went in the red almost as much as if no business had been handled. Its deficit was \$1,793,730.

The next year, 1891-1892, showed slight gains for the Santa Fe. The A&P and Midland continued to lose, but the Frisco netted \$586,618. The parent company made further gains in 1892-1893,

---

*The report was shifted from a calendar to a middle-of-the-year basis.

when gross was recorded as $37,301,771 and net revenue as $12,126,-
866. The drain of the A&P was $1,832,775 and the Midland lost
$489,366.*

Financiers at the helm of the Santa Fe had shifted securities
around like checkers. Many other changes had been put into effect.
Vice-president Reinhart revamped the accounting system "for the
prompt rendering of results and detailed and systematic arrangement and classification. The exhibits of operations are now made so
that they show minutely where economies may be exercised and
improvement in the working of the property secured." Special
statements were prepared in lengthy yet simple form so that outsiders would have a "Primer of the Santa Fe."

The affairs of the Frisco were given an economic housecleaning
similar to the one self-imposed on the Santa Fe. An awkward floating debt and need for new equipment as well as working capital
were pressing. The funded debt of $36,077,500 bore high rates of
interest on its many components. An issue of $50,000,000 in 4 per
cent mortgage bonds was prepared for the funding and refunding
operations. One-half of a second-mortgage issue of the A&P guaranteed by the Frisco was also replaced. The amount involved was
$2,800,000. A block of $4,500,000 in the new bonds was offered for
the outstanding first preferred on a dollar-for-dollar basis, thereby
accomplishing a reverse conversion.

The process, begun in 1890, of unifying the management of the
A&P, Frisco, and Santa Fe had been completed by 1891. The current ratio declined and the floating debt rose to new levels. The
distress was accentuated by the maturing on November 1, 1891, of
the $7,000,000 in guarantee fund notes. These notes had been is-

---

*Part of the difficulties of the Midland was attributable to vicious rate-cutting
against the D&RG. In the spring of 1893 a swimming pool (improved lake) was
opened at Glenwood Springs, Colorado. The Midland promptly adopted excursion
rates of a dollar from points on the line within forty miles. The nearby D&RG countered with a fifty-five-cent rate. The Midland followed with an invitation to all to
travel free as the guest of the Company. The capstone was added by the D&RG when
it offered free round trip transportation as well as a free ticket to the swimming pool.
Competitive rates on other parts of the system did not reach such fantastic proportions
but were cut as much as 90 per cent. See E. G. Campbell, *The Reorganization of the
American Railroad System, 1893-1900*, New York, 1938, p. 71.

sued in 1888 to ease the current plight of the Company. There was no choice when the notes came due. Redemption was impossible and extension was the alternative. The Company spent $135,109.45 to get the due date postponed two years.

The reorganization of 1889 to all outward appearances seemed a success during the next two and one-half years in spite of the incidental complications. Purchase of the Midland and Frisco had been a handicap and the floating debt problem was never conclusively solved. Traffic receipts were curtailed by an unprecedented series of reverses. Single lean years were not unusual, but the Santa Fe had light revenues for eight years. Common stockholders received no dividends, but the income bondholders had partial payments to the extent their interest was supposed to have been earned. Payments were:

Nine months ending June 30, 1890	2¾ per cent
Year ending June 30, 1891	2 per cent
Year ending June 30, 1892	2½ per cent

What followed was a catastrophic decision in the annals of the Santa Fe. Magoun and Reinhart decided that the time had come when prospects for earnings justified the refunding of the income bonds into fixed-charge obligations, provided some reduction in the rate of interest could be gained. The men were also prompted by the desire to whittle the floating debt and to raise money for much-needed equipment and repairs. They contemplated making the new issue larger than the old and using the difference for the added requirements. A total of $100,000,000 in second-mortgage bonds was authorized, divided into two classes. The Class A bonds amounted to $80,000,000 and were to be offered par for par in exchange for the outstanding income bonds. Maturity was set for 104 years. The rate of interest was staggered during the first three years at 2½, 3, and 3½ per cent, and the rate was set at 4 per cent from 1896 to 1996. The voluntary refunding was almost 99 per cent effective. The figures vary, but approximately $78,000,000 of the Class A 4s was issued. Costs of the readjustment were $1,514,436.

The Class B bonds were series bonds; that is, they were to be issued in installments at a rate of $5,000,000 a year during the next four years. The interest was 4 per cent. Records of the Santa Fe disclose that $5,000,000 worth was sold and $5,000,000 placed in the treasury. The latter was ultimately acquired by the present Santa Fe company and exchanged for preferred stock. The I. C. C. Valuation Reports show only $5,000,000, for which $2,942,722 was received from the sale of the $5,000,000 of par, less commissions and expenses of $95,237.[4]

Converting a contingent charge into a fixed charge was extremely dangerous in view of the fact that the Santa Fe had earned no more than the new fixed charges were to be. Earnings would have to improve to enable the Company to meet the obligations as the rates on the Class A bonds rose. Interest coverage of one is skirting thin ice. Perhaps the financiers reasoned that by the law of averages earnings were certain to advance from the depths. A rude awakening was in store. The readjustment of 1892 came on the eve of one of the most protracted depressions ever sustained by the United States. The Santa Fe entered the panic with $222,000,-000 in bonds and notes. Net worth was only half of the debt on the books and much less in the market. The current ratio was admittedly weak and in reality no strength could be added by transfusion.

The woes of the Santa Fe rested heavily on President Manvel. Work and worry brought their physical complications, and on February 24, 1893, Manvel died. He was succeeded by J. W. Reinhart, who enjoyed a wide reputation as an expert railroad accountant and financier.*

---

*J. W. Reinhart was born September 17, 1851, at Pittsburgh, Pennsylvania. While still in school he began doing railroad work on a part-time basis. After graduating from the Western University of Pennsylvania, Reinhart worked on a full-time basis for the Alleghany Valley Railroad, a branch of the Pennsylvania System. By 1875 he was a superintendent of transportation and rolling stock. The Richmond and Alleghany next claimed his services in 1880 as an auditor. Later he continued in the same capacity with the New York, West Shore and Buffalo and in 1886 was appointed general passenger and ticket agent of the Lake Shore and Michigan Southern. After a few months he resigned to hang up his shingle as an efficiency expert and consultant to railroads. Reinhart was only forty-one when elected head of the Santa Fe, but he was not lacking in experience.

Much of the execution of the reorganization of 1889 and the readjustment of 1892 had been handled by the new leader. Reaction to the new appointment showed a sharp cleavage. A. A. Robinson was the "people's choice." His wide acquaintance among employees and in the Santa Fe territory made his candidacy popular. Reinhart had support in financial circles where it counted.*

Behind Reinhart's assurances that all was well, events moved rapidly to a climax. Efforts to secure more passenger traffic led to ruinous local and transcontinental rate wars. The new fixed charges which had been saddled on the Santa Fe were difficult to meet. The reputation of the Company was soiled when costly pay frauds were exposed on the Missouri and Illinois divisions. The once-deferred guarantee fund notes were scheduled to mature November 1, 1893. Again the Company was unable to pay, and an emergency extension was necessary. The new day of reckoning was projected five years into the future at a cost of $760,000.

Rumors of impending insolvency of the Santa Fe were widespread. Reinhart refuted the charges. Almost every issue of the leading financial and railroad publications had a denial or an optimistic statement by the president. The floating debt was said to be small for a great railroad of 9,348 miles. Net earnings for the year ending June 30, 1893, were shown to be $16,065,538, a gain of almost a million. Reinhart contended that ample cash was available to meet all requirements. After receiving the plaudits of the board of directors at the annual meeting on October 28, 1893, Reinhart left for England. Well-founded rumors indicated that the trip was a money-raising mission to meet interest payments due in January. Near panic prevailed in the market for securities,

---

*Robinson and Reinhart were not of common clay. The methods of Reinhart were an anathema to the builder of the Santa Fe. Shortly after the appointment Robinson resigned as vice-president and general manager to assume the leadership of the Mexican Central. His administration was noted for high integrity and efficiency. For Robinson the failure to receive the presidency of the Santa Fe may have been a blessing in disguise. Without doubt receivership could not have been averted by any mortal man. From the viewpoint of the Santa Fe, the failure to advance Robinson was most unfortunate.

and Reinhart cabled repeated statements concerning the strength of the firm. He returned to the United States in mid-December and tried desperately to quell the uproar. Reinhart not only reiterated his contention that receivership was remote but also sharply criticized those who dealt in market gossip. The *Commercial and Financial Chronicle* quoted him as saying:

> The interest on the general mortgage bonds of the Atchison Company due January 1st will be paid. It seems hardly necessary to make this statement, because doubts as to its payment have, in my judgment, been created solely by speculators who have no substantial interest in the property. The Atchison Company, owing to the magnitude of its system, has large payments to make from time to time, and I have noted that whenever operators for short accounts could discover the dates of those payments they have circulated reports, calculated to throw doubt upon the ability of the Company to meet them. The public knows that since the reorganization the Atchison has met all of its obligations promptly, and every statement I have made in relation to such payments before they matured has been confirmed by the fact.
>
> My mission abroad has been a great success.[5]

Reinhart's mission was not the triumph which he claimed. He had evidently secured nothing better than assurances that funds might be advanced. The Santa Fe held several million in treasury or unissued stocks and bonds. These securities were to be pledged as collateral for money to meet the January obligations. Market suspicion of the weakness of the Santa Fe became so great that quotations tumbled. The proposed collateral no longer seemed adequate. George C. Magoun's death on December 20 removed the last support to the crumbling foundation. Actually Magoun's death should not have had any effect on Santa Fe securities. Illness had prevented him from taking any active role in financial affairs for several months. Reinhart had been the financial leader and was to carry on. But the market did not agree with such a view. Magoun was widely known and highly regarded. In the minds of traders his fortunes and those of the Santa Fe were inseparably linked. Magoun's death had hastened the inevitable: a cable to Reinhart from abroad, in short, read "No." The end was at hand.

On December 23, 1893, at Little Rock, Arkansas, J. W. Reinhart, John J. McCook, and Joseph C. Wilson were appointed receivers of the Santa Fe following the friendly complaint of the Union Trust Company acting for the bondholders. Receivers were appointed the same day for the Frisco, and the A&P followed into receivership the next month. Judge J. B. Johnson of Topeka was named special master of the Santa Fe.

Reinhart added insult to injury when he made the announcement of the receivership. The Company was described as fundamentally sound and well able to take care of all obligations if given a little time. The distress was trivial and temporary, and receivership offered the best means of preserving values while the minor difficulties were ironed out. The press assailed Reinhart and other officials with all the vitriol the editorialists could muster. The verdict was that Reinhart had been grossly misleading in his many utterances. Presidents of other firms had been more discreet, so that no one was betrayed. It is easy to understand why Reinhart had been reluctant to admit the plight of the Santa Fe. If he had openly validated the rumors, collapse would have followed immediately. Reinhart had gone to extremes, and when the inevitable came, both he and the Company were victims of many a barb.

The days of 1894 and 1895 were difficult ones for the rank and file who labored for the Santa Fe. The Company had long enjoyed a reputation above reproach. Perhaps the shame of those dark days accounts for the Company's concern for a clean record ever since.

Protective committees were quick to form. New York and Boston interests were led by Edward King, president of the Union Trust Company. Meetings of bondholders (the majority of bonds were owned in England) were held in London, and to Robert Fleming was delegated the task of going to America to survey the situation and look after English interests. Dutch investors organized and were represented by Hope and Company. A general reorganization committee was formed which represented a substantial majority of all claimants. The remainder aligned with the

Atchison protective committee. One of the first acts of the general committee was to retain Stephen Little, a well-known auditor, to make a searching investigation of the affairs of the Company. There was some doubt about the accuracy of the assets and liabilities shown in the elaborate annual reports of recent years. Little was specifically requested to ascertain the amount of the floating debt and to check the income account.

In spite of the lack of authoritative information on the finances of the Santa Fe, plans for reorganization were pushed. The first scheme was outlined for consideration on June 19, 1894. It was backed by the general committee consisting of R. Somers Hayes, L. A. von Hoffman, Edward N. Gibbs, Frederic P. Olcott, Louis Fitzgerald, George C. Haven, Charles C. Beaman, John R. Dos Passos, Adrian Iselin, Jr., William Rotch, and B. Rodman Weld, with Herman Kobbe as secretary. Briefly the plan suggested foreclosure by the junior bondholders. The capitalization was to be altered and enlarged. The existing first-mortgage bonds were to be undisturbed. An issue of $35,000,000 in second-mortgage bonds was to discharge the floating debt and provide funds for betterments and other purposes according to a staggered plan of issuance. The outstanding junior bonds were to be replaced with an equivalent in 5 per cent income bonds, and additional bonds in the same issue were authorized to acquire subsidiary securities. The stockholders were to be assessed twelve dollars per share, for which they would receive the par value in income bonds. Not only was the bonded debt to be increased $60,000,000, but the rate of interest was to be advanced on the income bonds over what the original second-mortgage bondholders were supposed to get.

The new plan had little appeal and was widely assailed. All lamented the lack of recent financial statements of the Santa Fe in attempting to evaluate the proposals. Various groups of stockholders objected strenuously. Any plan calling for an assessment or sacrifice on their part was unpopular. A group known as the Mutual or Atchison protective committee sought representation on the directorate through an attempt to get cumulative balloting at the annual stockholders' meeting instead of straight voting. The move was blocked in court.

While cold water was being poured on the initial plan of reorganization, Expert Little probed into the complicated records of the Company. His findings were not of the sort to reflect creditably on the honesty or ability of the recent administration. A preliminary report in July, 1894, intimated that there had been numerous irregularities. The formal statement was submitted on August 6 and revealed four years of book juggling and misrepresentation. The most startling discovery was the overstatement of earnings by $7,644,451 during the four-year period ending June 30, 1894. All of the inflation occurred in the Santa Fe proper except for $205,879 in the Frisco. The overstatement was accomplished in a variety of ways. Little disclosed that $3,700,777 on the Santa Fe and $205,879 on the Frisco had been returned to shippers as rebates. Instead of deducting the item from revenue, it was shown as an asset under the entry of "Auditor's Suspended Account Special." Some of the rebates eventually found their way into "Franchises and Property." Large sums totaling $2,488,000 were transferred from operating expenses to "Improvements." The Santa Fe had $305,844 due from a pool with the Union Pacific and the Southern Pacific. The debt was carried as an asset although the item was uncollectible. In the balance sheet for June 30, 1893, cash was overstated $602,525; bills payable, understated $1,930,000; accounts receivable, inflated $1,-640,844; and franchises and property, overstated $2,100,111. Other miscellaneous accounts revealed errors of $337,418.

The floating debt of the Santa Fe as of April 30, 1894, was set by Little at $12,834,223, with a net debt of $9,149,588. Unfunded obligations of the three major affiliated companies swelled these figures to $15,106,382 and $10,410,202. Numerous advances had been made by the Santa Fe to its subsidiaries. The total intercompany debt of the A&P to the Santa Fe and Frisco, and of the Frisco and Colorado Midland to the Santa Fe was $16,040,920. The true worth of the entry on the Santa Fe books was nil.

Earnings available for charges during the year ending June 30, 1894, sank to a new low. Only $5,956,614 had been earned. This was highly significant as a guide to proper formation of the new capital structure.

Receiver Reinhart countered with a vehement denunciation of Little's report but was unable to controvert effectively any of the specific charges. The debate between the two revealed more evidence of the loose manner in which the accounting had been juggled.

The disclosures of Little touched off another series of newspaper attacks and the Santa Fe sank lower in public esteem. People who had been close to the Company for many years were stunned by the revelations. Few employees apparently had known of the malpractices. Steps had been taken by Reinhart to short-circuit Edward Wilder, the treasurer, when he had questioned orders and payments. Others of the old Santa Fe had been kept in the dark or goaded into resignation.

Several features of the scandal were almost unique. None of Little's research ever indicated or intimated that the shortage in funds was anything except a write-up. Reinhart certainly did not have the $7,600,000 in earnings. Income had been overstated, not stolen. The same was true of the various asset accounts under fire. They were written up, not taken for personal gain. The motive was primarily to protect the position of the management. Reinhart hoped that earnings would recover and receivership be skirted. Certainly security values might have remained higher had not the plot been discovered. Even though Little had charged that rebates were shown as assets, the evidence was not conclusive that rebates were paid even though shown. The entries for rebates may have been merely a means of building up the "Auditor's Suspended Account Special." At any rate Reinhart was not convicted of rebating, following an indictment for violation of the Interstate Commerce Act. He retained to the last his lack of warmth and popular appeal. When notified of indictment, Reinhart is said to have declared, "The indictments don't amount to anything. I fear them no more than if I was the Mikado of Japan. They are purely technical." Whether Reinhart ever made the statement or whether the newspapers were getting even for the way in which he had duped them is not known. He contrasted sharply with the frank and forthright men who preceded and followed him as president.

All blame for what happened was thrust upon Reinhart. It is difficult to believe that he was a lone wolf, but responsibility was never attributed to anyone else. Thomas Baring, an influential director, asserted that no one could be more astonished than himself, "to find that there existed between the accountant appointed by the committee and the company's own accountant any serious difference of opinion." Baring claimed that he had accepted the annual statements and Reinhart himself with complete good faith. John J. McCook, general counsel, wished "to state most explicitly that if rebates had been paid by the Company, it had been done without his knowledge or approval. If there was any false accounting, it had been without his knowledge and of course without his approval." Other officials and directors made similar statements.

Reinhart's position as a receiver became untenable after disclosure of the Little evidence. On August 8, 1894, he severed his connection with the Santa Fe.* Aldace F. Walker was appointed to the vacancy. No more judicious choice could have been made. Walker had been one of the original members of the Interstate Commerce Commission. He had resigned in 1889 to be chairman of the Interstate Commerce Railway Association and later acted in the same capacity for the Western Traffic Association. The team of Walker, McCook, and Wilson gave the Santa Fe excellent administration. Wilson's death on September 18, 1895, was said to have been caused by overwork in the interests of the Company.

---

*The directorate underwent many changes the following month. On September 13, 1894, Baring, McCook, Peck, Purcell, and Libbey withdrew. J. W. Reinhart, Robert Harris, and B. P. Cheney, Sr., had previously resigned. The new board contained John A. McCall, F. K. Sturgis, James A. Blair, Thomas P. Fowler, Edward J. Berwind, and William L. Bull of New York; B. P. Cheney, Jr., Samuel C. Lawrence, Alden Speare, and George A. Nickerson of Boston; C. K. Holliday and C. S. Gleed of Topeka; and L. Severy of Emporia.

The final report on affairs of the Santa Fe was submitted November 15, 1894. The figure on overstatement of earnings was raised to $10,261,500. The increase stemmed mainly from refusal to write off doubtful accounts and worn-out equipment, which were carried as valuable assets. Close on the heels of the financial survey came an engineering report by Robert Moore on the condition of the physical facilities of the railroad. Marked deterioration had taken place. Maintenance had been skimped during the trying years. Approximately $14,000,000 was necessary to raise the line to a state of good repair. This figure was less than had been expected.

The second reorganization plan to attract attention was announced in December, 1894. The outstanding feature was the consolidation of bond issues of the Santa Fe, A&P, Frisco, and Midland into one mammoth issue $300,000,000 in 4 per cent first-mortgage bonds. Varying sacrifices were asked. The A&P bondholders were to realize 50 per cent in par. Enough of the new issue would be left over to raise cash for current needs. Simplicity was the only virtue. Fixed charges of $12,000,000 were too much.

Dozens of other schemes were advanced by various cliques of security holders. Each plan was characterized by heavy sacrifices on the part of everyone except the maker.

The final plan was the product of the joint executive committee. This body was a fusion of the three major bondholder groups: the general reorganization committee of the United States, the London committee, and Hope and Company representing the Dutch. Membership consisted of Edward King as chairman, R. Somers Hayes, Edward N. Gibbs, George C. Haven, Adrian Iselin, Jr., C. Sligo de Pothonier, Robert Fleming, John Luden, and Victor Morawetz, with Herman Kobbe as secretary. Morawetz and Charles C. Beaman acted as counsel. The joint executive committee proposed to foreclose under the general mortgage and "to vest the properties acquired at foreclosure sale in a new company" and to (1) reduce fixed charges to a safe limit, (2) provide for future capital requirements, (3) liquidate the floating debt and extinguish prior lien claims, (4) reinstate existing securities under equitable terms in their order of priority, (5) and unify the system in the interest of economy.

Although good management was deemed necessary, the committee went on record as opposed to voting trusts of the sort advocated in earlier plans.

The new body abided by its principles with fidelity. The plan of March 14, 1895, was probably the most successful one ever designed for the reorganization of any railroad. Certainly it represents the outstanding one developed outside of a governmental umbrella. The secured first-interest obligations were reduced from $224,933,586 to $109,462,117. Annual fixed interest charges were halved from $9,232,772 to $4,601,219. Fixed and contingent interest was whittled from $9,246,672 to $6,655,204. This was stiff medicine but no stronger than was good for the patient.

Holders of the old general-mortgage 4s were given $750 in new general-mortgage 4s and $400 in adjustment (income) 4s for each $1000 in par. The exchange cut the first mortgage from $129,320,777 to $96,990,586 and brought forth $51,728,310 in the 100-year adjustment 4s. Holders of the Class A and B bonds which were authorized in 1892 were assessed 4 per cent of par. Each Class A bond was exchangeable into $1,130 in par of 5 per cent noncumulative preferred. Class B commanded $1,180 in the same stock, and a few unconverted income bonds of 1889 were entitled to $1,130 in preferred. Holders of common stock were assessed $10 per share but received the equivalent in par of preferred and were able to trade old common for new on a share-for-share basis.* In all $111,486,000 in new preferred was to be traded. An additional $20,000,000 was authorized if it was desired to acquire certain securities of the Frisco, Midland, and A&P.

The committee provided additional general-mortgage bonds for the following purposes:

---

*The assessments were underwritten in England because no American financiers would assume the risk.

1. $1,500,000 to pay $1,500,000 in first-mortgage 6s of the Chicago and St. Louis Railroad.
2. $1,500,000 to pay for a dozen subsidiary issues.
3. $15,500,000 to pay for $9,000,000 in guarantee fund notes, $1,750,000 in equipment bonds, and $1,270,414 in car trust obligations.
4. $30,000,000 to finance improvements over a ten-year period.
5. $20,000,000 to combine with the earmarked preferred to finance construction of a new line to California in event the A&P were not acquired.

An issue of $17,000,000 in prior lien bonds could be issued to refund 1, 2, and 3 of the above if this were more feasible.

The committee's plan was favorably received in most circles, although the rigorous scaling-down was a shock. Some financial editors who had criticized previous schemes as too lenient wondered if the committee had not gone to the opposite extreme. A few criticized the increase in the capitalization to $20,000,000 over the cash secured by assessment. Even these critics admitted that the increase was more than offset by the reduction in fixed-interest-bearing obligations.

Deposits of old securities progressed rapidly. Between April 10 and June 1 almost three-fourths of the general-mortgage bonds were submitted. Two weeks later a majority of all bonds was deposited. The balky stockholders' protective committee announced withdrawal of its objections and stock was rapidly turned over. On September 19, 1895, the score was: stock, $100,078,200 out of $102,000,000; 4s, $127,795,500 out of $129,320,776; Class A and old incomes, $78,421,500 out of $79,191,107; and Bs, $9,-973,000 out of $10,000,000.

Steps were taken to substitute separate receivers for the Midland, and the reorganization of the subsidiary proceeded, relatively independently. Relations with the Frisco and A&P remained cloudy, and in November the court appointed a committee of three, E. P. Ripley, E. S. Washburne, and W. W. Findley, to iron out the wrinkles.

The work was rapidly drawing to a close. The foreclosure decree was entered late in August, and sale of the Santa Fe set for December 10, 1895. At 2 p.m. on the appointed day Judge

J. B. Johnson, master in chancery, carried out the sale of the Santa Fe in the stairway on the east side of the Topeka station. The steps were crowded by representatives of the Union Trust Company (trustee for the general-mortgage 4s), officers of the old and new companies, and newspaper men. A large crowd had congregated on the platform, curious to hear and see the sale. Most of the onlookers were disappointed and bored by the proceedings. Judge Johnson began the reading of a lengthy history of events leading to receivership and the sale. W. H. Rossington relieved Johnson. After the notice of sale, George H. Whitcomb lodged a protest on the grounds that control of the Frisco had not been acquired by legal means and that subsequent bonds of the Frisco were illegally issued and were properly the obligation of the Santa Fe rather than the Frisco. A second protest was read by Charles E. Small, representing London clients with $629,000 of unsurrendered bonds of the Chicago, Santa Fe and California. The two objections were to preserve rights of the claimants. Edward King, president of the Union Trust Company, bid $60,000,-000 for the property and its franchise. He acted for himself, Beaman, and Morawetz as had been planned. No other bids were submitted, to the relief of all. Rumors had circulated that eastern financiers might attempt to upset the procedure. The central figures then went to the Circuit Court for the District of Kansas, presided over by Judge Henry C. Caldwell, to hear Judge Johnson report the sale. Shortly after 6 p.m. Judge Caldwell signed the decree officially confirming the sale.*

The New Company

The Atchison, Topeka and Santa Fe Railway Company was chartered December 12, 1895. The incorporators were Edward King, Victor Morawetz, Charles C. Beaman, Edward N. Gibbs, R. Somers Hayes, and George C. Haven of New York; Edward

---

*The Topeka *Daily Capital* of December 11, 1895, reported that the new president, Edward P. Ripley, dodged the sale to look over the Santa Fe shops. He claimed he knew little about the line. Victor Morawetz was reported the smallest physically but largest mentally.

P. Ripley and Aldace F. Walker of Chicago; Benjamin P. Cheney of Dover, Massachusetts; William Rotch of Boston; and Charles S. Gleed, Thomas A. Osburn, Cyrus K. Holliday, and Edward Wilder of Topeka. The charter was brief and fully consistent with the reorganization plan.* On January 1, 1896, the Railway Company succeeded to the property and franchises.†

The financial structure of the new Santa Fe was in sharp contrast with the old. It comprised the following:

General-Mortgage 4s (100 years)	$ 97,295,716.60
Adjustment-Mortgage 4s (100 years)	51,346,000.00
Preferred Stock 5%	104,973,700.00
Common Stock	101,955,500.00
Miscellaneous and unchanged securities	12,391,516.93
Total	$367,960,433.53

Money was on hand to eliminate the floating debt. The public had already expressed confidence in the Company. Heavy fixed charges had been eliminated. Bonded indebtedness was down. Moreover, sacrifices had been equitably distributed.

The final plan of reorganization proved to be highly successful. Under the new management improved earnings were carefully husbanded and Santa Fe securities attained excellent quality. Financial manuals prefaced their surveys of the Santa Fe with the remark that "the Company's capitalization is a model among railroads." This conviction persists to the present time.

Under the presidency of Edward P. Ripley the operations of the Santa Fe were conducted on the highest plane of business ethics. The interlude of dark days was gone, never to return. The Santa Fe waxed rich in public esteem as receivership faded in the distance.

---

*See Appendix B for a reproduction.

†The receivership had cost $2,811,328.09. This figure was reasonable in view of the size of the Company and the creditable results.

VII

Peopling the Prairies

> If this invention has reduced England to a third of its
> size by bringing people so much nearer, in this country it
> has given a new celerity to time, or anticipated by fifty years
> the planting of tracts of land.—Emerson.

To trace the history of the land programs of western
railroads is to record conversion of the "Great American
Desert" into an expansive oasis. A vast area seemingly
forever relegated to the proprietorship of the coyote and
prairie dog was opened to new occupants. The task of subordi-
nating and converting an empire of waste into the West as it is
today was a monumental undertaking. Millions of acres of tough
virgin sod had to be "busted." Fences, houses, barns, schools, and
churches were to be built where the lack of wood could be offset
only by indomitable wills. So many trees were planted that later
generations were unable to visualize the early appearance of
the country. Kansas, Colorado, and other western states compressed world progress of man toward a bountiful way of life
into fifty years.

Early financing and promotion of traffic required Santa Fe
entry into the land business. Furthermore, this was in conformity
with the avowed policy of the Government to develop the West.
Acquisition of the Congressional land grant was described in
an earlier chapter. On March 3, 1863, President Lincoln signed
a bill which authorized the transfer of several large tracts of
land to Kansas for the purpose of facilitating construction of
certain designated lines. A year later Kansas officially accepted
the land and was ready to make it available to the railroads as
twenty-mile sections of line were completed in "good, substantial,
and workmanlike manner, as a first class railroad." The Santa

Fe was to receive every alternate section in a swath ten miles on each side of the line from Atchison on the east edge of the state to the western limit in the direction of Santa Fe, New Mexico.* The grant resembled a checkerboard when plotted on a map and, in all, enabled the Company to claim 6,400 acres for each mile of mainline track. In case the land was already settled the Santa Fe could not oust the claimant but could select an equal area within twenty miles of the rails. The value of the grant at the time it was awarded was negligible, although potentialities existed. Land without tillers and transportation was like a left shoe without a right. A definite ceiling on the price of land was incidental to the free and easy provisions for homesteading millions of acres of Government land.

POTTAWATOMIE LANDS

While the Santa Fe land grant was important to the development of the Company, the Pottawatomie lands at the outset possessed greater value. The Pottawatomie Nation in 1837 concluded a treaty with the United States to move westward. In return the Indians were to have the privilege of selecting a tract of land thirty miles square for their future home. Several years were spent in examining sites and finally an area was selected near the subsequent location of Topeka. The choice was well made and comprised some of the most fertile land in Kansas. No serious attempt was made to utilize the tract, and the Indians looked favorably upon the buying overtures of various organizations. Through the medium of the Government, the Leavenworth, Pawnee and Western Railroad secured a six-year option to buy unallotted lands in the reserve. The privilege was never exercised and by Congressional action on July 25, 1868, the Santa Fe succeeded to the purchasing rights of the LP&W. Thirty days were given to buy or reject the lands. The price was a dollar an acre,

---

*Also the Company was entitled to earn a strip to the southern boundary of the state if a line were built down the Neosho Valley. The same time limit of ten years for construction was set. The Neosho land was never acquired. The Santa Fe did come into possession of a railroad (LL&G) which had earned a grant in the general vicinity.

payment to be made within six years with interest at 6 per cent on
the balance. On August 7 the Santa Fe contracted to buy the lands,
338,766.82 acres in all. The Pottawatomie reserve was an asset of
some current value. Unlike the grant, the area was immediately
marketable and relatively independent of construction of the railroad. The lands were offered for sale in 1869 under the direction
of D. L. Lakin, first land commissioner of the Company. Prices
ranged from $1 to $16, with an average of $5. The terms were one-
fifth cash and the remainder in five equal annual payments. A
discount was given for all cash. The sale of the Pottawatomie
lands enabled the Company to net a sizable sum when payments
were completed. During the interim the Santa Fe pledged the
dwindling holdings as a basis for bond financing.

The Land Grant in Kansas

Attention was concentrated on the grant once construction
was under way. Although the award was to extend from Atchison to Colorado, scarcely any land was available east of Emporia.

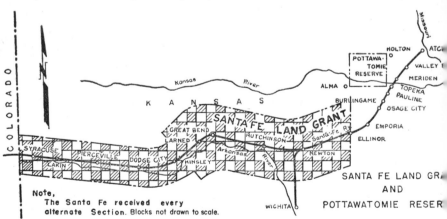

That portion of Kansas had already been settled. The substitution of equal acreage in the "lieu" area fell far short of full
compensation. The choicest part within the original grant was
in the eastern quarter of Kansas and could not be duplicated in
value by lands available for substitution toward the west. The

"lieu" lands selected were as far east as possible and had the effect of giving the Company a forty-mile swath of every other section between Cottonwood Falls and Spearville, Kansas.

Although the Santa Fe secured no land east of Emporia, the grant embraced excellent farming country. The rails followed the banks of the Cottonwood and the Arkansas rivers. The award therefore included much bottom land. This was especially important in an area where rainfall was scant.

The task of surveying and classifying the grant was enormous, yet it had to be done with celerity in order to establish Santa Fe claims and to use the lands for financing construction. Also, officials wanted settlers located at the earliest opportunity. A total of 2,928,928.54 acres was to be secured. It was unfenced, unmarked, unclaimed and unknown. In the spring of 1870 D. L. Lakin undertook to discover the extent and character of the Santa Fe's largest asset. The initial field party consisted of Lakin, a compassman, a flagman, a cook, an outfit boss, a wagon boss, and three appraisers—Colonel A. S. Johnson, Captain R. M. Spivey, and J. B. McAfee. Progress was slow but the work went ahead relentlessly. Indians, heat, cold, varmints, and other obstacles were met, endured, and sidestepped as the occasion dictated. Lakin's responsibilities for continuing the sale of the Pottawatomie lands and establishing the machinery for handling the eventual disposal of the grant prevented him from remaining with the surveying party. Plans were laid for opening the land offices in railroad towns as the line was extended. On August 25, 1870, Lakin and R. W. P. Muse, later a prominent judge and onetime agent of the Santa Fe, left Topeka to locate a land office west of Cottonwood Falls. Muse gave the following description of the journey:

During the day, and after traveling over thirty miles we had seen no human habitation or sign of human habitation, our way being through high prairie grass often standing above the height of our wagon wheels and bed. We varied the monotony of the journey by shooting at wolves, coyotes, antelopes, and prairie chickens. After reaching the cattle trail we were beset by swarms of buffalo gnats and mosquitoes, so ravenous that

Mr. Lakin declared that they bit his head through his hat. On going down the cattle trail to the mouth of Sand Creek, we had to pass by several droves of Texas cattle, en route to Abilene. The cowboys in charge of them would ride ahead of the cattle and request us to drive out of the road some two or three hundred yards to let their cattle pass, because on seeing strangers they would take fright and stampede as quickly as a herd of buffalo or antelope.

From time to time Lakin's field party forwarded reports to the land office in Topeka. Maps were prepared showing the location of each section possessed by the Company. Descriptive notes enabled Lakin and other officials to establish selling prices for the plots. In conformance with the grant, acreage could not be sold for less than $2.50. The objective was to prevent the Railroad's underselling the Government. The latter had doubled the price of its land lying in the area of the grant. The minimum was far below the intrinsic value of the land after the railroad was built.

Sale of the grant was just beginning to get under way in 1872 when Lakin's ill health prompted his resignation. He was succeeded by the dynamic and capable A. E. Touzalin. To the new commissioner should go most of the credit for organizing the land department. Touzalin had great administrative ability and won thousands of friends in his colonizing work, yet occasionally he was decidedly undiplomatic and indiscreet in dealings with fellow officials. The work of surveying and appraisal was continued. D. N. Heizer replaced J. B. McAfee as an appraiser, and a civil engineer named Armstrong was added to the corps.

Touzalin appointed agents in the new towns along the grant to push the sale of lands and to coöperate with eastern representatives. Throughout the East ministers, lawyers, school teachers, and newspaper editors were commissioned to sell people on Kansas. Tons of literature praising the merits of a home on the prairies were distributed. The lands were advertised everywhere. The whole program was conducted with a modest outlay of money. All of the agents were paid on a commission basis. Even the expenses of eastern agents when conducting inspections by land-seekers were borne by the salesmen. The Santa Fe eased the burden somewhat by providing free transportation on Company tracks. This concession was small indeed if the agent had started from Pennsylvania or New York. The land-seekers were given special rates, usually half-fare, and whatever was paid for tickets could be applied dollar for dollar on the initial installment on any land purchased. Often the eastern agent did no more than start the pioneers on their way and arrange for local agents to show the lands and close the deals. By the time the Santa Fe paid the commissions, conceded half-fares to all seekers whether they bought or not, hauled personal belongings and equipment free or at low rates, and paid for widespread advertising, little cash was netted. The extension of credit in some cases up to the full amount of the price of the land made the receipts in early years even lower. In spite of hell, high water, and grasshoppers, sales expanded. The number of buyers and total acreage for the first years are shown below.

Year Ending March 31	Number of Buyers	Amount Sold in Acres
1871	472	71,801.51
1872	277	45,328.81
1873	830	133,507.30
1874	1261	200,459.96

Prices ranged between five and six dollars per acre. Most sales were for 160 acres. The policy of the Company and the checkerboard nature of the grant precluded transfer of great blocks to land speculators. Home-builders were sought. The majority of the buyers came from states to the east. Of the 1261 purchasers during the year ending March 31, 1874, 461 came from Illinois, 327 from foreign countries, 122 from other parts of Kansas, 89 from Iowa, 52 from Ohio, 50 from Indiana, 30 from Massachusetts, and the remainder from 20 different states.

Notable among the early buyers were Mennonites from the east. During the winter of 1869-1870 Case and Billings, efficient agents for Marion County, sold 5000 acres to M. W. Keim and his brethren of Johnstown, Pennsylvania. This was the first of many sales to Mennonites. The earliest actual settlement of Mennonites in the Santa Fe territory, however, was southwest of the present site of Hutchinson. They were members of the Amish branch (Hook and Eye Dutch) and had emigrated from Pennsylvania, Ohio, Indiana, and Illinois.* Many in the colony selected lands before the Santa Fe had surveyed the area and sales were made by the Company to the late arrivals. The country being unsettled, the hardships endured by these God-fearing people were many. Their perseverance prevailed over the elements and, as usual, a prosperous and unostentatious development followed.

The so-called "Old Mennonites" followed Keim in Marion County. Two settlements developed about 1871 near Peabody and Marion. The communities were twenty-three miles apart, and in order to maintain communications a furrow was dug all the way between the two to serve as a guide over the open prairie. Another start was made by the Old Mennonites in 1874 in southern McPherson County. All these early migrations were merely the vanguard of the thousands of Mennonites who were to come to Kansas to seek homes and religious tolerance.

The metamorphosis of Kansas was rapid during the early 'seventies and the change was accelerated by the Santa Fe in the area contiguous to the line. In 1870 the population of Kansas was 364,234, and four years later it had increased 46 per cent to 530,367. The gain in thirteen of the eighteen counties now on the mainline was 64 per cent, jumping from 64,400 to 105,661. Equally impressive growth occurred in land under cultivation. In 1873 3,031,957 acres were worked in the state, and the following year showed a 21 per cent increase. The expansion in ten Santa Fe counties was 30 per cent.

The heroic migration of the Mennonites to America and, in part, to the land of the Santa Fe is one of the great religious migrations of the world. In the United States it was matched only

*The Amish and Old Mennonites, who settled in Kansas during the early 'seventies, were of old American stock. Their predecessors had emigrated from Switzerland, the Palatinate, Alsace, and nearby areas of Europe during the seventeenth and eighteenth centuries.

by the trek of the Mormons across the country to the future state
of Deseret. The occasion for the Mennonite journey to Kansas
grew out of a long struggle by the Mennonites to worship according to the precepts of their church. Mennonites, and there
are many kinds, apparently existed as a heresy in Italy as early
as the eleventh century. About the time of the Protestant Reformation the members became known as "Anabaptists" because
they did not believe in infant baptisms. Another appellation appeared as the numbers were expanded under a new leader, Men-
no Simons, a Catholic priest of Dutch descent, who joined the
Anabaptists about 1536 and systematized their views. Soon the
sect became known as "Mennonites." Churches were established
in Switzerland and the movement spread rapidly in Europe. In
some areas the adherents were termed "Biblicists" because of
the importance attached to the study of the Bible.

Mennonites from the first were victims of religious intolerance.
In Switzerland they suffered every conceivable indignity and
torture and even death. The causes of their persecution were
more complex than those accounting for the maltreatment of
other Protestant groups. The Mennonites held many views which
were anathema to Protestants as well as Catholics. Their absolute
refusal to bear arms or to take oaths was rather untimely in the
days of state-building. The persecution of the Mennonites persisted without abatement during the seventeenth century, although by the end of the period most of them had been driven
out of Switzerland. The majority of those remaining were de-
ported to Holland and East Prussia in 1711. There were many
Mennonites in the south German provinces, and hundreds of
Dutch Mennonites were induced to settle in various parts of
Prussia and Poland. Their fame as people of outstanding industry
made them welcome as settlers, although once they were established in a country, its rulers did not hesitate to extort money or
inflict punishments. When Frederick the Great came to power
the Mennonites hoped for peace at last. Frederick was religiously
tolerant, but he also relied heavily on an army; and Mennonites

did not serve in armies. For a time Frederick permitted the long-sought freedom of worship and did not ask the young men to join his forces.

When Poland was partitioned Frederick gained control over so many Mennonites that he felt special privileges could no longer be allowed to them. Both the King and the Mennonites proved to be compromisers, and in 1780 a charter was given to the groups guaranteeing continued liberties in return for an annual payment of five thousand thaler for the support of the military academy at Culm.[1] Various other imposts and regulations were subsequently provided. High excises were imposed on Mennonite transactions in real estate. Frederick William II, successor of Frederick the Great, obviously intended to deter the growth of the sect. Once again the long-suffering Mennonites felt it necessary to seek new homes. Their first destination was southern Russia. The Germanic Russian Czarina, Catherine the Great, was eager to improve the native stock and economy. The Mennonites, with their great reputation as agriculturists and men of industry, were invited to colonize the Crimea, the area around the Sea of Azov, and the vicinity of the lower Dnieper, Volga, and Don rivers. Freedom from military service was promised for one hundred years. About one-half of the Mennonites in the vicinity of the Vistula River accepted the invitation.

Under the Russian despots the sect enjoyed its most peaceful period. Catherine's promise was put in writing by her son, Paul, and the Mennonites felt secure. They were given free land and enjoyed the unmolested observance of their tenets and customs. Industry and thrift brought substantial prosperity to the estimated nine thousand immigrants.[2] Adaptation of farming methods to the limited rainfall was rapid but not without suffering. The Mennonites acquired herds of cattle and flocks of sheep. Wheat production became a specialty, although many concentrated on honey and silk. In time the colonies multiplied, and as usual schisms caused new factions to appear. In 1870 the termination of the special privileges granted to the colonists was announced to take place in 1880. Military service was to be compulsory, and Russian was to replace German in the schools. The Mennonites, horror-stricken, sent commissions to plead for continuation of the old order. Little easement was secured, though noncombatant service was proffered by officials at St. Petersburg. Again migration seemed necessary. The situation of the Mennonites was pathetic. Most of them lived narrow lives and possessed slight knowledge about other parts of the world. They had little idea where they should or could go. Some of the more worldly-wise members began to explore possibilities, and out of their efforts came the historic movement to the lands of the Santa Fe.

In 1871 Cornelius Jansen, a prominent Mennonite and Prussian consul in the city of Berdiansk, began correspondence with agencies in various parts of the world to find a new home for his brethren. He wrote to John F. Funk of Elkhart, Indiana, the editor of the *Herald of Truth*, to secure information concerning military laws, lands, and customs in America. News of the inquiries of Jansen and other leaders spread. Many states and several countries began to vie for the prospective emigrants. The Russian Government became alarmed over prospects of an exodus. Since Jansen felt his presence in Berdiansk was no longer consistent with safety, he migrated to Pennsylvania to continue his role as self-appointed agent.

A. E. Touzalin of the Santa Fe was fully aware of the opportunity to secure colonists among the Mennonites and spared no effort to develop correspondence with leaders and to arrange inspections of his land. In January of 1873 he hired C. B. Schmidt to assist in the work. The choice of Schmidt was wholly fortuitous. He was an implement salesman and grocer in Lawrence, Kansas, but had many Old World ties, having migrated from Germany in 1864 at the age of twenty-one. He was also a man of letters and served as a correspondent of several German newspapers. As a consequence he had developed numerous contacts with people who contemplated migrating to America. Cornelius Jansen had written Schmidt shortly after landing in America. Although

Schmidt was not a Mennonite, he was extremely sympathetic and understanding. In the course of his long dealings with the sect he became known as "the Moses of the Mennonites." During the summer of 1873 a delegation of twelve Mennonites from Russia visited America to inspect lands.* They examined the frontier from Manitoba to Kansas. Guaranty of military exemption in Canada seemed preferable in the opinion of some to the mere assurance of exemption in the United States. Schmidt spent a week during August showing the delegation lands in Reno, Sedgwick, Marion, and McPherson counties. The report to the worried brethren in Russia was enthusiastic and thousands resolved to leave their old homes. Meanwhile Cornelius Jansen traversed the grant with Schmidt and reserved 100,000 acres subject to the approval of others. Assent was forthcoming the following year. A small committee came from Illinois and another from Russia. They journeyed west as far as Great Bend, where the grasshopper hordes of 1874 were encountered. In spite of this, the option was commended and exercised. On October 14, 1874, the purchase of 100,000 acres of land north of Florence, Peabody, Walton, Newton, Halstead, and Hutchinson was consummated at Topeka.

In the spring of 1874 the scene in the Russian colonies was one of confusion. Everybody wanted to sell his property and go to America. Markets for real estate as well as personal property sagged. Alarmed at the likelihood of loss of 40,000 of Russia's most productive citizens, the Czar dispatched the renowned Adjutant General von Todtleben to induce the Mennonites to remain. The die was already cast by the strong minority. The others elected to take advantage of the concessions offered by von Todtleben.

First in the great exodus which began in 1874 was a party headed by elder Jacob A. Wiebe. Its members belonged to a faction that had lived in the Crimea and had come to be known as

---

*The delegates were: William Ewert, Jacob Baller, Tobias Unruh, Leonard Suderman, Andrew Schrag, Jacob Peters, Henry Wiebe, Cornelius Bom, Cornelius Toews, David Classen, Paul Tschetter, and Lorence Tschetter.

the "Krimmer Brethren." Bishop Wiebe's flock was not large
and the members scattered to several states. Thirty families followed Wiebe to Kansas. They were among the poorer Mennonites
who emigrated. Below is a portion of an account written by
Wiebe of the tribulations of his followers.*

We received our passports and could leave our earthly dearly loved
homes, as well as many friends, parents, brothers and sisters, May 30th.
July 15th, we arrived in New York. A great portion of our fellow travelers
went from Hamburg, Germany, direct to Dakota and Minnesota. Therefore we have emigrated with the Czar's approbation, and so faithful and
obedient as we have been to Russia, so far as God's word and our conscience allowed us, so we have a mind to be in America, and want to
seek the peace of the land, as long as our fathers' principle is not touched.
We thank God that we could live in this dearly beloved America these 38
years, according to our faith and principle, and that we can if we have a
mind to live our faith.

From New York we journeyed to Elkhart, Indiana, where we arrived
one Sunday morning. We knew John F. Funk through the newspaper,
"Herald der Wahrheit," he provided an empty house. Those of us that
had no room in this house were provided for in the church. Elder Funk
had announced that people from Russia had arrived, so many of the poor
were furnished with provisions. In the afternoon I was invited to preach
in the church to many hearers. Here our people lived for a number of
weeks, several of our brethren received work. Frank R. Janzen and I were
sent ahead to look for a suitable place for settlement. We traveled all over
Nebraska and Kansas, in Nebraska we were afraid of the deep wells, so
we decided for Kansas where we found the wells shallow. C. B. Schmidt
drove with us all over Kansas as far as Great Bend. On a hot August day
we ate our dinner under a tree on section 13 on the south Cottonwood
River, where Peter Harms now lives. The heat was great. Agent Schmidt
looked at his hands full of blisters, saying: I believe I have done my part.
Secretly he feared we might yet decide for Nebraska.

When we finally had bought the land, 12 sections, we let our people
follow us. Agent Schmidt offered to go for them to Elkhart, personally,
while we were to make preparations for their arrival. We hurried namely
to get ready with everything before the winter. I rented an empty store,
bought a stove, table, two horses and a wagon. While we waited for our
families it was very hot, so that we have not had a greater heat since. I
came into temptation on account of the high winds, everything was dry

*This version was written by Wiebe at the request of A. E. Case, an early land
agent of the Santa Fe. Mr. Case gave the original copy to John E. Frost, long an employee in the Land Department and one-time land commissioner. The manuscript is in
the possession of the Company.

and withered. The year before grasshoppers had taken all. I knew, soon our people would be here, the wind and dust swept through the street of Peabody. I on a sudden became afraid of the future whether we would make our living here or not. The great responsibility of having selected a place of settlement for so many poor people rested heavily on me. In my great grief I sat down on the steps, I thought of the poor families with their children, we had no provisions, no friend in the new world, the winter was nigh at the door, we were wanting of dwellings, provisions, agricultural implements and seed, everything was high in price, some of ours were old, weak and sick, the future seemed very gloomy, there were also no prospects of rain, only windy, dusty and very hot, all this fell over me, so I could not help myself but leave my tears free flow. While I was thus sitting on the threshold and weeping, Mrs. August Seybold came to me and asked: Mr. Wiebe, what ails you? I told her my grief, then she began to console me. She pointed to the street saying: Do you see those stones? They are sometimes entirely under water, it can rain very hard here, and it soon will rain. Oh Mr. Wiebe, be of good cheer, such people as you will even make their living. And so it was, it soon began to rain. On a Saturday night our people arrived at Peabody. Sunday we rode with a conveyance to get people, also Wilhelm Ewart, Mrs. Peter Funk and John Ratzloff sent teams. I took my family in my own wagon, it was the 17th day of August when we rode from Peabody onto the land, 14 miles northwest. I had loaded some lumber and utensils, and my family on top. So we rode in the deep grass to the little stake that marked the spot I had chosen. When we reached the same I stopped, my wife asked me, why do you stop? I said we are to live here. Then she began to weep. Several families moved into Mr. Funk's barn, where soon after old mother Abraham Cornelsen died—the first dead body of our people in America. We built light board shanties, dug wells, in three weeks it began to rain, there came a heavy rain. We rented some ploughed land from English neighbors, who lived on section 12 and 14. Seed wheat was seventy cents in price, corn was high priced, there had been no crop that year, it was $1.25, potatoes were $2.00 a bushel. The first sowed wheat brought a bountiful harvest the next year. We had not sowed very much, but that little brought much. That gave us courage.

Since we settled on section 11-R-2 Risley township, the 17th of August, 1874, we have fared well, although at the beginning we were very poor. We originally bought 12 sections of land of the railroad company in Risley township, later Liberty township, on ten years credit. We had to pay down some, and the dear friend and general agent C. B. Schmidt, and Case and Billings have treated us nicely and faithfully. We were all poor people many families owed their traveling expenses, they had to go in debt for their land, oxen, plow, farmer's wagon, and even their sod house, they had to have provisions for a year, there was no chance of earning something, so they had to go in debt for that too, so there was no other way, as to borrow money, but where? We were strangers, had no friends here, only Bernhard Warkentin of Halstead knew us from Russia, and he helped us through Elder Christian Krehbiel with a loan of a thousand dollars, when those were distributed it was said, brother Wiebe, we also need oxen and a plow to break prairie. Then Cornelius Janzen of Nebraska, the well known consul Janzen, loaned us one thousand dollars, when these were distributed, it was said, brother Wiebe, we have to buy provisions for a year, and some lumber to build little houses, then the Elder Wilhelm Ewart loaned us one thousand dollars. Then the time of payment for the land came, so Jacob Funk loaned us one thousand dollars. So we sat in our poor sod houses, some two feet deep in the ground, the walls of sod, the roof of long reed grass, that reached into the prairie. In part we were glad to have progressed so far before the winter, but we did not think of the great danger we were in, as we lived up to the knee middle in the prairie. But there we had a dear English neighbor on section 12, John Risley. The good man saw in what great danger we were, because we lived so, twenty-five families on one section of land, all in a row, as in a village. The dear friend, John Risley, had seen the prairie fire in the west, so he went for his five pairs of oxen and big prairie plow, and plowed five or eight times around the village with his five yoke of oxen, and brotherly told us: Now dear people, burn off the grass between the furrows, else all you have may burn you, and we followed his advice, thanks to the Lord.

The dear heavenly Father has a watchful eye, and has looked down on us with favor, we have had several good crops, and have repaid, and when the crops failed especially in the year 1879 grasshoppers came, and we could not make our payments at the appointed time. But the company had pity and patience with us. The dear Elder Ewart to whom I complained, that our brethren could not hold term, said: with nice buggies you are not riding yet, and two story houses you are not building yet, so are we obliged to wait. The preacher Ewart lived temporarily in a barn, and rode in a large farmer wagon with his delicate wife. He made little do, and helped other poor people. We have, thanks be to God, repaid everything, it is however to be regretted that some ventures are so much in debt, and since they gave their farms in mortgage, and through the high rate of interest had to turn over their farms to the company.

I am old now and will soon leave this world, and I pity the next generation. They no longer learn to ride with oxen nor to plow with hand-plow, but instead everything goes high out, instead with oxen with carriages or automobiles, though they stick deep in debt.

Jacob A. Wiebe.

Thousands of other Mennonites followed on the heels of Bishop Wiebe. Approximately one-half of all who came to the

United States headed for Kansas. Schmidt worked day and night to make arrangements for his charges. On September 23, 1874, some 400 families, estimated to contain 1900 people, arrived in Topeka. They brought with them drafts on American banks in the amount of $2,000,000. Their arrival was untimely as far as homemaking was concerned, and something had to be done to tide them over until spring. The Santa Fe agreed to let them use a large shop building which had been recently erected in Topeka. When the Mennonites appeared on the streets of Topeka they were subjects of ridicule. Their garb was the object of newspaper barbs, and Santa Fe officials were chided for bringing scarecrows into the state. When the Mennonites began to patronize local merchants and to display more money than Kansas had seen in years, public opinion executed an about face—now the Mennonites were the salt of the earth, the kind who would make Kansas. Governor Osborn was induced to hold a reception for the newcomers.

The fall of 1874 was a critical one in the history of Kansas. The agricultural reputation of the state was at a record low. Grasshoppers had consumed every vestige of green in large areas. Hopper sustenance was sought in fence posts, boards, and animals. Turkeys that had welcomed the vanguard were panic-stricken when the voracious hosts descended upon them. Crops were utterly laid waste, and hundreds of sodbusters forsook Kansas to return to the East. Courage and faith must have filled the hearts of the Mennonites in Topeka, who resolved to try Kansas in spite of the pall which had descended over the state. They resolutely turned the disaster into an asset and bought the equipment of those who left.

New arrivals came by the hundreds during the winter of 1874-1875. Shortly after the large contingent set up housekeeping in the shops at Topeka another sizable body arrived in Newton. On January 2, 1875, about 200 reached Great Bend. Barracks were provided by the Company to shelter the emigrants. Every assistance possible was given the movement. Prices charged for the land were materially reduced. Ministers and committees received free vessels. A Red Star Line steamer was chartered by the Santa Fe and sent to the port of Berdiansk to bring over household effects and implements. The cargo was landed at Philadelphia and shipped by rail to Kansas wholly at the expense of the Company. Free transportation of building material from the Mississippi River was given for one year. The Santa Fe guaranteed help in event of disaster. The policy was eminently successful and over 3000 took lands in 1874.

In the midst of the coming of the Mennonites A. E. Touzalin resigned as land commissioner. He had had frequent clashes with other Santa Fe officials. Touzalin shifted his allegiance to the land department of the Burlington and Missouri River Railroad. On August 10, 1876, Touzalin's successor, A. S. Johnson, wrote to President Thomas Nickerson: "Mr. Touzalin is giving us a good deal of trouble just now by sending his agents into our settlements and making inducements for those unsettled to go to Nebraska. And misrepresenting us in all manner of ways . . . ." Records of the Company indicate that Touzalin made strenuous efforts in New York to intercept Mennonites whom he had started toward Kansas. No great success attended his efforts, although he served the B&M well.

Colonel A. S. Johnson, the new acting land commissioner, continued the program mapped out by his predecessor.* One of his first decisions was to send Schmidt to Russia to recruit more Mennonites. The latter sailed from New York to begin his land mission. Schmidt's account of his midwinter trip from Danzig to southern Russia via Vilna, Minsk, Smolensk, Orel, Kursk, and Kharkov is richly romantic. He met a storybook Russian prince from the Caucasus, bedecked in rich silks and furs, who entertained him fabulously and, incidentally, ordered two Marsh Har-

---

*A. S. Johnson came of Kansas stock. He is said to have been the first white child in the state. The date of his birth was July 11, 1832, and the place was at Shawnee Mission, where his father, the Reverend Thomas Johnson, ministered to the Indians. Colonel A. S. Johnson had a notable military and political career before joining the Santa Fe in 1870. To Johnson more than anyone else should go the credit for the effective disposal of the land grant.

vesters. Schmidt apparently was still an implement salesman at heart. "The prince drove me all over the city [Kursk] in an elegant sleigh with three handsomely harnessed horses with jingling bells and waving plumes." Schmidt's first contacts at Alexanderwohl were discouraging. He was told that all the malcontents among the Mennonites had already gone to Kansas. Later he learned that his informers had misrepresented conditions. Schmidt crusaded through some fifty-six villages in the Molotschna Colony. Everywhere he was impressed with the well-kept farms and villages of the Mennonites. A warm reception was given him as he moved from place to place. The early migrants had written to the "old country" of his coming. Schmidt brought news of many and answered countless questions about America and Kansas for those who were interested. Chief worry of the Mennonites was not the grasshoppers or the fruitfulness of the soil but the Indians.* Being nonresistant, they thought migration to Kansas was suicide. Schmidt allayed their fears and started hundreds to the lands of the Santa Fe. Recruitment was halted when word came that the gendarmes were hunting for Schmidt, having in mind using him to help colonize Siberia.

The movement of the Mennonites to central Kansas persisted for almost a decade. In subsequent years strong efforts were made by Russia to deter emigrations, and those who were able to leave the country could not take their possessions. By 1883 an estimated 15,000 had located along the Santa Fe.† Twenty years later the local Mennonite population was said to have quadrupled from natural growth and further migration.

---

*Paradoxically enough, the Mennonites established missions among the Indian tribes. Many Cheyennes and Arapahoes worked for the Mennonites on their farms and were taught to read and write German. Schmidt was dumbfounded the first time he was greeted in Plattdeutsch by an Arapahoe woman.

†Mennonites who remained in Russia underwent great hardships. Many were granted liberties by going to remote colonies in the interior. During and after World War I the suffering of those who remained in south Russia surpassed comprehension. Hundreds were starved, slaughtered, or imprisoned. The Germanic culture of the Mennonites brought hardship again in World War II. Most of the sect were uprooted and sent to Siberia.

The contribution of the Mennonites to Kansas can hardly be overestimated. At the first opportunity they began to plow the dew under. They plowed deep and straight. Seeds were planted, growing crops diligently cultivated, and rich harvests reaped. Noble Prentis, a writer, revisited the Mennonite colonies in 1882 after an absence of seven years:

A great change had taken place in the country since my last visit. I left bare prairie; I returned to find a score of miniature forests in sight from any point of view. The wheat and corn fields were unfenced of course, but several acres around every house were set in hedges, orchards, lanes and alleys of trees in lines, trees in groups, and trees all alone. In many cases the houses were hardly visible from the road, and in a few years will be entirely hidden in the cool shade. . . We drove for miles with many Mennonite houses in sight, and the most promising orchards, and immense fields of the greenest wheat. I have never seen elsewhere such a picture of agricultural prosperity. . . .

The homes which replaced the temporary sod houses and huts were substantial. In the construction of the main partition they incorporated straw ovens which served to heat the rooms with a minimum of fuel. Like all emigrants the Mennonites attempted to transplant many of the industries and crops which they had known in the "old country." Mulberry trees were planted and silk culture was attempted. The experiment was relatively unsuccessful, but the Governor's wife received a silk dress made in Kansas. By far the most significant contribution made by the Mennonites to Kansas and the Nation was the introduction and propagation of Turkey red wheat. Eventually Kansas would have had hard wheat anyhow, but the Mennonites hastened the day.* Kansas farmers had been producing an inferior quality of spring and winter wheat. When the Mennonites came, they adopted the local practice, but they also experimented with small quantities of grains brought from Russia. Leader in the work was Bernhard Warkentin, a pioneer settler and miller at Halstead. Warkentin's father

*A small French Colony in Marion County is believed to have grown the first hard winter wheat in Kansas. The truth of this contention has never been established, but there is no doubt that the expansion of production stemmed from the plantings by the Mennonites.

had experimented in seed wheat in Russia and played a leading role in the introduction of Turkey red wheat from the Crimea to the Milk River colonies. The son and other Mennonites reasoned that climatic conditions were similar enough to warrant the use of Turkey red wheat in Kansas. Seed was planted in the fall, and extraordinary yields followed. For several years production was limited to the requirements of the colonists and not until 1885 was seed available to outsiders. Improvements in the system of milling arising out of the displacement of the buhr process by the roller system, dovetailed with the introduction of hard wheat and solved the grinding problem. Hard winter wheat eventually prevailed over the whole of Kansas and surrounding states. Kansas became the breadbasket of the Nation, producing hundreds of millions of bushels of wheat. Great mills were built, cornerstones of industrial development in towns and cities all over the Midwest.

The industry and integrity of the Mennonites have persisted over the years. Their farms are still models of orderliness and productivity. Visitors contend that they can spot the farms and farmhouses of Mennonites in mixed communities at a glance. Few permit their premises to deteriorate.

While the service of the Mennonites to Kansas has been great, they have had benefits in return. At last they had the coveted religious freedom. No despotic officials tore down their magnificent churches or burned their schools and colleges. No thought was ever given to punitive taxes or physical persecutions. During times of war they have been recognized as conscientious objectors. Little stigma, if any, has been attached to their status; certainly less than is ordinarily the case with pacifist sects. Everywhere the Mennonites have won and received respect. Santa Fe officials have always been proud of the Company's role in bringing these persevering settlers to Kansas. They were the sort who built the West. The Santa Fe colonized well when it brought the Mennonites. The seed yielded a hundredfold.

Dramatic and important as the Mennonites were in the history of the Land Department, they constituted only a phase of the vast operations of Colonel Johnson and his co-workers. Groups of one thousand or more buyers were gathered from all parts of the country and taken on excursions over the grant. Six experimental plots of twenty acres each were set aside in the spring of 1873 to carry on demonstration work in the culture of "forests" and crops. Settlers were urged to inspect the results as they traversed the grant. Literally millions of booklets, maps, and broadsides were printed and distributed. Some of the titles in 1874 were:

500 ACRES

OF THE

BEST FARMING AND FRUIT LANDS

LOCATED IN THE LIMESTONE AND BLUE GRASS REGION

OF KANSAS: IN AND ADJACENT TO

THE COTTONWOOD VALLEY

A HAND BOOK

OF

USEFUL INFORMATION:

FOR

IMMIGRANTS AND SETTLERS

HOW TO START A FARM

WHAT TO GROW AND HOW TO GROW IT

2,500,000 ACRES

IF YOU WANT

A FARM AS HOME

YOU SHOULD BUY OF THE

ATCHISON, TOPEKA & SANTA FE R. R. CO.

Although the lands were lavishly praised, almost every publication cautioned people not to try Kansas unless they had a nest egg of several hundred dollars. Agents on a commission basis did

not always act with as much restraint as officials of the Land Department. The following story is told of an agent who had a party
of landseekers out one day. They plied him with innumerable
questions. "Could you raise this?" and "Could you raise that?"
They shot questions until they knew the chances of every grain
that existed and a few more. "Gentlemen," the agent said finally,
"there is only one thing you cannot raise to advantage on this soil.
That is pumpkins."

"What!" they exclaimed. "How can you raise all the other
articles we have named and not pumpkins?"

"It's this way," came the deliberate answer. "The seeds come
up quickly. The plants blossom full. Pumpkins set and grow
about the size of a sugar barrel. Then the vines begin to grow and
run so fast that they wear the pumpkins out dragging them over
the ground until they die from exhaustion."

Despite this discouraging outlook some of the visitors bought
land and are said to have had the temerity to raise pumpkins.

The terms of sale offered the buyer a wide variety of methods
of payment. According to a booklet of 1874, five major choices
were given with minor variations.

No. 1   On purchase, 10 per cent down and 7 per cent interest on the
unpaid balance. No payments on the principal at the end of the first and
second years and then equal annual installments until the final payment
at the end of the eleventh year. If the settler improved and cultivated
one-fifth of his land by the end of the third year a 20 per cent reduction
was made in remaining payments.

No. 2   For the benefit of people with even less capital the second plan
required no principal payments for four years and then one-eighth annually. Interest was at 7 per cent. 10 per cent reduction in payments if
one-fifth were cultivated in four years.

No. 3   One-third was paid down and the balance in equal amounts
in one and two years. Interest was at 10 per cent but was more than offset
by a 20 per cent discount.

No. 4   If sales were made for cash a 20 per cent discount was given.

No. 5   Anyone selecting the first or second plans could pay the balance
at any time and secure discounts up to 18 per cent on the remainder.

If the rates of interest seem unduly high today, consider the
charges that prevailed in the West in the 'seventies. The usual

farm loan was made at 15 to 18 per cent. In 1870 the Santa Fe executed a mortgage upon the granted lands to secure a 7 per cent bond issue of $3,520,500. The market discounted the bonds 27 per cent so that the effective rate paid by the Company was about 10 per cent over the thirty-year life of the bonds.* The balance sheet for January 1, 1875, shows an issue of land-income bonds bearing a nominal rate of 12 per cent. A substantial indirect subsidy or discount was given purchasers through the medium of below-market rates of interest.

Chief problems of the Land Department, in order, seemed to be the Indians, grasshoppers, and temperance. Great difficulty was encountered in convincing people that their scalps would not be lifted. The number deterred could never be ascertained, but correspondence of agents indicates that thousands sought safer sites.

The grasshopper plague of 1874 set the land program back at least two years. Not only did many leave the area of the grant but still more shied away from Kansas. The role of the Company during and after the destruction was commendable. Supplies of all kinds, except coal and grain, were carried free of charge to the stricken people. The tariffs on coal and grain were cut substantially to the out-of-pocket cost of hauling. During 1875 a total of 9,972,-000 pounds of general goods was carried free to the grasshopper victims.† A moratorium was declared on the land payments. The Company advanced money to the settlers to buy seed, and in every way attempted to keep its earlier promises to help in event of disasters.

Rival states and companies attempted to make capital out of the plight of Kansas and the Santa Fe. Immigrants were asked, "Why go to Kansas and feed grasshoppers?" Such detraction was

---

*Equally large discounts were given in an issue backed by the Pottawatomie lands. The precise amount cannot be stated, because the Pottawatomie land bonds were part of a block sale. A portfolio of securities was sold, consisting of $768,500 of 7 per cent Pottawatomie bonds, $192,000 of 7 per cent Santa Fe bonds, $150,000 of Shawnee County bonds, and $960,000 in par of common stock. The amount realized was only $955,700. The stock was valued at a trifling sum and absorbed much of the discount, but a substantial portion was borne by the land bonds.

†The same report indicates that Mennonite contracts accounted for 1,798,000 pounds of free freight.

difficult to counteract. The best antidote was a master stroke of
Colonel Johnson. He conceived the idea of inviting editors of midwestern newspapers to make a tour of the land grant in 1875 to
see for themselves that the grasshopper damage had been only a
temporary reverse. All expenses of the excursion were to be borne
by the Santa Fe. The response to the offer exceeded Johnson's
fondest expectations. Every editor wanted to go. Approximately
225 made ready. Johnson timed the trip perfectly. It was made between June 24 and 27, when Kansas was at its peak. The golden
fields of wheat were a sight to behold. Pastures were lush. The
stand of new corn was good. The prairies were in bloom. Everywhere the editors were astounded at the development of the country, its fertility, the spirit of the people, and the generosity of the
Company.* Editorials which came in the wake of the excursion
exerted a greater influence than any amount of direct advertising
could have accomplished. Johnson gathered clippings from the
various newspapers and prepared a booklet which was given wide
circulation. The cumulative effect of all the indorsements was
powerful and undoubtedly was a factor in the revival of sales.

The final harvests in 1875 were excellent and seemed to be
conclusive evidence that 1874 was simply "one of those years."
Johnson began the use of testimonials in his advertising and the
success stories from the "Garden of the West" probably served
their ends. The grasshopper year was never fully erased from the

---

*At a meeting of the editors in Granada, Colorado, the following resolutions were
enthusiastically adopted:

"*Resolved,* That we fully appreciate the wisdom and courtesy of the Atchison,
Topeka & Santa Fe road in extending an invitation to so large a number of members
of the press in the States bordering on the Ohio and Mississippi rivers, to visit the yet
undeveloped portion of the Great West, through which their road extends, and particularly we appreciate the untiring efforts of the officers and agents of said Company
and its connections to make the excursion so enjoyable and instructive.

"*Resolved,* That we have been profoundly impressed with the immense agricultural
resources of the country traversed by the Atchison, Topeka & Santa Fe road, the
evidences of which we have witnessed; that we are convinced that its capabilities for
raising cattle, corn, and all the products necessary to the sustenance and comfort of
human life, can hardly be realized and appreciated until they have been seen.

"*Resolved,* That having seen and believed, we are compelled to repeat in earnest
what we have often quoted in derision, the advice of a distinguished member of our
profession—'Go West, young man, go West.'

"*Resolved,* That the ladies along the road have our warmest thanks for the kindness and distinguished courtesies which we have received at their hands."

minds of the settlers or the officials. Neither were the other hardships and risks of sodbusting. A pamphlet issued by the Land Department in 1879 admonished Easterners not to be hasty.

> We cannot advise any married man to come here with less than $800
> to $1000, to make a start on a farm, or any single man with less than $500
> to $600, and then it will require plenty of grit, hard work and rigid
> economy to get through the first year or two. . . If you are happy in the
> East, stay there. . . Living costs are moderately high. A house 16x28
> of 1½ stories can be erected plainly for $375, neatly for $450. . . Steaks
> are 8 cents to 10 cents per lb.

Besides the editor's tour Johnson took another avenue to miti-
gate the grasshopper publicity and to boom Kansas. When the
Centennial Exposition was held in Philadelphia in 1876 Johnson
sent an elaborate display of agricultural products from the land
grant. The finest fruits, vegetables, and grains were shown and
they attracted much attention. Clippings from eastern papers indicate that Johnson had arranged the outstanding exhibit at the
Centennial.

The effect of the temperance movement on immigration to
Kansas has probably been exaggerated in the records of the Santa
Fe. C. B. Schmidt was firmly convinced that no greater calamity
ever befell the state than prohibition. One of his blasts appeared in
The Commonwealth, July 23, 1881. Part of the heading was "How
a Continued Effort Is Made Useless by an Obnoxious Prohibition
Law and Its Chief Promoter, the State's Own Governor." Schmidt
wrote:

> Gradually the impression gained ground and was encouraged by the
> press of Germany, and the governments, that this law prohibiting the
> manufacture of liquors of all kinds, including wine and beer, had become
> a necessity in a State which was populated chiefly by outlaws, gamblers,
> and drunkards, who had congregated there from all parts of the Union.
> The work of years and the expenditure of thousands was at once neu-
> tralized. Letters began to come into the offices at Hamburg, London and
> Liverpool containing inquiries as to the prohibition law; soon the agents
> reported that people did want to hear nothing more about Kansas; that
> many who had fully made up their minds to go there were changing their
> destination, because they thought it could not be safe for people who had

anything at stake to live in Kansas. The comments of the press were aggravating in the highest degree, and it was impossible to overcome its influence. Large colony organizations started with a view to settlement in Kansas, moved or are moving to other States, as for instance a company of winegrowers from Rhenish Bavaria, who are now going to Missouri; a colony of Saxons organized by myself, now are going to Arkansas.

Schmidt cited dozens of cases in which parties were alleged to have forsaken the destination of Kansas. A portion of one of the letters received by the Hamburg agent is supposed to represent the typical reaction to the colonizing efforts of the Santa Fe.

Thank you heartily for all your trouble and the detailed information you have given us, but am sorry to have to inform you, that on account of the temperance business we have altered our destination and shall not go to Kansas. We go to another State and are ready to start next week. None of my friends can fancy themselves living under such stringent laws and think it can not be good where such laws are considered necessary, which are only in order for drunkards and not for sober, industrious farmers, who require a drop of liquor occasionally with their hard work. Moreover the prices of wheat and other products must be much impaired.

The temperance legislation of Kansas probably exerted more influence than warranted, for the obvious reason that the wet-dry controversy has always been unduly magnified. On the other hand, there is a possibility that many people came to Kansas because it was supposed to be bone-dry. Wets may have migrated to the Sunflower State in spite of the law, believing the facetious assertion that "Kansans will vote dry as long as the voters can stagger to the polls." The argument might be advanced that even though the number of newcomers may have diminished, the quality was better. Actually, the Santa Fe secured more settlers during the early 'eighties than at any other time.

The machinery for handling colonization was perfected as the disposal of the lands progressed. By 1875 the Santa Fe had sixty "foreign" real estate agencies. They were not foreign in the sense of being abroad, but were outside of Kansas. Eleven states and Canada were represented in the out-of-state firms. More than half were located in Iowa and Illinois. There were twenty-three loca-

agencies on the railroad line. All of the representatives were en-gaged in the general business of real estate, but the Santa Fe deal-ings constituted a sizable per cent of their operations. Men of high quality were selected, and they became the leading citizens in many of the communities which they fostered. The office of the Land Department in Topeka acted as a central clearing house for the multifarious problems of the system. Tons of literature were sent to the Eastern agents for distribution. Colonization meetings were held among young farmers of Iowa, Illinois, and Indiana. Plans were made for inspection tours and small parties mustered by agents were merged as they neared the lands of the Santa Fe. Special trains were ordered. Groups of one thousand were com-mon by the time the consolidations ended and Topeka was reached. Local agents hustled to show the lands to best advantage. The guests were well treated whether they bought or not. There was much merit in taking the excursionists in large units, because a few purchases often had the effect of generating a buying wave. An idea of the diverse sources of the home-seekers is evident from a breakdown of the 708 in a party which passed through Newton February 21, 1878: Illinois, 172; Indiana, 79; Iowa, 154; Wiscon-sin, 33; Pennsylvania, 17; Ohio, 28; Michigan, 26; New York, 15; Virginia, 1; California, 1; and Missouri, 14.

Colonel Johnson established contacts with shipping lines and was informed regularly of immigrant arrivals in Atlantic ports. His agents were on hand to persuade the newcomers to continue traveling until they reached Kansas.

Operations east of the Missouri River became so active in 1879 that administration and direction from Topeka were no longer feasible. The territory was divided into four sections, and salaried Traveling Agents were assigned to coördinate the work of the local agents in each area. Later the title of Traveling Agents was changed to General Agents of the Land Department. The men chosen differed widely in background, but all were experienced. Captain W. R. Linn supervised Ohio, Michigan, and western Pennsylvania; Judge George B. Dusenberre of Geneva, New York, had the territory east of Captain Linn's; the Reverend George W. Gue, a Methodist minister, took charge of Indiana and eastern Illinois; and John E. Frost, later Land Commissioner of the Santa Fe, assumed control over western Illinois, Iowa, Wisconsin, and the Northwest. The new arrangement was much more effective, and a steady stream of buyers converged on the land grant.

The work of C. B. Schmidt among the Mennonites in Russia was deemed such a success that he spent a large portion of his time in succeeding years in Europe. Shipping firms, travel agencies, and real estate men were enlisted in the movement. The Santa Fe sponsored groups from Sweden, Germany, Switzerland, Belgium, France, England, and most of the other nations of Europe. Great care was taken to prevent the theft of the parties. On arrival in Kansas the Irish were shown sandy soil adaptable to the growth of potatoes, and the Danes taken to sites where dairy cattle might prove profitable. Newspaper men of Europe were given many inducements in the form of railroad passes and partial expenses if they would visit the land grant.*

---

*The Treasurer's office in Topeka has an interesting vestige of one of the early acceptances. It is a small card outlining the privileges of a pass and reading as follows:
"The undersigned beg to introduce as the guests of the Atchison, Topeka and Santa Fe R.R. Co. the following named Gentlemen, Representatives of the European Press:

Chevalier Ernest de Hesse Wartegg
Special Correspondent 'Illustrirte Zeitung,' Leipzig 'Wiener Fremdenblatt,'
Vienna and 'Lloyd,' Pesth.
Leo von Elliot
Special Artist 'Illustrie Zeitung,' Leipzig and 'Le Monde Illustre,' Brussels.
S. N. Townsend
Correspondent 'The Field,' London.
Count Adam Steenbock
Lieu. of the Horse Guards to H. M. the Emperor of Russia, St. Petersburg.
F. W. Bornemann
Correspondent 'Phoenix,' and 'Bunte Welt,' Leipzig.
Henry De Lamonthe
Correspondent 'Le Temps,' Paris.
Prof. Paul Oeker
Special correspondent 'Vossische Zeitung,' Berlin.

T. J. Anderson   A. S. Johnson
General Passenger Agent   Land Commissioner
C. B. Schmidt
Gen'l. Foreign Agent.

As activities in Europe were enlarged, the Land Department established a branch in London in 1880 to serve as headquarters for all the foreign emigration work. Schmidt, who had been shuttling back and forth across the Atlantic, took charge. He organized the work on a pattern similar to that used in the eastern United States. The number of agents was greatly enlarged. During the first fourteen months the London office distributed over 300,000 pamphlets. They were issued in all of the languages of the northern countries. The French were given thousands of opportunities to learn official facts about Kansas. If interested, they were to get in touch with J. F. de Baesere, Agent, *special du departement territoriale, a Bruxelles, Belgique, la France, le Grand-Duché de Luxembourg, la Hollande, l'Alsace et la Lorraine.* Branches of the London office were established in Liverpool and Hamburg. Night meetings were arranged for factory workers to acquaint them with opportunities in Kansas. Schmidt asserted that every shipping company in Europe was supplied with information about the Santa Fe. All were offered liberal commissions for directing emigrants who bought a portion of the grant. Ingredients for the melting pot came thick and fast. There were Swedes, Bohemians, Welshmen, Scots, and people from all the other European nations.

The recruiting force of the Santa Fe made heavy inroads on the land grant. Each year substantial portions passed into private ownership to provide homes and jobs for the buyers and more traffic for the Company. Below is the sales record from 1875 to 1893.*

The slackening of sales in 1880 and 1881 was the aftermath of lean years when Kansas was the victim of drouths. During the boom of 1885 more than 25 per cent of the total grant was sold.

Sales prior to 1881 were in the portion of the award to the east of Dodge City. A final appraisal of the land to the west had never been made. Colonel Johnson assigned the task to his faithful associate, D. N. Heizer. The latter had worked with the grant from the first days of the colonization program and was well qualified

---

*For figures for 1870-1874 see above, p. 223.

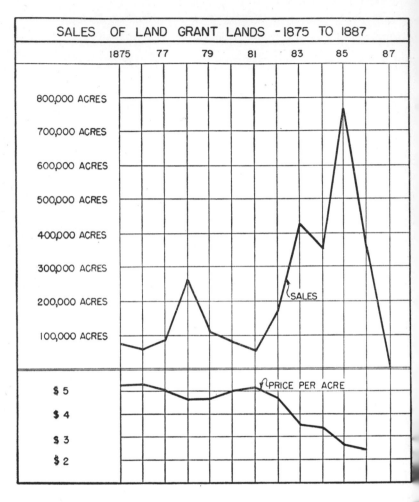

in land evaluation. A party was put in the field in April, 1881, and
the work completed before the end of the year. Heizer estimated
that he rode three thousand miles on horseback in the course of
the job. Detailed descriptive notes were made for every section and
quarter. When Heizer had finished, local agents were appointed
at Garden City, Cimarron, Lakin, and Dodge City to handle the
expected business. Lands west of Dodge were not as desirable as
those sold earlier by the Company and as a consequence the average price paid per acre declined. The adjacency of the River was

a bolstering influence. Water was available for irrigation, and numerous projects were begun. These were private ventures, but they were aided by the Company. Irrigation companies were given right of way over railroad lands, and much equipment was hauled at reduced rates. Where man made up for the Maker's deficiency in supplying water, the country began to resemble eastern Kansas. Orchards and shade trees made rapid growth. Settlers on the western lands installed windmills and built reservoirs to help solve the water problem. In time the area became highly productive, although extensive agriculture was the rule. Garden City became known as the sugar-beet capital of Kansas.

Acreage in the land grant was exhausted during 1886, and remaining operations of the Land Department were confined to collecting outstanding debts and reselling lands that were repossessed because of default. Little land had to be recovered after 1886, although the reverse had been true in prior years. The liberal terms involving no down payments prompted some to renege at the first crop failure or symptom of homesickness. Kansas is a state that requires a stoic philosophy in farming. On the average incomes are high, but the mean develops out of fat and lean years.

New responsibilities were thrust upon the Land Department as sale of the grant tapered off. When the Santa Fe purchased the Denver Circle Railroad in 1887, a sizable quantity of platted and unplatted land was acquired in and about Denver. These holdings were advantageously sold by the Department. Dispersal of other properties in the vicinity of Las Cruces and Mesilla Park, New Mexico, was undertaken, with creditable results.

In 1887 the Land Department was assigned the operation and management of the Santa Fe Town and Land Company as well as several other town companies. The SFT&L Company had been incorporated to develop townsites on the Chicago extension. Commendable work was done and several towns were organized. Their continued growth confirms the wisdom of early decisions. Marceline, Missouri, is one of the model products.

Laying out towns along the railroad required the utmost tact. The Santa Fe naturally desired to secure the increments that attended town development along the line. No opportunities for profit could be neglected. Yet any goose that might lay golden eggs had to be pampered. Towns had to be encouraged. Excessive profit-taking on lots at the outset would have been shortsighted. The Company attempted to balance the conflicting interests. Utmost secrecy attended early operations of town companies, to prevent speculators from interfering. News of activities had to be suppressed even among employees lest some would develop side-line enterprises.

Prior to the time the Land Department became concerned with town development, most of the work was done by the affiliated Arkansas Valley Town and Land Company. The officials had long been connected with the Santa Fe. Alden Speare was president; George L. Goodwin, secretary and treasurer; and Colonel W. G. Dickinson, general manager. Between 1870 and the end of 1886 approximately one hundred towns were launched. Sites were selected and sold. Dickinson claimed that he could organize a town in twenty minutes. A typical performance was the establishment of the town of Burdett, Kansas. The site was determined on May 6, 1886. A week later, May 13, the survey of the lots began, and by the end of the day $34,000 in transactions had taken place. Burdett was born in adult form and has neither expanded nor contracted since.

Ill health caused Colonel Johnson to discontinue his leadership of the Land Department in 1890. He was succeeded by John E. Frost. The work of liquidation went on. Various small parcels of land were sold. Frost successfully worked himself out of a job by 1898. Few landholdings remained and they were bought by Frost. Included in the final sale were the remnants of several town companies.

A&P Holdings

Land operations were not to cease with the disposal of the original land grant. Through the A&P the Santa Fe was to fall heir to a vast kingdom in Arizona and New Mexico, the land grant of the old A&P. The acreage was enormous. But no other government grant contained such a high percentage of wasteland. The A&P for the most part traversed desert country. In some areas nature in the raw has been ameliorated by irrigation projects, but improvements have been possible only in a small number of locations. Limited grazing was practicable in certain areas.

The A&P was granted every alternate section of nonmineral land for a distance of forty miles on each side of the Railroad on all mileage across territories. The amount per mile was, therefore, 25,600 acres, and the total to which the road was entitled for building between Isleta, New Mexico, and the Colorado River near Needles, California, was 14,325,760.* The Company had the privilege of selecting substitute lands for the mineral lands found in the original grant. The "in lieu" zones were ten miles in width on each side of the principal grant. By the time the line was definitely located, 1,120,337 acres within the award had been disposed of by the Government and replacement had to be made.

The A&P undertook the sale of its allotment. The nature of the land made for extensive rather than intensive agriculture and sales in terms of acres were large. No colonization comparable to the Santa Fe program in Kansas was attempted. By 1897 a total of 5,320,398.72 acres had been sold. Selling prices ordinarily ranged from fifty cents to a dollar an acre. Receipts from all land sold up to 1897 plus rentals and royalties on the entire grant were $4,611,-015. Expenses of selling and management and taxes were $756,-325.31.

The A&P encountered financial reverses like the Santa Fe and was in receivership for a period of three years, 1894-97. The Santa

---

*The net amount of the grant was slightly less, since 8,230.81 acres were used for right of way and station grounds. The area would have been obtained whether or not a land grant had been forthcoming. The Santa Fe proper has acquired various parcels of land in New Mexico and Arizona by purchase. Some of the grant in Kansas west of Dodge City was not salable and was returned to the Government. Scrip was given to the Company, and portions of the public domain were selected in New Mexico. Some acreage was obtained by direct purchase.

Fe purchased the equity of the Frisco.* The assets of the A&P, however, were bought by the Santa Fe Pacific Railroad Company, which in turn was controlled by the Atchison, Topeka and Santa Fe Railway. Possession was taken June 30, 1897. The Santa Fe Pacific continued the liquidation of the land holdings. A substantial reduction was made when portions of the grant were in the area set aside for the Grand Canyon Forest Reserve and the San Francisco Mountain Forest Reserve under an act of June 4, 1897. Approximately 1,306,000 acres were turned over to the Government. The Santa Fe Pacific had the right to select an equal area of public lands but elected to take scrip representing the claims. The scrip was sold to the general public, and the buyers made the choices. The last scrip was sold in 1920.

Control of the old A&P lands passed in 1903 from the Santa Fe Pacific Railroad Company to a new corporation, the Santa Fe Pacific Development Company. The railroad portion of the assets was deeded to the Atchison, Topeka and Santa Fe Railway. In less than a year the lands were returned to the Santa Fe Pacific Railroad Company and have been held in its possession ever since.

The dispersion of lands has continued to date. Sales between 1897 and 1916 were 2,681,489 acres. The average price ($2.40) was higher largely because of the settlement of Arizona and New Mexico. A total of $6,462,883 was received from sales, rents, and royalties. Expenses were slightly under $1,000,000. The quality of the residual after 1916 became progressively lower as the process of skimming the cream persisted. Much land was unsalable and as better areas were sold, the average quality diminished. By 1940 the remnant of the original grant amounted to 4,300,000 acres. About 60 per cent was located in Arizona and the rest in New Mexico. More than half of the holdings are leased on an annual basis for grazing, and slightly over 25 per cent let on a long-term basis. Over 400,000 acres in Arizona are unleased. Most of this is unsuitable for grazing. The land is often used without payment,

---

*For several years the Santa Fe had had indirect control through its investment in the Frisco.

because it is not feasible for the Company to build fences or to police the holdings. Annual rentals are extremely low. Land in Mohave County, Arizona, is let for 1½ cents an acre per year, but the bulk elsewhere earns 2½ cents. No pointed program for sales exists and no colonization efforts are made. Bids for land, however, are entertained.

The Santa Fe Pacific is only one of several members of the Santa Fe corporate family to hold land in Arizona and New Mexico. The parent Company has several non-carrier parcels. The Santa Fe Land Improvement Company acquired a limited acreage from the Santa Fe Pacific and from other sources. The diverse activities of the Land Improvement Company in Arizona and New Mexico as well as in other states will be considered in the chapter dealing with operations between 1896 and the present.

The Santa Fe and its subsidiaries have waged a long struggle with the Government over land claims in the Spanish-tempered states. Disagreements remain and many points are yet to be settled. Under the Transportation Act of 1940 a total of 400,000 acres of claims to unpatented land in Arizona was forfeited in return for a discontinuance of land-grant rates charged for the transportation of United States mail.

Colonization after 1900 in Texas and Kansas

Discontinuance of the Land Department of the Santa Fe in 1897 did not end the colonization endeavors. A special department was established to encourage settlement in the Santa Fe territory. Efforts were concentrated in Texas, where various private land operators had secured large tracts of land. The Santa Fe coöperated in advertising the opportunities. Special freight and passenger rates were given to land-seekers. During the first three months of 1907 the Department of Colonization and Immigration arranged for the transportation of 1340 cars of emigrant outfits (two families per car) to the vicinity of Amarillo, Texas. Thousands more poured into the Lone Star State. Prices charged by the private landholders exacted the last dollar of current value. The Santa Fe aided in settlement in order to build traffic. Officials of the Company often remarked that each homestead meant $300 per year in gross revenue. The labors of the Colonization Department continued into the depression of the 1930's. Efforts were then diffused among several other departments of the Santa Fe.

Reëntry into the land business in Kansas was made in 1909. The Company contemplated construction of a line into the southwest corner of the state. In order to make the project financially sound the area had to be developed and peopled. The motive for the line was not restricted to the establishment of a volume of local traffic, but was prompted in part by the desire to provide a new cutoff for transcontinental traffic. The Company expressed the intention of eventually extending the projection to Colmor, New Mexico. Not only would a substantial reduction in miles be made but expensive operations would be avoided in the mountainous area near Raton. Agents of the Santa Fe Land Improvement Company quietly bought 340,000 acres along the right of way. Remoteness from any existing railroad made for acquisition on a favorable basis.

Construction of the line from Dodge City to Elkhart was under the legal umbrella of the Dodge City and Cimarron Valley Railway, which had been incorporated November 11, 1911. Sale of the lands was begun early in 1912 about the same time as grading. A nationwide advertising campaign was set up to attract progressive young farmers. The same liberality which featured the disposal of the land grant was again outstanding. Settlers could pay as little as one-eighth down. Only taxes and interest (6 per cent) had to be paid at the end of the first year, but one-eighth of the principal had to be added for the succeeding seven years. A unique requirement was the stipulation that buyers had to pursue a special cropping plan for three years. The plan was outlined by the agricultural experts of the Company and borrowed from the Kansas State Agricultural College. Crop rotation and diversification were the salient features of the scientific program. By June, 1915, over 150,000 acres had been sold at an average price of $15. The range was from $7.50 to $22. These prices covered the original cost and expense of administration plus nominal profits. Final sales in the tract were in the early 'twenties. Notwithstanding the severe reverses sustained in the dust bowl between 1933-37, the project has been successful over the years.

The Santa Fe launched a colonization program in Texas about the same time as the second one in Kansas. The results were quite different. The Pine-land Colonization Project of east Texas was begun with high hopes and promptly collapsed. In 1912 President Ripley approved a plan for buying cut-over pine-land to reclaim for agriculture. Initially 3,000 acres were purchased at ten dollars per acre. Later, 1368 acres were added. The stumps were removed and the land was divided into eighty-eight farms of fifty acres. The economic objective was almost transcended by the importance Santa Fe officials attached to the humanitarian angles of the project. Hungarian and German steel workers and their families from congested districts of Lackawanna and Buffalo were to enjoy clean, invigorating air. They were to be returned to the soil from whence they had sprung in their native lands. The project was also to serve as a guide to land utilization; a solution to the old problem of what to do with cut-over forests. Forty of the contingent arrived October 10, 1913. They were followed the next month by thirty. Six arrivals in December swelled the total to forty-two families. The group had little money, but the colonization company of the Santa Fe was ready to finance distress. It offered liberal contracts which concealed substantial subsidies. The colonists decided the life of a human guinea pig might entail too much work, and all but two families rejected the contracts. Sponsors of the project were disheartened at failure before a fair trial had been given. Local farmers were induced to utilize the land, and in the end the Pine-land Colonization Project attained moderate success.

The Santa Fe and its subsidiaries acquired several hundred thousand acres of land all over the system. Such projects are not considered in this chapter, because the primary objective has not been for purposes of agricultural colonizing. Treatment will be found in the section dealing with operations from 1896 to date. Several of the holdings were secured to integrate operations; e. g., timber lands and lumbering facilities for ties and oil, and coal lands for fuels. Other properties were obtained to push plans for industrial colonization.

Three sections of the system were built with the aid of land grants made prior to the time title was gained by the Santa Fe. The Leavenworth, Lawrence and Fort Gibson Railroad extending south from Lawrence, Kansas, received 114,401.76 acres at the same time the Santa Fe gained its original grant. The land was sold under trying circumstances for $492,000. Expenses of $114,000 rendered the net aid $378,000. The Leavenworth, Lawrence and Galveston Railroad succeeded the LL&FG and received $154,429 as the proceeds of an additional grant sold by Kansas for the benefit of the Railroad. The Southern Pacific had land aid to build from Mojave to Needles. None of the grant was transferred to the Santa Fe when the land was purchased. Texas gave the Gulf, Colorado and Santa Fe an area so large that something was realized in spite of the cheapness of the land. Although the GC&SF was entitled to 3,554,560 acres of actual land, officials elected to sell the certificates or scrip rather than the land itself. Net receipts amounted to $211,168.

LAND-GRANT RATES

All the federal aid to the Santa Fe and its predecessors was not without strings. Grants to railroads invariably had a proviso that "said railroads and branches shall be and remain public highways for the use of the Government of the United States, free from all tolls or other charges for the transportation of any property or troops of the United States." The wording of donations to canals had been similar. The interpretation placed on the restriction was that the Government had the right to use the roadway of land-grant lines but had to furnish its own carrying equipment. Lacking rolling stock, the Government elected to pay land-grant railroads for all services rendered beyond the utilities provided by the roadbed. Until 1874 a discount of 33⅓ per cent was taken on Government business. The Court of Claims was then given the right to determine payments to the railroads. Finally, by Congressional action on June 30, 1882, during the Granger days, the compensation was set at a maximum of 50 per cent of established rates. Later the limit was advanced to 60 per cent, but payments continued to be made at 50 per cent. Although nothing in the original grant to the Santa Fe called for discounts on mail, Congress in 1876 prescribed charges of 80 per cent of those exacted on non-grant lines.

The land grant to the Santa Fe seemed to be satisfactory to both parties during the fifty years following the award. The Government had accomplished its objectives. The chief motives were to hasten the building of the West, to unify widely separated areas and develop national solidarity, and to facilitate movements of military supplies and personnel. Without doubt the savings in the form of reduced rates or free use of the roadway were decidedly secondary in importance. As indicated by the Santa Fe's role in peopling the prairies, the Company carried out its responsibility in an eminently satisfactory manner. No more effective colonization program can be visualized. Moreover, the line was pushed into remote areas at an early date, if anything too early, and served to enlarge the federation of loyal states. As a military adjunct the Santa Fe lived up to all expectations. Any apparent financial loss to the Government was actually offset by the doubling of the prices of the alternate sections of Government land lying within the outer limits of the grant. The enhancement of the land which attended the building of the railroad was more than double, so that public lands were especially attractive and their occupation was accelerated. Company lands were taken second.

The increase in value of lands was not restricted to the confines of the grant and was a factor in inducing settlement in the general area contiguous to the award. Feeders for the mainline had to be built. These were without grants and they multiplied the advantages to the Government. The mainline, furthermore, did not remain within the termini of the grant. As the Santa Fe was extended the Government enjoyed all of the advantages incidental in the land-grant area except the reduced rates.

The task of comparing the amount received by the Santa Fe and its predecessors from land grants with the rate discounts given by the Government involves several imponderables, but some observations are worth while. Net receipts from the original grant in Kansas, as far as can be ascertained from incomplete records, were $9,495,091. This was secured over a period of twenty-eight years. If the varying net secured each year were discounted at the going rates of interest to the date of the donation, the original value of the grant would have been approximately one-fourth of this amount. A&P lands sold down to 1916 netted $9,341,703 after expenses. The selling period was thirty-five years. Certainly in 1881 the grant had only a low speculative value. If the future receipts were discounted back to 1881, only a fractional portion of the actual receipts could be considered as the value of the land in 1881. The discounted value of all of the lands to which the Santa Fe succeeded has been estimated at slightly over $6,000,000. Over $23,000,000 has been realized since the awards were originally secured.

Reduced freight rates and mail rates which the Santa Fe conceded have proved to be sour grapes for the Company. When the land was secured, officials did not regard the concession as an important perpetual liability. The role of government was limited, the old laissez-faire dictum prevailing. The less government, the better. The amount discounted for many years was low. Between 1879 and 1916 the saving to the United States in transportation of freight, passengers, and mail over the land-grant portion of the system amounted to $2,405,761. The total amount did not especially alarm officials, but the trend was ominous. The annual average for the whole period was $63,000, but during 1914, 1915, and 1916 the mean was $106,900. During the first World War the concessions soared into the millions each year. Later they subsided, so that the balance for the whole transaction favored neither party.

The advent of the New Deal with the far-reaching activities of its alphabetical agencies made the scales weigh heavily in favor of the United States. The Government entered fields of endeavor which had always been in the province of private enterprise. Grains, livestock, building materials, and hosts of other items moved in enormous quantities at 50 per cent. Those who minimized the pump-priming influence argued that in the majority of cases Government shipments replaced private traffic. General freight and passenger rates were, in effect, reduced. Land-grant railroads combined to protest the burden placed on them by the entrance of the Government into diverse activities. The companies also objected to the 20 per cent discount on mail traffic on the grounds that no such concession was specifically required in the grants. Congress was sympathetic, and full rates were authorized on mail under the Transportation Act of 1940. The Government was to pay commercial rates on transportation of its personnel and property except for movements of military or naval property and members of the military and naval forces and their property while traveling on official duty. The railroads were to surrender all claims to unpatented lands in exchange for the easement.

The Santa Fe yielded rights to vast acreages in the Far West in order to secure the benefits of reform. Title to a portion of the lands had been challenged before the restoration was made. Some of the grant of the old Atlantic and Pacific Railroad in northwestern Arizona had long been the stamping grounds of the Hualapai Indians. Representatives of the United States, as guardian of the tribe, asserted that title to lands within and outside the Hualapai reservation which were also in the land-grant area belonged to Indians. The Company became engaged in a long-drawn-out controversy. Judgment was favorable to the Santa Fe from the lower court to and including the Supreme Court of the United States. The Company, however, quitclaimed the lands in January, 1941, almost a year before the final verdict was rendered.

The relief afforded the land-grant railroads under the Act of 1940 was substantial, yet it was more than offset by the burden imposed by the requirements of the war economy which followed. Unprecedented quantities of war materials dwarfed the previous volume of Government freight which carried preferred rates. Reduced charges were claimed not only on goods in possession of military divisions but on raw materials destined for processing in war plants leased or operated by private enterprise. The amount of the discount skyrocketed. Net receipts of $23,000,000 from the sale of all lands are dwarfed by the magnitude of the land-grant deductions listed below.

| | | Rate Reductions | |
Period	Freight	Passenger	Total
1942	$ 18,250,936	$ 4,663,677	$ 22,914,613
1943	33,841,772	9,079,211	42,920,983
1944	46,154,324	8,579,731	54,734,055
1945	44,496,642	10,046,672	54,543,314
1946	8,500,099	5,882,900	14,382,999
	$151,243,773	$38,252,191	$189,495,964

Citizens who lament the continual duping of Uncle Sam in financial affairs should be particularly pleased with the above statistics.

The discount given by the Santa Fe was properly interpreted as an opportunity loss, yet the business of the Government was not unattractive even at the reduced rates. Non-grant competing railroads voluntarily matched land-grant railroad rates. The unique situation arose out of the peculiar nature of railroad expenses. The practice has always existed of accepting many commodities at rates which do not cover average costs of transportation but which would not be shipped unless lower tariffs were given. The rates charged, however, had to be in excess of the out-of-pocket or variable costs incurred in handling the merchandise. Railroads gained some income to apply on fixed expenses. The alternative was nothing. Non-grant roads found that rates equalizing those on the land-grant lines were feasible. Out-of-pocket expenses could be more than covered. This did not mean that commercial freight rates were too high. If land-grant rates had prevailed on all shipments, the returns would have been grossly inadequate to meet fixed charges. The willingness of non-grant railroads to handle Government business at lower rates eased the problem for the grant lines. Otherwise traffic would have flowed over the grant lines as far as possible to the exclusion of commercial business. The Santa Fe would have had a larger volume to carry at a lower average yield per ton or passenger mile. The anomalous situation developed that non-grant roads in land-grant regions were more disadvantageously affected than the companies which received grants. A broad inequity was largely in favor of lines in non-grant areas where the full commercial rates apply with minor adjustment. Inasmuch as the Government received far more than full compensation for the original donations, no basis remained after the 'thirties for the continued inequity other than the original agreement, which had become economically obsolete.

The astronomical concession of $189 million shown in the table was expected by the Company to be lowered approximately $30 million. The Transportation Act of 1940 had narrowed the scope covered by land-grant rates to "military and naval property of the United States moving for military or naval and not for civil use" and "members of the military or naval forces of the United States (or property of such members) when such members are traveling on official duty." What constituted military and naval property not for civil use became a mammoth bone of contention. The largest single item in the dispute amounted to $20 million and involved the applicability of rate concessions on construction materials shipped by the United States Maritime Commission for incorporation in cargo vessels. The next largest item was lend-lease shipment. The Supreme Court of the United States in a series of three decisions on March 3, 1947, ruled against the bulk of the claims of the land-grant lines. The Court upheld the railroads' arguments on shipments of a portion of lend-lease material clearly intended for civilian use. The refund due the railroads including the Santa Fe was nominal. Land-grant discounts on all military supplies and personnel were ended by Congressional action as of October, 1946.

Although the controversy between the Government and the Santa Fe and other land-grant lines attracted much attention, other aspects of the donations are of greater significance. The grant was vital to the early financing of the Santa Fe. The support was small but nevertheless essential. The Company utilized the lands to highly commendable ends consistent with the public interest. The development of states and territories was greatly hastened. Substantial people were induced to settle in the region of the Santa Fe. They converted untrodden prairies and deserts into fruitful gardens, farms, and orchards. Mines were opened and yielded coal, gold, silver, and innumerable other products sought by man. All of these developments constituted the basis for the rise of commercial cities and towns to handle the products of the fields and mines and to provide the supplies for further production. In time local manufacturing began and finished goods spread out over larger and larger concentric circles until the cities of the Southwest were factors in the national and international economy. The empire of the Santa Fe progressively bought more and more from other regions. Today its affairs are inextricably mingled with the business of the Nation. Important as the role of the Southwest is at present, new frontiers yet remain. The Santa Fe no longer owns the lands, but the makers of an empire do.

VIII

Meals by Fred Harvey

Fate cannot harm me—
I have dined today.

STAUNCH ALLIES have helped to round out the service of the Santa Fe. Three of them—Western Union, Pullman, and Railway Express—serve all railroads, and there is very little to differentiate their relations with the Santa Fe from those with any other railroad. But the fourth ally is distinctive. Other railroads have their own arrangements for feeding passengers and employees, but the Santa Fe's clientele and force dine with Fred Harvey.

The institution of Fred Harvey needs little description, because everybody seems to be familiar with this unique adjunct of the Santa Fe. Its reputation does not spring from any high-pressure advertising program, but from a judicious cultivation of good will arising out of a service that is well-nigh fabulous in the West. Fred Harvey's role as purveyor of fine foods has even been described as the "greatest civilizing influence in the West." Quite as unusual as this influence on social development has been the association between the Harvey and Santa Fe companies. The two have complemented each other and worked together in a manner almost unparalleled in the history of American business. The two have never been legal partners, yet companies have never coöperated or labored any more in each other's behalf.

HASH BEFORE HARVEY

Relations between Fred Harvey and the Santa Fe began in 1876. Prior to that time the budding railroad had done little to solve the problem of feeding its passengers and crews. As a matter of fact, no railroad had provided adequately for the needs of travelers. A few primitive dining cars were in operation in various parts of the country, but the food elicited little praise. Travelers usually brought their own provisions whether eating stops were made or not. The problem was more formidable for passengers than might be imagined on first consideration. Schedules were slow, and the time spent on journeys was three or four times as long as required today. Trips of seventy-five miles occasioned belt-tightening or a lunch. No "butchers" provided milk and sandwiches, nor was there refrigeration for any perishables the passenger brought. The problem of supply was especially complicated on long trips. Either many meals had to be prepared in advance, or the larder had to be restocked. In the summer, maintenance of palatability was difficult without refrigeration. Flies, gnats, and other insects had lifetime passes over every line.

Some passengers preferred to take their chances on eating places at railroad stops. The prevailing custom was to hold the train for about twenty minutes while passengers bolted whatever was to be had. Irregularity of train schedules and poor spacing of stops were a source of much irritation. But the greatest objection voiced by passengers was directed at the quality and prices of servings. The customer was usually given his choice as long as he ordered black coffee (made once a week) and dry, salty ham. Questionable eggs, fried in rancid grease, were used as a filler for two slices of stale bread. No pretense at good service was made, since the trade was transient in nature. The dishes were washed occasionally but by persons without phobias on the subject of uncleanliness. Prices exacted the maximum gain possible in the monopolistic position. The alternative was hunger, which many people preferred. In the East, the intolerable situation was improved, standards becoming more bearable at an early date. The struggle in the West was confined to establishing eating places of any type, rather than to ameliorating the existing places.

The Santa Fe did little during early years to provide for the food requirements of passengers and crews. The rule was "Bring your own or go hungry." When the line was extended across Kansas in 1872, several towns enjoyed mushroom growth beside the tracks. These developments enabled a man to get a drink while the train stopped even if he could not order a meal. Rude structures were erected and provisioned at the end of runs where crew members could prepare their own meals of buffalo, corn bread, long sweet'nin', and coffee. A secondhand story can be heard of a crew of three who had a daytime layover in Granada. The town had a few houses but no place where the trio could bed and board. They induced the proprietress of a sod house to rent sleeping quarters. She made the deal without the knowledge of the husband, who worked a land claim some distance away and spent one day a week with his wife. Hence the agreement was on a six-day basis. All went well, although the three men found the one bed rather uncomfortable, until, unannounced, the fearsome husband returned in the middle of the week. The wife was able to warn the men, but no escape was possible. They grabbed their clothes and scrambled under the bed. The unwelcome man of the house must not have been observant, because he did not discover the crew, although he sat on the edge of the bed. But fear of discovery was not what made the occasion memorable to the trainmen. A rustling, buzzing sound seemed to spring from the ground near their feet. Three minds had a single thought—a rattlesnake! Cold sweat poured out of the terror-stricken men. The engineer later remarked that they would have rolled from under the bed, husband or no husband, if they had not been petrified with fear and unable to move. The sounds continued for more than an hour. Could men have been in greater anguish? The sounds subsided, finally, and the husband left. The crew scrambled out, vowing never to return. The wife kept up a running argument to retain her income.

The noise, she contended, was merely a hen that had taken refuge under the bed to escape the heat of the day. The Santa Fe began construction of facilities for the men the following week.

The Santa Fe made its first real efforts to provide suitable eating accommodations in Topeka, where a combined station and office building had been erected in 1872. The site was somewhat removed from the commercial area of Topeka where food might be obtained. In 1874 or 1875 Superintendent C. F. Morse determined to make arrangements for service near the station. The Company lacking money to erect and equip a new building, space was found in the old one. Since the first floor was already fully utilized, resort was made to the upper story. Peter Kline of Topeka contracted with the Santa Fe to operate the new venture. Fragmentary evidence indicates that Kline successfully met the urgent needs, although the food and service were no more than passable.

A Harvey Lunchroom in 1876

Kline did not stay with the lunchroom long. In the spring of 1876 he sold his furnishings and supplies to Fred Harvey of Leavenworth, an employee of the Burlington. The transaction had the unqualified approval of Superintendent Morse. The latter had also worked for the Burlington. The new proprietor was not of the common run of hash slingers. His background was different and, what was more, he had boundless ambition plus a firm conviction that the traveling public would appreciate and reward anyone who began the reformation of the lowly restaurant.* Harvey secured a fellow townsman in Leavenworth,

---

*Frederick Henry Harvey was born of English-Scotch parentage in London on June 27, 1835. His childhood years are obscure. At the age of fifteen Harvey migrated to America. Like most immigrants, he landed in New York with little money. A job as bus boy in the Smith and McNeill Cafe yielded $2 per week. Harvey subsequently turned up in New Orleans, where he won a bout with yellow fever. Late in the 'fifties, he entered a partnership to establish and operate a restaurant in St. Louis. Business thrived until the War, when the partner absconded with the remaining liquid assets. Fred Harvey was more fortunate in the choice of a partner for life. In 1859 he married Barbara Sarah Mattas, who was to prove loyal through adversity as well as prosperity.

Guy Potter, to assume the management of the lunchroom. He did not give Potter full authority, for he had no intention of becoming the sort of absentee investor who passively waits for the profits to be mailed. He had well-thought-out ideas about every detail of food and service. Potter was not retained to operate the lunchroom as he might be inclined, but was sent to Topeka to operate the lunchroom precisely as Fred Harvey wanted.

The obscure lunch counter slowly but surely attracted attention. The magic touch of Fred Harvey was already in evidence. The place was spotless, the dishes sparkled, and patrons had a favorable impression at the outset. The menu offered variety, something unprecedented at the time. The food looked attractive and tempting. Its taste was even more delightful. There were zestful flavors that were new and some that were old but had been ruthlessly suppressed in the average restaurant. Strange but true, the prices were moderate. The news of the changed order spread rapidly. The small quarters bulged with patrons. Skeptics wondered when the manager would decide that the business was large enough to lower the standards. To their continued amazement there was no letdown. The quality of food and service improved as Harvey and Potter discovered better sources of supply and tempting recipes. Contemporaries went so far as to express concern for the westward movement. They contended that there was danger that settlers en route to western Kansas

---

A wide variety of jobs provided a livelihood during the next years. Harvey finally secured a clerkship on a mail car on the Hannibal and St. Joseph. Leavenworth, Kansas, became his headquarters. He held progressively higher positions on the North Missouri Railroad, the Hannibal and St. Joseph, and the Chicago, Burlington and Quincy. These companies were affiliated. At the time Harvey began operating the lunchroom in Topeka he held the rank of General Western Agent of the CB&Q. In the course of his travels Harvey became disgusted with the general run of restaurants available to railroad patrons. He was convinced that the opportunity was present for highly profitable operations if the right type of accommodations, food, and service were offered. Harvey and Jeff Rice acquired two eating houses on the Kansas Pacific in 1875 at Wallace and Hugo, Kansas. Although the enterprise prospered, Harvey summarily ended the partnership in a few months for inexplicable reasons. Attempts to induce the Burlington to coöperate in establishing eating houses were unsuccessful. Harvey began negotiations with C. F. Morse of the Santa Fe, and after receiving the approval of President Nickerson, succeeded to the rights of Peter Kline.

would stay in Topeka to eat at the new lunchroom. One reporter wrote, "Traffic was blocked and it became absolutely necessary for the Santa Fe to open similar houses at other points that the West might not be settled in just one spot."

A HARVEY HOUSE IN 1877

Expansion came late in 1877, the site being Florence. Again Harvey did not open a new place, but merely took over an existing establishment. A converted eating house and hotel had been opened on April 1, 1876, by Ben Putnam. The structure was on private grounds, but Putnam had a contract with the Santa Fe to erect a larger hotel on railroad property. Patronage of the original inn was excellent in spite of the bedbugs and unappetizing food. Putnam ordered material for the new hotel. Before much work had been accomplished, his creditors intervened, and Putnam sold the uncompleted structure to J. A. Pike and Company. The hotel was opened on June 14, 1876. The quality of construction may be surmised from the fact that the building time was less than two months. J. A. Pike and R. T. Battey were the co-owners. In December, 1877, Fred Harvey visited the hotel at the suggestion of C. F. Morse. He inspected the building and furnishings and submitted a bid, which Pike and Battey accepted. The building went for $4,370 and the furnishings for $1,000. Harvey was said to have been reluctant to buy the properties and wanted the Santa Fe to provide them. The latter was financially weak and assured Harvey that he would be reimbursed when affairs permitted. The Santa Fe kept its word and later bought the building.

Working arrangements between Fred Harvey and the Company were laid down in a contract effective January 1, 1878. The ground at Florence on which the hotel stood was leased to Harvey for five years. No rent was to be paid, but a reasonable standard of service was to be provided. At least two mainline trains were to be stopped each day for meals. The lease was terminable by the Santa Fe on thirty days' notice. All improvements of property were subject to review by the Santa Fe.

The contract of January 1, 1878, was the last written agreement between the two parties until 1889. Business relations between the two during the interim were enlarged and complicated by the opening of a dozen or more eating houses and hotels and the establishment of service on diners. William B. Strong, an old friend of Harvey, had shifted from the Burlington to the Santa Fe in 1877. Both were men of the highest integrity. A gentlemen's agreement amply fulfilled all of their needs. The arrangements for the first house were applied to new houses as they were added. The Santa Fe supplied the buildings and Fred Harvey equipped them. Coal, ice, and water were provided by the railroad; employees and supplies were hauled free. Problems of joint concern were solved as soon as they were noticed. "Whatever is fair" was the guiding principle.

M. Fisher was sent to operate the hotel at Florence in the prescribed Harvey manner. The old routine was turned upside down. Fred Harvey had as many revolutionary ideas about the running of a hotel as he did about an eating place. The building was completely refurnished with a view toward making the accommodations pleasing to the eye and to the tired body. Before, a man paid for a bunk; now he was to pay the same amount for the maximum in comfort. A high-salaried and incredulous chef was induced to leave a post in one of Chicago's leading hotels to assume responsibility for the cuisine. What the expert did with the bountiful wild game of the prairies was a lasting delight to the hundreds who came to Fred Harvey's first dining room. The Clifton Hotel, as it came to be called, gained such wide fame that the westward movement was enabled to continue from Topeka to Florence.

Fred Harvey resigned from the Burlington when he assumed control of the hotel at Florence. The new chain began to expand so rapidly that divided activities were no longer possible. Eating houses and hotels were added steadily. In 1879 Harvey succeeded Guy Potter at Lakin. The latter had left the lunch stand in Topeka in 1876 to open the Lakin hotel. The Santa Fe tore the building down in 1880 and used the material to reëstablish a Harvey house at Sargent (now Coolidge).

The most imposing responsibility thrust upon Harvey during the early expansion was the management of the cuisine of the fabulous Montezuma Hotel near Las Vegas, New Mexico. The Montezuma catered to the wealthy from all parts of the world. Harvey service more than met the most discriminating tastes of those whose purses bulged. Completion of the line to Guaymas in Mexico added variety to the Harvey menus. Fresh vegetables and fruit were obtained throughout the winter. Epicurean Harvey boasted in his quiet way that canned goods were never served in the Montezuma. As a special treat for the guests, a buyer for Harvey contracted with the chief of a tribe of Yaqui Indians to supply green turtles and sea celery from the Gulf of Lower California. The turtles were shipped alive to Las Vegas, where they were put in a specially provided pool and fed well until needed for steaks and soup.

The public demanded, and the Santa Fe was happy to provide, more Harvey Houses. The number of eating establishments operated by others was gradually reduced. Fred Harvey assumed exclusive control of all meal service on the Santa Fe from Topeka to El Paso. In May, 1883, Santa Fe passengers were assured the inimitable "Meals by Fred Harvey."

CIVILIZING THE WEST

Harvey Houses were so successful on the enlarged basis that Santa Fe officials decided the service should be introduced on the A&P. Eating places west of Albuquerque were a disgrace. They were never adequate in number, and their quality rendered them scarcely better than nothing. C. W. Smith, first vice-president of the Santa Fe, made a local survey and declared that reform was an absolute necessity. Again Fred Harvey was willing, and in 1887 he dispatched his right-hand man, David Benjamin, to

take over the beaneries. The task was not easy, because many
of the proprietors had shaded their operating functions into
price gouging. The clever Benjamin maneuvered to arrange
deals on a reasonably satisfactory basis. He was horrified with
what he encountered. At Kingman the eating house was primarily a saloon. Liquor stocks were ample, but the food was
scarce. At another point the dining room had been moved up-
stairs to make more space for gambling.

Units on the A&P were rapidly raised to the prevailing
standards. Harvey service was available from Topeka to California and Mexico. Then followed the golden days which have
excited the poet and writer. Fred Harvey began to "civilize the
West." His fame spread partly from fact and partly from fancy.
The reserve of Harvey officials prompted imaginative talk. Harvey was a rare combination of dignity and color. He did things
with dramatic effect. He would have been a success in any business and hundreds of stories would have been told of his exploits.
The West has a great treasure chest of Harvey lore as well as
stories of the manner in which the Houses led in the transformation of raw western life into a refined and orderly social structure.

The typical Harvey House of the romanticized period was
of frame construction. The railroad station was usually under
the same roof. Hotel facilities were provided at less than half
of the sites, depending upon the need. Staffs of Harvey Houses
were necessarily large regardless of how small the stations were.
The lunchrooms were not wholly dependent upon local trade
but were primarily designed to serve passengers. The business
was not diffused but was highly concentrated at two or more
times in the day or evening. Since the train was to be detained
a minimum length of time, the service had to be rapid. Only a
large number of waitresses could fulfill the requirements.

Telegrams were sent from speeding trains to indicate any
unexpected numbers or delays as the trains neared the Harvey
House. The employees hustled to have everything in readiness

for the guests. When the train came to a stop a gong sounded the way. The passengers alighted and entered the pleasing atmosphere of a tastefully decorated lunchroom or dining room. Meals were table d'hote and the choice was limited, although variety was offered. The menus were cunningly planned to be most appealing. Travelers in desert country were offered sour salads and fruits which tempted the palate on hot days. Passengers on east-bound trains from California were offered freshwater fish rather than salt-water on the assumption that they might appreciate a change from sea foods. Exotic dishes which had been unknown to the self-sufficing West were regularly on the menus. The meals were deftly served in a manner designed to secure inconspicuous speed. Although the time allotted for stops was seldom more than thirty minutes, the service was so smoothly organized that patrons had the impression of leisurely dining. Another sound of the gong and it was time to entrain. The mad scramble, familiar on other railroads, to bolt the last half of a meal was missing. The customers unknowingly ate on schedule. The stop was relaxing and the food excellent. Fred Harvey had won new friendships and strengthened old ones.

Personnel of the Harvey Houses was about equally divided between men and women. The manager and the chefs were invariably men. They were recruited from all parts of the East and Europe. Regardless of previous experience the men were retained to follow Harvey methods rather than their own. Serving was done by waitresses. These were recruited in eastern states. Most of the waitresses were young. The selective process was rigid. Observers all agreed that those in charge of hiring selected intelligent and refined girls. What was more conspicuous was the eye for beauty possessed by the recruiters. The girls were given rigorous training for their work. A Harvey patron was served in a minutely exact manner. The slightest deviation from the pattern was inexcusable.

Rooms for Harvey employees were incorporated in the Houses. The girls were supervised by a matron. Strict hours had to be kept and good morals observed.

In the case of the waitresses, the problem of labor turnover was consistently serious. The girls were well paid and working conditions were ideal. The trouble was the adverse ratio of women to men in the new country. Harvey girls would have had suitors in the most settled community. In the womanless West the girls were wooed by ranchers, trainmen, and miners. The conservative uniforms, which have persisted to the present, were supposed to have been introduced in an effort to temper the natural beauty of the waitresses. As a rule the girls married after a year in the service. Their level of refinement caused associations with a high type of men. Consequently, they married leaders of the West. No one knows how many thousands of girls went west to work in Harvey Houses but soon shifted their endeavors to homes of their own.

Operating Methods and Agreements

The excellence of Harvey meals continued to amaze travelers from afar and to delight those who dined regularly at the Houses. Notables, one and all, were lavish in their praise. An English nobleman, asked to relate his most pleasant experience in America, replied, "Breakfast in Arkansas City, Kansas." The praise was earned by conscientious and ingenious efforts to utilize every bit of imagination and resourcefulness in the preparation of food. In order to secure a dependable supply of the proper quality of poultry and dairy products, farms were integrated into the organization. Milk products and chickens were produced at Newton, Kansas, and Del Rio, Arizona. For a time, costs of production at the latter were far in excess of the prices charged for final products in the desert Houses, but the obligation to maintain standards had been met. Additional dairies were operated at La Junta, Colorado, Las Vegas, New Mexico, and Temple, Texas. Experts in judging meat selected prime carcasses for the system. The meat was not accepted for immediate delivery, but was put in coolers for proper aging. Quantity purchasing with care was as important to success as the painstaking preparation and impeccable service.

Numerous stories are told of Fred Harvey's perfective bent. Tables had to be set as if a king were to dine. A misplaced napkin or spoon was inexcusable. On one occasion Harvey walked into a dining room at the same moment his manager entered by another door. One of the tables had not been set quite properly. Luckily no guests were present.

"You know better than this," Harvey shouted as he seized a corner of the cloth and jerked the tableware to the far corners of the room. "Now fix it right."

A near phobia about cleanliness kept all hands busy maintaining an immaculate condition. Fred Harvey's inspections struck mortal fear into the hearts of the employees lest he discover something amiss.

The guiding business philosophy of Fred Harvey was that profits would accrue in the long run if excellent service were provided and maintained in spite of an initial or temporary period of losses. Many a House operated in the red for years. A smaller loss with no change in volume of patronage required an explanation. The worry was not that the ham might be cut in too few slices but too many. Accountants labored over statistics to make certain that there was no skimping in the interest of today's profits at the cost of the whole future.

Rooms in Harvey Houses had their standards too. The furniture reflected a discerning regard for style and comfort. A perpetual battle against dirt and blemishes was waged. Harvey Houses became objects of civic and regional pride. They set standards for backward competitors and were a powerful influence in raising the quality of their rivals.

Harvey eating places were put on wheels shortly after the Santa Fe began service to Chicago in 1888. Below is a reproduction of the first menu issued on the new diners:

Little Neck Clams on Shell

Consomme Printaniere Royale

Fillets of Sole, Tartar Sauce
Sliced Cucumbers   *Pommes Persillade*

Boiled Westphalia Ham with Spinach

Roast Beef   **Spring Lamb, Mint Sauce**
Young Turkey, Cranberry Sauce

New Asparagus on Toast   *New Green Peas*
Mashed Potatoes   *New Potatoes in Cream*

Fillet of Beef with Mushrooms
Sweetbreads Braized, Jardiniere
Spanish Puffs, Strawberry Sauce

Punch Benedictine

Broiled Plover on Toast

Mayonnaise   **Chicken Salad**
Sliced Tomatoes   *Lettuce*

Apple Pie   **Pieplant Pie**
Sago Pudding, Brandy Sauce

Strawberries and Cream   **Assorted Cake**

Vanilla Ice Cream

Edam and Roquefort Cheese
Bent's Water Crackers   **French Coffee**

Meals 75 Cents.

CAR REDONDO.

Another menu of the same year featured prairie chicken. The efficient service offered by the eating houses by the side of the road deferred the widespread introduction of diners on the Santa Fe west of Kansas City.

By 1889 the working arrangement between the Santa Fe and Fred Harvey had attained a large and complicated scale. A written contract signed on May 1 codified most of the oral agreements. Newspapers intimated that the men who were displacing the Strong regime were responsible for the discontinuance of coffee-cup relations. Some thought that the contract was urged by Strong in order to preserve the status of the two allies if he should be ousted. The most plausible explanation attributes the contract to early railroad regulation and to the need for an explicit agreement arising from the enlarged scope of activities.

Fred Harvey was to enjoy the first choice of all sites on owned or leased lines. The Santa Fe continued to have arrangements with others for eating places at the less desirable points.

The team of Manvel and Reinhart proved to be rather skeptical and unappreciative of Harvey. They interpreted the contract of 1889 to mean that Harvey was given priority over other persons outside of the Santa Fe in the matter of eating houses but that the Company could operate its own diners if it chose. Manvel started to put diners in service west of the Missouri River. The value of Fred Harvey's business was threatened. In August, 1891, an injunction was secured preventing the Santa Fe from operating diners west of the Missouri and from refusing to stop trains for meals. Harvey estimated that his business at the time served five thousand daily and that he had about $150,000 invested. A few conferences between the parties and further consideration by Manvel restored harmonious relations. Soon Manvel was as firmly convinced as Strong had been that Fred Harvey service was one of the best features of the Santa Fe.

Among the first actions of the receivers of the Santa Fe was the extension of the 1889 contract. Judge Caldwell, however, insisted on a few inconsequential modifications. Later in the period of receivership a major supplemental agreement was attached covering the extension of dining-car service. The Santa Fe was to furnish all cars used by Fred Harvey. The latter was given exclusive control. Early operation of dining cars on other railroads demonstrated that losses were inescapable. The very nature of the difficult circumstances under which the meals were served made for costs in excess of what the traveling public would pay. Railroads which operated their own diners simply took the loss. Since Fred Harvey was a separate business unit, a provision for reimbursement was made.

The economics of train meals is generally misunderstood. The unknowing often charge the railroads with everything up to extortion for the prices exacted. They believe that every line tries to make up for the lack of traffic by profits on meals. Diners are actually a source of much happiness to sellers of red ink. No railroad has ever been able to show real profit from them. Increased volume of diner business does not necessarily mean less loss.* Likewise, lower prices usually mean a great financial setback. The president of one railroad estimated that his company spent seventy-five cents on each person served regardless of whether the order was water or a multi-course dinner. The allocation of constant costs was too much to put meals on a self-sustaining basis. The actual cost of food, the president observed, was a rather unimportant matter. Therefore, a 50 per cent reduction in the amount of food in a diner could not reduce the cost to passengers by much more than 10 per cent. Most large railroads lose hundreds of thousands of dollars annually on dining-car service and are criticized too.

---

*The only exception to this occurs in extraordinary times like those during World War II. Much more intensive utilization of existing dining cars made for broader allocation of overhead costs. Patrons were inconvenienced but had to accept the congested condition. The number of dining cars was limited and could not be increased owing to priorities. If the same increase in passenger travel occurred during peace times, the public would insist that more dining cars be made available. The Company would provide the facilities in advance of the demand. The Santa Fe would probably have doubled its fleet in 1943 in order to serve its patrons had additional cars been obtainable. This move would have increased overhead costs sharply and eliminated many of the current economies.

The Santa Fe-Fred Harvey working agreement has been the outstanding solution of the meal problem on trains. No other company has been as successful in transposing an unproductive expense into a potent medium for attracting business. "Fred Harvey" means more than the satisfying of hunger pangs; it means delightful dining. Those most devoid of epicurean sensibilities cannot fail to be pleased by the extraordinary creations of Harvey chefs, by the courteous and dignified service, and by the discreetly appointed surroundings. Harvey dinners are memorable. They are topics of conversation whenever food and travel are mentioned. In short, "Meals by Fred Harvey" are one of the most powerful advertising forces of the Santa Fe. Maintenance of standards far above the national average has changed the nature of the deficiency payment from an unproductive subsidy to a fructifying expense.

The acquisition of the Frisco by the Santa Fe opened up additional opportunities for Fred Harvey. Much delay ensued in expanding the service to the newly acquired line and not until 1896, while the Frisco and Santa Fe companies were separating, were Harvey meals made available to Frisco patrons. Operations continued on the smaller road until 1930.

During the first year of Ripley's presidency a new and comprehensive contract was negotiated between the Santa Fe and Fred Harvey covering dining cars, lunchrooms, and the Houses. The contract of 1896 introduced profit-sharing clauses for the first time. The usual care was taken to specify that relations between the two did not establish a partnership.

Existing contracts were superseded in 1906 by another comprehensive contract. One provision required that Fred Harvey secure Santa Fe consent for operations. A complicated basis of division of profits was introduced. Profits were divided on a progressive basis. Service at the Grand Canyon was governed by a separate tripartite agreement made later in the year, the third signer being the Grand Canyon Railway Company.

The regime of Ripley beginning in 1896 cemented the co-operation of the Santa Fe and Fred Harvey even more closely than in the days of William B. Strong. Ripley was fully cognizant of the value of Fred Harvey service, and as time passed he recommended heavy outlays to provide building facilities more consistent with Harvey standards.

The death of Fred Harvey in 1901 was a severe blow to the Santa Fe and to the Southwest. Yet in the hour of darkness there was already evidence that Fred Harvey was not entirely gone. He had left an indelible imprint on the empire of the Santa Fe—an influence that time could not erase even if the business founded by Harvey should perish. More than this, Fred Harvey left a smooth-functioning organization of his own design. It was oiled, greased, and wound for years of service. Lieutenants steeped in Harvey tradition remained. The survival of the old order was assured by Harvey's flesh and blood. Two sons had developed under their father's watchful eye. Three years of illness had necessitated a shift in leadership to the partners and sons. When death came, the Harvey machine was not without engineers to guide it. The sons, Ford and Byron, were youthful replicas of their father. They had the same executive ability, ambition, respect for food and tradition, and all of the gentlemanly traits requisite for carrying out their portion of the contract with the Santa Fe.*

---

*The "coat rule" of the father was carried out just as religiously by the sons. Fred Harvey from the beginning was determined to maintain an air of refinement and good taste in his dining rooms. Accordingly he laid down the rule that all patrons must wear coats. Harvey obviously had extraordinarily strong convictions of decorum to attempt to enforce such a rule in raw, rough country where coatless gunmen were not unusual. Nevertheless, the rule was unflinchingly put into effect. Since many travelers were without coats, Harvey supplied each dining room with a number of dark alpaca coats. Few balked at donning the garments. The atmosphere of the dining rooms was such that the most insensate usually recognized the propriety of the attire.

In 1921 the Corporation Commission of Oklahoma ordered the coat rule set aside, charging discrimination among patrons. The decision was appealed and in 1924 the Supreme Court of Oklahoma set aside the holding of the Commission (229 Pac. 428, 1924) to the obvious relief of the second generation of Harveys. The pronouncement of the Court was a sparkling essay on customs and manners. Below is a portion:

"Society in America has for years assumed jurisdiction to a great extent to dictate certain regulations of dress in first-class dining-rooms, and these conventions of society cannot be entirely ignored, without disastrous results to those who serve a metropolitan

The trustees of the estate of Fred Harvey continued the business operations as the deceased had designated. In 1906 the trustees organized Fred Harvey, a closed corporation, chartered by New Jersey. The new firm entered a contract with the Santa Fe which embodied the provisions previously sketched.

The period around the turn of the century brought many changes to Fred Harvey. Many new Houses and lunchrooms were opened. Service was started in the Galveston Union Station in 1897 and at the Dearborn Union Station in Chicago in 1899. When the San Francisco and San Joaquin Valley Railroad was purchased, Fred Harvey had new fields to conquer. In 1900 the Santa Fe authorized offline service in the St. Louis Union Station.

AFTER 1900

Harvey Houses in the 'nineties, although well-kept, were built for the maximum of utility and the minimum of outlay. Restricted finances of the Santa Fe precluded a series of "Montezumas." The regime of Ripley brought financial strength. A noticeable change

---

public in such capacity. Civilized society has developed the masculine attire from the breech-clout to the coat and trousers. Always a part of the masculine garb, and often a major portion of feminine dress, is worn as an adornment to satisfy the conventions of society rather than for bodily comfort and protection. Unlike the lower animals, we all demand the maintenance of some style and fashion in the dining-room, but where to draw the line between the breech-clout and the full dress suit, tailored in Paris or New York, presents a question often affording great difference of opinion and that is the trouble here. . . .

"To abrogate this rule and require the dining-room manager to draw the line of dress at mere cleanliness would lead quickly to personal disputes over differences of opinion. To permit the coatless to enter would bring in those with the sleeveless shirts, and even the shirtless garb that we frequently see where no formality is required. Man's coat is usually the cleanest of his garments, and the fact that he is required to wear a coat serves notice that decorum is expected and creates a wholesome psychological effect.

"Fred Harvey equips these dining-rooms with most luxurious furnishings, pleasing to the trained and appreciative eye, satisfying to the esthetic taste, and places the patrons amidst surroundings best calculated to stimulate the appetite. Food seldom elsewhere excelled is served by well garbed and efficient attendants. Certainly it is not amiss to require the gentleman who would there dine to don a coat for twenty minutes, as he sits in front of the cooling electric fans always there afforded. Our nation's chief executive has recently well said that 'a true citizen of a real republic cannot exist as a segregated, unattached fragment of selfishness, but must live as a constituent part of the whole society, in which he can secure his own welfare only as he secures the welfare of his fellowmen.' Complaints against such rule, by those unwilling momentarily to endure a slight discomfort, out of regard for the feelings, tastes and desires of others are few compared with the storm of protests the abrogation of the rule would ultimately produce."

took place in Harvey Houses. No architect had been given a free hand to develop the hotels of the early period. Beginning about 1900 the Santa Fe engaged the finest talent to design Harvey Houses and stations. The objective sought was conformance to geographic and historical background of the Southwest. Both Edward P. Ripley and Ford Harvey were keenly interested in the change. One of the first of the new order was erected at Albuquerque. The building remains to this day as one of the finest adaptations of the well-known Spanish-mission style to the modern requirements of a hotel. The name chosen was "Alvarado." Most of the Harvey Houses of the second era were given names which were historically harmonious with the area.* A second architectural style was also utilized. It was the motif of the early city of Santa Fe—a blend of sixteenth-century Spanish and Indian design strongly modified by the environs. The general effect was low and long—a clinging and blending to the earth. Façade lines were horizontal, with relief offered by roof beams, inset porches, fire-wall apertures, and flanking buttresses. An outstanding early example of Santa Fe style was El Ortiz at Lamy. La Fonda in Santa Fe is one of the more recent triumphs.

Statistics on operations of Fred Harvey are few. Being a sole proprietorship and then a closed corporation, it had little reason for divulging facts and figures. Enough driftwood is available to give a rough idea of the scale of operations. When Harvey died in 1901 the business was reported to be conducted in fifteen Houses, forty-seven lunch and dining rooms, and thirty dining cars. The payroll in 1902 included approximately 2,000. Consumption by patrons may be gauged by the monthly use of 20,000 chickens. In 1907 the larder had a turnover of 500,000 pounds of ham, 500,-000 of chicken, 300,000 of butter, 150,000 of lard, 3,000,000 of flour, 2,000,000 of beef, and other edibles in proportion. An item in the Kansas City *Star,* December 24, 1911, stated that between sixty and

---

*Some of the names and locations were: the Bisonte at Hutchinson; El Vaquero at Dodge City; the Sequoyah at Syracuse; the Castaneda at Las Vegas; the Fray Marcos at Williams; El Tovar and Bright Angel at the Grand Canyon; the Escalante at Ash Fork; El Garces at Needles; and the Casa Del Desierto at Barstow.

sixty-five eating places and a dozen hotels were in operation. The number of employees was estimated in excess of 4,500. The last figure probably should be discounted almost 50 per cent, since the number was set at 2,300 in an article appearing in the *Santa Fe Magazine* in 1916. Statistics of purchases were given for 1915. The gain between 1907 and 1915 is evident from a poundage comparison of the few items for which information is at hand.

	1907	1915
Chickens	600,000	750,000
Flour	3,000,000	4,500,000
Potatoes	3,000,000	5,000,000
Sugar	1,000,000	1,500,000
Lard	150,000	365,000
Butter	300,000	500,000
Coffee	333,000	500,000

Harvey Houses in operation in 1916 were not nearly as large in number of rooms as their outward appearance and nationwide reputation suggested. Only nine had in excess of thirty-five rooms. The largest was the Alvarado with eighty-nine. Seven had approximately sixty rooms.

The business of Fred Harvey soared during World War I in perfect correlation with the passenger volume of the Santa Fe. After the War, traffic was even heavier, but a steady decline began in 1920. Harvey interests were able to buck the adverse trend. A higher percentage of the traveling public patronized the diverse services. The improvement of the Houses continued, and their number and size increased. New fields of endeavor had to be entered to maintain the rate of growth. Newsstand operations were expanded with due regard to matching standards of other departments. Fred Harvey began the display of the old Southwest to tourists. The work was under the direction of the capable John F. Huckel, a son-in-law of the founder. In coöperation with the Santa Fe, historic sites were widely advertised. Travelers were invited to visit Indian ruins as well as pueblos where tribes carried on unmindful of the passing centuries. The various Indian tribes of New Mexico and Arizona had eked out a subsistence on Government aid, agriculture, and the selling of hand-manufactured items. The latter had a highly imperfect market and the amount realized was small. When the Santa Fe united with Fred Harvey to boost vacation lands in the Southwest, Indian handicrafts were given a potent stimulus. Fred Harvey undertook to sell the products—pottery, rugs, blankets, beads, silver ornaments such as rings, belts, and bracelets studded with turquoise, and many other articles. The application of modern merchandising methods was a boon to the decadent arts. The demand was enormous, and hundreds of Indians applied their native skill to works of beauty. Connoisseurs engaged by Fred Harvey evaluated the products properly so that ultimate consumers could rely on the final price as a measure of quality. From the impetus given by the associated companies, profitable employment in natural pursuits has been provided the Indians. Their products attained a nationwide demand and are marketed through a host of agencies. Collateral phases of Indian culture have been preserved and New Mexico and Arizona beckon more visitors every year.

Various developments in facilities have been undertaken with a view toward stimulating travel. In 1926 the Santa Fe Land Improvement Company acquired La Fonda Hotel at Santa Fe. The structure at a corner of the plaza was on the site of an historic ruin of the same name which had been the rendezvous of early traders of the Trail. Operation was turned over to the Harvey interests. La Fonda was substantially enlarged and became one of the show places of New Mexico. Operations were integrated with the Fiesta, and La Fonda became the hub of the colorful celebration commemorating the triumphant return of the Spanish into Santa Fe under the leadership of Don Diego de Vargas in 1693. The Hotel also served as a base for excursions to neighboring Indian ruins and pueblos.

The Bright Angel and El Tovar at the brink of the Grand Canyon fulfill the same purpose as La Fonda. The Santa Fe has erected two magnificent lodges to serve visitors. Numerous side-line projects are conducted. The business at the Canyon is heavy and profitable. The greatest returns, however, accrue to the Santa Fe in the medium of increased passenger revenues. The good will generated defies estimate. Prices for the various attractions and products at the canyon are in keeping with the general Harvey policy. They are neither high nor low. They represent the intent to have more patrons five, ten, or twenty years from now rather than an effort to maximize gains today. Fred Harvey is in business for the future as well as the present. Moreover, sales are made and services rendered in such a manner as to relegate money matters to a subordinate position. What is most important to the Company is that the guest enjoy his meal or art object or room. If this is the case the money matters generally take care of themselves. Of course, Fred Harvey is not a benevolent institution or a private community chest for the benefit of the traveling public. As in any other business enterprise, profits are the objective. Fred Harvey differs only in the approach to profits.

Station operations expanded steadily during the present century and at some points new types of enterprise have been undertaken. A drugstore, gift shop, book store, and toy shop are operated in the Union Station at Kansas City. The lunchroom and dining room are available to patrons of all the lines as well as to the people of Kansas City. In 1925 Fred Harvey assumed control in the Union Station in Chicago. This was the second major station which was served by Harvey but not entered by the Santa Fe. The other was at St. Louis. In 1930 Fred Harvey went far afield and invaded the near East by installing the system in the magnificent Cleveland Terminal. Declining railroad passenger travel was more than offset. An attempt to provide meals on a transcontinental airline in 1929 was not profitable.

Changes in travel habits and in the West itself have necessitated many readjustments in Fred Harvey. The increased use of automobiles siphoned traffic away from the Santa Fe and Fred Harvey. The time came when signs were erected to direct highway users to local Harvey Houses. At San Francisco and Newton rail and bus terminal facilities were unified and "Meals by Harvey" made available.

Increased speed on the Santa Fe has been the greatest problem of its ally. This has been brought on by the demands of the public and the technological progress of the railroad. Competition of other companies and buses has been an important factor. Faster trains necessitated fewer stops. In fact, a speed-conscious generation objected to any stops. Diners continued to displace Harvey Houses. Many lunchrooms were closed, including the original one at Topeka.

A final adverse factor has been the gradual narrowing of the gap between Fred Harvey and the West. In the early days Harvey Houses were the only places where fine food was obtainable. The growth of the western cities has brought rivals. None can match the peerless service of the old institution, but they have narrowed the differential to the point where convenience in location of the rivals is becoming the deciding point in patronage. Fine hotels have been erected which can vie effectively for business. Fred Harvey has neither declined nor stood still. Great progress has been made. No evidence is at hand to indicate that Fred Harvey has relinquished the role of pace-setter of western good things of life. Development of agriculture in the West made possible the discontinuance of Harvey dairies and poultry farms. Adequate quantities of chickens, eggs, and milk products could be had from local producers from Illinois to California.

WORLD WAR II

The advent of World War II brought an unprecedented volume to the Santa Fe and Fred Harvey. Passenger travel increased more than 600 per cent. Shortages of vital materials rendered the number of dining cars constant, and more trains stopped again at the Houses as of yore. The old practice brought back nostalgic memories to veteran travelers. The speed of modern times is a heavy price to pay for the delights of meals by the side of the road.

The dining cars emulated the Houses in most respects, but the atmosphere was not quite the same.

War rationing proved doubly difficult to Fred Harvey. Sumptuous meals were no longer possible on the usual scale. A characteristic display of ingenuity enabled the chefs to lessen the consequences. The effect of rationing on the waiters in dining cars seems to be more pronounced than on the patrons. Coffee was one of the first products to be restricted in use. Fred Harvey coffee had a nationwide reputation as a marvel of perfection and uniformity. Diners reveled in a first cup, and the waiters beamed as they poured a second or a third measure from the individual pot served with meals. Rationing meant only a single cup. The frustration of the colored waiters was painful. They had long delighted in climaxing meals with "Mo' coffee, suh?" Some in desperation attempted to compensate by offering unlimited pats of butter. Soon a shortage of fats prevented this individual bit.

Increased labor turnover incident to the war economy and the deluge of business made deliberate dining impossible at times, but the organization never functioned any better than it did in the early 'forties. Operations at resort points were curtailed, but elsewhere business attained record proportions. Two of the eating places had to be reopened to meet the requirements of the public. Over the entire Harvey system the traditional standards were maintained with the greatest fidelity.

The swarm of new employees was integrated into the wartime beehive as quickly and effectively as possible. Training films speeded up the process. Indoctrination was not always perfect. Byron Harvey, Jr., sheepishly admitted that an incident in the Chicago Union Station was virtually repeated a distressing number of times over the system. Ray Barbour, the tactful manager of the restaurant in the Union Station, noticed a new bus boy loading his tray in the dining room in a noisy manner. Ray said politely, "Couldn't you be a little more quiet?" The bus boy snarled back, "You keep your —— —— nose out of my business and I'll keep mine out of yours." Ray retired as gracefully as he could. About two hours later the bus boy shyly approached Barbour and said, "I'm awfully sorry I was rude to you, Mr. Barbour. I didn't know that you were the manager—I thought you were a customer."

Employment soared to over seven thousand during the war. A surprising number were and are second-generation employees. Loyalty of the rank and file of personnel and especially at the supervisory level enabled the Company to cope with the troubled time. Long-established purchasing channels also served the Company well. Buying policy had been to find responsible firms and deal with them without resort to competitive bids. When the days of short supply came Fred Harvey was rewarded.

The wartime peak is evident in the gastronomical figures for 1945:

    5,000,000 pounds of potatoes
    8,500,000 pounds of meat, fish and poultry
    1,679,000 dozen eggs
    41,000,000 meals
    20,000,000 cups of coffee
    1,000,000 gallons of milk and cream

Relations between the Santa Fe and Harvey today are on the same amicable coöperative basis as they were when Fred Harvey and William Strong bound their companies during friendly conversations. The contracts have been supplemented or new ones written in recent years.* Each party is ready and anxious to revise the contract if it becomes unduly burdensome to the other. The Santa Fe wants Fred Harvey to prosper, and Fred Harvey wants to please the Santa Fe. No finer spirit of corporate teamwork can be found.

Santa Fe officials travel too much on their own line and eat too many "Meals by Fred Harvey" to be uncoöperative. The way to a man's heart, be he railroad official or passenger, is through his stomach.

---

*Operations comprising dining-car and news service, hotel and eating facilities predominantly serving railroad passengers and employees, and vending machines in railroad stations have become railway operations under the supervision of Fred Harvey, managing agent. All persons engaged in such operations are now railway employees. Other hotel, eating-house, and newsstand facilities, including those at the Grand Canyon, are leased to Fred Harvey for a rental figure based on profits.

IX

Labor Relations

"It's work all day for damn sure pay
On the Atchison, Topeka and Santa Fe."

THE HISTORY of the labor relations of the Santa Fe shows a sharp cleavage about the time of World War I. During the first period the Company dealt only with its employees. Unions were recognized and negotiations were conducted with representatives of the various employees. For the most part strife was minimal, and an excellent spirit of coöperation and a feeling of trust existed. Wages and working conditions were kept abreast of those of competitors as well as those in other industries. Management went much further and provided, in effect, a broad system of social insurance. This was not done to forestall the organization of the employees; rather, it was a part of a program of enlightened selfishness of the sort epitomized by Henry Ford's revolutionary wage scale of five dollars a day. A happy, well-paid employee was more productive. He was apt to stay on the job, thereby reducing costly labor turnover. He became a booster for his company and indirectly brought business. The collective contentment of all the employees made for better coöperation and smooth teamwork.

Through judicious and forthright administration the Santa Fe developed a family spirit and an intense loyalty on the part of its personnel. The regime of E. P. Ripley following 1895 marked the climax of goodwill. There were some malcontents, but on the whole they were an obscure minority.

Ripley was succeeded by men no less desirous of perpetuating the wholesome labor relations—men thoroughly schooled in the Ripley tradition—but conditions had changed and they were no longer able to deal with a free hand with their own labor force. Abetted by the years of government operation, labor organization had been greatly enlarged. Employees of the Santa Fe joined forces with employees of other railroads. Uncle Sam had convincingly demonstrated that in the future the labor problems of the railroad industry were to be on a national rather than a company basis. The stimulus to unions was substantial. Employees began to look to the Brotherhoods rather than to management, and soon the Brotherhoods were to look to Uncle Sam and to bargaining with the collective management of the railroads. Eventually federal social security was to supersede Santa Fe social security, and countless rules and regulations born of union and governmental wedlock were to partition the province of management. A uniform front was formed on both sides. Differences in spirit and substance yet remain. Old employees retain the loyalties of yesterday, and newcomers still absorb the proud feeling that typifies a man of the Santa Fe.

During much of the early history of the Santa Fe, the number engaged in building the railroad was greatly in excess of those in operation. Little attention will be given to the builders for two reasons: first, the majority were not, in a strict sense, employees of the Company but were retained by contractors; and, second, they were not permanently identified with the railroad but were more or less transient and casual laborers, or local residents who desired some extra income.

The Original Force

The regular force of the Santa Fe was initially small, in keeping with the length and means of the budding project. On June 15, 1869, the Company had over a dozen men in service. W. W. Fagan was the one and only conductor; George Beach, the locomotive engineer; Al Dugan and William Bartling were the brakemen; Britt S. Craft was the fireman; and Jonas Stafford bossed a small section gang. The general office was located in a room over the Costa and Hanley butcher shop, now 612 and 614 Kansas Avenue, Topeka, Kansas. M. L. Sargent and James Knox had little difficulty in doing all record-keeping of the firm. A flimsy partition was installed to segregate nails and tools from the remainder of the general office. When supplies were required on the line the men went to the office and took what they needed. Sargent served not only as chief clerk but also as paymaster, storekeeper, janitor, and general freight agent.

The combination of limited resources and the small number of employees made for an identity of interest of all those on the line. Each man had great responsibility. His failure meant the failure of all. The men who hitched their fortunes to the Santa Fe were men of courage and ability. They did their tasks well and continued in the service for many years. One and all later nostalgically recalled their early experiences. There were no regular hours of work. Each man labored as long as there was something to be done and usually there was plenty to do. The train crew reported daily, and twelve to fourteen hours was a normal day. Overtime was unknown. Since most of the men were on a monthly basis the paycheck was the same regardless of the long hours. The Santa Fe was jokingly accused of being unwilling to hire a man who owned a watch. The rising and setting of the sun were the limits for labor. A slogan of the workers epitomized the give and take: "It's work all day for damn sure pay on the Atchison, Topeka and Santa Fe."

As the road lengthened employees were added and specialization began. Soon the head of a department was not the whole staff but had assistants. The Santa Fe boasted a train dispatcher, a superintendent of bridges, buildings, and water service, a master painter, a superintendent of telegraph, a master mechanic, and a general superintendent. Sargent's manifold duties were parceled among new men. James Moore took over the increasing duties of paymaster.

Meager records and reports indicate that wage payments during the 1870's were consistent with the time and place. Peter Tellin's wages were raised to $3.25 per day when he was advanced in 1872 from fireman to engineer. Avery Turner, who had an illustrious career from the early days to maturity of the system, wrote that conductors were paid $60 per month in 1876. Brakemen received a minimum of $45 plus a good growth of calluses. Section laborers earned about $1.10 per day. Advancement to foreman brought 40 or 50 cents more. Wages were not as low as they might seem on first consideration. Purchasing power of money was far greater in 1875 than today. General standards of living were much lower and enabled workers to obtain the current necessities. Three dollars in 1875 no doubt satisfied more desires than ten dollars would now. Difference in purchasing power of the dollar was only one factor. Differences in wants and goods were equally important. Paddy on the section could "keep up with the Joneses" when Jones clerked in a general store or worked in a mill. The Santa Fe was a good employer. Money was scarce in the territory as well as in the Company's treasury. In short, seemingly low wages were in reality high wages. Apart from the willingness of the Company to recognize the loyalty and productivity of its personnel, the "safety valve of the West" guaranteed a minimum of reward and working conditions. Fertile land was to be had for the asking and with the advent of the Railroad a ready market was assured. The Railroad had to match other opportunities of individuals. Sodbusting was not a great temptation to the men. There was infinitely more drudgery and less romance to it than contemporary writers usually assign. Breaking the prairie often was accomplished by physical and financial breaking of the pioneers. Some waxed rich, others made a comfortable living, still others eked out an existence, and many failed miserably. The combination of a highly mobile labor supply and the simple state of the arts tended to make for a rapid labor turnover. These factors were more than offset by the desirable wages and working conditions offered by the railroad. Already present was that indescribable attraction felt by men who have once worked for a railroad. To them the call of the rails is like the call of the sea to an old tar. Once a railroad man, always a railroad man.

Wages in the 'Seventies

Wages were not uniform in the early days as they are at present. The salary was tailor-made for the man and locality of the work. Men in train service in settled areas were paid less than those whose runs were through the wilds. The bonus at the front was well earned if the testimony of Engineer A. R. Glazier is representative. Glazier ran a train in the vicinity of Lakin, Kansas, during the winter of 1872. He wrote:

. . . our headquarters were at Lakin. That is where we got for a lay-over at night when we got to layover anywhere. We slept in a little boxed building, twelve by twelve, built for the operators. We had it lined and carpeted with green buffalo hides. We had no blankets and the night operator would keep the fires going so we could sleep.

In those days we never got any train-running orders. We ran exclusively by smoke and headlight. We never had any collisions, excepting with buffalo. My conductor was a character. He never wore a coat, he had been a rustler and an ox skinner in the West for years and had never worn a coat since he had been there, and only one heavy flannel shirt. Our food was buffalo meat. Our eating-houses were all in dugouts, and the buffalo meat was piled up outside these dugouts. We would go out and cut off just what we wanted for each meal. The bread came from Lawrence, Kansas, and by the time we got it, it was hard enough to knock down a buffalo with. Black coffee and sorghum molasses completed the menu, and the only change we got in our meals was when we would go to Dodge City to get the engine washed out.

When I first went to the front I learned one of the lessons of my life. I was complaining to Alex Swan, Mr. Criley's roadmaster, about our fare. He replied, "Young fellow, what we have been standing for the last six months I guess you can stand for a few days, for it will take only a few days to relieve you." It did not take me long to tell Mr. Swan that he need not relieve me, as I could stand all that he could, that $140 per month at the front beat the extra board at Topeka about two to one.

The series of lean years during the middle of the 'seventies was a severe strain on the struggling Company. Revenues were impaired by alternate floods and drouths as well as grasshoppers and a national panic. A substantial fall in the general wage level followed. The Santa Fe went counter to the decline for a time. Finally in 1877 the pressure to cut salaries could no longer be resisted.

The wage scale below was reported to have prevailed prior to the paring:

Conductors..............Up to $100 and $120 per month
Engineers................$3.50 to $3.75 per 100 miles (roughly, a day)
Firemen.....................$1.57 to $2.05 per 100 miles (roughly, a day)
Extra crews..............$45 per month but docked for idle days
Trackmen.................$1 per day

A five per cent general cut was ordered for August 1, 1877, and conductors were notified of a top of $75. The first strike on the Santa Fe occurred shortly before the deadline. The stoppage was confined to the men on the freight trains and was conducted ineffectively.

Dissatisfaction persisted after the strike of 1877. The brother-hoods of the firemen and engineers were resisting cuts throughout the Nation and seemed anxious to test their newly developed strength. Without warning the two groups in freight service called a strike on April 4, 1878. The dispute centered at Emporia, Kansas, and developed into alarming proportions. Superintendent C. F. Morse wired Governor George T. Anthony that there was "a large mob about our depot threatening violence." The local sheriff was reported busy trying to organize a posse for protection. Passengers and mail trains were delayed. By the sixth the situation was critical. Anthony sent the militia to Emporia. About $2500 in state funds was expended. The brew was unfortunately stirred when a member of the militia accidentally killed an innocent by-stander. A gun was unintentionally discharged and the bullet struck the Rev. O. J. Shannon, who was sitting in a railroad coach. Tempers were further inflamed but cooled off as the strike efforts waned. By April 9 trouble was at an end.

Ensuing years were to be relatively free of labor strife. The Santa Fe embarked upon a farsighted policy designed to develop the best possible relations with the employees. There is an old saying that "every strike is a mistake of management." While not strictly true, the proverb did not circulate without reasons. Those in control of the Santa Fe were to make few mistakes. They seemed to anticipate the desires of the employees before desires became demands. The result was that the benefits appeared as gratuities and were pleasantly received. But much that was done was not intended to avert trouble. The Company did not make negative objectives predominant. What was done was done in a positive manner, with a frank and open statement of the purpose. Officials believed, within limits, that good pay and working conditions were economical. Sweatshop labor was high-cost, inefficient, and undependable. Benefits were extended to the employees as rapidly as the limited resources of the Company permitted, and when financial strength was developed under the presidency of E. P. Ripley, Santa Fe employees were the beneficiaries of a broad program of social security. The Company developed a spirit of loyalty and coöperation that was never equaled before or after.

The Railroad Y.M.C.A.

Media for creating good will were many, such as support of the railroad Y.M.C.A., hospital association, and employees' magazine, an apprentice system, improved disciplinary methods, a pension program, reading rooms, a death benefit plan, and, lastly, countless other schemes for acquainting workers with their supervisors and administrators.

Railroad Y.M.C.A. work on the Santa Fe began in Topeka in 1882 when the Company donated an old passenger coach for a meeting place. Physical facilities were improved when A. A. Robinson gave the "Y" quarters in a house owned by the Santa Fe. Membership soon outgrew the plant, and Robinson was helpful again. Late in 1884 or early in 1885 he provided a large, two-story frame building. Secretaries John Caldwell and Thomas E. Prout waged war against debt, dirt, and the devil for the benefit of railroaders. The Y.M.C.A. provided a place for recreation after the day had ended in the shops or the crews had come to Topeka after a run. In the hallowed atmosphere a common-sense verdict was rendered to the effect that billiards and cards did not mean eternal damnation. A small circulating library distributed the latest and best books and periodicals. Plays, dances, and various other forms of entertainment were encouraged. Classes were organized in electricity, rate-making, welding, telegraphy, typing, and most of the other subjects pertinent to the needs of the men and the railroad. The "Y" and the Company provided the instructors. Bible-study courses were established which were well attended and did inestimable good. Men engaged in road work were especially benefited by the "Y." The rooms provided for overnight lodging were economical and clean. The importance of this service can hardly be overemphasized. John Purcell, who climbed the Santa Fe ladder from the bottom to the top, recalled that in the early days saloons and dives were the only places for train crews to go. Hotels were few and beyond the means of a fireman. Consequently, he tended to choose the easy way by going to a saloon, buying a schooner, and flopping in a back room. Purcell was so impressed with the plight of both the worker and the Company that he took steps to organize a "Y" in Kansas City. Clean beds and baths were ten cents each. The worker was better off financially, mentally, and morally, and the Santa Fe reaped rewards too.

The "Y" in Topeka was leveled by fire in 1902. The Company was so impressed with the good work done in the past that President Ripley committed the Santa Fe to a pledge of $20,000 for a new structure and $2,000 for furnishings, plus a land site. The "Y" raised $18,000. President Theodore Roosevelt laid the cornerstone on May 1, 1903, before a crowd of 17,000. The Santa Fe not only helped to finance the building but supplied approximately $2,300 annually in money or services (lights, water, heat, etc.) for operation. Patronage swelled. In 1910 the Topeka "Y" provided 36,000 baths and 12,363 beds. Local membership touched 1,600. Other cities on the System had "Y's" too. The Santa Fe was a heavy contributor at all points. The year 1916 saw the peak of the movement. Membership was as follows:

Albuquerque	610
Argentine	312
Cleburne	802
Kansas City	477
Las Vegas	403
Temple	659
Topeka	1572
Pueblo	810

The development of hotels and wholesome recreational facilities in the cities tended to lessen the once acute need for the services of the "Y." The good work, however, persists to the present.

Hospital Associations

Long before group health insurance and hospital associations were common over the Nation, the Santa Fe took steps to assure employees of adequate medical attention. Railroading in the early days was a hazardous occupation. In the unsettled territory of the Santa Fe the consequences were especially severe. Good physicians in the West were few, and quacks and charlatans tortured the helpless public. Primitive methods and facilities multiplied the pain and suffering which attended the many accidents. Employees of the Company were in great need of some program which would systematically meet their requirements. Management recognized this and in 1884 coöperated to establish the Atchison Railroad Employees' Association, with Dr. Sheldon as chief surgeon and Dr. G. H. Hogeboom as assistant. The Railroad furnished financial support, although the lifeblood of the organization was the payments of the member employees. The charges ranged from twenty-five cents to a dollar per month, depending upon salaries, and the check-off system was used. The early hospitals were logically located where existing facilities were most limited. The first one was opened at Las Vegas, New Mexico, on October 11, 1884, one month prior to the completion of a second at La Junta, Colorado. Hospitals were soon opened in other cities. The Santa Fe usually provided the lands as well as funds for the original building and equipment. The Association paid all expenses of treating em-

ployees as long as the injury or disease was not contracted as a
result of "personal quarrels or vicious or intemperate habits."
There were a few additional exceptions as well as a time limit of
four months. Membership was open only to Santa Fe employees
during their period of service.

During 1887 the original Association was supplanted by the
Santa Fe Railway Employees' Association. The scope of the work
was greatly enlarged. In 1887 Dr. John P. Kaster began his career
with the Association. He was to be its chief surgeon over forty
years and to spend more than half a century in building a magnificent system—mute evidence of his own greatness.

Continued enlargement of the Santa Fe family occasioned additional changes in the hospital system in 1891. Four associations
were established to minister to the four major divisions of the
railroad. The original association was rechartered as the AT&SF
Hospital Association. The GC&SF Hospital Association was incorporated in Texas on June 10, 1891, to take care of the employees on the Texas lines of the Gulf, Colorado and Santa Fe
Railway. The Southern California Hospital Association (Santa Fe
Coast Lines Hospital Association after 1904) was to handle cases
in the Far West. The fourth organization, the Atlantic and Pacific Hospital Association (later the Santa Fe Pacific Hospital
Association and finally the Santa Fe Coast Lines Hospital Association), completed the coverage. Purchase of the A&P by the Santa
Fe accounted for the disappearance of the fourth hospital association.

Each of the associations is nominally independent. Those of the
AT&SF and the GC&SF are each managed by seven trustees, three
officers of the companies and four representing employees. There
are nine members of the Board of the Santa Fe Coast Lines Association, with the employees represented by five.

Many hospitals were erected which incorporated the latest developments in architecture and medical science. By 1916 there
were seven well-equipped hospitals in the AT&SF Association and

many more provided for the other associations. The largest hospital was at Topeka and drew patients from a wide area. Other buildings were at Clovis, Mulvane, La Junta, Fort Madison, Ottawa, and Las Vegas. Approximately 40,000 employees were serviced 57,000 times during the year ending June 30, 1915. Facilities were expanded from time to time as needs increased and existing structures became outmoded. A hospital was built at Albuquerque in 1926, and in 1931 and 1950 imposing additions were made to the "mother" structure at Topeka.

The Santa Fe Coast Lines Hospital Association was centered at Los Angeles, with branches at various points on the Railroad. The major unit represented an investment of one and one-third million dollars in 1940.

Not as large as the other associations but just as efficient is the organization on the Gulf Lines. The focal point is Temple, where an ample, well-staffed hospital is maintained. There Dr. A. C. Scott did for the GC&SF Association what Dr. Kaster did in Topeka. Dr. Scott was Chief Surgeon for forty-seven years. Sisters of Charity of the Incarnate Word cared for the patients from the first until 1949. The start was modest. The original staff of four doctors received total monthly wages of $297.95. Monthly receipts were $1,753.75. By 1940 there were twenty-five staff specialists who treated 2,000 cases in one year.

All three associations engage several hundred local surgeons at places where the number of employees is large. Dispensaries are also maintained. Although the associations are ostensibly on a self-sustaining basis the element of subsidy has ever been present. The good as well as good will fostered cannot be overemphasized. Employees have been provided the best in care and protection at a modest cost.

READING ROOMS

The reading rooms of the Santa Fe were established to serve ends similar to those of the railroad Y.M.C.A. They were located where employees had long layovers at points remote from bright social life or where the moral and social tone of cities was not of the best. Reading rooms provided a wholesome place to kill time. Beds and baths, in some cases meals, were available. Prior to 1898 the project was not supported strongly. There were several rooms, but they were ill-equipped and poorly supervised. President Ripley, aware of their possibilities, directed the Reverend S. E. Busser to take charge of the program. New rooms were opened; librarians and attendants hired; books and pool tables purchased; and extensive programs of entertainment planned. This was part of Ripley's policy of fair treatment of employees, but he declared, "We make no pretense of unselfishness—we aim only to practice enlightened selfishness; we want better men, and we are willing to spend money to make them better, because they will do their work more intelligently and more conscientiously, besides being much happier themselves. We concern ourselves with no man's religion or politics—we only ask in him the qualities that make him valuable to the company, which are also the qualities that make him a good husband, good father and good citizen."

The revivified rooms became the social hub of many localities. Members of the employees' families and townspeople were invited to participate. Assignments to desert towns were no longer feared as they had been. Swimming, bowling, libraries, dances, pool, and lectures were to be enjoyed in the most unexpected places. By 1909 eighteen rooms were in operation. Sleeping quarters were available in five. Evidence of the scale of activities is apparent from the statistics for 1909: labor cost of 46 attendants at $150, $25,000; newspaper subscriptions, $2,500; entertainment, $8,000; improvements and renewals, $50,000; total investment, $250,000; library size, 17,500 volumes with a daily check-out of 386; and room use, more than 7,000 each day.* Superintendent Busser modestly wrote, "Garnishment for gambling debts is a thing of the past. Our general superintendent reports the reading rooms con-

---

*The reading rooms enabled development of a hybrid pension system. Employees who were incapacitated for their chosen assignments were given jobs around the reading rooms. A fireman who lost an arm was useful and self-supporting as a librarian.

stitute the best prohibitory system of temperance in the world, beating Kansas and Maine. . . . You never hear a Santa Fe employee applying hell epithets to his officials. . . . Wrecks from carelessness or the violation of rules have been practically eliminated and our property is handled more carefully and life is very nearly safe on the Santa Fe." Busser may not have accomplished quite all that he claimed, but his work had a wholesome influence. The reading rooms were the town halls of many a western upstart. Entertainment and education were provided which otherwise would never have been available. Some of the programs featured Ted Shawn, Waldemar Geltch, Carrie Jacobs Bond, Norma Gould, glee clubs of universities such as Chicago and Oklahoma, distinguished lecturers and professors including Robert A. Millikan, and small symphony orchestras. The circuit was made just as a vaudeville troupe might play to a chain of theaters. Widespread publicity heralded coming events as if a circus were in store. Attendance was excellent. The talent received no fee but did have a generous all-expense tour. In 1911 Busser went to Europe to seek new blood for the programs. He reported that splendid companies had been secured, "among them being the famous Swedish chorus and twenty artists who are talented enough to sing in four languages." Old posters reveal that an extraordinarily high plane of entertainment was offered.

Development of the program continued into the 'twenties. Thirty-five reading rooms were in operation. Later years halved the number of rooms. The entertainment circuit was eliminated in 1938. Reading rooms had been superseded by country clubs, schools, movies, radios, commercial recreation centers, and other things which came with maturity of the West. The machinery for centralized management had been scrapped. The use of available beds has increased in recent years and the reading rooms still afford pleasure and service, but they have not held their predominant position of two or three decades ago.

APPRENTICE SYSTEM

Another plan for the mutual benefit of employees and the Company was the Apprentice System of the Santa Fe. While many railroads have had plans for training skilled shopmen, none have had such a well-developed program. The Santa Fe had long made a practice of securing the majority of its mechanics in the open market. A few were home-grown but not many. Boys in their late 'teens were hired and after puttering around and standing in the way for several years were considered mechanics. No orderly attempt was made to instruct the newcomers, and they were dependent upon occasional advice from any of the mechanics who were inclined to give it. Shortly after the turn of the century, John Purcell's fertile mind conceived the idea of holding classes for the apprentices. Purcell happened one day to be eating in a room with shop employees of Shopton. He sat close to some of the young men who were being apprenticed in the haphazard manner of the time. Out of curiosity he asked them if they knew anything about a blueprint drawing he had at hand. None seemed to know the bottom from the top. Purcell, as an experiment, selected two of the boys for instruction. They went to his hotel for an elementary explanation in the preparation and use of blueprints. The boys were fascinated by the new field opened to them and told the other thirty apprentices. They wanted to learn too. Purcell was petitioned for more information. He was convinced that the boys needed a regular instructor who would explain all phases of shop work to them. Purcell hired a teacher at his own expense, bought paper and lessons, and carried on for four months. It took $45 per month out of his $175 salary. When Purcell was shifted to Topeka the experiment ended for a time.

Following 1900 the Santa Fe had great difficulty securing requisite numbers of skilled craftsmen. Vice-president Kendrick was not well satisfied with the products of the Company's aimless education. When he heard of Purcell's plan, he was impressed and decided that mechanics could be manufactured if they could not be hired. Purcell was directed in August of 1907 to establish his school system, only this time the Company would pay the bills. F. W. Thomas was named Supervisor of Apprentices. A program of careful selection of candidates was developed. Instructors were hired and classrooms provided. Detailed lessons covering every phase of work were arranged for the four-year course. The apprentices combined class work with shop work. A streamlined course enabled the more talented helper apprentices to finish in three years. There was also a three-year training period for graduates of technical colleges and universities. The apprentice system was quick to yield results, and the Santa Fe soon had an abundance of excellently trained men. In 1924 almost 1900 were in school. The supply of graduates exceeded the Santa Fe demand but not the demand of other railroads. Placement was easy. More than 8000 have completed the program since it was established. During the 'thirties few were indentured, but the number swelled as business recovered.

The Company not only trained the boys to work but assumed a paternalistic interest in their behavior. Bands, glee clubs, football, baseball, and basketball teams and college scholarships were sponsored in an effort to achieve maximum development of well-balanced employees. Good timber must have been found and cultivated, for nearly all the supervising officials in the Mechanical Department since 1912 have been onetime apprentices. The program has been a great boon to the Company and to the employees. Union rules have not always permitted the unfettered operation of the system.

Training activities were reduced during the 'thirties but expanded with the subsequent increase in business activity. Over nine hundred apprentices were in various stages of their three- or four-year programs in 1946. Twenty full-time instructors had charge of twenty-nine centers scattered over the system. Coöperation of shop supervisors provided practical as well as theoretical instruction.

SANTA FE MAGAZINE

The strongest single influence working to weld together Santa Fe employees has been the *Santa Fe Magazine*. It was started in 1906 at the suggestion of Albert MacRae, stenographer to Vice-president Kendrick. MacRae was directed by Ripley to assume the editorship. Since that time every employee has received the monthly publication. Circulation has been as high as 80,000.

The accomplishments of the *Magazine* have been many. Employees have become acquainted with each other. Common problems have been threshed out in the columns, and suggestions interchanged on how to fire a locomotive, how to manage a section gang, how to do the multiplicity of things that must be done to operate a great railroad. The personnel have gained a better idea of what constitutes their source of livelihood. A company of far-flung holdings ordinarily has difficulty in securing a community of interest. Through the medium of the *Magazine* freight solicitors in California had a better idea of what facilities and service the Santa Fe had in Texas. One western Santa Fe man was reported to have routed traffic consistently over the Texas and Pacific in preference to the Gulf, Colorado and Santa Fe because of the two competitors he liked the former. Imagine his chagrin on learning that the Gulf, Colorado and Santa Fe was a subsidiary of the Santa Fe. The *Magazine* has done much to eliminate the possibility of errors of this sort. The advantages of a well-informed personnel are inestimable. Countless articles on problems of other railroads as well as on the industry as a whole have given new perspective to the thousands who make up the "family."

In the early years of publication the *Magazine* was tempered by a crusading spirit against loan sharks, tobacco, and drink. Approval was given to various get-rich-quick ventures such as eucalyptus groves and pecan orchards. A few years of seasoning eliminated such extraneous matter. Each issue has had its joke section, thus assuring all readers of an adequate repertoire for every occasion. Poetic souls on the Santa Fe found an outlet for their better offerings. Especially outstanding were the efforts of S. E. Kiser, who contributed regularly in early years. "Among Ourselves," devoted to local news of the doings of employees all over the system, has been a major attraction.

The format has long been the model for "house organs" and compares favorably with that of the best magazines offered for general circulation. Some sort of medium is absolutely necessary in any large company, especially one whose operations extend over a wide area. The Santa Fe has met the need well—almost too well: an official facetiously remarked that the men were so anxious to read the magazine that they did not wait to take it home but sat down and read on Company time.

The Brown System

During the early days of the Santa Fe, employees were seldom disciplined for infractions of rules—they were fired. Later they were suspended for varying lengths of time depending upon the gravity of the offense. Finally, the Brown system of discipline was adopted and provided a systematic approach. It prescribed that merits and demerits be put into bookkeeping form as debits and credits to the account of each man. The debit may be offset with credit marks granted afterward because of a perfect record. An accumulation of sixty debits in excess of credits was cause for suspension or dismissal. The employee was notified of debits and therefore forewarned. Continuity of employment and better work were thus secured, to the benefit of employer and employee.

Pensions and Death Benefits

One of the most potent factors in cementing the bond between management and labor was the pension system for retiring aged employees. The plan was voluntarily established by the Santa Fe and wholly financed by the Company without any tax on salaries such as is deducted under the present federal plan.

Preliminary to the actual establishment of the pension system, a survey was made to ascertain the number of old employees. A Topeka timekeeper was assigned to the local task. At that time the Santa Fe had a pair of Irishmen who had lived since the late days of Methuselah. They were skeptical of the motives of anyone who inquired about their age—fearing that the boss was thinking they should be let out. The two, Owen Callahan and his friend, Peter Cart, were laying some pipe when the timekeeper asked their age. "None of your God-damn business," said Callahan. "The boss's orders," replied the timekeeper. "We're both thirty-five," Cart averred. The two centenarians were enraged when the pension system went into effect, and the Superintendent told them that they were not eligible because they were only thirty-five.

Officials of the Company had been contemplating a pension system for some time. Retirement programs were already in effect on a few roads. Hundreds of men in service had labored long and loyally for the Company. They deserved a rest, their output had declined, yet they needed income. A pension system was the fair solution.

On December 12, 1906, the Board of Directors adopted a voluntary pension system, to become effective January 1, 1907. Administration was by a five-man "Board of Pensioners," appointed by the president. Pensions were to be paid to any retired officer or employee who had been continuously in the service of the Company during fifteen years preceding the date of retirement at the age of sixty-five or the date of incapacitation. Service with companies acquired by the Santa Fe counted. Employees hired at fifty or over were not eligible (few were hired). Retired men could engage in other work not prejudicial to the Santa Fe and get pensions. No contractual rights were conferred. The amount of the pension was to be 1¼ per cent of the first $50 of the highest average monthly pay during any consecutive ten years, plus ¾ per cent of the excess over $50, but under $300, multiplied by the total number of years in service. The minimum was $20 and the maximum was $75 unless exceptional service warranted up to 25 per cent more. The following example gives a better idea of the method and amount. Assume an employee labored twenty-eight years and that his highest ten-year average of monthly pay was $90. He would receive 1¼ per cent x $50 x 28 plus ¾ per cent x $40 x 28. The monthly pension would be $25.90.

The Santa Fe was never a happier family. The benefits were more than a gesture of good will; they represented a substantial annuity at no out-of-the-pocket cost to the employees.* Salary checks were undisturbed. An increase in the number of pensioners was a function of the increase in the number of employees. The seniority system worked to hold up retirements in the face of declining numbers of employees during the 'thirties.

On June 16, 1937, notice was given that the June 1, 1937, checks were the last ones to be paid under the voluntary pension plan of the Santa Fe. A federal plan had been drawn under the Railroad Retirement Act of 1937 and the Carriers' Taxing Act of 1937 which gave promise of constitutionality. Two previous plans had been ruled invalid. Payments to employees in most cases were increased substantially under the new plan, but the source of 50 per cent of the stipends was deductions from salaries. The remaining 50 per cent was a tax on the railroads measured by payrolls. The monthly payment was computed on a basis of the average monthly wage between January 1, 1924, and December 31, 1931, rather than the ten-year high used by the Santa Fe. Payment was 2 per cent on the first $50 of the average, 1½ per cent on $51 to $150, and 1 per cent up to $300. The rates were revised in 1948 to 2.4 per cent on the first $50, 1.8 per cent on the next $100, and 1.2 per cent on the remainder up to $300 per month.

Maximum payment under the federal plan was originally $120 but was later raised to $144. All employees were covered immediately, and the scheme was retroactive in that employees

---

*It is rather interesting that Ripley was so enthusiastic about the retirement program, for he snorted when an interviewer quizzed him about retiring at seventy-two.

"Experience of the centuries has taught that the busy man is the happy man. I want to keep happy, so I keep busy. My advice—if it were asked—to men over middle age would be to fasten their minds on the kind of work that will last to the end of their days; not make retirement from business their goal. No man should retire—if he would get the most out of life. The Lord made man for work, and he should be willing to let the Lord fix the quitting time."

eligible for retirement could receive the newly authorized payments notwithstanding the fact that no contribution had been made. Employees who retired immediately after the act and all of those retiring to date gained enormously at the expense of those who are to retire under the plan when it has been in operation longer. Younger men were immediately asked, in effect, to subsidize older men.

The federal plan provided for lump-sum payments to the estate of employees in event they died before retirement or before they received as much as they had paid under retirement taxes. This feature will be explained and compared later with the death benefit plan of the Company.

The average age for retirement under the federal plan, as shown in the chart, was about the same under the Santa Fe program. Average single-life annuities under the federal plan were $69.42 in 1939, and $75.98 for 1946. These figures may be compared with Santa Fe payments of $46.38 in 1935 and $63.67 in 1936. If the upward trend of the Santa Fe had continued, the difference would be little if any.

Since the Santa Fe payments did not involve contributions by the workers, the Railroad Retirement Act appears to be disadvantageous. Of course, the coverage under the federal act was much broader, so that thousands were included who would have received nothing under the Company's plan. In reality, adequate figures are not available for comparison. The Company plan was substantially more favorable to disabled employees. If a man was incapacitated at thirty-five, for example, after fifteen years of service, he was pensioned. Under the federal plan the man has to have either thirty years of service or have attained the age of sixty. The 1946 amendment to the Railroad Retirement Act liberalized the provisions. Annuities were payable to individuals disabled for their regular employment with twenty years of service or aged sixty and individuals with ten years of service or aged sixty who could not engage in any regular employment.

PENSIONS OF SANTA FE EMPLOYEES

Calendar Year	Number pensions or annuities awarded by calendar years	Average Age at date of retirement		Average years of continuous service at date of retirement		Average pension or annuity
		Yrs.	Mos	Yrs.	Mos.	
1907	55	70	8	24	3	$24.23
1908	59	67	4	24	7	21.78
1909	54	66	11	23	9	24.34
1910	40	66	10	21	9	22.14
1911	49	63	11	22	11	24.44
1912	69	64	1	24	1	24.56
1913	82	63	11	23	6	23.84
1914	69	64	10	24	5	25.10
1915	75	64	4	24	6	25.70
1916	81	65	7	26	1	27.07
1917	73	64	1	26	5	28.67
1918	61	67	1	27	2	30.51
1919	63	65	6	27	10	31.78
1920	76	66	11	27	4	31.69
1921	174	66	2	26	5	30.31
1922	113	63	11	26	8	35.27
1923	120	64	10	28	0	37.24
1924	168	65	8	29	4	42.69
1925	212	66	9	28	11	39.40
1926	156	65	8	28	2	39.89
1927	163	64	10	30	6	42.69
1928	207	65	2	29	10	47.56
1929	208	65	2	28	9	45.46
1930	322	66	3	29	4	45.38
1931	307	64	9	28	7	44.46
1932	325	66	1	28	8	42.54
1933	243	64	7	28	2	44.11
1934	185	63	4	27	4	42.71
1935	277	64	7	30	2	46.38
1936	567	69	6	26	0	*
1937	1,236	67	9	24	6	
1938	937	66	1	24	7	
1939	710	65	11	26	5	
1940	598	65	3	27	6	
1941	516	64	6	27	8	
1942	403	64	4	28	5	
1943	553	64	6	28	10	
1944	638	65	0	29	7	
1945	731	65	3	29	11	
1946	577	65	7	31	0	
Jan.-July 1947	670					
Total	12,222	65	9	27	6	

*Comparable figures after 1937 are not obtainable. The Company pension system was

The great boon to railway employees in the federal program was independence of benefits from service with any one
railroad. A man could shift from one company to another and
take up where he left off at a later date. Or, he could quit and at
the age of sixty-five enjoy payments based on early earnings.
Prior to 1937 the Santa Fe pensions were a powerful factor in
decreasing the mobility of labor. Employees developed a heavy
vested interest which was nontransferable. Men thought twice
before changing to another position. No specific information is
available on the extent to which a greater turnover of labor has
stemmed from the new program. A strong influence has been
exerted, and the acute labor shortage during World War II has
contributed to the increase in the turnover. Seniority rules with
their key to promotion and existing job levels remain as deter-
rents to changes. No large number of "labor tramps" or "floaters"
can be said to have developed out of the Act, but under it the link
between the Santa Fe and its employees has been weakened. The
same may be said of any other railroad's relations with its personnel. Employees are much less dependent on the Company and
less stable, and they look to Uncle Sam to protect them during
the twilight of life.

During the years of peak payments the Santa Fe expended a
million dollars annually for the pension program. When the
Federal Act superseded the Company program the burden of
the pension program took the form of taxes. The cost under the
new program was two and a half times greater in early years.
Employees contributed the same amount as the Company. The
number covered was substantially in excess of the number benefited under the Company program but not in proportion to the
increased cost. An estimate which admits several imponderables
indicated that three or four times as many were covered in 1941

---

terminated May 31, 1937.
    Employees granted Company pensions, and granted government annuities in a later
year, Company pensions being canceled, are reported in this statement in the year in which
the Company pensions were granted.

at six times the cost. The figures below show the comparative cost of ten years of the Santa Fe Benefit System with twelve years of the Federal System.

Federal System		Santa Fe Benefit System	
1937	$2,294,004	1927	$ 475,888
1938	2,038,838	1928	530,974
1939	2,109,090	1929	599,480
1940	2,377,310	1930	692,215
1941	2,886,344	1931	799,717
1942	3,714,155	1932	920,970
1943	4,921,228	1933	986,023
1944	5,661,095	1934	998,906
1945	6,168,624	1935	1,060,475
1946	6,596,768	1936	1,156,217
1947	11,242,149		
1948	12,043,162		

The burden of retirement annuities was raised substantially in legislative changes made during 1946. The Railroad Retirement Act was amended to provide for greater coverage and liberalization of benefits. The changes were so far-reaching that a higher tax schedule was recommended to assure actuarial soundness. The tax schedule was advanced to 11½ per cent of payrolls for 1947 and 1948, 12 per cent for the next three years, and 12½ per cent in succeeding years. Equal division of the rate was made between employer and employee. Payrolls of 200 million will call for retirement contributions of over 24 million split between the Company and its personnel.

The second leg of Santa Fe social security was the death-benefit system. Like the pension program the cost was borne entirely by the Company and payment was a gratuity. The minimum was $250 and the maximum $3,000. The basis for determination was 5 per cent of the last year's salary or wage times the number of years in service. A man needed only two years of employment to be eligible. Beneficiaries had to be designated this rule was rigidly enforced. Selection of the earnings of the final year was more generous than is immediately apparent. In industries where position and payment are based on merit, many older employees sustain cuts or are fired and find jobs that in effect entail cuts, but seniority in railroading tends to make salaries go up with years of service. The last year prior to death is likely to be the peak year. The benefits were extended to pensioned employees shortly after the original announcement.

The amount conferred by the Company may be judged by sample cases and a table of total payments. Assume that the man used in the pension examples died at sixty-five. He had averaged $75 per month for twenty-eight years with a ten-year high of $90, and should have earned $100 during his final year. His beneficiary would receive $1,200x28x5 per cent or $1,680. A man earning $2,000 his last year of a twenty-year career would provide a nest egg of $2,000 for his heirs. Payments over the years were:

DEATH BENEFIT PLAN
May 24, 1934
Operations from July 1, 1916 to June 1, 1934

Year	Payments	No. of Cases	Av. Pay	Av. Age	Av. Service
1916 (6 mo.)	$ 54,306.81	71	$ 764	51	14
1917	123,472.73	168	734	53	14
1918	148,645.52	207	718	51	13
1919	259,817.61	345	753	56	13
1920	217,051.05	233	931	54	14
1921	257,142.92	247	1,041	53	15
1922	307,443.55	289	1,063	50	15
1923	337,056.60	295	1,142	56	16
1924	303,808.09	272	1,117	53	15
1925	329,985.95	328	1,006	54	15
1926	330,009.41	341	967	54	15
1927	391,816.29	382	1,025	54	16
1928	381,581.52	350	1,090	63	17
1929	455,779.68	412	1,106	56	17
1930	514,377.88	433	1,186	56	19
1931	431,808.75	376	1,148	57	19
1932	540,479.89	503	1,075	58	19
1933	420,884.54	408	1,032	57	20
1935 (5-mo. estimate)	171,743.83	172	999	58	21

Classification of Beneficiaries to year ending December 31, 1933

Number of Cases	5,660	Aunts	4
Widows	4,765	Cousins	2
Children	496	Mothers-in-law	2
Parents	234	Sisters-in-law	4
Brothers and sisters	112	Daughters-in-law	3
Nieces and nephews	23	Deaths from accidents on duty in 1933	10
Grandchildren	10	Deaths from all other causes	398
Husbands	5		

Classification by Occupations December 31, 1933

	Number	Total Pay	Average Pay
Officers	123	$358,318.08	$2,913.16
Clerks	478	492,590.95	1,030.53
Engineers	487	774,235.69	1,589.81
Firemen	66	61,358.93	929.68
Conductors	271	519,039.29	1,915.27
Brakemen	168	177,390.42	1,055.90
Switchmen	121	127,654.39	1,055.00
Station Agents	178	218,824.97	1,229.35
Telegraph Operators	122	132,076.27	1,082.59
Machinists	426	337,822.29	793.01
Car repairers and carpenters	456	338,565.48	742.47
Section foremen and laborers	558	305,369.14	547.26
All others	2,206	1,962,222.30	889.49
	5,600	$5,805,468.20	$1,025.70

When the Railroad Retirement Act of 1934 was passed the Santa Fe announced that death benefits would not be given after July 25, 1934. The increased burden on the Company plus the protection of the federal plan was mentioned as the reason for this action. Under the national system as it finally crystallized, the employees' heirs were entitled to the difference between the annuity amounts paid and 4 per cent of the creditable compensation after December 31, 1936, if the latter were greater. No payment was in order if the pensioner lived a long time. The lump sum paid under this plan was much less than that paid by the Santa Fe. The percentage used for computation was 1 per cent less, annuity payments being deducted, and actual earning, rather than a last and likely peak year, times service being used. Average lump-sum benefits paid through June, 1941, were $149.75 with a final year of $218.64. These figures were far below the Santa Fe averages. Company coverage was broader for death benefits than for pensions, and no wide disparity in coverage existed between the federal and Company plans for payments to heirs of railroaders.

The inadequacies of the federal plan for death benefits were eliminated somewhat by statutory revisions in 1946. The previous system had definitely proved unsuccessful and few employees had elected to use a joint-and-survivor annuity.

The Santa Fe provided no counterpart to the program of unemployment compensation launched by the Government. Unemployment insurance for railway employees was originally a part of the Social Security Act of 1935 and was handled by various state agencies. Beginning on July 1, 1939, the Railroad Retirement Board took over the administration on a nationalized basis. The most that could be said for the Santa Fe was that the management had always tried to lop off the peaks to fill the

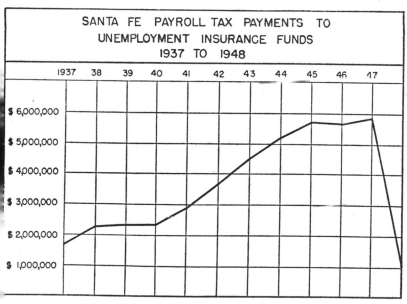

SANTA FE PAYROLL TAX PAYMENTS TO
UNEMPLOYMENT INSURANCE FUNDS
1937 TO 1948

valleys in the curves of cyclical and seasonal employment. Costs of maintaining the federal program rest solely on the railroads.

During war years the unemployment insurance tax payments were many times in excess of the benefit payments arising out of conditions of full employment and the increase in wage rates in relation to a set scale of benefits. Upward revision was made in the payments to employees and the payments period in 1946. The cost of unemployment insurance was borne solely by the Railroad by means of the payroll tax of 3 per cent. Under the Wolverton Act the tax was reduced to ½ per cent effective January 1, 1948. A graduated scale of rates was to apply up to 3 per cent if the Railroad Unemployment Insurance Account declined to designated levels. Unemployment arising out of sickness calls for benefits similar to those for involuntary idleness. The same statement is true for maternity benefits. The length of period for payments is strictly drawn with some relation to the physiological processes involved. "Such a [maternity] period is defined as beginning 57 days before the expected birth of the child and extending for 116 days or at least until the 31st day after the day the child is born. If birth takes place after the 84th day of maternity period, no benefits will be paid for the days after the 84th and before the date of the birth. . . . The daily benefit rate will be the same as for unemployment and sickness except that the benefit rates for the first 14 days of the maternity period and the 14 days immediately following the birth of the child will be 1½ times the regular rates." The Santa Fe's increased employment of women in recent years will occasion application of maternity benefits with far greater frequency than would have been possible in earlier years had the program of social security been in existence.

The total cost of social security may therefore be 15½ per cent of payrolls plus hidden costs of red tape, which will be very great. In order to obtain continuity in the discussion of social security for the Santa Fe, parts of the story of labor relations have been told prematurely. Thus far little has been said of the full record beyond the 'seventies.

WAGES AND CONTROVERSIES

Peace reigned between the Santa Fe and its personnel during the 'eighties. Wages were high by comparison, for agriculture had its troubles. With beefsteak ten cents a pound in Kansas, a man did not need many dollars. The following table from the *First Annual Report of the Bureau of Labor and Industrial Statistics of Kansas* gives an accurate summary of wages paid on the Santa Fe during 1885 in Kansas.[1] For the sake of comparison the statistics of other railroads in the state are included. Engineers, firemen, conductors, and brakemen were assumed to work 365 days and the remaining employees 306.

	Monthly	Average of Other Railroads in Kansas
Superintendents	$295.18	$249.62
Clerks	58.27	55.42
Train Dispatchers	98.52	105.38
Station Agents	53.11	49.44
Master Mechanics	107.10	150.71
Local Engineers	104.63	106.40
Local Firemen	58.70	58.06
Passenger Conductors	103.72	94.85
Freight Conductors	75.13	84.21
Brakemen	52.01	56.24
Machinists	61.96	58.65
Watchmen	38.76	36.21
Section Hands	33.66	32.64
Telegraph Operators	47.47	46.67
Laborers	35.44	33.46
Flagmen and Switchmen	59.00	45.39
Others	50.74	44.11

The average earnings of Santa Fe employees amounted to $581.07, slightly over the average of other railroads. Wages during the next years averaged $562.25 in 1886, $629.84 in 1887, and $660.27 in 1888. The great Gould strike did nothing to upset the peaceful scene on the Santa Fe, although a few struck sympathetically when

Burlington employees were out. The strike of the locomotive engineers in 1888 was widespread, but enough men remained on the job to operate the engines. During 1890 the Company made substantial concessions to the men in train service, further raising its prestige as a good employer. The Bureau of Labor and Industrial Statistics reported:

A notable instance of this new departure in the conduct of railroad affairs was furnished by the Santa Fe last summer, when after a lengthy conference, a comprehensive agreement was entered into between the management and the men engaged in train service. The September, 1890, number of the *Trainmen's Journal* thus alludes to the matter:

"A Valuable Agreement"

"The recent agreement between the trainmen of the Atchison, Topeka & Santa Fe and the company is a valuable one, and the employees whose persistent and determined efforts secured it have reason to be proud of their work. It is profitable to pay good wages to toilers . . . .

"This agreement went into effect August 1, and provides that passenger conductors on Eastern, Middle, Southern Kansas, Southern and Western Divisions shall receive $125 per month, and passenger brakemen $60 per month; for New Mexico and Rio Grande, conductors, $130 and brakemen $65 to $70; freight conductors on local trains will receive $90 per month of 26 days, and brakemen $60."

This action on the part of the Santa Fe might have been profitably followed by other railroad corporations. The complicated dual basis of payment of men in road service was already in existence, as well as seniority provisions. Detailed rules were agreed upon for overtime, turn-arounds, and other points at issue.

Wages remained at almost the same money level from 1890 to 1900, although real wages rose substantially after 1893. Employment rolls were cut as an outgrowth of diminished freight and passenger traffic and the acute financial straits of the Company. Average daily wages of 9,847 employees in Kansas were $1.91 in 1898. Hours had been shortened to ten or twelve, though train crews often had consecutive assignments which kept them on duty for longer periods.

The first of three major strikes of the shopmen occurred in 1893. The other stoppages were in 1904 and 1922. Although the

Santa Fe territory had been harried by economic distress during the first three years of the 'nineties, wage rates held up well. General business conditions were good, and money wages on all railroads advanced slightly, though lagging behind prices of consumer goods. Negotiations were instituted between the brotherhoods and the Company. The joint grievance committee of the Brotherhood of Railway Conductors and the Brotherhood of Railway Train Men found the Santa Fe very approachable in 1892. Wages were raised; the major increases were on runs west of Dodge City. Various working rules were altered, as well as bonding arrangements.

About the same time that the agreement was reached with the conductors and trainmen, the grievance committee of the Order of Railroad Telegraphers met for the first time to press for an upward revision of the pay schedule. Demands and counter offers were made in the best spirit and an amicable settlement was reached. Increases of $2 to $20 a month were scattered among all the 900 men in telegraphy service over the Santa Fe. The cost to the Company was set at $80,000.

The terms given to telegraphers and dispatchers on the Santa Fe proper were offered to men on the Gulf Lines. The GC&SF contingent was not satisfied and began a strike during October, 1892. Events took a strange twist, and the strike was unintentionally expanded into one of major proportions. A more unexpected walkout never occurred than that which followed. The case is so unusual that the complete story as published in the *Report of the Bureau of Labor and Industrial Statistics for Kansas*[2] is reproduced:

The fake telegraphers' strike on the Santa Fe system occurred at 10 o'clock on Monday morning, October 17, 1892, without previous warning. The telegraphers employed in the various offices along the Santa Fe railroad left their instruments, and for the next 10 hours chaos reigned, so far as the traffic of the road was concerned. The trouble originated through H. N. Barker, an operator employed at Dodge City. A strike was in progress among the operators of the Santa Fe southern line, and of the Gulf, Colorado & Santa Fe. Mr. Barker, knowing the fact, left the following "message" on his table, as a joke, he says, on the manager:

"Galveston, October 16, 9:30 a.m.—All dispatchers and operators: In view of the fact that the Gulf, Colorado & Santa Fe is controlled by the Santa Fe road, I therefore declare a strike on the entire Atchison, Topeka & Santa Fe system, to take effect at 10 o'clock a.m. Monday, October 17. See that no telegraphing is done, no tickets sold, and that nothing is done to injure our cause. See that the company's property is cared for until you are regularly relieved.

"D. G. Ramsey, Grand Chief."

The following history of the affair is taken from the **Topeka Capital** of October 18:

The first man who came in saw the dispatch, wondered that he had not heard of it, and wired it to Nickerson to ask the operators there if it were true. Nickerson received the purported order, and in an instant had flashed it on to the next station, and away it went over the whole system like wild-fire. Everywhere it was taken for genuine, and at 10 o'clock the men walked out.

"To all Operators and Dispatchers   Dodge City, October 17.

"The message from Galveston, of the 16th, signed D. G. Ramsey, order-ing a strike, is a fraud, written by me simply for a joke on Manager Swett.

"H. N. Barker, Operator."

But the men were all out, and the first message was believed, and the second one was thought by them to be the fake, instead of the opposite, as was really the case.

The strike, coming just at a time when the road has such heavy freight business, was particularly unfortunate, and all but the scheduled trains were greatly interfered with. In the general offices 10 men were kept busy all the time. Yesterday the room presented a rather lonely appearance. Super-intendent Gemmell and Assistant Superintendent Sperry and one other man were the only ones to finger the keys the whole day. Mr. Sperry held the Chicago lines open from morning till the strike was over, but it was the only one the strikers would allow to be used.

Whenever an attempt was made to connect with any of the smaller stations the striking operators would break in with cross messages and interruptions, nor would they stop here, but would send vile epithets over the line to the men at headquarters, calling them "scabs," and cursing them in indecent language.

It was just 8:12 p.m. when the general office operators returned to work, upon receipt of the following telegram:

"All Dispatchers and Operators: Emporia, Kans., October 17

"The message dated Galveston, Tex., October 17, signed D. G. Ramsey, has been proven to be a bogus message. All men will return to work on receipt of this message. This does not apply to men out on Gulf Colorado & Santa Fe.

"J. D. Somers, Chairman."

The feelings of the irate chief, on hearing that his name had been forged to a message ordering a strike, are shown in the following message received last evening:

"R. B. Gemmell: East St. Louis, October 17

"The man who sent out the forged bulletin should be arrested. I thought my deputy, Mr. Tobey, now at Galveston, had issued the request, he having full authority in the adjustment of the Gulf, Colorado & Santa Fe. Please bulletin this, my order, to all our Santa Fe members, except the Gulf-Colorado line, to immediately return to work.

"D. G. Ramsey."

It is safe to say that Chief Ramsey's suggestion that Barker ought to be arrested meets with the approval of most of the men whom he has placed in such an unfair position. There were many mutterings of disgust to be heard coming from the little group of telegraphers who gathered yesterday and last evening to talk about the strike. They denounce the sender of the bogus telegram in the strongest terms for the manner in which he led them into this trouble.

The railroad company is feeling hard towards the telegraphers for the utter disrespect in which they held the rules adopted April 1. The last rule, as it appears over the signatures of both parties, is as follows:

"The Atchison, Topeka & Santa Fe Railroad Company on its part, and the dispatchers and operators on their part, do hereby agree that they will perform the several duties and stipulations provided for in this agreement, until 30 days' notice has been given by either party to the other, requesting a change in the same.

"J. D. Somers, Chairman AT&SF Committee
"D. G. Ramsey, Acting G.C.T.
"H. R. Nickerson, Gen. Supt.
"R. B. Gemmell, Supt. Telegraph.
"Approved: A. A. Robinson, Second Vice President
"and General Manager."

Under this rule, it will be seen the men agreed not to quit work without 30 days' notice. Yesterday morning, when the bogus dispatch was received, they gave just 20 minutes' notice.

The telegraphers of the western division of the Santa Fe did not go out on strike, because the fake Ramsey message having been started east, first, the later message from Barker saying that it was only meant for a joke reached the western division first.

The men here have no grievance whatever, and when they went out yesterday on an order supposed to have come from Ramsey, it was only with the idea of helping the striking telegraphers on the Gulf, Colorado &

Santa Fe, who are striking now over the adoption of practically the same schedule adopted in this city after a long wrangle last April.

Galveston, October 17.—The telegraph operators' and station agents' strike on the Colorado & Santa Fe railroad is in a status quo condition to-night. The schedule of wages demanded is $65 minimum salary, and at one-man stations 5 to 10 per cent on ticket sales. All operators, and station agents who are operators, are out except about 10. Twelve operators from the auditor's office were sent up the road today to help out the system.

Wichita, Kansas, October 17.—Trains from this point commenced running at 8 p.m. as usual after being tied up since 10 a.m. All the telegraphers went to work at 7:30, in obedience to the order of their chief telegrapher. Shippers here are jubilant over the result.

Kansas City, Mo., October 17.—A little after 10 o'clock this morning the Santa Fe operators in and about Kansas City received the message to go out. To many of them it was something of a surprise, but as soon as each man wrote the word "Ramsey" he took his hand from his instrument, and from that time forth he was deaf to any business message over his ticker. All he could hear was when some brother operator called up to talk about the strike. At 10:30 o'clock, for all practical purposes, the lines along the Santa Fe were as dead as though every one was grounded.

The operators and train dispatchers at Argentine quit as promptly upon receipt of their bulletin as did those in Kansas City, and things at the Santa Fe yards there are in a nice tangle. No train has gone out since 9 o'clock this morning, and this afternoon 50 train crews are lying idle, not being able to take out a train because they can get no orders.

The operators will carry a train until it gets to a place where it can switch, but after that it can get no further orders.

John Altberff, in charge of the Western Union office of the union depot, called up all the Santa Fe operators on his circuits after they went out, but could not get a single response. It is absolutely impossible to tell just where any train is on the whole system, or to find out anything about it.

The men could not have chosen a better time to inaugurate their tie-up. The Santa Fe system, from one end to the other, is just now doing a heavy freight business all through the great grain regions of the West, and has more business than it can well look after, and is having a hard time to prevent blockades.

The Santa Fe was slow to match small wage increases granted to shopmen by other lines in the Southwest. Dissatisfaction grew and other grievances appeared in 1893. Two detailed accounts of following events were filed with the Bureau of Labor and Industrial Statistics. One was submitted by the Company and one by labor leaders. The variance in the versions was noticeable, yet there was full agreement on the presentation of the fundamental issues.

Various shop crafts had had agreements with the Company for several years. Late in January of 1893 a convention of machinists assembled in Topeka to formulate a new labor contract. The workers wanted increases in rates of pay, especially in Colorado and New Mexico, where Santa Fe wages had lagged. Provision was made to restrict the use of apprentices, to limit the working day to eight or ten hours, to provide time and a half for overtime, to advance by seniority, and to require investigation for establishing the basis for discharge. The machinists, boilermakers, and blacksmiths were aggrieved. John Player, superintendent of motive power of the Santa Fe, indicated that the Company would raise wages to match other lines, but he refused to enter into the remainder of the agreement. While negotiations were still under way in Topeka the machinists suddenly walked out on January 28 at Raton, New Mexico. On learning that wage increases had been ordered they returned on Monday, January 30. Company officials continued to balk at signing the agreement. The situation was further aggravated when a machinist named Hoffman was discharged at Las Vegas for allegedly soldiering on the job and for insubordination. Fellow workers demanded reinstatement or investigation and were refused. Workers on the New Mexico division walked out in protest on February 22. Two weeks elapsed before the Topeka committee representing the workers and the Company were able to meet and reach a decision concerning Hoffman. The Santa Fe agreed to an investigation and further agreed to reinstatement if the charges leading to dismissal were unfounded. The men returned to their places March 9 and the case of Hoffman was reviewed. All agreed that there was good and sufficient cause for the discharge.

The boilermakers and blacksmiths joined the committee of machinists negotiating in Topeka and a new agreement was proposed. This was rejected by management. The issue was not so much wages as greater union recognition. On April 3, Mr. Player indicated that the Company would not only match but exceed wages on competing lines, and on April 7 and 8 the increases were announced. At noon of April 8 the men went out in all the shops. The strike was conducted more peacefully than most, but the Company did secure a restraining order under injunctive proceedings to curb activities of the strikers. Largely through the mediatory services of leaders of the brotherhoods in train service, a satisfactory compromise was drawn on April 22.* The men returned to work, both sides regretting the whole affair.

Peace prevailed until 1900, although minor disorders occurred during July of 1894. The telegraphers of the Gulf Lines set off the torch in 1900. An agreement had been signed between the Company and the telegraphers on the Santa Fe proper. The contract was to be operative for one year subject to renewal. Similar terms were offered to employees of the GC&SF but they refused to sign, and struck. The agreement on the Santa Fe proper had been in force only two months when the contract was ignored and on December 8, 1900, a sympathetic strike spread over the whole system. About 50 per cent of the workers went out under the leadership of M. M. Dolphin. This was the second time that Santa Fe telegraphers had violated their agreement to give notification of a strike as well as to strike while a contract was in force. The Company was adamant, and by December 21 the strike had been broken. The result was disastrous to the union, because the management refused to sign a contract on any terms, charging that the irresponsibility of the men prevented the formulation of an agreement that would be observed. Not until federal control were relations resumed.

With minor exceptions the strike history of the Santa Fe had alternately featured the telegraphers and the shopmen. The turn of the machinists in the shops came in 1904. On March 23 the district lodge of the International Association of Machinists presented the Company with a schedule of desired rules for employment

---

*An agreement of August 1, 1892, was reaffirmed and provision made for taking the strikers back.

and wages. The pay revisions were modest, but the other changes were not. The qualifications of machinists were set forth in detail. No discriminatory classifications could be set up like the alleged current ones. Handy men, helpers, and laborers were not to be moved into machinists' work. Apprentices were to be restricted. Any dismissals were subject to elaborate review. Passes, overtime, exemption from the hospital association, and minimum wages constituted the other points of issue. One unusual demand was that "any and all machinists now or hereafter employed by the above-named company shall not be required to fill out any form of application for employment, and shall not be subjected to or have to undergo any form of physical examination."

The demands of the machinists were rejected by the Santa Fe on the ground that all the requests embodied new conditions which would be attended by decreased output and efficiency. Some officials thought that a closed shop could be read into the union demands. A strike vote was taken in all the shops, and the strike was ordered for nine o'clock on the morning of May 2. The Company declared a lockout for seven o'clock that morning in Topeka. The strike was bitter and protracted. Most of the 800 machinists went out. The union claimed that 296 left the service in Kansas. Violence was reported at nearly all the twenty-one shops and roundhouses. On May 6 revised demands were made which eliminated the wage changes but retained most of the other terms. No doubt the new proposal would have been accepted if it had been offered at first, but relations had become so strained that the management was balky. Disorders increased. An injunction of May 9 designed to curb activities of the strikers had little effect. Notice was given by the Company that all those who failed to report for work on May 9 were to be classed as if they had resigned. Mass meetings were held and broadsides circulated. One was headlined:

"Santa Fe Excursions are Unsafe for You to Patronize
"Standard Oil Greed
"Incompetent Workmen, Small Wages, Rush Work,
Workmen Dissatisfied."

A. E. Ireland, a leader of the machinists, branded the Santa Fe as "a monopolist of the worst type, the only purpose of which was to get the better of the working man."[3]

The Company succeeded in retaining some of the original force and gradually added newcomers as well as a few who went out on the strike. The battle continued for several years before the union admitted defeat.

Uncle Sam in Labor Relations

Storm clouds threatened in 1916 when men in train service of the Nation united in demands for an eight-hour day. Strike ballots were distributed over all lines including the Santa Fe. President Wilson and Congress capitulated because they feared paralysis of the whole economy in the face of war. The Adamson Act went into effect in spite of the vigorous protests of officials of all the railroads.

Uncle Sam proved to be a very generous employer during the period when the Government operated the railroads. Unions were formed and recognized. Wage increases were freely given and working rules liberalized. Checks for larger amounts could be made out easily with no unpleasant consequences, because the companies were to pay the bills.* Dozens of disorders outcropped in an effort to hasten distribution by Santa Claus.

The period of government operation was one of nationalization of labor relations in the railroad industry. Wages and working conditions were made relatively uniform throughout the country. Workers were organized in many fields of labor in which they had hitherto been unorganized. The new unions were recognized and began to function as a unit. Pressure was brought in Washington rather than in a state capital or with a single company. The Government provided machinery for handling disputes. Decisions were to involve cross sections of all railroads rather than a single concern.

---

*Railroads were paid by the United States amounts beyond expenses, but after the return to private control the railroads were stuck with the wage rates which had been granted so freely.

Title III of the Transportation Act of 1920 established the Railroad Labor Board with broad jurisdiction.* The new body was promptly asked by the brotherhoods to grant pay increases. The rise in the general cost of living was weighed heavily by the board, and the employees received average advances of 22 per cent. About the time the new wage schedule went into effect, net operating revenues of all the railroads were in a precipitous decline. Increases were granted in freight rates, but relief was obscured in the continuation of difficulties. The railroads then appealed to the Labor Board for a wage reduction. The Board listened attentively to testimony concerning the decline in the cost of living and wage reductions in other industries and ordered an average cut of 12.2 per cent during the summer of 1921. Both sides were disappointed. Strike votes were taken by most of the brotherhoods. Railroad executives began steps to secure further reductions. Meanwhile hearings were conducted on the working rules. Under the United States Railroad Administration, national working rules had been adopted which governed starting time, methods of determining wages, overtime, physical examination, and almost every other phase of employer-employee relations. The carriers wanted the national agreements set aside in favor of local rules. The decision of the Board was a compromise and did much to foster the swelling antipathy between the shopmen's organizations and the carriers.

In the spring of 1922 hearings were held on the additional wage requests of the carriers. On May 28 the decision was announced, to be effective July 1, 1922. The "Big Four" were unaffected. Maintenance-of-way employees were cut 5 cents per hour except foremen, mechanics, and mechanics' helpers, who were cut 3, 4, and 1 cent respectively.[4] In a second decision in the series shopmen were cut from 5 to 9 cents, with the majority sustaining a decrease of 7 cents.[5] A third decision affected stationary engine and boilerroom employees, clerical forces, and those in the signal department.

---

*The act was pushed in order to avert a strike which threatened.

The decisions were bitterly received and the shopmen were especially resentful. On July 1, 1922, the first nationwide strike on the railroads occurred. Some 400,000 were reported to be out in the shops.

The Santa Fe, like other railroads, was confronted with the strike. Though the issues were identical for all, the carriers waged the struggle relatively independently of each other as part of their attempt to get labor relations off a national basis. The shopmen of the Santa Fe had been at odds with the management following the layoff of 15 per cent of the men during 1921. As in the machinists' strike of 1904 the battle was fierce and long. It was waged all over the system while the larger battle was fought in Washington.

Shortly before the outbreak of hostilities the Company posted a notice for the six shop crafts that all strikers would lose their pension, death benefit, and seniority rights. This induced many who were on the fence to join those who had planned to remain on the job.* On July 6, 2896 were at work in the shops, so that the Santa Fe was short 10,662 or 78½ per cent. Employment in Topeka was 51 per cent. Charges and countercharges were made and the Company enjoined certain strike activities. The men claimed that the law-enforcement officials were dominated by the Company, which sought pensioners to help keep the trains mov-

---

*One employee wrote this account of his pathetic position:

"As the dinner pails were opened each noon at the Topeka Shops during the latter part of 1921, groups of mechanics, helpers, and laborers, as well, entered into glib discussions of the ever present problem of capital and labor. These discussions were precipitated largely by the organizers of the American Federation of Labor.

"In each man's heart there throbbed an unfailing sense of loyalty to his fellow workers engaged in his craft and inversely, in most cases, there was, also, a sense of loyalty toward the management of the railway shops. Early in 1922, important developments placed these workers in an extremely embarrassing situation. The labor organization decided to strike. Torn between two alternatives, the workers had to decide whether the balance of his loyalty would swing toward the labor union or toward the company.

"The wide-eyed children in a family whose head was to be affected by this situation listened eagerly from day to day as the father discussed developments with the mother, particularly those regarding the sources of much impending unhappiness for that home. Two days before the strike was called, however, this bread-winner suffered personal injury at his work. Over a week's hospitalization was necessary for recovery. The decision was temporarily delayed but had to be reached. The decision was—to resign! Thus, the risk of inviting the contempt of his fellow workers already on strike was avoided and, in a measure, the record was kept clear with the company. Capital and labor had both taken their toll!"

ing. There was great difficulty in keeping the rolling stock in condition. Efforts to secure strikebreakers were concentrated at Shopton, Iowa, which was regarded as the bottleneck of the Santa Fe. The shopmen were aided by occasional stoppages by men of other brotherhoods. Some three thousand passengers of the Santa Fe were marooned in the deserts of Arizona and California when train crews abandoned their posts.

The Santa Fe held out although several railroads signed the Baltimore Agreement, which permitted the return of the workers on essentially the carriers' terms. New men were gradually added and the strikers rehired (as if they were newcomers). The strike had been costly for both sides.

Since 1922 there have been only two strikes on the Santa Fe. One was the national strike of 1946, and the other was the firemen's strike against four selected systems (including the Santa Fe) in May, 1950. The Company can no longer pursue an independent policy in coping with trouble. Legislation has unified the front of management and the brotherhoods. Wage disputes and controversies over working conditions are now processed through an elaborate machinery created by a legislative process of trial and error.

A general view of the labor history of the Santa Fe reveals relatively few disorders. The number of strikes was low not only in the absolute sense but also in the relative sense. The troubles after 1910 were part of a national struggle, and those before 1910 were infrequent and either of short duration or limited extent.

GROWTH AND CHANGES IN THE FAMILY

As the mileage of the Santa Fe lengthened and the Southwest was settled, the number of employees steadily increased. Employment reached a peak during World War I, sagged, and then went up again. During the depression of the 'thirties employment fell to less than half what it had been during the first World War. Preparedness for the second period of hostilities was accompanied by another increase in personnel. In 1940 the average number employed was 41,300 and by 1942 the number was 53,890. The number in service continued upward but remained far under the early high of 80,000 notwithstanding the fact that more ton miles of

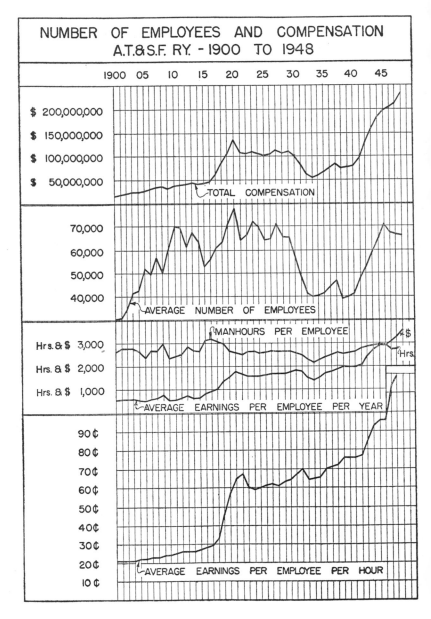

freight and more passenger miles were recorded. The chart given above shows the changes in number, hours, and earnings since 1900.

Many changes took place in the personnel of the Company in the course of time. In the early days the Santa Fe like other railroads relied heavily upon the Irish. The lure of politics proving too strong for them, the percentage of Irishmen in service declined gradually, though they are still prominent. Paddy was replaced on the section by Mexicans. At first the latter were used only in Arizona and New Mexico. By 1910 they were to be seen in service all over the system. Mexicans made excellent track workers if handled properly. Displacement of the Irish was signalized in 1913, when the Santa Fe issued Spanish dictionaries to all track foremen. Mexican nationals were used extensively during World War II under an emergency agreement between the United States and Mexico. The peak came in June, 1945, when 11,725 were on the payroll of the Company. Acute labor shortages in many departments accounted for utilization of many of the Mexicans in work other than track maintenance. Re-located Japs were also made available and proved to be excellent workers.

Indians were used in numbers up to several hundred on the Atlantic and Pacific lines down to 1900. They were chiefly Apaches, Navajos, and Mojaves. Their early refusal to wear clothes was a source of much embarrassment to passengers. Oddly enough, they did excel all others as shovelers. Indians sent with wrecking crews invariably turned the occasion into one of gross thievery. Many found employment in the shops in Albuquerque. They were replaced to a certain degree by Japanese. The education of the Indians has improved their quality, and many of them are currently employed. The Santa Fe has engaged Negroes from its earliest days. Their use has increased somewhat over the years.

The employment of women has expanded since Mrs. Caroline Anderson was hired in 1874 as a clerk at the Topeka station. Most of the women were engaged to do clerical and stenographic work in the offices, but some became telegraphers, station agents, and car cleaners. None have ever been hired for work on the section. During the first World War the number was greatly increased because of the general labor shortage. Peace brought a diminution. The number employed in 1929 was estimated at one thousand. World War II increased that figure to 3,500 in 1943, one-third of these being engaged in work ordinarily assigned to men.

Women served as signal tower operators, agents, freight handlers, turntable operators, yard clerks, track sweepers, drill press operators, sheet metal workers, engine wipers, fire builders, and timekeepers, and in countless other positions in which the fair sex had never been engaged before. To the surprise of many oldtime employees who had the usual skepticism about the weaker sex, women showed equal and in many cases superior efficiency in tasks that only men had been believed capable of performing. Decades of prejudice melted away, and the post-war role of women in railroading in general will be much more important than in pre-war days. The type of women engaged during the period of acute labor shortage was substantially different from that in preceding years. The women were not lassies filling the gap between the last day of school and the first day of marital bliss. They were older and in many cases working for more than the means with which to acquire a trousseau. Wives, mothers, and sisters of soldiers plus women not otherwise classified contributed to the war efforts in one of the most direct ways possible—working for a railroad.

Railroading is no longer the last redoubt of men. A special department of women's personnel was established in 1943 to integrate the swelling numbers into the working force.

Annual wages of Santa Fe employees at the turn of the century averaged slightly less than $700. Hours of labor were long. By 1915 earnings had risen to $854.81 (excluding officials). These figures may be compared with $548 in 1900 for all railroads and $815 in 1915.[6] Hours were simultaneously being shortened. The average employee of the Santa Fe received 27.2 cents per hour and worked a little over 60 hours a week. His status was relatively unchanged as far as purchasing power was concerned. The war boom was responsible for a sharply increased pay check. A bonus of 10 per cent of annual salaries was given in December of 1916. Another bonus of 10 per cent of six months' salary was paid July 1, 1917, and a third January 1, 1918. Wage payments had doubled by 1920. The cuts discussed in connection with the strike of 1922 curtailed money wages, but real wages were not adversely affected over the years. Money wages on the Santa Fe in 1923 were 79 per cent above those of 1915, and the hours of labor had declined 17 per cent. Real wages advanced, although the gain, about 12 per cent, was less impressive. A series of increases stemmed from the various negotiations incidental to the Railway Labor Act of 1926. Early in 1932 employees of the Santa Fe as well as those of other railroads voluntarily accepted a 10 per cent cut. It was to last one year, but because of the continuance of the depression, the period of the cut was extended twice for a total of seventeen months. In 1934 leaders of the railroads agreed with the brotherhoods to a gradual restoration of salaries. By April of 1935 the 1931 level had been attained.

RECENT WAGE DISPUTES

Improved traffic conditions in 1937 prompted a move for higher wages. A committee was set up by the carriers. Negotiations failed and the case went to the National Mediation Board. The resulting boosts averaged about 8 per cent for all employees, including those on the Santa Fe. Once again the increase seemed poorly timed. Net railway operating income vanished into thin air. An attempt was made by the carriers acting as a unit to secure a 15 per cent increase in freight rates. The Interstate Commerce Commission conceded a disappointing 5 per cent. Relief was then sought in the form of a 15 per cent reduction in wages. The case went through the usual channels to the National Mediation Board. The latter was unable to induce agreement, and the President was asked to appoint an Emergency Board. After hearings were conducted, the cut was not advised. The railroads accepted the report and a strike was averted.

Increases averaging 41 per cent were sought in 1941 by the operating and nonoperating employees. The gamut of stopgaps was run and the opinion of the Emergency Board rejected by the brotherhoods. The Board was reconvened to act as a special Board of Mediation. Employees in the transportation group were given an increase of 76 cents per day and the rest 80 cents. The estimated burden on the Santa Fe was set at $12,500,000, based on 1941 payrolls (47,569).

Labor unions representing the nonoperating employees requested an increase of 20 cents an hour and a minimum wage of 70 cents an hour in 1942. Early in 1943 the operating employees asked for wage increases of 30 per cent or $3 per day, whichever was greater. Once again the negotiations were begun under the cumbersome mechanism of handling labor relations in the railroad industry. An Emergency Board appointed by the President recommended an increase of eight cents per hour for the fifteen nonoperating unions. Both the railroads and employees agreed to the finding, but the proposal was disapproved by the Office of Economic Stabilization. In the meantime the request of the operating organizations was refused by the Emergency Board. An increase of four cents per hour was recommended and rejected by the employees.

Both the operating and nonoperating groups called strikes for December 30, and the President made unsuccessful attempts to induce arbitration. The War Department was then ordered to take possession of the railroads on December 27, 1943, in order to avoid interruption of the war effort.

Federal control was terminated January 18. The final agreement worked out by the Emergency Board amounted to nine cents per hour for the operating organizations and a one-week vacation with pay. The nonoperating unions were awarded increases of nine to eleven cents an hour, which was from one to three cents more than they had agreed to accept. Demands for higher pay in Diesel engine service which were made in 1941 were repeated in 1944. Increased rates in pay on Diesels were authorized. Pressure of work during the height of hostilities prevented employees from enjoying the vacation periods which had been provided in the agreements reached early in 1943. Extra payments were made in lieu of vacations, and the total expenditure in 1944 was $2,747,000. Requests of 1944 for more liberal vacations for nonoperating employees were successfully mediated in 1945, increased vacation allowances being provided after five years of service. The operating employees asked for pay increases of 25 per cent.

More significant than the wage increases themselves were demands for revision of working rules. The request of nonoperating employees eventually took the form of an addition of thirty cents per hour to existing rates of pay. Differences with the nonoperating organizations and three of the five operating unions were arbitrated in 1946 and resulted in an increase of sixteen cents an hour, retroactive to January 1, 1946. The finding of the arbitrators was not satisfactory to the unions, and notice was served of new demands for the balance of fourteen cents of the original request for thirty cents. A fact-finding board appointed by the President of the United States awarded the engineers' and trainmen's unions an increase of sixteen cents an hour, along with minor concessions on rules. The recommendations were acceptable to the carriers but were rejected by the employees, and a strike was ordered for May 18, 1946. The President obtained a five-day postponement of the strike and urged both parties to accept the sixteen-cent increase plus a 2½ cents per hour increase effective May 22, 1946. The engineers and trainmen refused the proposal and went on strike May 23, 1946. Trains rolled to a stop, travelers were stranded all over the nation, and city dwellers worried about their food supply. President Truman made an appeal to workers without success. He was castigating the unions before a joint session of Congress with recommendations for anti-strike legislation when news of the capitulation of the engineers and trainmen was made public.

During the two-day strike the Santa Fe was able to operate the Chief and a few mail trains. Government control was relinquished on May 26. The proposals which the President had recommended were applied, resulting in an increase of 18½ cents in the wage scale. Continued inflation in 1947 led to demands for further wage increases. Nonoperating unions were accorded increases of 15½ cents an hour effective September 1. The gain was equivalent to an increase of 15 per cent. A like increase in cents per hour was granted to the trainmen and conductors effective November 1 along with revisions in working rules. Agreement could not be reached with the remaining three operating brotherhoods, and negotiations continued, only to lead to governmental seizure of the lines in May, 1948.

The Government relinquished control on July 8, after agreement on 15½ cents. By August of 1948 requests for wage increases were pending which involved all organized employees. Increases of ten cents an hour for operating unions were agreed upon. The nonoperating employees asked for a forty-hour work week with the same pay as had been received for forty-eight hours. The unions also sought time and one-half for Saturday, double time for Sunday, a minimum of eight hours on either of these days, and a 25-cent increase. An Emergency Board recommended, and both sides accepted, the shorter work week, effective September 1, 1949, with no reduction in weekly pay and with a 7-cent hourly increase. Penalty payments on week ends were denied, but time and one-half was awarded for the sixth and seventh days per work week. Separate terms applied to yardmasters and marine service and dining car employees.

Late in 1948 both the engineers and firemen sought to revive part of the earlier Diesel requests by requiring assignment of another engineer and firemen on multiple unit road locomotives. An Emergency Board denied the engineers and sustained the argument of railroad officials that the request amounted to "featherbedding." Another Board denied the demands of the firemen. An unsuccessful strike followed on four major systems, including the Santa Fe, in May, 1950.

Pros and Cons of Featherbedding and Seniority

The labor relations of the Santa Fe and the railroad industry reveal an impressive array of uneconomic practices. Railroads in recent years have had more downs than ups, but an examination of their labor relations discloses that the railroads are doing surprisingly well in the light of crippling regulations. Train-length laws, full-crew laws, starting-time rules, onerous limitations on spheres of workers, dual bases of payments in train service, and seniority combine to put a heavy burden on operations. The Santa Fe shares the handicaps along with other railroads.

Oklahoma and Arizona have harried the Company from time to time with laws which placed limits on the length of trains. The avowed purpose was to increase safety, but the real objective was to increase job opportunities. Arizona, California, and Texas have been responsible for the imposition of another "make-work fallacy" by full-crew legislation. Costs of operations on branch lines swelled and led to abandonment of feeders. The California law was repealed by referendum in 1948. The legislature having failed to give relief, the railroads took their problem to the voters. The full-crew law was set aside and a measure adopted which gave the public ample protection without subjecting the companies to unwarranted expenses. Featherbedding exists on the Santa Fe in about the same degree as it does on any other railroad. Starting-time rules are identical and job classification equally restricted. The dual bases of payment of crews and employees on passenger trains does not vary from company to company. An engineer on a passenger train has done a day's work when he has traveled a hundred miles or worked five hours. In 1900 a hundred miles or five hours amounted to the same thing, but the speed of trains has been greatly increased. A train may run a hundred miles in two hours now and qualify the crew for a full day's pay. Exorbitant hourly earnings are possible. Monthly earnings of individuals are checked by union limitation on mileage in order to spread the work. A basic day in freight service is eight hours or a hundred miles and involves financial burdens on the Company similar to those in passenger service. Improved locomotives, rolling stock, and better roadbeds have speeded trains so that a hundred miles may be covered in much less than eight hours.

The seniority system is probably the greatest of all drags on railroad efficiency. Seniority prevails on the Santa Fe as on all other roads. Seniority is an employee's rank in point of service relative to others performing the same task within a given district. The system determines promotions, layoffs, demotions, recalls, and filling vacancies. Employees begin at the lowest job in any sequence. As men die off above or jobs are created, advancements from the bottom are determined by the length of service. The ability of the Company to weigh merit has steadily declined, so that an especially promising man cannot be favored over one who can just "get by." Seniority in any one district or line cannot be transferred. If a man is an extra fireman in California he cannot transfer to Illinois and retain his seniority, nor can he point his efforts toward becoming a train dispatcher instead of an engineer and retain his seniority even if he stays in the same area. The general result is that employees are not always advanced on the basis of merit and ability.

Railway labor unions have sought seniority rules from the beginning, and as indicated earlier in the chapter the Santa Fe accepted seniority in some crafts as early as 1890. Recognition has spread. Great impetus was given during the United States Railroad Administration when agreements embodying seniority were obtained by virtually all organized groups. Today seniority is an integral part of the complicated railway labor structure.

Small power of perception is needed to see the shortcomings of the seniority system or the few good features. Promotions do not go to the most able. Advancement of capable and ambitious employees is checked. The quality of those holding the higher jobs is diluted. The more capable are frustrated and normally tend to withdraw to other work at early stages in employment. A larger number probably refuse railway employment at the outset rather than enter into strait-jacketed channels. Seniority combined with the absence of piece payments fosters "get-by" performances and stultifies initiative.

The lessening of job turnover incidental to seniority is said to avoid costly attendant expenses. Actually seniority often causes a half a dozen break-ins when only one might be necessary in the absence of seniority. The system not only works to deter workers from going from one company to another but, worse yet, precludes movements within a company. A young man might begin in the shops and after ten years realize that his aptitudes were better suited to train service. Seniority would probably cause him to remain in shop work and where he would no doubt be advanced.

All that has been written about its demerits does not mean that seniority should be totally ignored. Men should be rewarded for their loyalty. The best reward private industry offers is continuity of employment—not promotion. Often the reward is demotion in preference to outright firing. Merit measured not only by past performance but by potentialities should be the basis for promotion if any company is to function in keeping with the tenets of our capitalistic order.

Damning seniority in the Santa Fe or any other railroad is idle folly, for the system is so firmly entrenched that only a revolution or some other catastrophic event could dislodge it. At times the cloud has its silver lining, and during the period of a general labor shortage such as World War II certain advantages are apparent. The security and certainty of tenure possessed by employees with seniority cause them to resist the lure of higher wages in booming industries.

The offset to seniority is an extraordinarily strong personnel department. Young men should be selected who will develop as more responsible openings appear. Much greater care should be taken to hire men of promise in railroading than in any other field. Most important of all, the personnel department should have general jurisdiction. A candidate's aptitude should be examined and he should be placed where he is fitted.

The Santa Fe did not have a personnel department for many years. The one finally established limited its scope of activities to handling problems arising out of union working agreements. No attempt was made at centralized record-keeping. Workers were seldom transferred from one department to another, and if they were the personnel department had nothing to do with the transfer. Circumscription of union rules, seniority obstacles, the compartmentalized organization of the Company, and lack of centralized control over hiring postponed or deterred development of an active personnel department. Within the last decade a positive program has been inaugurated. Greater selectivity is being exercised, and centralized record-keeping has been instituted. Widespread training programs for supervisors and junior officials have already yielded excellent results that show even more promise of being a tonic for business efficiency. The program for the future embodies two features: more careful choice of personnel and systematic training once it has been hired.

The independence of the Santa Fe as an employer has declined. The Santa Fe in the past pursued a liberal policy and won the support of its family. Pensions, death benefits, and good wages and working conditions rendered employment very attractive. Young men in their prime stayed with the Company at times when labor turnover for most industries was high. Today, the conditions of labor are uniform over the nation. No single company can deviate from another in thousands of matters which seem more properly in the sphere of management if any vestige of independence were to be shown. Wages are substantially the same over the country with inadequate regard to local conditions—nor can the Santa Fe alter them. Pensions and death benefits no longer make men specifically grateful to the Santa Fe but, instead, to Uncle Sam. This change will no doubt make the highly productive men of younger age more mobile while seniority will effectively exert its influence over those who are in the period of decline. The latter stayed before and will continue to remain.

A single railroad has difficulties in maintaining a more progressive program of labor relations than other railroads. The
avowed intention of unions is to maintain uniformity of wages
and working conditions throughout the country. There is a question whether employees of the Santa Fe gain by national bargaining. One of the most potent arguments for the united front of
railroads during wage negotiations, as they are now conducted, is
the ability-to-pay theory. (Perhaps "lack-of-ability-to-pay" would
be a better appellation.) Mediatory and emergency boards have
given considerable weight to the contention of the railroads that
their financial distress was too great to permit increases or to retain existing levels. If bargaining were on a basis of individual
lines the argument would be invalid. Over the years the Santa Fe's
productivity has been outstanding. Few railroads have more ability
to pay or willingness to pay.

In Retrospect

Recounting of railroad wage disagreements and recitation of
examples of featherbedding tend to be misleading. These difficulties may well be minor annoyances in a system which is essentially good. Relations between the Santa Fe and its family of
employees compare favorably with those prevailing in any other
company. An examination of the wartime performances of the
Railway discloses many accomplishments supporting the conclusion that management and labor coöperated far more than they
disagreed. The spirit of the employees is still good, and Santa Fe
management, which has risen from the bottom, has the common
touch.

X

Pruning and Controlled Growth

Come, all ye bold Wagoners, turn out man by man,
That's opposed to the railroad or any such a plan;
'Tis once I made money by driving my team,
But the goods are now hauled on the railroad by steam . . . .
It ruins wheelwright, blacksmiths, and every other trade;
"Damned" all the railroads that ever was made!
—John Omwake, *The Conestoga Six-Horse Bell Teams of Eastern Pennsylvania.*

EFFICIENCY AFTER REORGANIZATION

THE ATCHISON, Topeka and Santa Fe Railway was judiciously managed following receivership. Great care was taken to avoid the assumption of any property or obligations which might prove burdensome. The early period of loose accounting gave way to one of accuracy and conservatism. If any doubt existed whether a certain expenditure was an operating expense under maintenance or an addition to the capital investment, the former was favored. Ex-president Reinhart would have chosen the latter. The worship of size or length of the lines gave way to a sense of responsibility to make each mile of track justify the continuation of its operation from the point of view of profitable investment. Management was determined to make the reborn Santa Fe as efficient as possible.

The general receivership committee coldly examined the advisability of retaining the Colorado Midland and took no moves to maintain control. Bondholders of the Midland foreclosed, and the Santa Fe forfeited its investment in stock. All contracts between the two companies were set aside. Acquisition of the Midland had been a costly venture, but Santa Fe officials were satisfied to accept the loss before it became larger.

The decision to split with the St. Louis and San Francisco was unanimous. The Santa Fe had invested about $25,000,000 in the Frisco, and, although the money was lost, the management found the facts difficult to accept. Control of the Frisco meant access to St. Louis and contacts with many eastern railroads. Yet these connections had not been profitable in the past. Ripley and his associates saw little to be gained by holding the smaller line. The common stock held by the Santa Fe was recognized as valueless, but some worth was attached to holdings in senior securities. The latter were sold to the majority bondholders of the Frisco after a long period of negotiation. A total of $5,633,000 in par netted $1,971,550 on a basis of 35. Mutual cancellations of inter-company floating debts and claims was made. In the spring of 1896 the two firms were separated.

The A&P posed special considerations not present in the cases of the Midland and the Frisco. The line from Isleta, New Mexico, to Mojave, California, was a fundamental part of Santa Fe plans from the earliest days. Without the A&P the Santa Fe was merely a middle-western road; with the A&P the Santa Fe was a transcontinental railroad. While cross-country traffic had not been remunerative in the past, the millennium seemed at hand. California was developing prodigiously in agriculture and commerce. The long-waited traffic gave promise anew of the wisdom of a California outlet. The heavy investment of the Santa Fe in railroad mileage in the southern part of the state made the retention of the A&P essential to preservation of property values unless another line should be built by the Santa Fe across New Mexico and Arizona. The A&P was excellently located, and any new line would be disadvantageously routed. Although the A&P has often been regarded as a bridge between eastern New Mexico and California, local traffic had begun to develop on a modest scale. Santa Fe officials admitted that the western line was entitled to a more equitable division on through traffic receipts which would improve earnings.

During the period of receivership, groups of A&P bondholders, who blamed the Santa Fe for their woes, attempted to split the two companies. The parent company blocked the moves. In December, 1895, Aldace F. Walker and John J. McCook of the Santa Fe resigned as A&P receivers. They were succeeded by Charles W. Smith, ex-president of the A&P. The appointment served to placate the aggrieved interests. Receivership of the A&P overlapped the Santa Fe's in duration. Composition of sharp differences was time-consuming. A three-man board of arbitration was created to ascertain the proper distribution on through traffic over the A&P, Frisco, and Santa Fe. The men were instructed to determine what split, if any, should be made in the rent paid by the A&P to the Southern Pacific for the line between Needles and Mojave. A report was issued on the problems during the summer of 1896. The share of the A&P on-through business was advanced from $15,000 to $20,000 per month. The Santa Fe was to pay one-half of the rental on the Mojave division, thereby relieving the A&P of a burden of $18,000 per month. The Board reported that earnings during the first half of 1896 had shown a remarkable gain.

While steps were taken to arrange a foreclosure sale, Edward King and Victor Morawetz of the Santa Fe were busy negotiating with the A&P bondholders. A deal was arranged for the purchase of the entire issue of $16,000,000 in Western division first-mortgage 6s of the A&P. Payment was by $8,400,000 in par of the general-mortgage bonds of the Santa Fe and 92,000 shares of preferred. These securities had been authorized and reserved for acquisition of the A&P. The Santa Fe also paid $530,000 in cash and agreed to assume the outstanding obligations of the A&P receiver. Foreclosure was later completed under the mortgage covering the bonds purchased by the Santa Fe. The sale of the property was confirmed by Judge Collier at Albuquerque on May 4, 1897. The Central division was taken over by the Frisco. A new corporation, the Santa Fe Pacific Railroad Company, was federally chartered to assume possession of the vital line from Isleta west.

The last of the dead limbs of the Santa Fe was sawed off in March, 1897, when the Company arranged to exchange the line to Guaymas for the Mojave division. The invasion of Mexico had been another losing project. Rails south of Benson were logically in the territory of the Southern Pacific. The mileage was held by the New Mexico and Arizona Railroad as far as the border, and by the Sonora Railway to Guaymas. The Mojave line, owned by the Southern Pacific, was properly a part of the Santa Fe. The trade was mutually satisfactory. Both lines were in deplorable condition. Mileage was comparable. The Santa Fe had to pay $156,750 to make up the difference in the valuations of $6,718,000 and $6,874,750 respectively. The transaction carried out the intention of William B. Strong when the Mojave division was originally leased from the Southern Pacific in 1884. Although the trade was for all purposes completed in 1897, titles could not be assigned until 1911.

INTENSIVE DEVELOPMENT OF LINES

The effect of the pruning of the Santa Fe was to reduce the mileage of the Company to slightly less than 7,000 miles. But what remained was hardy and capable of resisting the severest blight.* What had been eliminated was good riddance and what had been retained reflected the utmost sagacity.

The assumption is frequently made that the great building era of the Santa Fe had ended by the time of receivership. But this conclusion is wholly unwarranted. The Santa Fe more than doubled in size after the post-receivership pruning. The expansion, however, was intensive rather than extensive. The perimeter of the territory had been well defined by the end of the century. Within the area were naked limbs. Feeders were few save in Kansas. The Company was to build, purchase, or acquire a dense growth of branches. Contemporaneously this meant a heavy flow on the trunk and

---

*One minor portion of the system conspicuously lacked strength. This was the isolated St. Louis, Kansas City and Colorado Railroad Company projecting fifty-seven miles from St. Louis to Union, Missouri. Efforts had been made to sell the defunct line and a sale was finally consummated November 30, 1899.

double-tracking, grade and curve reductions, heavier rails, stronger bridges, improved roadbeds, and block systems. The Santa Fe had to rebuild old lines, duplicate tracks, and double the mileage. The period was characterized by a more scientific approach to expansion. The feasibility of new mileage was coldly calculated. Injection of business and engineering analyses in no way lessened the romance in construction. Each project had new and interesting aspects. The West was far from settled. New lines were projected through pioneering country. Other lines were built in well-developed communities where the significance was equally great. The so-called "romance of railroad construction" is a function primarily of technological and social progress. Given a lapse of years so that old methods are outmoded and imaginations play on facts, the days gone by develop an aura of heroism. Acute discernment would reveal greater romance in the current operation of any company as it wrestles with the innumerable problems of everyday affairs.

The post-receivership expansion of the Santa Fe was under excellent guidance. Victor Morawetz, the general counsel, was one of the most capable corporation lawyers of his time. Aldace F. Walker, chairman of the board, was a man whose impromptu decisions reflected the wisdom of years. Edward P. Ripley,* the president, was an admirable example of an American "Captain of Industry." He was without doubt the outstanding personality associated with the administration of the Company until the time of his death.

----

*Edward Payson Ripley was born in Dorchester, Massachusetts, October 30, 1845. His ancestors had settled in the vicinity in 1630. Ripley's only ancestral boast was that there were nine blacksmiths on the family tree. Educated in the local grammar and high schools, he entered, at seventeen, the employ of a Boston dry goods house. In 1868 he was engaged by the Pennsylvania as a contracting agent in the freight department. Two years later the Burlington claimed his allegiance. Ripley successively advanced from a clerkship to New England agent, general eastern agent, general freight agent, traffic manager, and general manager. He resigned in 1890 to become a vice president of the Milwaukee and came to the Santa Fe at the end of receivership.

As president of the Santa Fe, Ripley more than restored the good name of the Company. He had no equal in public-relations work. Ripley developed a spirit among the employees which belied the great size of the Company. Last but not least, he expanded judiciously and operated soundly. Under Ripley the Santa Fe finally became the sort of Company envisaged by its early promoters.

The triumvirate wisely decided to concentrate initially on renovating the existing Santa Fe lines. Purchase or construction of new mileage was deferred until the foundation of the new Company was firmly settled. A year and a half of the new administration had passed before any additions were made. The expansion was begun when the Texas, Louisiana and Eastern Railroad was purchased July 26, 1897, to extend the Conroe branch 29.6 miles into the loblolly pines of East Texas. A short line in New Mexico and one in California were also acquired during the year.

In the spring of 1898 the Santa Fe, through a subsidiary, took a short but significant step toward the development of a great railroad web emanating from Amarillo. The Southern Kansas Railway Company of Texas had been built to Panhandle City about thirty miles short of Amarillo. During the 'nineties an independent line was begun from Pecos to Amarillo via the rich Pecos River Valley through Carlsbad and Roswell, New Mexico. Santa Fe officials were anxious to make a connection and also to have a portion of the heavy trade developing around Amarillo. On April

---

The Topeka *Journal* of April 22, 1915, described Ripley as ". . . massive of head and features; tall, broad, flat as an athlete at the abdomen; huge of chin, nose, and mouth; gray of eyes and leonine—a man, in short, as one would picture on a tremendous black horse, armor-clad, and carrying a heavy sword and a long lance, a terror to his foes and a sure bulwark to his friends; worn clothes; short of vision but no spectacles." His sense of fairness was renowned. A traffic manager of the Burlington once had a dispute with a Santa Fe official:

"I'll arbitrate the case," said the Santa Fe man eagerly.

"All right," replied the traffic manager, "I am willing to leave it to Mr. Ripley, your own president."

"Go to thunder."

Most characteristic was Ripley's disarming frankness. His business methods were forthright, and he never hesitated to say exactly what he thought. Ripley damned state regulation, politicians, and government ownership, yet he was a staunch advocate of well-formulated federal control. Ripley lamented the attempt to establish competition in a field where coördination was essential to the avoidance of economic waste.

Ripley's marriage was fully as successful as his business career. Friends of the great leader never forgot the touching tribute he paid to his wife on the occasion of a dinner celebrating his seventieth birthday. Notables had gathered at the Blackstone in Chicago to honor the dean of American railroads. At the end of eloquent testimonials Ripley arose and raised a glass of water to a gray-haired lady in the balcony whose eyes were glowing at the numerous recitals of her husband's achievements, saying:

"Before proceeding I desire to pay tribute and praise to her who forty-four years ago joined her fortunes to mine and who ever since has provided the comforts and rest of a quiet home; who twice has accompanied me through the valley of the shadow of death; who has watched over me mentally, morally and physically, and who is mainly responsible for such success as I have had in conserving mind and body. I ask you, friends, to join in drinking to the health of my wife."

20, 1898, the Panhandle Railway Company, running 14.5 miles from Panhandle City to Washburn, was leased. Later in the year the line was bought at a receivership sale. Trackage rights were secured during the same year from Washburn to Amarillo over the Fort Worth and Denver City Railway. All of this gave a desirable but circuitous entrance into the capital of Llano Estacado. Ten years later the old route was superseded by a direct course built under the charter of the Panhandle and Santa Fe Railway.

Purchase of the San Francisco and San Joaquin Valley Railway

The first major expansion of the revitalized Santa Fe was the purchase of the stock of the incomplete San Francisco and San Joaquin Valley Railway.* Arrangements were made in December, 1898, to authorize the acquisition and the deal was formally concluded November 1, 1899. During the intervening months completion of the line was vigorously pushed. The unfinished portion was between Stockton and Point Richmond opposite San Francisco on the Bay. In addition to securing a long-sought entrance to San Francisco and lines in the rich San Joaquin Valley, the Santa Fe gained another valuable asset in the person of William B. Storey, Jr.* He had directed the construction of the Valley Road

---

*The early history of the Valley road was sketched in Chapter IV, "Wars of the Santa Fe."

*William Benson Storey, Jr., was born in San Francisco on November 17, 1857. His father was an express, stage, and newspaper agent. Frequent assignments moved the family from place to place, but in 1866 permanent settlement was made in Colfax. There young Storey received an early baptism in railroading as an errand boy for his father. He attended the local village school until 1874, when he went to Oakland to attend high school. Limited resources forced him to work for room and board. During the vacation of 1876 Storey secured his first railroad work as a stake driver in an engineering party working on a line between Oakland and Berkeley. The summer's employment netted twenty dollars, and Storey was convinced that a career as a civil engineer would be proportionately more profitable and interesting. Graduation from high school came in 1877. Storey remained out of school for a year and a summer while he saved railroad construction earnings to finance a college career. By dint of much work and with the help of a loan, Storey graduated from the University of California with a degree in mechanical engineering. He soon was attached to a surveying party of the Central Pacific which was sent into the wilds of Idaho, Utah, and South Dakota. During the 'eighties and early 'nineties Storey had many assignments for the Central Pacific and Southern Pacific all over the west coast. When panics led to a cessation of construction Storey was usually released. During one interlude he entered an engineering partnership and on another occasion he served as assistant engineer for the

from the first and was a highly capable engineer and executive—a suitable successor to any of the great engineers who had been identified with the Santa Fe. Storey continued for a time with the Valley Road while the finishing touches were given the line. Completion of mileage between Stockton and Point Richmond involved a series of difficult engineering feats. Two were outstanding. One was the crossing of the tule swamps and the other was the burrowing of the Franklin Tunnel through the coastal mountains. Between Stockton and the San Joaquin River was a swamp with ten to twenty-five feet of living and dead tule plants. Walking was almost impossible in the bog. Storey ordered canals dredged on each side of the proposed line for the necessary distance of sixteen miles. As the material was removed, it was piled high in the middle to form a base of 100 to 130 feet. Clay and sand were added in alternate layers with the tule plants after the water had drained out and the top had dried. Then the tracks were laid. Slides were a nuisance and difficult to stop. Sparks occasionally ignited the highly inflammable peat foundation when the surface of clay on the roadbed cracked. The soundness of the project was admitted by all of the many skeptics who had predicted failure for any line across the swamps.

Franklin Tunnel between Glen Fraser and Christie, California, was 5,560 feet, one of the longest on the Santa Fe. The task of boring was arduous but no more so than had been anticipated. The difficulties developed in trying to maintain the completed parts in proper form. The tunnel was timbered as work progressed. Surrounding earth absorbed moisture and swelled. Pressure developed against the timbers and they broke like matches. Provision had been made for limited pressure on the top but none on the

---

California Debris Commission, charged with the regulation of hydraulic mining on navigable rivers.

When the San Francisco and San Joaquin Valley was organized Storey was selected as chief engineer. Shortly after purchase by the Santa Fe he became chief engineer of the system and was in charge of construction of hundreds of miles of new lines and improvements on old lines. Vice-presidency came in 1909 and in 1917 he became federal manager. When the period of Government operation was over, Storey was advanced to the presidency and remained in office until retirement in 1933.

sides where the greatest exertion of pressure occurred. Dampness caused extensive rot and hastened the collapse of the supports. Long before the headings met on July 6, 1899, parts had to be re-timbered. Chief Engineer Dun of the Santa Fe despaired of any solution and suggested abandonment of the tunnel and the use of switchbacks. Storey refused to give up. He had noted a diminution in the rate and extent of swelling as time passed. By excavating behind the timbers as they were removed he provided a margin which absorbed the remaining expansion.

Reclamation of the China Basin for terminal use in San Francisco was a formidable undertaking. The Santa Fe Terminal Company did the work. China Basin was a mud flat well under water when the tide was in. A sea wall had to be built, the basin filled, slips erected, and tracks laid. Over four million cubic yards of rock were used in addition to large quantities of mud. Trouble was encountered in securing a substantial foundation for the slip. It sagged three times, and finally a new and more satisfactory location had to be selected.

On May 1, 1900, freight operations began over the new line and passenger service started July 1, 1900. The last of the great objectives of the promoters of the Company had been attained. C. K. Holliday, "the father of the Santa Fe," had been denied the opportunity to witness the formal triumph by only a few weeks, having died on March 29, 1900, though the line was actually complete at the time of his death. His span of life and worldly goal had dovetailed perfectly.

The Valley Road had extended southeast as far as Bakersfield. The nearest point on the Santa Fe line was Mojave, a distance of sixty-eight miles through the Tehachapi Mountains. The Southern Pacific had already built between the points and was willing to share the use of its line. A deal was made to the mutual economy of the companies.

SHORT LINES

Several minor additions and changes were made in mileage. On the last day of 1898 the Wichita and Western Railway extending 79.77 miles from Wichita to Pratt, Kansas, was bought at fore-closure sale. The mileage had been operated previously as a part of the Santa Fe-Frisco compact. A portion of the old Manhattan, Alma and Burlingame (owned jointly with the Union Pacific) was purchased outright.

The uncompleted Kansas, Oklahoma Central and Southwest-ern was purchased and projected from Kansas south toward Tulsa in Indian Territory. Oklahoma was entered again to the west by the acquisition of the Hutchinson and Southern. The line stretched 142 miles from Hutchinson, Kansas, to Cross, Oklahoma. Both were expected to be heavy feeders.

East Texas pineries which were tapped by the Conroe branch were further penetrated by the purchase and continued construc-tion of the Gulf, Beaumont and Kansas City. The line extended northeast from Beaumont to Rogan and on toward San Augustine. Later the sixty-mile gap between the new line and the Conroe branch was bridged to provide excellent lines into an area hitherto inaccessible. The acquisition was one of several enterprises backed by John H. Kirby, a resourceful leader in the industrial develop-ment of lumbering in Texas. The Santa Fe coöperated with Kirby projects over a period of many years.

Numerous short segments which were intended to serve the rapidly growing needs of the territory of the Santa Fe were built or purchased between 1897 and 1901. The next major addition to the System was at the outset of 1901 when the Santa Fe obtained con-trol of the important Pecos Valley and Northeastern Railway. This line was 370 miles in length, stretching from Amarillo to Pecos, via Texico, Roswell, and Carlsbad. The route traversed the fertile Pecos Valley, a source of heavy traffic if adequately irrigated. The Santa Fe was able to buy the securities of the Pecos Valley and Northeastern on favorable terms, acquiring over two-thirds of the bonds and 96 per cent of the stock for $2,675,902. Additional bonds were acquired later. Admittedly the line was not up to Santa Fe specifications, but it was obtained for less than a $10,000 per mile basis. The purchase climaxed extensive financial aid extended to the project. It had been launched in 1890 by J. J. Hagerman, a notable figure in the history of New Mexico. Previously he had been interested in the Colorado Midland. The New Mexico line and its immediate corporate predecessors were part of a plan to develop the Pecos Valley by irrigation. Hagerman had begun the project in 1890 between Pecos and Carlsbad (formerly Eddy). The river was dammed by the affiliated Pecos Valley Irrigation Company. Colonists were induced to locate on the reclaimed lands. Large numbers of Italians were attracted. The results were disappointing. Rampages of the fickle Pecos destroyed the dams, inundated the farms, and washed out tracks. The segment between Carlsbad and Roswell was begun in 1893 and was also dependent on agricultural development. Results on the new portion were also disappointing. Years later the Pecos was somewhat tamed, and Gardens of Eden contrasted with outlying desert wastes. In 1898 work on the portion between Roswell and Amarillo began simultaneously at both ends. The Santa Fe advanced $750,000 to enable completion.* Passenger service was offered from Amarillo to Pecos on February 10, 1899. The Santa Fe integrated operation of the Pecos Valley lines into the system on July 1, 1906. After 1907 the property was held by the Eastern Railway Company of New Mexico, a Santa Fe subsidiary. Title passed to the present company in 1912.

The program of expansion by purchase continued in 1901, when the Santa Fe purchased the Santa Fe, Prescott and Phoenix Railroad. This was the first branch owned in Arizona and gave exclusive control over a promising territory. The Pea Vine, as it was called, had a complicated background arising out of the struggle of Prescott and nearby copper mines to secure a railroad outlet.† The United Verde mine at Jerome was long handicapped

---

*Lack of finances prevented Hagerman from undertaking construction of a line to El Paso. He had proposed to build from a point south of Roswell west through Surveyors' Pass over the Sacramento Mountains.

†The name "Pea Vine" stemmed from the tortuous course through the mountains. Even though curvature has been greatly reduced since original construction, especially at Hell Cañon, the engineer is still able to pass his tobacco to the brakeman on the hairpin curves. The scenery around Prescott justifies travel over the Pea Vine, if only for the sights. The sun has a special way of bringing the day to a close.

by the lack of transportation. A decline in the price of copper in the early 'eighties rendered the use of mule trains to the A&P prohibitive in cost. The cure-all was thought to be a railroad. Largely through the activities of Governor F. A. Trittle, the Central Arizona Railroad was organized May 10, 1884.* Surveys were made and county subsidies sought. Authorization from the territorial legislature, later known as the "Thieving Thirteenth," was secured. The Southern Pacific interests, operating as the Maricopa and Phoenix Company, blocked every move to secure county aid for extension of the line south to Phoenix. The rival wanted to handle all Phoenix business over its own lines to the south. The Central Arizona could not make headway under its early managers. In June, 1885, the Arizona Central was organized with a capital of $3,300,000 to build a narrow gauge to the A&P. Minnesota interests headed the company. One week later T. S. Bullock with New York backing organized another Central Arizona with a capital of $1,875,000. The old Central Arizona collapsed. Each of the new companies made surveys that zigzagged over the rival line, and mudslinging almost prompted leadthrowing.[1] Bullock seemed to have better support from the A&P with an agreement for reduced rates on building supplies. In 1885 the rivals united as the Prescott and Arizona Central under Bullock. Construction began in July, 1886. The rails were light discards of the A&P; ties were few and far between; bridges were weak; and curves and steep grades prevailed. The road between Prescott and Seligman was opened January 1, 1887. A locomotive belonging to the A&P was used on the initial run, because vandals had disabled both of the ancient engines of the Company. Service over the new line was so uncertain that little relief was afforded the distressed area. The *Arizona Weekly: Journal Miner* gave the following account of the telegraph service:

> The present line has been so imperfectly constructed that communications over it are at best uncertain. It runs through a section of country

---

*In 1883 Governor Trittle had incorporated the Prescott and Thirty-fifth Parallel Road which never reached the stage of organization.

devoted largely to grazing, and when an animal's side itches it invariably uses a telegraph pole for a 'scratcher.' Pieces of barbed wire were wrapped around the poles about a year ago, with a view of preventing this rubbing process, but the prickly prongs of the wire seem to be more satisfactory to stock to rub against than bare poles, although of course less damage to poles is done.[2]

The scratchers were so poorly set that they were pushed over by the animals and leveled by strong winds. Bullock and his railroad were widely assailed and plans matured for a new line to liberate Prescott.

The Santa Fe, Prescott and Phoenix Railway Company was incorporated on May 27, 1891. D. B. Robinson, general manager of the A&P, was the president and F. M. Murphy, the secretary. The

latter was the main driving force. Construction began soon. Grading was interrupted frequently around Iron Springs when workers found traces of gold in cuts. Tracklaying began at Ash Fork on August 17, 1892, and the first passenger train entered Prescott from the north April 26, 1893.* Construction toward Phoenix was pushed rapidly. Meanwhile Bullock's line was auctioned for salvage. A great celebration in Phoenix on March 13, 1895, heralded the arrival of the first locomotive from the north. In 1897 a subsidiary, the Prescott and Eastern Railroad, was created to coöperate in building a branch of twenty-six miles to Mayer.

The Pea Vine, unlike many other purchases of the Santa Fe, was not bought at a forced sale. The line had a record of always covering the interest charges, although the margin was never wide. The Santa Fe had early developed close ties with the SFP&P through traffic agreements and gradually took steps pointed toward purchase. All of the stock and $2,963,000 of second-mortgage bonds (one bond of $1,000 withheld) were obtained for $2,889,935. Outstanding first-mortgage bonds amounted to $4,940,000. The new line was already a heavy feeder and interchange between the two continued on the upgrade. Soon after the accession of Santa Fe the line to Mayer was extended to Poland and Crown King under the charter of the Bradshaw Mountain Railroad. The Santa Fe, Prescott and Phoenix sponsored the Phoenix and Eastern, which built southeast from Phoenix toward Winkelman to the indignation of the Southern Pacific. This extension was sold in 1907 to the rival company.

A second important branch was added in Arizona in 1901. Control of the line to the Grand Canyon came after financial ties had been tightened over a period of months. Soon after the A&P had bisected Arizona a substantial volume of tourists visited the Canyon. Most of them traveled by stagecoach from Flagstaff and then had to "rough it" to reach their destination and to return. The Grand Canyon would draw hundreds of thousands of sightseers if

---

*Mines at Jerome secured an outlet by construction of the United Verde and Pacific in 1894 east from the Pea Vine.

better facilities for reaching the chasm were provided. Numerous independent lines were contemplated between the A&P and the south rim. Ripley welcomed all prospective builders. In 1897 he offered right of way over Santa Fe Pacific lands to the proposed Santa Fe and Grand Canyon Railroad. The promoter was Lombard, Goode and Company, and its owners were identified with copper mines in Arizona. The threat of rival construction prompted the start of active construction-building on May 29, 1899, after much procrastination. Progress was as fast as a full measure of financial woes permitted. The Santa Fe Pacific supplied second-hand 56-pound rail at $41.66 a ton payable in bonds at par. Freight rates on materials used in construction were also payable in bonds at a rate of one and two-thirds cents per ton mile. Other concessions were made by which the Santa Fe Pacific acquired some stock. Anita Junction was reached by rail April 12, 1900, and eight more miles were completed before financial prostration brought a halt on September 5, 1900. The reorganization committee completed the line to the Canyon. Under the reorganization, the Santa Fe Pacific received $201,300 of preferred and $529,000 of common for $324,000 of old bonds and an advance of $200,000 to the committee. Other bondholders received $676,000 of common for an equivalent amount in par of old bonds. The Santa Fe Pacific made many improvements in the line and invested over $250,000 in tourist facilities at the Grand Canyon. Fred Harvey assumed the operation of the lodges and incidental projects.

During 1901 and 1902 the Santa Fe bought or built several short segments over the system. The Sunset Railway was constructed jointly with the Southern Pacific to Sunset, California. Extensions were continued toward Maricopa and eventually to Shale. The California Eastern was purchased to tap the territory of the Ivanpah Valley. The Randsburg Railway from Kramer to Johannesburg, California, was purchased on an advantageous basis. Steps were taken to give access to Oakland and Berkeley. Numerous branches were begun in Oklahoma in anticipation of growing requirements in the territory.

By 1902 the Santa Fe had added almost one thousand miles of lines to the system since the post-receivership pruning. The new mileage had been purchased or built with a critical view toward financial soundness. The Ripley administration was determined not to buy a Colorado Midland. Certain Ripley principles of expansion were already evident and were to be applied consistently as time passed. First, lines had to have confirmed profit possibilities before purchase or construction could be justified. Second, railroadless territory with a good traffic potential should be promptly preëmpted to forestall permanent loss to rivals. Finally and most important of all, in the event that rivals appeared on the scene at the same time or prior to the Santa Fe there should not be any duplication of facilities. Ripley regarded competitive construction of parallel lines as a blight on railroading. Invariably he endeavored to reach an agreement for joint construction or some other plan so that two lines would not be built where only one was needed. There are countless cases in point to illustrate his aversion to economic waste of excessive mileage. Ripley applied his own test of "convenience and necessity."

Major moves begun by the Santa Fe in 1902 and 1903 gave further proof of adherence to the Ripley principles of expansion. One was the Belen cutoff connecting the southwest line from Kansas to Amarillo and the Pecos Valley with the mainline across New Mexico and Arizona in the vicinity of Albuquerque; the other was the extension from San Francisco into the redwood empire of California.

Belen Cutoff

The Belen cutoff, or a line in the vicinity, had been contemplated from the earliest days of the Santa Fe. Long before the Company entered New Mexico, engineers prospected for an easier route than a right angle to the north with the accompanying steep gradients. Most of the surveys were north of the present Belen cutoff except one made by Lewis Kingman in 1878. The records of the latter were destroyed in the fire which gutted the general office building in 1889. The substantial increase in transcontinental traffic which followed the reorganization caused renewed interest in a low grade route. Acquisition of feeders in the booming states of Arizona and California accentuated the need. Purchase of the Pecos Valley and Northeastern from Amarillo through Texico caused the Company to shift the line southward. One of the most cogent factors accounting for the decision was the public declaration of rivals that they planned to build in the area. Ripley and the directors resolved to act promptly. Early in 1902 Chief Engineer Dun ordered the taciturn F. Meredith Jones to "go out and see what you can do." Jones organized three field parties and spent most of his waking hours during the next seventeen months in a buckboard. The men who made the survey all believed that Portales, New Mexico, was the logical junction rather than Texico, but Dun felt otherwise. Final location of the Belen cutoff was completed in December of 1902 and the grading contract was let December 30. Work was held in abeyance between August, 1903, and the following spring because of the current business doldrums. As usual the Santa Fe supplied materials but engaged contractors for the construction. Lantry and Sharp of Kansas City began the project, but the Sharp Construction Company assumed responsibility for completion. C. J. Lantry or Lantry Brothers did most of the Santa Fe construction during this era of expansion and also built many other lines in the Southwest.

Progress on the Belen cutoff was checked, and tracklaying did not begin until 1906. On July 1, 1908, the line was turned over to the operating department. The cutoff had certain marked advantages over the Raton Route besides being slightly shorter. Two high mountain ranges were avoided. The highest point on the new line was 1100 feet under the level of the Raton tunnel. The maximum gradient at Raton was 184.8 feet per mile and 158.4 in the Glorieta Mountains. The cutoff had a maximum of 31.68 feet, except for 25 miles at Abo Pass, where 66 feet prevailed. Curvature was also reduced appreciably. The savings to be realized in fuel and wear and tear on rolling stock loomed large.

E. P. RIPLEY
president 1896-1920

W. B. STOREY
president 1920-1933

S. T. BLEDSOE
president 1933-1939

EDWARD J. ENGEL
president 1939-1944

FRED G. GURLEY
president 1944-

The Belen cutoff became the transcontinental freight line of the Santa Fe. The route was less scenic than the old line but more economical and had the effect of double-tracking the Santa Fe from central Kansas to Belen. Its construction required rebuilding of much of the line northeast from Texico to Kansas in order to sustain the heavy traffic. Tracks between Texico and Cameo were

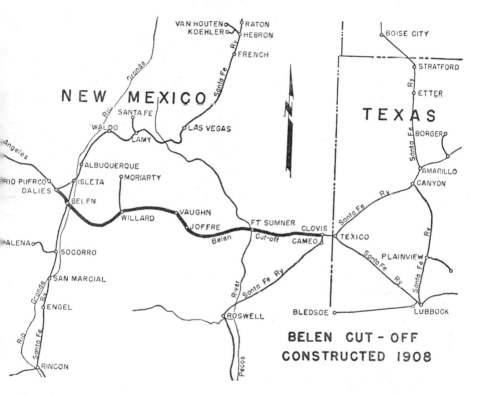

BELEN CUT-OFF
CONSTRUCTED 1908

taken up in favor of a new outlet of the Pecos Valley lines from Cameo to Clovis on the cutoff. When the new link on the transcontinental line was finally forged, newspapers announced that the Santa Fe (Eastern Railway of New Mexico) had spent "Millions to Save Less than a Quarter of a Mile"—only the quarter of a mile was straight up.

The second enterprise which exemplified the Ripley principles of expansion was the invasion of the redwood empire of northern

California. The area had a threefold appeal to the Santa Fe: first, existing railroads gave inadequate coverage and service; second, the extensive forests promised a large volume of traffic, especially in view of declining stands of marketable timber in other regions; and, lastly, the forests would provide a splendid source of ties for the Company's coast lines. Wood-treating methods gave redwood a longevity comparable to that of treated hardwoods. The Santa Fe began its invasion by the purchase of two small railroads far removed from itself. The Eel River and Eureka Railroad and the related Pacific Lumber Company line extended forty-two miles southeast of Eureka and the California and Northern connected Eureka and Arcata. Title was vested in the San Francisco and Northwestern Railway, a newly formed subsidiary of the Santa Fe Land Improvement Company.

MORE SHORT LINES

The Santa Fe hoped to purchase several short lines between the San Francisco and Northwestern and the Bay Area. The Southern Pacific, however, had ambitions in the redwood forests and succeeded in obtaining the mileage coveted by the Santa Fe. William B. Storey was then detailed to examine the territory and pass judgment on the feasibility of construction south along the Eel River. Southern Pacific engineers were busy contriving a route to the north on the opposite bank. The lines crossed many times, and it was apparent that duplication would be wasteful. Although each company began to extend its mileage toward the other without any noticeable signs of coöperation, officials of the two railroads looked forward to a unification of effort.

On January 8, 1907, the Northwestern Pacific Railroad Company was formed to engulf the many small lines owned by the Santa Fe and Southern Pacific. The stock of the new firm was equally divided. Total mileage involved was approximately 500. One hundred and three miles, however, had to be built between Willits and Chively before the desired access to the north would be obtained. Contracts were made for immediate construction, but the panic of 1907 intervened to deter action for two years. The link involved extraordinary difficulties. Heavy winter rains made transportation of supplies virtually impossible. The mountainous topography necessitated cuts, fills, and tunnels. Thirty tunnels ranged up to 4,335 feet in length. Attempts to freight supplies by wagon were unsuccessful. The country roads were quagmires for months at a time and paving was too expensive. In 1912 an attempt was made to use trucks, but daily breakdowns discouraged the builders. Experimentation with various makes isolated one serviceable truck and a fleet was bought in 1913. Every conceivable sort of natural obstacle was encountered, and the line was not put in operation until July 1, 1915. Service was offered as far north as Trinidad, California, close to the Oregon line. Ferries were necessary to connect the southern terminus of Sausalito with Point Richmond and San Francisco.

The Santa Fe, Prescott and Phoenix had not been in the corporate family very long before Santa Fe officials speculated on construction of a more direct line between Phoenix and the Coast. The Salt River Valley area was developing rapidly, and Phoenix assumed increasing importance as a wholesaling center. Building on the Phoenix and Eastern had strengthened the case for a new southern, low-grade line to California. A hypotenuse from Phoenix to the mainline in California was expected to command heavy ore shipments. W. C. Bashford, who made a reconnaissance trip, reported in glowing terms on the fabulous mines to be served. The final argument for the proposed segment was the safety factor of continuity of operations by having two lines in place of one. Through trains could be routed circuitously around any obstacles or washouts occurring on the mainline west of Ash Fork.

On September 10, 1903, the Arizona and California Railway was incorporated to serve the manifold objectives. Grading began March 3, 1904, north of Wickenburg, Arizona. The Santa Fe, Prescott and Phoenix constructed the line. Progress was hampered by a shortage of laborers who would toil under the scorching desert sun. Bridging the Colorado at Parker was the most formidable problem. The mainline was contacted at Cadiz. Operations as far as Parker began June 17, 1907. The current panic halted construction, and the entire line was not opened until midsummer of 1910.

ACROSS TEXAS AGAIN

The greatest building program of the second Santa Fe was launched in the vicinity of the North and South Plains of Texas. The main portion of the work was the linking of the Gulf, Colorado and Santa Fe with the new transcontinental line opened by the Belen cutoff. The project carried out the early objective of the GC&SF for a route into the northwest.* The chief end, however, was to secure a short line for traffic between Texas and the Pacific. Hitherto, shipments from the bustling cities of southeast Texas had to be sent north into Kansas and then southwest over the mainline. Effective competition with the Texas and Pacific and the Southern Pacific was impossible. The roundabout course was slow and costly. Matching rates precluded profit possibilities. Another strong inducement to build was the latent traffic in the comparatively railroadless area. As early as the 'eighties the GC&SF had made surveys in the general area of northwest Texas. Union with the Santa Fe and the period of financial distress suppressed plans for extending the Gulf Lines beyond San Angelo.† Interest was renewed about 1900 and Chief Engineer Dun wrote Ripley that any of three short cuts was possible. One was along substantially the line eventually taken, and the other two were far to the south, from San Angelo to Roswell, and Ballinger to Hagerman. Another period of quiet followed. In 1904 the Santa Fe again became active. J. V. Key made a preliminary survey from Canyon

---

*Early promoters of the GC&SF planned to build into southern Colorado or at least to a union with the D&RG at Santa Fe, New Mexico. The inclusion of Colorado in the corporate name probably was taken from this distant objective rather than from the Colorado River of Texas along the proposed route.

†Preliminary surveys are supposed to have been made shortly after control passed to the Santa Fe. A. A. Robinson directed Philip Smith to establish a course between Texico and Coleman.

to Plainview and from Dickens east of Lubbock to Brownwood.*
C. M. Wood examined the country between Plainview and Lubbock. Final location between Canyon and Plainview began August 15, 1906, with the supervision of Meredith Jones. Construction proceeded under the Pecos and Northern Texas Railway. The
line was completed and turned over for operations in February,
1907.

Attention shifted next to the cutoff from the south. The Santa
Fe in its efforts to build along the most feasible route from a transportation standpoint became embroiled in a bitter controversy
among towns and counties. What Texas towns lacked in size, they
compensated for in ambition and fighting spirit. The new cutoff
loomed as the key to prosperity, and sharp rivalry ensued on the
assumption that good lobbying would determine where the railroad would be located. Abilene and Brownwood were aligned
against Sweetwater and Coleman. At the outset Abilene was presumed to be favored because of a personal preference of Chief Engineer Dun. Little credence can be attached to the belief. Another
story indicates that Abilene lost out because its leaders were unfriendly to Meredith Jones. The town fathers are supposed to have
doubted that Jones was a duly authorized representative of the
Santa Fe and to have demanded credentials. Jones was unprepos-
sessing in appearance but not a man to be challenged or doubted,
and he is said to have withdrawn vowing to build elsewhere.
Doubt exists as to this novel version of the loss by Abilene. Like
Dun, Jones was too good an engineer to be swayed by trivialities
when millions were at stake.

During 1907 Jones surveyed the Coleman-Sweetwater route to
Texico. He was impressed with the marked advantages of the
course over the one through Abilene, but his conclusions remained
a dark secret as far as the town fathers were concerned. Any pre-
mature pronouncements would have touched off a wave of speculation in town sites.

---

*Announcement was made that the Gulf, Santa Fe and Northwestern Railway Com-
pany was incorporated September 13, 1905, for the purpose of sponsoring construction
of the cutoff from Brownwood.

The intervention of the panic of 1907 and anti-railroad legislation in Texas deferred construction of the new line but in no way
lessened the enmity between the rivals.* In the spring of 1909 the
Santa Fe was ready to resume the project. Officials who visited the
scene were beset and beseeched by local committees. An Abilene
contingent even went to Chicago to plead their cause before Rip-

ley. They were frankly told that the location of the route was not
for sale and that construction would follow the most practical line.
The decision to build via Coleman, Sweetwater, Snyder, and Lubbock was not difficult to reach, because there were marked supe-
riorities. Abilene was irreconcilable and its leaders sought the aid
of Tom Campbell, the governor, in order to accomplish by political pressure or action what could not be accomplished on economic
merit. According to contemporary accounts the governor was cooperative.[3]

---

*Grading was completed between Farwell and Lubbock during this period of relative
inaction.

Having in vain appealed to President Ripley to make his straight-line cutoff sinuous for the benefit of these objecting interests, the Texas governor declares loudly that what he has been unable to accomplish by diplomacy he will bring about by the rigors of Texas law, and that therefore, he will summon a special session of the statute makers to teach the Santa Fe System that it can't monkey with vested rights down where the cattle grow.

Abilene tycoons during the period of dormancy developed a "hedge" which was difficult for the Santa Fe. They had incorporated and built a short railroad, the Roscoe, Snyder and Pacific. It began at Roscoe on the Texas and Pacific and extended through Snyder to Fluvanna. The newcomer was cheaply made and zigzagged over the line staked by the Santa Fe. The strategy was twofold: having preëmpted a portion of the alternative line of the cutoff, the Abilene route might become preferable; or, being first on the scene, the Santa Fe might well pay for costs plus a substantial nuisance stipend. To the chagrin of Messrs. F. W. James, E. S. Hughes, H. D. Wooten, and others the Santa Fe balked on both evils and announced plans to build through the same area. The line was relocated between Hermleigh and Snyder. Leaders of the RS&P and the governor were indignant at the threat to parallel and crush the short line. The special session of the legislature seemed inevitable until the governor was reminded that his crusade might not look so righteous if the rumors of his own financial interests in an Abilene bank gained wider circulation. Actually the governor did not own stock in the new bank, but he feared the damage of false rumors. Also, he was admittedly impressed with a demonstration of the comparative merits of the chosen course. The matter was dropped, to the delight of Sweetwater and the dismay of Abilene. The Santa Fe suffered heavily in the struggle in which it was an unwilling participant. The plight was summarized by W. B. Storey when he wrote to S. D. Myres of Sweetwater.[4]

. . . We regret extremely that our choice of route should have aroused the animosity of communities in your section, as we would prefer to be on good terms with all your Texas people. It is manifestly impossible for us to go through every town in West Texas and we, therefore, must make a selection by the route that seems best for all parties, namely: for the people of that portion of Texas, and for the railroad, and we, of course, must be the judges of such route for the reason that we are furnishing the means to build the road. I am sincerely hoping that the sane people in the communities not touched by us will ultimately see the justness of our position, and that the resentment against us will die out.

Grading was begun early in May, 1909, between Plainview and Lubbock. This link was to be used for east-west traffic until the longer line between Lubbock and Texico was built. The work was pushed and trains entered Lubbock on January 9, 1910. Meanwhile grading had started at Coleman and Sweetwater and soon crews were also busy at Lubbock. All the new work between Plainview and Coleman was under the corporate shelter of the Pecos and Northern Texas Railway Company. G. W. Harris was the chief engineer. With him came increased use of power machinery and a hastening of the transition from handicraft construction using mostly brawn to scientific methods that made greater use of heads than any other portion of the body.

Work was delayed near Sweetwater when the T&P stubbornly refused to permit a grade crossing. The Santa Fe finally had to erect an overhead crossing. Securing the right of way was easy in some places and tedious in others. Citizens of Sweetwater, Lubbock, and other towns were generous in their support. R. C. Crane, C. W. Post, and Thomas Trammell, leaders in the area, gave time and money to ease the way. Condemnation proceedings were necessary at places where asking prices seemed extortionate. The most difficult construction was northwest of Post where the Cap Rock had to be surmounted to the higher plains. By May, 1911, tracklaying was completed on the cutoff and on December 1, 1911, the line was available for operations. Trains from Galveston no longer traveled at a right angle for one-third of the mileage to their objective. The fraction was greatly reduced but not to a minimum. Pacific-bound trains still had to vary from a crow's route between Lubbock and Farwell. The line connecting these points had been graded between March, 1907, and August, 1909, but no more had been done. Through trains were routed around two sides of an equilateral triangle via Canyon Junction. In 1912 construction was begun under the personal direction of Joseph Weidel, later the valuation engineer of the Santa Fe. The first regular train went over the finished product on March 1, 1914. The area was almost as wild and woolly as Kansas had been forty years before, but rapid taming followed completion.

STILL MORE SHORT LINES

The major projects undertaken after 1903 in no way lessened the rate of acquisition or construction of short but essential branch lines. Below is a table which summarizes the facts to 1938.

Year	Corporation	Pur. or Const'd	Location	Mileage
1902-04	Eastern Oklahoma Ry. and subsidiaries	C&P	Newkirk to Pauls Valley, Indian Territory	184
			Guthrie to Cushing, Oklahoma Territory	48
			Ripley to Esau, O.T.	40
			Seward to Cashion, O.T.	11
			Pauls Valley to Lindsay, I.T.	24
1903	Cane Belt	P	Sealy to Matagora, Texas	104
1903	Gulf, Beaumont & Great Northern	C	Rogan to Center	78
1904	GC&SF	C	Bragg to Saratoga	9
1904	Oakdale Western	C	Riverbank to Oakdale, California	6
1904-08	Jasper & Eastern	C	Kirbyville, Texas to Oakdale, Louisiana	81
1905	Arizona & Utah Ry.	P	McConnico to Chloride, Arizona	22
1905	AT&SF	C	Owasso to Tulsa, I.T.	11
1906	Eastern Oklahoma Ry.	C	Davis to Sulphur, O.T.	9
1906-10	Texas & Gulf	P&C	Longview to Carthage to Timpson to Grisby to Center to Gary, Texas	96
1907	Denver, Enid & Gulf	P	Guthrie, O.T., to Kiowa, Kansas	117

Year	Corporation	Pur. or Const'd	Location	Mileage
1907	Denver, Kansas & Gulf Ry.	P&C	Kiowa to Belvidere, Kansas	49
1907	Barnwell & Searchlight Ry.	C	Barnwell, Calif., to Searchlight, Nevada	23
1907-08	Holly & Swink Arkansas Valley Rd.	P&C	Holly to Rocky Ford, Colo. (excluding branches)	68
1908-09	Sunset Western (with the Southern Pacific)	C	Pentland to Fellows, California	15
1908-10	Llano Estacado Ry.	P&C	Plainview to Floydada, Texas	27
1910	Concho, San Saba & Llano Valley	P&C	Miles to Paint Rock, Texas	17
			San Angelo to Sterling City, Texas	44
1910	Pecos & Northern Texas	C	Slaton to Lamesa, Texas	53
1911	Garden City, Gulf & Northern	P	Garden City to Scott City, Kansas	38
1911	Kings River Ry.	C	Wahtoke to Piedra, California	11
1911	Laton & Western	C	Laton to Lanare, California	15
1911	GC&SF	C	Lometa to Eden	98
1911-13	Verde Valley Rd.	C	Cedar Glade to Clarksdale, Ariz.	38
1912-13	Dodge City & Cimarron Valley	C	Dodge City to Elkhart, Kansas	119
1913	St. Louis, Rocky Mountain & Pacific	P	Des Moines to Ute Park, New Mexico	106
1913-14	Minkler Southern	C	Minkler to Exeter and branches	40
1914	Oklahoma Central	P	Chickasha to Lehigh, Oklahoma	133
1914-15	Oil Fields & Santa Fe	P&C	Cushing to Pemeta and Jennings to Drumright, Oklahoma	30
1915	Crosbyton-South Plains	P	Lubbock to Crosbyton, Texas	38
1917-18	South Plains & Santa Fe	C	Lubbock to Seagrams, Texas	64
1917-19	Barton County & Santa Fe	C	Holyrood to Galatia, Kansas	32

Year	Corporation	Pur. or Const'd	Location	Mileage
1917-20	North Texas & Santa Fe	C	Shattuck, Oklahoma, to Spearman, Texas	85
1919-20	Buffalo Northwestern	P&C	Waynoka to Buffalo, Oklahoma	53
1921	California Southern	P	Rice to Ripley, California	49
1922	Dodge City & Cimarron Valley	C	Satanta to Manter, Kansas	54
1922-23	Osage County & Santa Fe	C	Owen to Pawhuska, Oklahoma	35
1923-24	Eldorado & Santa Fe	C	Ellinor to Eldorado, Kansas	42
1923-24	Santa Fe & Los Angeles Harbor	C	El Segundo to Wilmington	13
1924	Salina & Santa Fe	P	Salina to Osborne	81
1925	South Plains & Santa Fe	C	Doud to Bledsoe	65
1925	Elkhart & Santa Fe	C	Elkhart, Kansas, to Felt, Oklahoma	59
1926	Healdton & Santa Fe	P	Ardmore to Ringling and branch to Healdton, Oklahoma	36
1926	New Mexico Central	P	Santa Fe to Torrance, New Mexico	116
1926	Panhandle & Santa Fe	C	Panhandle to Borger, Texas	31
1926-27	Dodge City & Cimarron Valley	C	Manter to Pritchett, Kansas	56
1927	Osage County & Santa Fe	C	Pawhuska & Osage Junction, Oklahoma	27
1928	Central California Traction	P ⅓	Stockton to Sacramento, California	55
1928	Clinton & Oklahoma Western	P	Clinton to Cheyenne, Oklahoma	58
1928-29	Clinton-Oklahoma-Western	C	Cheyenne to Oklahoma-Texas line	24
1928-29	Clinton-Oklahoma-Western of Texas	C	Oklahoma-Texas line to Pampa, Texas	57
1929-31	Cane Belt	C	Cane Junction to Thompsons, Texas	34
1931	North Texas & Santa Fe	C	Spearman to Morse, Texas	19

Year	Corpor- ation	Pur. or Const'd	Location	Mile- age
1930-31	North Plains & Santa Fe	C	Amarillo to Texas- Oklahoma line	101
1930-31	Elkhart & Santa Fe	C	Texas-Oklahoma line to Boise City, Oklahoma	21
			Felt, Oklahoma, to Clayton, New Mexico	24
			Mount Dora to Farley, New Mexico	36
1936-37	Dodge City & Cim- arron Valley	C	Oklahoma-Colorado line to Las Animas, Colorado	90
1937	Fort Worth & Rio Grande	P	Birds to Brady, White- land to Menard	216

Imposing as the above list is, it is far from inclusive. Countless lines up to ten miles in length were built or bought. A glance at any recent map of the Santa Fe will reveal innumerable short branches.

The table reflects varied policies and programs of the Santa Fe. Some lines were built to serve oil fields, coal, iron, copper, or potash mines, and forests. Other mileage was built to provide short cuts, speed service, and reduce expenses. Much new construction was intended to develop hitherto railroadless agricultural or industrial areas. The effect was to provide a capillary system which gathered or distributed a vastly swollen volume of traffic over the main arteries and veins.

PURCHASE OF THE ORIENT

One major enlargement was made after World War I. In 1928 the Kansas City, Mexico and Orient was purchased. The Orient extended from Wichita, Kansas, to Alpine, Texas, a distance of 737 miles, and also included 289 miles in Mexico. The history of this mileage had been turbulent. The Orient was originally promoted by A. E. Stilwell, who relied heavily on visions and intuition to guide him in business transactions. Stilwell projected and built the Kansas City, Pittsburg and Gulf (the Kansas City Southern) as a short line to salt water. He lost control to others, including John W. "Bet-a-Million" Gates. A period of mental depression followed, and friends planned a banquet to raise Stilwell's morale. The promoter happened to be on the rebound. Apparently without any forethought he calmly announced that the "Cannibals of Finance" had not devoured him and that he had a bigger and better project. Stilwell called for a map and, using a piece of string, he demonstrated that the shortest line to Pacific salt water came out on the Mexican coast in the vicinity of Topolobampo. The Kansas City, Mexico and Orient was suddenly born. The new line was 1659 miles in length and 400 miles shorter than any other. Topolobampo was described as an excellent landlocked harbor capable of accommodating the largest vessels and appreciably closer to the Orient and South America than California ports.

Stilwell threw himself into the promotion with characteristic zest. He incorporated the Orient in 1900 about two months after the birth of the idea. Surveys were made, and it was planned to top the Sierra Madre Mountains with forty miles of 14 per cent cog road. Later three 2½ per cent lines were supposed to have been located. Grading was begun in Harper County, Kansas, in June, 1900, and on July 4, 1901, the first rail was laid at Emporia. Terminal facilities were secured in Kansas City and work over the line progressed rapidly. In 1908 a total of 729 miles was completed and 241 graded.* Construction methods evidenced Stilwell's flair for promotion rather than engineering. The ties were untreated, ballast was disregarded, and bridges were light. Construction began northeast of Topolobampo but did not penetrate the mountain barrier. The line was financed in England, and America was entitled to Mexican subsidies of $3,000,000. Much water was injected into the structure, and the outstanding securities more than doubled the actual investment. Lack of finances harried the enterprise, but Stilwell kept a bold front. Early in 1912 he wrote:

The Kansas City, Mexico and Orient Railroad is one of the greatest enterprises of today; it opens one of the treasure houses of the world in the mines of Mexico. It will build a port that will rival any on the Pacific

---

*Pancho Villa had one of the subcontracts for grading in Mexico.

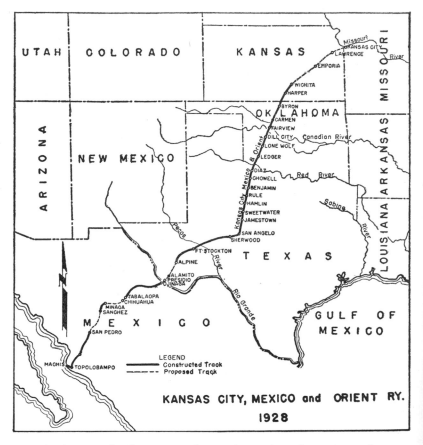

KANSAS CITY, MEXICO and ORIENT RY.
1928

coast; it shortens the line across the continent; it makes a great short-cut to the west coast of Mexico, Central and South America. On the line of this road, when finished, there will be three smelting centers—the smelters now at Chihuahua, smelters at the border and a smelter at the coast. The lumber of the Sierra Madre Mountains will find a market as far north as northern Oklahoma. It will supply all the ties for western Texas. Along the line of the finished road will be great plants treating the ore from the dump heaps placed there in the years of long ago; along the road there will be two or three cities which will equal Cripple Creek as mining centers.

The port of Topolobampo will be one of the great cities of the Pacific; it will have its line of steamers to the Orient, Central and South America, New Zealand, and Australia. The early vegetables, oranges, etc., which are one month earlier than those in California, will come in train loads to Chicago and eastern markets and the one hundred miles of the Fertile River Valley, as rich as the valley of the Nile, will contribute great earnings to the road. The hundreds of thousands of acres of level land east of Chihuahua will be irrigated and the cultivation of sugar beets and cotton furnish northern Mexico with all these products it can use.[5]

Notwithstanding the glowing account of the future, the current factors proved controlling, and March 7, 1912, Edward Dickinson, the vice-president, was appointed receiver. With the exception of a period between 1914 and 1917 the Orient remained in receivership. Governmental upheaval in Mexico not only barred completion of the line but also prevented orderly operations on the portions which had been finished. On several occasions abandonment of the entire venture was contemplated. William T. Kemper of Kansas City successfully cajoled bondholders, employees, and taxing and regulatory bodies into stays of execution. Finally a deal was arranged whereby the Orient was sold to Kemper, Clarence Histed, and others for $3,000,000. In 1923 "black gold" was discovered in west Texas. For the first time in its history the Orient showed signs of standing on its own. Development of the oil pool raised the dollar volume of oil and oil supplies shipped over the Orient to 48 per cent of gross revenue. The boom station of McCamey is supposed to have grossed $750,000 in one month. The fortuitous revival of the line caused the old investors to attempt to regain control, but Kemper was able to block the move.

The Orient needed more than oil to prove reasonably profitable. The territory was capable of substantial growth, but the Orient had had too many lean years to meet the challenge. The roadbed was in wretched condition and the rolling stock wholly inadequate for the need. The locomotives were light, old, and worn-out. Kemper and his associates decided the task was for someone else and elected to sell. Negotiations were begun with the Santa Fe, and sale was made at a figure in excess of $14,000,-000. The Santa Fe had a twofold objective. The Orient cut through the middle of Santa Fe territory. The latter feared purchase by a rival and therefore made a defensive move. The Orient at $14,000,000 with its oil traffic was obviously low-priced. Moreover, there was reason to believe that profits could be improved.

The Santa Fe had rolling stock to spare and could easily meet the requirements of the handicapped Orient. Lines of the new addition could serve as cutoffs for the parent company and afford further economies. The Santa Fe planned an active development program of a type the old company could never finance.

Inclusion of the Mexican mileage was more or less windfall. It consisted of 289 miles between Ojinaga on the border and Tabala-opa, Minaca and Creel, and El Fuerte and Topolobampo. The unconstructed portions in the mountains totaled 215 miles. President Storey urged prompt sale, and in 1929 B. F. Johnston, a land and sugar operator, bought the lines. He paid $650,000 in cash, and the Santa Fe carried a mortgage of $900,000. Johnston endured great financial reverses with the lines and paid the interest on the loan for a time out of his personal wealth. Later he defaulted. In 1940 the Mexican government took over from Johnston in conformance with its program of nationalizing the railroads. The government suggested that the Santa Fe cancel its debt, but later a token payment of $90,000 was made in full discharge of the obligation.

The line to Topolobampo was never completed. The gap between Alpine and Presidio, however, was filled by securing trackage rights to Paisano and building beyond to the Rio Grande. On November 2, 1930, a special train brought Santa Fe officials into Presidio en route to Chihuahua. A branch between Del Rio Junction and Sonora which had been started in 1910 was completed in 1929 and 1930.

From time to time reports of the Mexican government intimate that a portion of Stilwell's dream will be realized. The Orient conceivably could be built over the Sierra Madre. The remainder of the promoter's dream, dealing with the heavy volume of freight, would still remain far from reality.

RECENT CHANGES

While the Santa Fe was in the process of buying the Orient, disposal was made of the half interest in the Northwestern Pacific. The Southern Pacific, which had been the co-owner, made the

TOPEKA STATION, 1880

TOPEKA STATION, 1900

purchase. The Northwestern Pacific had never been integrated successfully with the Santa Fe. Interchange in the Bay area was awkward. The excellent results obtained by tie treatment and the tapering off of new construction reduced the necessity for access to the forests.

A short, but important, extension of Santa Fe lines was made during World War II. Determined efforts to secure trackage rights into Long Beach, California, began in 1941 and culminated in the inauguration of freight service on December 15, 1945. Long Beach had become an industrial giant and its products moved over Santa Fe lines through interchange of freight. The Company was unable to secure a large volume as long as direct service to shippers was not offered. Freight could now be moved directly from Chicago or points on the system to Long Beach and vice versa.

EFFORTS TO ENTER ST. LOUIS

With the termination of World War II the Santa Fe endeavored to bring to final fruition one of its oldest objectives—entry into St. Louis. C. K. Holliday had included a line to St. Louis in his earliest dreams. No move was made toward accomplishment until the summer of 1887. The Santa Fe acquired terminal rights in St. Louis by purchase of the St. Louis County Railroad. Construction toward the main line in Missouri between Kansas City and Chicago was begun by a subsidiary, the St. Louis, Kansas City and Colorado Railroad. The new line was built as far as Union, Missouri, which was short of a connection. Three years later the Santa Fe entered St. Louis indirectly through the purchase of the Frisco. The entry was not in the manner in which the Company desired. The line of the Frisco west from St. Louis was not well integrated with the Santa Fe system.

Neither of the two attempts to serve St. Louis developed satisfactorily. Financial difficulties of the Frisco were too heavy for the weakened Santa Fe to bear. The companies were separated following the reorganization of the Santa Fe. The stub northwest to Union was sold. Outsiders of the Santa Fe expected entry into St.

Louis to be made by means of construction between Pekin and St. Louis. The plan was once given serious consideration by officials and service was offered for three years following 1890. This was shortly after acquisition of the Frisco and was made possible by the use of various trackage rights.

During the next forty years the Santa Fe contemplated reëntry to St. Louis but was diverted by other activities, two world wars, and a depression. Aggressive steps were taken upon cessation of hostilities in 1945. The Santa Fe and the Burlington Railroad applied to the Interstate Commerce Commission in June, 1946, for approval of a plan to enter St. Louis. No initial construction was involved, and the objective was to be attained by a logical yet complicated series of contracts. The Santa Fe and Burlington were to acquire the 156-mile line of the Gulf, Mobile and Ohio (Alton) from Kansas City to Mexico, Missouri. The Santa Fe and Burlington were to pay $24,000 for the stock interest in the line, which was nominally held by the Kansas City, St. Louis and Chicago Railroad. Both companies were to guarantee the interest, sinking fund, and principal of the outstanding bonds of the owner ($2,093,980). The sum of five million dollars was to be expended in rehabilitation of the line within five years. The Gulf, Mobile and Ohio was to benefit by a $100,000 per year reduction of terminal charges incurred as a proprietary line of the Kansas City Terminal Railway. The Gulf, Mobile and Ohio was to retain trackage rights over the Mexico-Kansas City line and to provide the Santa Fe and Burlington with trackage rights over two and one-half miles of line between Mexico and Francis. The Santa Fe was to secure trackage rights over the Burlington line between Francis and St. Louis and reciprocate by giving the Burlington rights over the Santa Fe main line between Bucklin and Sheffield. The Santa Fe planned to utilize facilities in St. Louis held by the Terminal Railroad Association. The city of St. Louis, the St. Louis Chamber of Commerce, and other public interests gave strong endorsement to the proposal. An equally vigorous reaction was registered by the Missouri Pacific, the Frisco, the Rock Island, the Cotton Belt, the

T&P, and other lines operating out of St. Louis. The rivals were opposed to additional division of traffic, regardless of the benefits.

A glance at the map of the Santa Fe system reveals the logic of the extension to the Company. St. Louis in addition to Chicago is a natural gateway to the East and a logical point for interchange of traffic between the West and the East. The city is the terminus

PROPOSED KANSAS CITY
ST LOUIS LINE

of several large eastern railroads. Both the service of industry and the strength of the Santa Fe would be improved by the entry. I. C. C. approval, nevertheless, was denied. Sound business principles are certain to revive the project in years to come. The Commission may be even more reluctant to grant rights to the Santa Fe because permission was given the Burlington in a later request.

ABANDONMENTS, DOUBLE-TRACKING, YARDS, RAILS, TIES, BALLAST, AND BRIDGES

Construction between 1896 and the present was by no means limited to the building of new mileage in railroadless areas. Equally important was the great building program of old lines. The original Santa Fe was in a sense duplicated by double-tracking. Also, as portions deteriorated and the need for repair arose, the replacement of parts did more than restore the original condition but advanced the line to new standards. Millions of dollars were spent reducing grades and curvature, strengthening or replacing bridges. The requirement of the traffic volume underwent great changes as the years elapsed.

As the needs of business changed, the Santa Fe modified its mileage. Branch lines were abandoned where the volume of traffic no longer justified operation. New lines were constructed to serve growing communities with their expanding industry, commerce, and agriculture. Changes in mileage were not as great as cursory examination of the annual reports of the Company indicates. Some of the changes represented shifts of operated mileage from subsidiaries to the parent company in the interests of corporate simplification.

The Santa Fe abandoned eighty-six miles of its lines in 1937 and 1938. Some of the mileage was between Havana and Cedarvale, Kansas, and the rest in California. In the following year thirty-one miles was retired. Elimination of mileage continued. A washout on the line of the Oklahoma Central Railroad between Purcell and Chickasha led to discontinuance of service. Operations had not been profitable, and when the disaster occurred no basis existed for restoration. Corporation simplification during the year accounted for the internal shift in the legal title to 391 miles of line.

The exigencies of the war forced the Company to accelerate abandonment in order to conserve manpower and materials. During 1942, 257 miles was abandoned. Leading casualties were:

> Florence to El Dorado, Kansas, 31 miles.
> Anthony, Kansas, to Cherokee, Oklahoma, 34 miles.
> Port Bolivar to High Island, Texas, 27 miles.
> Koehler Junction to Ute Park, New Mexico, 40 miles.
> Boise City, Oklahoma, to Clayton, New Mexico, 60 miles.
> Mt. Dora, New Mexico, to Farley, New Mexico, 37 miles.

Part of the mileage between Boise City and Farley was controlled by the Elkhart and Santa Fe Railway. Its dismantlement sealed the fate of a short line to a junction at Farley, New Mexico. The remainder of the line represented trackage rights on the Colorado and Southern mainline between Clayton and Mt. Dora.

Builders of the Santa Fe had regarded the mileage as a significant cutoff which might become a mainline of the system. The steep grades of the Raton Mountains were to be averted by the new cutoff. The Company came within a few miles of completion of the project only to stop work and eventually abandon the stubs. The rail from the abandoned mileage went to the Metals Reserve Company, an agency of the Federal Government. Some of the materials became a part of a line extending from the Persian Gulf north toward Russia.

Abandonments combined with shifts in legal title in 1942 accounted for a deduction of 821 miles in operated main track. This was offset by additions and transfers of legal title to the extent of 540 miles. Service was extended during the year on many miles of sidings and branches which were financed by agencies of the government.

An era of corporate simplification ended in 1942, and from 1943 to 1948 few adjustments were made, the exception being the entrance to Long Beach. Beginning in 1948 the work of simplification was resumed.

In 1897 the Santa Fe began double-tracking the congested bottleneck between Emporia and Florence. The project was completed in 1899 and afforded much-needed relief. A steady increase in traffic, however, soon necessitated double track to Newton as well as duplicate lines all of the distance into Chicago. By 1904 the work was under way or authorized on many sections of the line and in the vicinity of Raton. At the latter a second tunnel was bored during 1907 and 1908. The new passage was 2790 feet in length, approximately one-third longer than the old tunnel. The line was carefully located and effected a marked reduction in grade to 0.5 per cent through the new tunnel.

Double-tracking the Illinois division covered a span of eight years through 1911. Similar work was pushed in the Missouri division. At the outset of 1941 almost 1,000 miles had been paralleled. The growth of transcontinental traffic had prompted work on a second line from Albuquerque to Needles. The new tracks

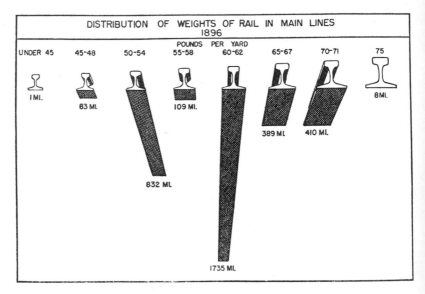

deviated from the old at points in order to cut the ruling grade from 1.4 per cent to .6 per cent. The reduction was partially at the expense of an increase in curvature.

At the end of 1925 the Santa Fe operated 1,596 miles of double track, 39 miles of third track, and 6 miles for fourth track. Twenty years later (1945) 340 additional miles of double track was in service; 5 miles of third track and 4 miles of fourth track had been added. The total of second, third, and fourth track in 1948 was approximately two thousand miles. The dual routes between Kansas and New Mexico via the Panhandle and Colorado had the effect of providing double track from Chicago to California with an offshoot to Denver.

Less spectacular than construction of new mileage or double-tracking was the building of yard tracks and sidings. These were of the utmost importance to the proper handling of shipments and trains. The construction was widely scattered over the system but intensified at the major cities. Although the individual projects were ordinarily small, the collective result was large. Between 1903 and 1945 approximately 4,000 miles of sidings and yard tracks was added, raising the total to 6,010 miles. A notable improvement was a new electric "hump" yard, put in operation at Argentine, Kansas, in 1949.

The qualitative changes in the trackage of the Santa Fe were as significant as the quantitative. The standard weight of the rails was steadily increased. In 1897 a weight of 75 pounds per yard was

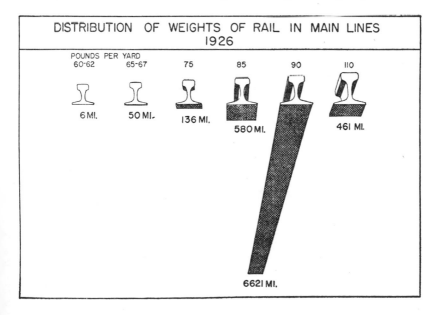

DISTRIBUTION OF WEIGHTS OF RAIL IN MAIN LINES
1926

POUNDS PER YARD
60-62   65-67   75   85   90   110

6 MI.   50 MI.   136 MI.   580 MI.   461 MI.

6621 MI.

adopted. This was raised to 85 in 1902; 90 in 1910; 110 in 1925; 112 in 1934; and 131 in 1939 for the transcontinental main tracks. The standard is now 132. Weights of 130 and 131 were introduced in mountain areas as early as 1928. As heavy rails were introduced the old rails were relegated to branch lines where they exceeded the originals in strength. Below is a chart showing the weight distribution of rail on the main track of main lines at selected dates:

Weight	Jan. 1, 1896	Jan. 1, 1916	Jan. 1, 1926	Jan. 1, 1942
131	....	....	....	276
112	....	....	....	1928
110	....	....	461	3547
90	....	3378	6621	2210
85	....	2800	580	225
80	....	....	....	....
75	8	880	136	....
70-71	410	7	....	....
65-67	389	189	50	....
60-62½	1735	83	6	....
55-58	109	142	....	....
50-54	832	4	....	....
45-48	83	....	....	....
Under 45	1	....	....	....
Total	3567	7483	7854	8216

Heavier rails and trains meant greater wear on ties. In 1902 the Santa Fe adopted the use of tie plates on soft wood ties to lessen the cutting effect of the rails. Later the use was expanded to include hardwood ties. As the rails grew so did the plates, ties, angle bars, and other rail accessories. The standard mainline rail adopted in 1939 called for tie plates twelve inches wide. Continued experiments were made in anti-rail creepers and rail joints which gave great assurance of stability of the track.

A railroad can be judged by its ballast. Lack of it is excusable on lightly traveled lines, but on main arteries the absence of ballast means rough riding, frequent repairs on rolling stock, short-lived ties and rails, and poor drainage. Beginning in 1896 officials of the

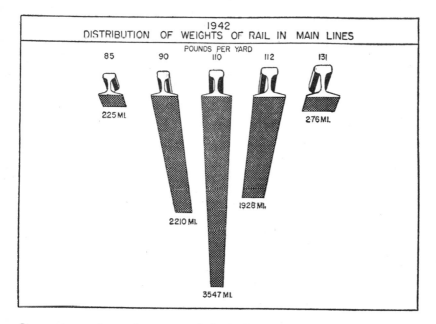

1942
DISTRIBUTION OF WEIGHTS OF RAIL IN MAIN LINES
POUNDS PER YARD

Company undertook to extend the ballasting as well as to improve the quality on lines previously surfaced. The statistics below measure the progress:

Ballast on Main Tracks of Main Lines

Kind	Jan. 1, '96	June 30, '09*	Jan. 1, '16	Jan. 1, '26	Jan. 1, '42
Crushed Rock	322	1429	2864	3325	4617
Slag		82			
Pit-run Gravel	587	2148	....1874†		
Engine Cinders	67	161	.... ⎫1019‡		
Volcanic Cinders		444	.... ⎬		
Burnt Gumbo	137	115	2923	3105	
Other		103			
Total Ballasted	1113	4482	5787	6430	7510
Oiled Roadbed		1261			
Unballasted	2454	1636	1696	1386	706
	3567	7379	7483	7816	8216

*Main lines.
†Also screenings.
‡Also gypsum and shell.

The per cent ballasted rose from 31 per cent in 1896 to 86 per cent in 1932. Crushed rock was used on much of the increase and offered the finest support known. The per cent of branches ballasted was lower and the per cent of sidings still less. Light traffic and intermittent use reduced the need for a cushion on this mileage.

A special department was established in 1944 to improve the methods and machinery used in maintenance of way. All phases of roadbed care were assigned to the department, including ballast cleaning, joint oiling, weed control, and track grouting. Chemicals developed during World War II for control of the terrors of the garden have been adapted to use on railroad rights of way.

The Santa Fe like other railroads has long battled the problem of soft track due to water pockets. Certain types of clay tend to squeeze out under the ballast section under the action of wheel loads when the clay is wet. Restoration to sound condition has been costly and time-consuming. Tracks have been repaired by driving ties and poles under the tracks where the ballast has become depressed into the subgrade. The latest and best means of coping with this type of soft track is to pump a grout composed of cement, sand, emulsified asphalt, and water into the ballast. The water is forced out and replaced by the grout, which has properties of weak cement, yet does not have the shortcomings of solid concrete. Results on the hydraulic grouting of 450 miles of soft track led officials to believe that a successful and economical solution has been found to one of railroad's oldest problems.

Notable betterment was made in the ties. An earlier chapter mentions the beginning of tie treatment at Las Vegas in 1885. Impregnation of ties with creosote or some other medium greatly increased the resistance to rot and insects. The Las Vegas plant was unable to meet the requirements of the system, and for many years the majority of the tie replacements remained untreated. A second plant was built at Bellemont, Arizona, in 1895, but it burned in 1905. Two years later the one at Las Vegas also went up in smoke. After the Santa Fe gained access to the pineries of east

Texas a mammoth installation for wood preservation was erected at Somerville. A major plant at Albuquerque replaced the loss at Las Vegas. Somerville and Albuquerque provided the Santa Fe with nearly all of its requirements until the Orient was purchased.

Many untreated ties were stored at National City, California, for aging and eventual insertion after 1911. During 1923 facilities were erected there for treating ties. The plant investment at National City was large. Output was halted during the war and heavy operations were resumed in 1947.

The Santa Fe used the Orient plant at Altus, Oklahoma, for treating hardwoods. In 1930 these operations were shifted to Wellington. The Company was a leader in many improvements designed to give greater longevity to ties. In order to prevent spike killing, holes were bored where the spikes were to be driven. Certain softwood timbers had hard wood dowels inserted as a further precaution. Screw spikes were utilized to give added strength. Ties were bored, trimmed, and adzed before treatment so that there would be no raw exposures. Inserted ties were dated, and their performances carefully observed. Since 1896 the life of ties has been doubled. At the present time, 58,000,000 cross ties are in service and they are replaced at a rate of 1,800,000 annually.

The Santa Fe was early handicapped by the lack of hardwood forests contiguous to the lines. Company representatives were sent to foreign countries in an effort to establish sources of supply. In 1907 E. O. Faulkner visited Hawaii, the Philippines, Japan, China, Manchuria, Korea, and Australia. Later, South and Central American sources were investigated. Between 1906 and 1912 over 6,000,000 ties were imported from Japan. They were primarily oak. Beginning in 1908 ohia ties were brought from Hawaii at an annual rate of 125,000.

The most interesting outgrowth of the exotic prospecting was an attempt of the Santa Fe to grow its own ties. Thousands of eucalyptus trees were planted in 1909 in the vicinity of Rancho Santa Fe in southern California. Supposedly hardwood ties would be available in fifteen years. The experiment of the Company attracted wide attention and led to a general boom in eucalyptus silviculture of the sort that dashed the hopes of thousands of investors in pecans and tulip bulbs.*

Vestiges of the eucalyptus ventures yet remain. The Santa Fe turned increased attention to tie treatment as the best means of reducing costs.

The program of bridge renewals begun in 1893 was pushed until 1899. Untreated wood yielded to treated timbers, steel, and concrete. The loading adopted during the 'nineties anticipated future requirements although higher standards were set later. The five major bridges over the Illinois, Mississippi, Missouri, Colorado, and Little Colorado were replaced and double-tracked.

The new double-track bridge over the Colorado at Topock was placed in service in 1945. The old structure had been built in 1890 and had been strengthened twice. The Santa Fe took advantage of the opportunity to improve the track alignment on the California side. The new bridge has already proved its merit.

The third spanning of the Canyon Diablo was opened for service in 1947. The double tracks are 222 feet over the floor of the Canyon. Company needs should be adequately served for decades to come.

Acquisition of countless lines of diverse clearances necessitated standardization. The work was time-consuming and persisted over many years. River control work has been another important phase of the engineering department. Thousands of dollars were expended on various strait jackets for rampaging and meandering rivers.

More technological progress has been made on the Santa Fe's lines than meets the eye. A cross section of road at present as compared with a cut in 1896 embodies as much contrast as a small steam locomotive, aged 50, and a modern streamlined Diesel

---

*The Santa Fe was much less visionary than one midwestern road which decided that the catalpa was the solution to the tie problem. The trees were planted along the right of way. They were expected to mature rapidly and to beautify the line. The plan obviously required no added acreage. A portable sawmill was to go up and down the line cutting the ties where needed. Great economies in transportation loomed. Subzero blasts decimated the saplings and ended the Utopian dreams of officials in the tie department.

freighter. The qualitative changes had matched strides with the quantitative. The Santa Fe represents over 13,000 miles of substantial well-kept main track. All the heavily traveled portions are double-tracked to handle peak loads with dispatch and safety. Numerous branches project wherever a profitable volume of business is present. Hundreds of sidings give door-to-door service for industry and agriculture. The Company is alert, ready to improve existing facilities, build new lines, or retire old mileage as changing circumstances warrant.

XI

Steamline to Streamline

"I'll put a girdle round about the earth
In forty minutes."—Shakespeare,
A Midsummer-Night's Dream.

GROWTH IN TRAFFIC

DURING THE YEAR ending June 30, 1897, revenue traffic of the Santa Fe amounted to 243,052,426 passenger miles and 2,062,483,268 freight ton miles. In 1948 the Company recorded 2,263,822,110 passenger revenue miles and 32,993,968,000 revenue freight ton miles. The one was almost ten times greater and the other sixteen! Freight revenue traffic in the early year did not even equal volume hauled for Company use in 1948! This tremendous development of volume did not spring miraculously from numerous lamps of Aladdin nor did it come steadily and easily. It came in surges of progressively larger proportions intermixed with recessions.

A portion of the growth was like Topsy's, but most of it was the product of assiduous cultivation. Much of it came in spite of rival railroads, trucks, ships, pipelines, and airlines; some of it because of them. Government regulations, droughts, floods, and countless other influences impinged with varied effects upon the fortunes of the Company in a manner which tended to diffuse the casual relations of growth. But the two factors remained sharply defined; one was the economic expansion of the territory, and the other was the contemporaneous effort of the Company to be the pacemaker or at least to keep the pace. The two were related in a fashion remindful of the old problem of the hen and the egg. During the period between 1869 and 1896 the Company led territorial development by a narrow margin; afterwards, the Southwest and the Santa Fe marched together. The area waxed rich in part because of the Santa Fe, and the Santa Fe waxed rich because of the area.

The operational history of the Railway may logically be divided into several periods—1896 to 1917, a time of uninterrupted growth; 1917 to 1920, Government operation; 1920 to 1930, maintenance of wartime volume in a period of peace; 1930 to 1940, depression and adjustment; after 1940 war and post-war volumes.

The management proceeded cautiously in the years which followed receivership. Changes in policy were carefully analyzed before decisions were made. Emphasis was shifted from construction and acquisition to the enlargement of traffic on a paying basis. President Ripley was determined that the Santa Fe would pursue a model business program. This was especially important because the difficulties of preceding years had centered public attention on the efforts to restore good will and respectability.

The Santa Fe of 1896, while a bit run-down, was considered one of the leading railroads of the Nation. Its territory was relatively settled and rapidly emerging from the extractive stage in historical development. There were, however, extensive portions where the marks of civilization were yet to be etched. Millions of relatively fertile acres were cropped by rabbits, antelopes, and widely separated herds of cattle. The subjugation of nature was rapid during the early years of the twentieth century. Westerners were equipped with ingenious mechanical advantages which compressed the progress of a decade into the span of a year. Railroads were a substantial leverage factor.

EQUIPMENT

The Santa Fe was ill-equipped in 1896 to carry out its chosen role. The lean years had scarred the trunk and branches. Equipment had not been maintained and had become obsolete. The locomotives were light, and the rolling stock was lacking in modern safety appliances. The shops, stations, and yards needed vast sums spent for repair. The new administration, though anxious to preserve a strong liquid position, aggressively embarked on a plan to modernize its plant and equipment. At the outset the improvement of old rolling stock seemed a wiser policy than purchase of new. Most of the freight cars and many of the locomotives were without automatic brakes and couplers. In the year ending June 30, 1897, the old link-and-pin combinations were replaced on 6,206 cars, 25 per cent of the total. The number equipped during the next two years was even higher. By 1900 virtually all cars had this essential labor-saving device.* The installation of airbrakes had been continued during the receivership and was completed by 1898. The carrying capacity of freight cars was raised at a rate from 500 to 1500 cars annually. The increases were usually 20,000 pounds above the old ratings of 30,000 or 40,000. The effect on train loads quickly became apparent. In one operating year (1898-99) a gain of 14 per cent was shown on freight trains. Heavier and more powerful locomotives, along with new methods of handling freight, were responsible for the showing.

The repair of rolling stock was emphasized. The general average of the fleet was much improved by the annual expenditure between 1896 and 1902 of approximately $2,700 per locomotive, $700 per passenger car, and $75 per freight car. The amount of work accomplished was substantially in excess of the current rate of depreciation. The increase in the carrying capacity between 1896 and 1917 is indicated in part by the statistics on equipment in service.

Combining numbers times the increase in tractive power gives the gross gain in locomotive power. Every year showed not only an advance in number but an advance in the pulling power, since the additions were invariably bigger and better. In the year ending June 30, 1904, an astounding gain of 13.55 per cent was shown in the tractive power per engine. Considering the fact that only 156 were added to a fleet of 1309 (32 retired), the new locomotives had to be much more powerful in order to show such an

---

*Required by the Safety Appliance Act of 1894.

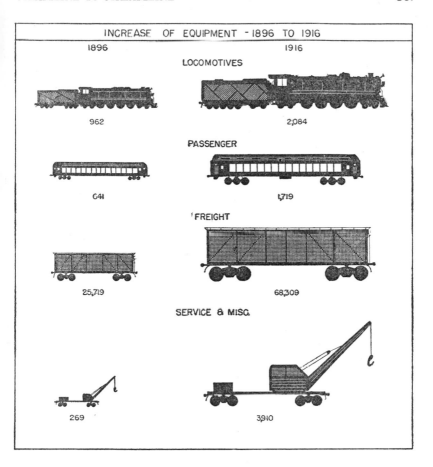

advance. In 1903 the average tractive power was 22,526 pounds and by 1916 it had risen to 34,535. Between 1904 and 1916 the weight per locomotive rose from 74.91 tons to 98.83. A fleet of 83 Mallets weighed over 200 tons per locomotive. The Santa Fe experimented with many designs in an effort to develop the types best suited to its requirements. Many of the engines were built at the Topeka and San Bernardino shops, but chief reliance was placed on the Baldwin Works. In 1911 the Santa Fe built a series of ten Mallets which were the largest locomotives in existence. They had a 2-10-10-2 wheel arrangement and a tractive power of 111,600 pounds. The overall weight was 616,000 pounds. The experiment was not successful, and the ponderous engines were remade into twenty locomotives. The increase in power combined with the program of grade reduction made for faster handling of heavier trains.

The fuel-supply problem on the Coast Lines of the Santa Fe was greatly eased by the local production of oil. Conversion from coal burners began, and by the end of 1900 locomotives in California were oil-fired. Later Williams, Arizona, became the dividing point. The abundance of petroleum in Texas enabled conversion there.

A small navy was provided to handle traffic between Galveston and Port Bolivar and in the San Francisco Bay. The Company acquired tugs, ferries, and car floats. Probably the most unusual additions to the rolling and floating stock of the Santa Fe were some motor coaches which were bought for rail service about 1910. They were streamlined in a revolutionary style that would have been quite acceptable thirty years later. A snub-nosed front and tapered rear made them the first streamlined railroad equipment ever put into service. The windows were of the porthole type. The design failed and the cars lived and died without propagating.

Specialized freight cars of certain types made marked gains between 1896 and 1917. Oil and refrigerator cars constituted a much higher percentage at the end of the period than at the start. The Company discontinued listing twelve beer cars. They were reclassified as "ice cars," perhaps to please Kansans. In passenger-train equipment the expansion of smoking, dining, and chair cars was most pronounced. Replacements and additions were consistently better, and the average level of comfort and safety was steadily advanced.

The outstanding passenger train put in service during the prewar era was the Santa Fe De Luxe, which began weekly runs to the Coast on December 12, 1911. It was the first extra-fare train on the system and operated on a 63-hour schedule. The surcharge was $25 each way. Passengers had the last word in current train comfort, with the added advantage of a barber shop, ladies' maids, stenographer, market reports, and telephone connections at terminals. This luxury train is supposed to have been a great success.

Special Trains, Including the Coyote Special

Special passenger trains were made up for breath-taking runs which captured the public's fancy. In 1899 the Huntington Special, carrying the president of the Southern Pacific, made a fast run from Pueblo to Chicago. Record-breaking time was made in March, 1900, when the eastbound Peacock Special negotiated the distance between Los Angeles and Chicago in 57 hours and 56 minutes. It carried A. R. Peacock, vice-president of the Carnegie Steel and Iron Company, who was on his way to Pittsburgh.

The performance of the Peacock Special remained unchallenged until 1903. H. P. Lowe of the Engineering Corporation of America was in New York when notified of serious illness in his family in Los Angeles. He immediately left for Chicago, where a special was in readiness. The trip was made in 52 hours and 49 minutes. The occasion was particularly memorable to some of the crew members. All who beat their schedule were given $50. The total elapsed time across the country was 73 hours and 21 minutes.

In January of 1904 a special was made up at Winslow, Arizona, to rush Charles W. Clark to his wife's bedside in Chicago. The train made an average speed of 44 miles an hour, including stops. The total time was 37 hours and 22 minutes.

The special which attracted the most attention of all on the Santa Fe or any other railroad was the Coyote Special of Death Valley Scotty. As in the case of the famous Nellie Bly, the run was made solely for the passenger's publicity purposes. On July 8, 1905, John Byrne, general passenger agent of the Santa Fe, was busy at work in his Los Angeles office when a stranger entered. He was cowboy-clad except for a cheap blue suit. After Byrne asked the puncher's business, the latter replied, "I've been thinking some of taking a train over your road to Chicago. I want you to put me there in forty-six hours. Can you do it?"

While Byrne speculated on the possibilities the stranger began to peel thousand dollar bills from a roll. Several minutes of rapid figuring followed, and Byrne accepted the challenge and $5,500. Departure was scheduled for the next day. News of Death Valley's run was flashed all over the country. Newspaper readers had a new interest. At the appointed time a crowd estimated as high as 20,000 congregated to see the start. Death Valley Scotty made a speech from the tender and entered the Pullman with his wife, F. N. Holman, and C. E. Van Loon. The Santa Fe assigned its best engineers to the run. They were known later as the "Nervy Nineteen." Holman in an article on the historic race contended that the Santa Fe picked only engineers who thought that there were no curves on the mainline. Chef Beyer of Fred Harvey fame supervised the meals in spite of his wife's entreaties to have a care for her and four little ones. Geyer's creations were superb. Dinner was served while Fred W. Jackson was at the throttle. The menu was specially prepared for Scotty.

Caviar Sandwich a la Death Valley   Iced Consomme
Porterhouse Steak a la Coyote,
two inches thick, and a Marvel of Tenderness
Broiled Squab on Toast, with Strips of Bacon au Scotty
Stuffed Tomatoes
Ice Cream with Colored Trimmings
Cheese   Coffee   Cigars

Unfortunately deliberate dining was impossible. Engineer Jackson gave the following account of the complications:[1]

> . . . we got the train going in a very short time to sixty miles per hour or more. Three miles from town Needles we hit the first bad place on a curve, which took Scotty's his wife's and newspaperman Mr. Van Loon's suppers from the table to the floor including the table cloth in a clean sweep. However, the engine and train straightened out again without any other bad effect. By the time we got to the Colorado River bridge (which we passed over about fifty miles per hour) we practically got used to these rough places. . . . We had not got very far before things began to fall to pieces in the cab of the engine. We only had three cars in the train, but it took both injectors to supply the boiler with water most of the time—the fireman Sam doing the cutting in and out with his in

jector, but the rigging to this injector fell apart. The engine was rolling so badly he was afraid to let loose his hold he had on the side of the cab with his left hand, which made it impossible to work with only one free hand. This high-wheeled engine was rolling so much that he was even afraid to get off his seat. . . . I let Mr. Doran run the engine while I went over and got the injector working again.

On account of the expected crowd at Kingman, Arizona, we decided to take water at McConnico and run Kingman, which we did. It may have been a disappointment to the folks there, but if we had stopped it would have made quite a delay and some may have been hurt. The whole town was around the depot when we passed through. . . .

There is one other part of this trip for which I wish to give credit to Mr. Doran, the extra engineer. Every time the engine was about to roll completely over he would rush to the high side of the engine cab. His extra weight on that side seemed to balance the engine back to normal again.

Van Loon wrote steadily and his dispatches were flashed to newspapers all over the Nation. Every crew experienced exciting moments as the maximum speed was exacted from the locomotives. Hot boxes developed. Rough track was encountered where heavy rains had fallen. Each man brought his engine to a stop ahead of schedule. Scotty greeted the curious throngs who congregated to see his Coyote Special. East of La Junta and across Kansas on the "race track," speeds of 85 and 90 were recorded. Part of the time Scotty rode in the cab and assisted in the firing. He tipped crew members liberally. President Roosevelt received the following telegram from Dodge City:

An American cowboy is coming east on a special train faster than any cowpuncher ever rode before; how much shall I break the transcontinental record?

The train crossed Illinois at an average speed of 60 miles per hour, including stops. A record-smashing top of 106 was attained. The exuberant Scotty arrived in Chicago after a total elapsed time of 44 hours and 54 minutes, having averaged 50.4 miles per hour, with all delays included in the estimate.

The run meant more to the Company than the fare or even the nationwide publicity and advertising. The Coyote Special was an ideal test of Santa Fe coördination of manpower and of locomotives, roadbed, and tracks. The run presaged the speeds to come and revealed the improvements necessary to swifter service. A booklet of the Santa Fe on the Coyote Special commented:

> And this miner from Death Valley incidentally helped advertise the fact that by going Santa Fe the journey from Pacific Ocean to the Great Lakes may be made in less than forty-five hours when necessary.

The next specials of the Santa Fe had more excuse for being than mere western exhilaration. A. D. Thomson was at Montreal in 1914 when notified of his son's illness at Raton, New Mexico. He immediately ordered a special for a Chicago physician and followed in another. The son was returned to Kansas City. All three runs were made at average speeds in excess of 50 miles per hour with a peak of 100.

Not all trains of the Santa Fe reflected such precise coördination and regard for time. Considerable tolerance of leisurely performance on the branches and in the frontier country was taken for granted. Old-timers in train service amaze the current generation of crews with stories of the early nineteen hundreds when railroading was not an exact science. Probably the best of the tales had its setting in Panhandle, Texas, when the chief recreation was bronco-busting.[2] Stakes were made up and everybody congregated at a plot near the station to watch the punchers try the outlaws. The crew of a northbound passenger train out of Amarillo (via the dogleg before the direct line was built) enjoyed the contests and tried to make up time so that they could linger for more of the show. On one occasion when a horse proved too much for its rider, the conductor leaned out the vestibule door and averred that he had $20 which said that the Pullman porter could not only do better than the previous performance but could ride any other bronc that citizens could wrangle.

"Bring on your porter, we'll get the hoss."

The event was scheduled for the next day. A record run was made from Amarillo and the crew covered all the bets their limited resources permitted. "Bones" jovially but confidently mounted the bronc. The sight was rather ludicrous, for the porter was still wearing his white jacket. The outlaw tried every trick that had upset others but to no avail. The porter rode the horse to a standstill while the fireman blew the whistle and the crowd roared. The crew pocketed their winnings and pulled out. Later the news spread that Bones had little seniority as a porter. One of the spectators had recognized him as a former professional bronco-buster from Colonel Charles Goodnight's great ranch.

Death Valley Scotty had established the record for speed on the Santa Fe, but almost as much publicity was attached to a record for slowness, or a record for speed by slow means. Early in 1910 Edward Payson Ripley, the president of the Company, received a letter from 71-year-old Edward Payson Weston, a renowned pedestrian. He asked for permission to use the Santa Fe right-of-way from Los Angeles to Chicago on a proposed cross-country jaunt. Ripley more than acquiesced, offering to provide rest stations and meals.* A small tricycle motor carried what provisions Weston needed between stations. The feat captured the fancy of a nation susceptible to such exploits. Crowds collected along the line to see the famous Weston stride. Chambers of Commerce had delegations pace Weston in and out of towns. A side-trip to the Canyon added two days. A great celebration was planned in Chicago, but Weston refused to put in an appearance, because he thought the publicity and arrangements inadequate. He reached New York on May 2 after ninety walking days. Mayor Gaynor and fifteen thousand were on hand. Although Weston extolled the merits of the Santa Fe roadbed for walking purposes, increasing numbers elected to ride.

SHOP IMPROVEMENTS, BLOCK SIGNALS, STATIONS, AND OFFICES

The passing of years and growth of traffic brought many changes to the Company. Shops, offices, stations, depots, and other buildings were renovated, replaced, built, or retired. Probably the great improvements were made in the shops. An excellent picture

---

*It is said that Weston was given almost unlimited authority and that he flagged down the California Limited and ordered meals.

of "before and after" at Topeka was given in 1916 by M. J. Drury, superintendent. He had worked there in 1889 and returned in 1912.

. . . The whole of the old shop could be put in our present blacksmith shop, but it sufficed for the day. Our power was light and our demands were not so exacting as in this competing age. The land upon which our new locomotive shops now stand was, during my first residence here, covered with homes and boarding-houses, gardens and shade trees. The locomotive has crowded the freight car out, and the latter has a new, modern home a mile east of the old homestead. In the eighties we employed four hundred men in the Topeka shops. Today we employ nearly three thousand. In the eighties no traveling cranes were in use. Today we have seven, varying in capacity from five to eighty tons.

Then we had torches and tallow candles for light at night, these making the darkness visible. Today we have 4,045 electric lights. Since that day pneumatic hammers and drills have come into general use. Autogenous and electric welding have become common, and the rate of pay for machinists has increased from twenty-two and one-half to forty cents per hour, and every comfort possible is shown our employees.

In the construction of our former shop and roundhouse buildings, apparently very little consideration was paid to the comfort of the men so far as lighting, heating, ventilation and so forth were considered. The new shop buildings at Topeka are models so far as the above mentioned factors are concerned. They are splendidly lighted, for, with the exception of very dark days, no artificial light is necessary during working hours. The drinking water for all the shop employees is boiled and cooled by indirect radiation, no ice being put directly into the water. In the winter fresh air, after passing over the steam coils to be heated, is blown into the shop, and in the summer months fresh air is passed over cooling coils and blown into the shop, insuring fresh cool air for the workmen at all points . . . . Ample stationary and portable lamps are provided during the necessary hours, which relieves the strain of the workmen's eyes. Goggles are furnished all mechanics engaged in work that may endanger their eyes through flying particles of steel. First aid stations are located for the comfort of the injured, and an automobile ambulance has been provided for the rapid transit of the seriously injured from the shops to the hospital.

The shops elsewhere underwent similar metamorphoses.* The Purchasing and Stores departments were greatly enlarged. A steel

---

*The other principal shop and engine houses were at Albuquerque, San Bernardino, Cleburne, Fort Madison, Chicago, Kansas City, La Junta, Clovis, Winslow, Prescott, Needles, and Barstow.

mill at Corwith in Chicago processed scrap gathered from the system. A rail mill at Newton manufactured guards, frogs, and switches. Reservoirs were built in arid regions to provide the Company with dependable water supplies. Marked improvement was made in water treatment, which prolonged the life of locomotive flues. Water tanks and coal-loading devices incorporated the latest in technologies.

Large expenditures were made to facilitate faster and safer movement of trains. In 1898 the installation of block signals was well under way. By 1914 the Company had 891 automatic block signals and 188 interlocking plants. In coöperation with Western Union the telegraph system was thoroughly overhauled. The Santa Fe was a leader in the adoption of train dispatching by telephone. Costly track elevation was carried out in Chicago between 1898 and 1904. The city had passed an ordinance calling for grade separation, and a "roof garden" plan for various lines was devised. For a time officials expected that the Chicago Electrification Ordinance of 1909 would require an outlay of several million. Ripley caustically seared the City Council. The measure was never enforced.

The most obvious improvement on the Santa Fe was the painting and repairing of depots and stations. The old administration had not offset wear and weather. Ripley urged prompt action and the task was soon completed. Ripley went beyond redecoration and had better buildings constructed at many places. Combined Harvey Houses and stations were distinct architectural achievements. The Santa Fe coöperated with other companies to erect union stations at such points as Joliet, Wichita, and Kansas City. The cost of the Kansas City Terminal was estimated as high as $40,000,000 but was shared through the Kansas City Terminal Company with a dozen railroads.

Office facilities were outgrown as rapidly as a small boy's trousers. The general office building in Topeka had to be enlarged in 1906-07. The relief afforded by the new wing lasted a short time. Facilities being severely taxed by 1909, a new white brick structure was built beside the old one of red brick. Though the colors clashed, the office force of 979 had ample space.

General offices in Amarillo were housed in an old frame building which had been moved in sections during 1903 from Roswell. Several additions were made, none of which reduced the fire hazard. At Galveston a four-story station and office building of red brick was erected for the home of the GC&SF. A white brick building of eight stories was added in 1913. Elsewhere the Company provided whatever facilities the business required.

TRAFFIC GAIN TO 1917

The improved methods of the Ripley regime brought immediate results. Each year the *Commercial and Financial Chronicle* marveled at the comeback staged by the Santa Fe. In 1914 the *Chronicle*'s review of the annual report began in the usual manner: "Probably there is no other railroad in the United States that has been able in recent years to present such uniformly satisfactory results, in good and poor periods alike, as the Atchison, Topeka and Santa Fe Railway Co."[3] Beginning in 1896 the Company went steadily forward. When general business activity declined the Santa Fe either went ahead or slipped much less than was expected. The statistics below reveal a relentless forward movement that overcame diverse depressing influences and made the most of advantageous factors. The sharp rise for 1916 and 1917 was largely attributable to World War I.

Passenger travel between 1896 and 1917 rose over 600 per cent. Although the rate per passenger mile had varied from year to year, the same level existed at the beginning and end of the span. For the year ending June 30, 1897, the charge was 2.293 cents per mile as compared with 2.276 cents in the year ending June 30, 1917. The number carried rose from 3,536,968 to 14,200,421. The outstanding change was the lengthening of the average trip. Passengers in 1896-97 went 68.72 miles each, while in 1916-17 they bought longer tickets good for 101.23 miles. There were diverse causes for this change, all of which benefited the Santa Fe.

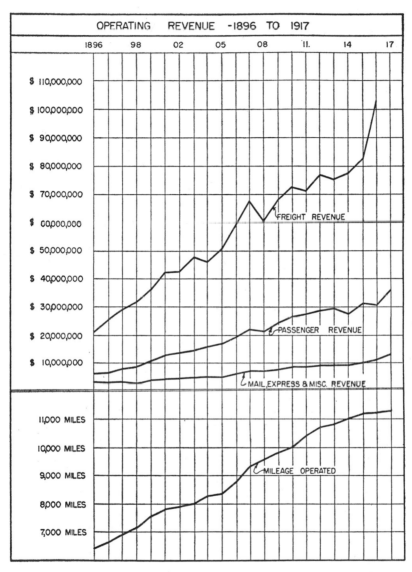

OPERATING   REVENUE   -1896 TO 1917

The swollen passenger receipts were the outgrowth of the development of the territory. To a certain extent they were the direct result of a carefully executed advertising program. The Passenger Department undertook to aid in the promotion of the western states for eastern vacationers. A substantial volume of travel to and from California was encouraged. The Company, however, concentrated its efforts on the lures of the Grand Canyon of the Colorado. If any railroad executive were asked what natural phenomenon he would like to have appear miraculously in the vicinity of his line, he would no doubt reply, "Another Grand Canyon." The drawing power of the mighty chasm has gathered strength in geometric ratio. Each personal visit has eventually meant several return trips as well as original trips of others. Part of the beauty of the Canyon from the traffic standpoint is its remote location. A long haul is assured. The nature of the environs makes for a minimum of competition with other forms of transportation. A further advantage is in the magnificent size of the spectacle. It is so big that millions of sightseers and souvenir hunters cannot disturb, mar, or in any manner alter the original beauty. Having an indescribable appeal that artists have never fully captured has enabled the Canyon to retain its monopoly. The finest canvas has been no better than a still picture of a fraction of the whole, ever-changing scene. The Canyon has to be seen at least once, preferably many times, to appreciate the interplay of color and size.

After the line was acquired to the south rim of the Canyon and Fred Harvey luxuriously encamped, the Santa Fe advertising men had their cue. Artists, lecturers, and writers were encouraged to visit and linger in the vicinity. The Santa Fe bought their better paintings and writings. Copies were widely distributed. Posters went out by the thousands. The amount of money allocated for newspaper advertisements was increased. These diverse channels of enticement reached millions who were previously unaware of the Canyon. Each year brought increasing numbers. None were ever sold a false bill of goods. The Grand Canyon has always been an unmatched spectacle.

Expositions in San Diego and San Francisco, linked with the development of the Panama Canal, enabled the Company to offset the blow at future freight traffic by ticket sales to tourists.

The gain in freight traffic in tons between 1896 and 1917 kept pace with passenger travel. The increase in freight revenue, however, lagged owing to the decline in rates. Receipts advanced over 550 per cent. During the operating year of 1896-97 the average rate per ton mile was 1.07 cents. In 1916-17 the rate had fallen to .927. Three factors served to offset the ill consequences. The average tons per freight-train load increased from 142 in 1898 to 497.75 in 1916-17. The second lever was the gain in the average distance per ton from 251.3 miles in 1896-97 to 341.82 in 1916-17. The ratio of empties to loaded cars declined 10 per cent as a result of greater care in making up and handling freight trains. The one-way nature of much Santa Fe traffic, such as the movement of grains toward the Gulf ports and citrus fruit to the East, precluded greater reduction.

The classification of freight tonnage strikingly revealed the alternations taking place in the Southwest. Below are comparable figures and percentages for the years ending June 30, 1897, and 1917.

Although the comparison of single years fails to recognize many temporary factors, the two years selected are reasonably representative except for corn in the second test year. In 1916, for example, 838,310 tons were hauled. The most noticeable changes during the two decades were the greater increases in the volume of mineral and manufactured products. In 1897 they constituted 41 per cent of the total tonnage and in 1917 over 61 per cent. Outstanding gains were shown in wheat, oil, and fruits and vegetables. The table reveals on the whole a maturing of the economy. A more refined and diversified tonnage became evident. The Santa Fe began to carry its eggs in many baskets, and each basket contained other things besides eggs.

The gains of the Company were in the face of sharp competition which was refereed by the Interstate Commerce Commission. The days of rate wars had passed. On four occasions the Santa Fe was accused of forgetting and charged with rebating. Suits were filed, but the indictments were not sustained. The cases involved coal, salt, oil, and lime. The Company admitted a technical guilt in the coal case, but not in the others. The lime case was

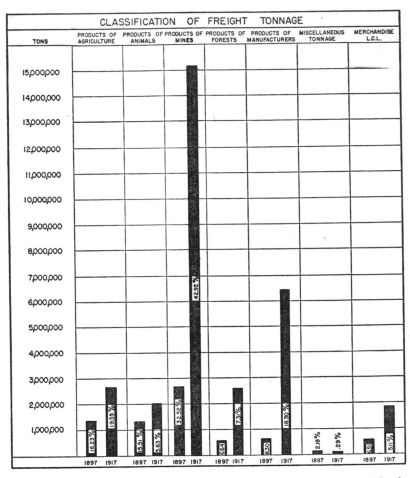

the most interesting because of a national aspect which suddenly developed. The trouble began in Nelson, Arizona, where the Grand Canyon Lime and Cement Company had a small loading car which was used to carry lime to the Santa Fe. The car was said to hold 800 pounds; therefore, fifty unloadings should have filled a California-bound freight car. The shipper was accordingly billed for 40,900 pounds. After regular shipments had been made for a period of months, it was discovered that on arrival at destination the lime weighed much less. Either it was never loaded or was lost en route. A Santa Fe clerk, acting without official authorization, made a deal with the shipper to refund the estimated overcharge as well as to continue the old billing but to weigh the cars each time and refund the difference. Some of the correspondence while innocent in the light of all the facts was incriminating if isolated. A disgruntled employee who had been jailed for embezzling Company funds appropriated some of the correspondence and turned it over to authorities. Teddy Roosevelt, the trustbuster, came into possession of one of the stolen letters and built a message to Congress around the missive. The Santa Fe was stunned by the surprise attack. Before it recovered, Judge Welborn of the U. S. District Court in Los Angeles had fined the Company $330,000. The case went to the Circuit Court of Appeals and the decision of the lower court was set aside, Judge Welborn sharply criticized, and a rehearing ordered. The complete account was given at the second trial and the Santa Fe fully exonerated.

The policy of Ripley was diametrically opposed to rebating or cutthroat methods. The vast and complicated nature of railroad rates caused borderline cases to outcrop in the same manner as on all railroads then and later.

Traffic and facilities between 1896 and 1917 had many blows of natural and man-made origin. Droughts, blights, and floods occurred in some localities almost every year. The Santa Fe extended over such a wide area that it enjoyed a loss similar to that sustained by large insurance companies. Losses in occasional years from floods were unusually heavy and hampered the Company more than would ordinarily be expected. In June, 1913, the Kansas (Kaw) River went on its greatest sustained rampage. The mainline from Topeka to Kansas City with minor exceptions was inundated from three to sixteen feet. Terminal facilities at Kansas City were severely damaged; boxcars were lost; engines rolled over; and two feet of silt was deposited over the Company's property. Train service was interrupted for weeks. Great damage was done to growing crops. Santa Fe employees coöperated wholeheartedly in battling the waters. At Topeka a large ferry was hastily constructed to rescue several hundred who were marooned. When the Topeka waterworks ceased to function, the Santa Fe connected its water supply with the city lines and was able to pump quantities adequate to avert disaster.

Destructive floods ravaged southern Texas in the spring of 1903 and revisited eastern Kansas in 1904. During the operating year of 1904-05 portions of the system were out of service almost continuously. Damage was heaviest in Arizona and New Mexico. The cost of repairs exceeded $2,000,000, only a fraction of the loss borne by the Company.

The various strikes discussed in the chapter dealing with labor relations hampered operations considerably. A coal miners' strike in Colorado and New Mexico beginning in November, 1903, was more damaging than any walkout of Santa Fe employees. The Company had depended upon the mines for locomotive fuel as well as commercial freight tonnage. The estimate of the loss arising out of the enhanced cost of fuel and revenue decline was set at not less than $1,500,000.

In addition to the misfortunes which brought general destruction to Company property and the contiguous revenue-producing area, several more localized disasters affected the Santa Fe. On September 8 and 9, 1900, the Galveston hurricane devastated the island city and wrecked the facilities of the Gulf, Colorado and Santa Fe as well as $30,000,000 worth of other property. Notable relief work was performed by the Santa Fe and the Southern Pacific by marshaling equipment to rush relief supplies to the stricken area. In 1915 a second great hurricane lashed the city. Better protective barriers restricted the damage. The GC&SF loss at Galveston and Port Bolivar was $300,000. After the storm, relief trains were rushed to Texas City, where supplies and personnel were transferred to barges and landed at Galveston. The general office building was converted into barracks and afforded shelter for an estimated 3,000 to 4,000. Locomotive tanks were drained to provide drinking water. Switch engines furnished steam to pump water from abandoned wells for cooking and watering stock.

Comparable assistance was given to the people of San Francisco following the earthquake and fire of 1906.

ARDMORE DISASTER AND CLAIMS

The catastrophe of greatest import to the Santa Fe was the "Ardmore, Oklahoma, Explosion" of September 27, 1915. The GC&SF held a tank car of highly volatile casing-head gasoline on a spur in Ardmore pending orders from the Ardmore Refining Company, the consignee. About noon of the fateful day employees noticed a whistling sound of vapors escaping through safety valves. The day was hot and apparently pressure was being developed within the tank. Guards were posted and the consignee was sought. The refinery representative removed the dome cap and a stream of gases and vapor shot upward and later settled over a circular area estimated to have a radius of 300 feet. Without warning a terrific explosion rent the air. Buildings collapsed as if made of straw. The blast was heard for twenty miles. Flames broke out and the screams of hundreds of the maimed and terrified added horror to the scene. Relief crews were quickly organized and the leveled business district was mined for the dead and injured. The death list was set at forty-eight and ten times that many had been injured. Governmental investigating committees rushed to the scene. There was much debate over assignment of responsibility. Although representatives of the GC&SF and Santa Fe believed that the Company would probably be exonerated, there was strong feeling on the part of the townspeople. Long-drawn-out litigation seemed inevitable; then suddenly the Santa Fe made an announcement almost as startling as the original explosion. On October 4, President Ripley sent the following telegram to Mayor Val Mullen:

During its entire life the Santa Fe has never declined to pay any just claim, and in the face of the terrible calamity which has overtaken the people of Ardmore, I am not disposed to await the judgment of the court upon the liability of the railway company.

I therefore propose that a careful investigation of claims for death, personal injury and property be entered upon by the committee of your citizens

which you have appointed and that a statement be prepared and submitted
to us with a view to prompt adjustment of such claims in cash upon a
reasonable basis. Mr. Pettibone will see you Wednesday to confer as to
details.

No action of the Company could have been more warmly received. The press of the Nation and even Europe was so startled
that more space was devoted to the unprecedented action of the
Santa Fe than to the original disaster. Ardmore citizens promptly
erected a large billboard on which appeared a Santa Fe emblem
with the words:

GREAT IS THE "SANTA FE"

Ripley   Pettibone

ONE CORPORATION "WITH A SOUL"

A committee of six leading Ardmore residents received the claims
and negotiated with representatives of the Santa Fe. The latter had
some of its legal staff and claim investigators on hand. S. T.
Bledsoe and John S. Douglas did outstanding work for the Company. Douglas was later given a $1,000 bonus and Bledsoe made
progress toward eventual presidency of the Santa Fe. The fairness
of the Company had wide appeal and was a keen disappointment
to the large number of shysters who had descended on Ardmore.
Most of the settlements were made during the following month
and by May, 1916, a total of 1967 cases had been settled involving
48 fatalities, 504 personal injuries, and 1415 property claims. The
total awards amounted to $938,546 at the time and later soared to
over $1,000,000. Only one lawsuit was tried, the plaintiff receiving
$1,000 less than the Committee had recommended. In a few
instances attempts were made to defraud the Company, but they
were readily exposed. One Negro mammy asked for a large award
because of her husband. The latter was a roustabout and was play-
ing pool when the explosion occurred. His cronies were killed and
their bereaved received thousands of dollars. This particular
mammy was asked why she petitioned for more money. The calm
reply was "Cause mah husbin' lived!"

The Ardmore explosion was wholly regrettable, yet the exemplary conduct of the Santa Fe did much to assuage remorse. The decision to assume the damages was a characteristic action of the Ripley regime. The President abhorred lawsuits and permitted the Company to become involved in them only when no other course was feasible.

The "Ardmore Explosion" was the only major setback sustained by the Ripley administration in its efforts toward reduction of claims against the Company. A broad educational program was prosecuted among shippers and employees regarding proper packaging and handling of consignments. The rate of losses was pared and more cordial relations with shippers were established. Complete elimination of claims was never achieved. Patrons of the Santa Fe sometimes paid unexpected amounts and offset claims. The treasurer received a letter from an ex-tramp who enclosed five dollars explaining:

> I am now a member of the Salvation Army. That's why I pay for the meat. I would like to pay for the rides I stole, but I can't do it now. The meat is the only thing I ever stole, except rides. A brakebeam ride is, I think, worth only half a cent a mile. If I can settle on that basis sometime my conscience will be clear.

The refund sent by a farmer was larger:

> Three years ago a Santa Fe train killed four of my pigs, which had broken out of the pen and gone on the railroad track. I put in a claim for damage, and the Company turned it down. I knew that it was my fault that the pigs got on the railroad, but just the same I was sore. One night, to get even, I led a worthless blind horse out on the track, and a train came along pretty soon and killed the critter. I put in a claim for damage and received $30. I had a change of heart later, turned from my wicked ways and joined the church. My work with the blind horse was cruel and criminal. Perhaps I ought to be in jail. Anyhow I will do the next best thing to ease my conscience. I am returning the $30 to the company paid for the horse, with interest, and as I also beat my way on several passenger trains on account of the pigs, I am making the full amount $50, which ought to cover everything. I couldn't sleep with this in my system.

The period between 1896 and 1917 saw the complete transformation of the Santa Fe from a company weakened by many ills to one of the most virile organizations in existence. Improvements had been made in every phase of operations. Freight solicitors sought and cultivated tonnage throughout the territory as well as in areas remote from the Santa Fe. Shippers were pleasantly surprised to receive interim reports of the movement of their consignments and plans could be made to receive cars. Faster service was offered. Damages were reduced and valid claims were paid promptly. The regime won the loyalty of employees and the public alike. The former were the recipients of various forms of social insurance. A far-reaching safety program was set in motion by Isaiah Hale for the mutual gain of the employees and the Company. The good will of the public was cultivated by improved service and more directly by increased contacts between officials and the clientele. Ripley insisted that Santa Fe executives meet their friends as well as critics. "Harmony" specials were organized. Lawrence, Kansas, for example, might be visited by a dozen top-ranking officials who came for a friendly chat with local farmers and business men. Cordial relations were established and Santa Fe policy was better adjusted to requirements of the community.

World War I Operation

Near the end of the era of traffic expansion the increase became in large measure attributable to World War I. The volume flowing over the Santa Fe began to tax the carrying power. Eastern railroads were deluged by the flow of traffic from the western lines as well as that of local origin. Terminals at Pittsburgh, Philadelphia, Baltimore, and New York were hopelessly congested. Cars were blocked as far west as the Missouri River. Thousands of off-line Santa Fe cars were caught in the snarl and could not be recovered. An attempt was made to ease the situation by working through the Railroads' War Board. The combination of fear, antitrust prosecution, and adherence to competitive methods did not provide the necessary relief. The companies were hampered by lack of equipment and faced mounting labor costs. Assumption of Government control was announced by presidential proclamation to be effective December 28, 1917. For more than two years the railroads of the country (except most of the short lines) were operated under the jurisdiction of Director General William G. McAdoo and his successors. What happened to the Santa Fe was substantially the same as the experience of other lines. The personnel remained unchanged except at the top. Duplicate leadership was provided. Ripley and several others continued to safeguard the interests of the stockholders while the second set of Santa Fe officials shifted their association to the Government. William B. Storey became the federal manager. Walker D. Hines, the general counsel, resigned to become McAdoo's assistant and later succeeded him. The Government obligated itself to maintain and preserve the condition of the line and to pay a rental based on the average earnings during the preceding period of three years. Various regional and functional officials were appointed, with more or less jurisdiction over the federal managers. The four leading express companies were consolidated and taken over by the railroads as the American Railway Express.

Far-reaching changes were made in the operations of the Santa Fe. Off-line offices were closed and freight and passenger solicitation ceased everywhere. The city ticket agencies were combined with those of other lines. Industrial, agricultural, and colonization work, as well as advertising and public relations, were discontinued. The Company made repairs in shops of former competitors and the latter used Santa Fe facilities. At San Francisco and Oakland all railroads used ferryboats of the Southern Pacific. Rolling stock of the railroads was pooled and Santa Fe boxcars wandered far afield. By the end of the period the car accountants had lost track of many and had no inkling of the condition of others. Passenger service was curtailed. The Santa Fe was given the preference in Chicago-Los Angeles travel but had to concede the Chicago-San Francisco business. Shippers lost their right to designate routes. This accounted for many changes in old procedures. Terminal facilities were shared at many points and some significant economies effected. Competing passenger train service was cur-

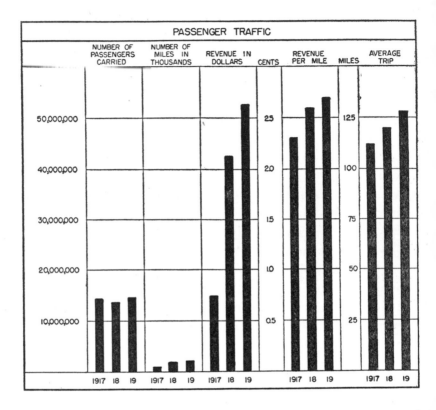

tailed. Parlor, observation, and dining cars were either eliminated or operated in reduced numbers. *Per diem* charges were waived on cars on foreign lines and each road was to keep the supply on hand in good repair. This directive obviously led to trouble. In spite of innumerable administrative mistakes the railroads assumed a larger volume than ever before and the operation was reasonably successful. Losses were incurred for understandable reasons, such as high wages, relatively low rates, and the pressure for speed.

The Santa Fe carried its share of the burden. Below are graphs of selected statistics for passenger and freight traffic. The year 1917 is included to serve as a guide.

In the two years of operation ending December 31, 1919, the number of locomotives owned by the Santa Fe increased 126, and a gain of 3656 was recorded in all types of cars. Many of the com-

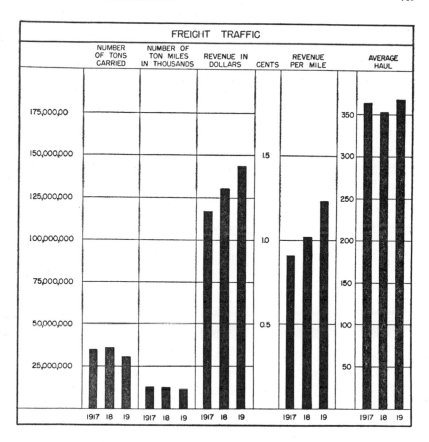

FREIGHT TRAFFIC

pound locomotives were converted into simple types. The amount spent for maintenance of equipment advanced from $2,406 per mile in 1917 to $4,002 in 1919. Maintenance of way and structures rose from $1,787 per mile to $2,550. Rising costs of labor and materials offset much of the increased rate of expenditure. Santa Fe officials declared that the railroad and its equipment suffered severe deterioration. The most important bequest of the Government to the Santa Fe was the new labor relations. Railway labor emerged from the War on a nationalized basis, but distressed by countless narrowly drawn working rules all of which resulted in raising operating costs for the new plateau of hourly rates of pay.

The Roaring 'Twenties

The end of Government operation came with Wilson's signature on the Transportation Act of 1920. On March 1 private control was restored. Great celebrations were held all over the Santa Fe. Old stationery, stored since 1917, was brought to light. Car accountants dug into the task of locating the rolling stock and clarifying ownership of cars on Company tracks. There were 60,142 cars, representing almost every road in the Country, on the lines. The Passenger, Freight, and other departments took measures to recreate the facilities and methods which had proved successful in the days of old. Once again the Santa Fe was on its own and ready to continue its progress. Unfortunately the old engineer was no longer at the throttle. President Ripley had ended his final run at the close of 1919. He remained as chairman of the board until February 4, 1920, when the Santa Fe lost its peerless leader. William B. Storey succeeded Ripley, relying on those principles which his predecessor had used with such impressive results.

The experience of the Santa Fe between 1920 and 1929 was typical of the experiences of railroads in general. The year 1920 was a peak followed by a slight decline in gross operating revenue. Another rise came in 1926, a recession in 1928, and a new high in 1929. The range of variation was surprisingly narrow. The lowest gross was recorded in 1921 as $228,925,070, and the highest in 1929, $267,189,178. Fundamental changes, nevertheless, had occurred in the sources of income. Passenger receipts had declined every year except for a slight recovery in 1922. This loss was offset by the favorable showing in freight revenue. Widely divergent factors were at work in the transportation field, and stress and strain impinged upon the Santa Fe with mixed results. The whole period was one of the most satisfactory in the Company's history. Facilities were fully utilized. Efforts were successfully concentrated on improvements rather than expansion. The general business outlook was good, with assurance of two chickens in every pot.

Santa Fe officials were deeply engrossed during the ten-year period of 1920-29 inclusive in improvements of the line, equipment, and service. The astronomical total of $296,176,004 was spent for additions and betterments of road and equipment. The results were manifest in every phase of the business. Changed methods were equally evident.

Decline in passenger traffic made itself felt in passenger-train cars. The melting away of volume occasioned an excess of retirements over replacements. But the margin was not wide. At the end of 1929 the Company had 823 passenger-carrying cars other than diners as compared with 1057 at the beginning of the 'twenties. Gains were recorded in certain types which represented an attempt to adjust the equipment to conditions. A net of over 170 coaches was withdrawn. These were cars that were obsolete and badly worn and represented 36 of the original number. The retirement of chair cars was less significant. There were increases in combination cars, which were put into service on branch lines where traffic was light. A gain from 42 to 55 in the number of dining cars indicated a quickening of train service to attract customers and meet competition. Smoking cars dwindled from 169 to 88. The Santa Fe acquired its first lounge cars and added a new type of express. The inventory of 1929 showed 42 refrigerated express cars.

Speeds of passenger trains were advanced on most runs, although the Chief required the same time in 1928 to reach California from Chicago as the Santa Fe De Luxe required seventeen years earlier. In 1929 the running time was cut to 58 hours each way. The California Limited and the Grand Canyon Limited were changed to faster schedules.

Other means were adopted to bolster passenger traffic. Historic and scenic points in the Southwest were widely advertised. Elaborate itineraries by Harvey cars to Indian pueblos and ruins were integrated with transcontinental travel on the California Limited and the Navajo. Californians were urged to spend their vacations in the East, and eastern residents were invited to forget their troubles in sunny California. A substantial shuttling was encouraged.

A twofold effort was made to improve passenger operations. The first has already been discussed under efforts to induce travel. The second approach was to whittle costs. Service was not skimped; in fact, it was immeasurably ameliorated. Expenses of operation were curtailed by intensive research for greater efficiency and longevity in locomotives. Improved design, better methods of firing, and other developments enabled substantial economies. In 1929 the Santa Fe acquired a fleet of gas-electric cars for branch lines. These were of the combination coach-smoker type with or without baggage and mail facilities. Lower costs of operation enabled more effective competition with busses. The all-in-one feature was better adjusted to the light requirement of traffic on branches. No longer did the lack of balance exist between motive power and train load.

The trend in freight cars was the reverse of that for passenger cars. The annual report for the year ending December 31, 1919, listed 71,992; a decade later there were 87,060. Nor did the mere addition in number measure the transformation. The average capacity per car was advanced from 36.09 ton to 40.63. It was the same old story of stronger construction on all additions and overhauls. The general state of repair was steadily raised. Although all types showed gains, disproportionate increases were made in refrigerated and oil cars. The development of the Winter Garden of Texas and the amazing growth of fruits and vegetables in California and, to a lesser extent, in Arizona accounted for the addition of the first type. Large icing facilities were erected for maintenance of low temperatures on shipments en route. The heavy drain on oil pools in Kansas, Oklahoma, Texas, and California occasioned purchases of tank cars for transporting oil and its derivatives.

Changes in locomotives in the 'twenties were concentrated on raising efficiency rather than increasing the size. Super-heating steam, mechanical stoking on coal burners, heated feedwater, and booster engines were among the multitude of features which were introduced or expanded. A crude gauge of the net result is the gain in tractive power. At the beginning of 1920 the average was 36,741 pounds; at the end of 1929 the figure was 49,736, a gain of 35 per cent. The number of engines had declined from 2,195 to 1,993, but the total pulling power had risen almost 25 per cent. Increased speeds and superior utilization enabled the smaller number to travel more train miles.

The most interesting engine put into service during the period was not distinguished by either size, speed, or advanced design. A fireless locomotive was obtained for switching cars under the great warehouses and jobbers' mart built by the Santa Fe in Dallas. The boiler conformed more to thermos bottle specifications than anything else. A stationary boiler in the heating plant of the development charged the fireless locomotive with sufficient steam pressure for several hours of work. Lack of a firebox caused the appearance to be decidedly abbreviated. Absence of smoke made the engine admirably suited to subterranean service.

The Santa Fe replaced countless station buildings during the 'twenties with substantial structures of pleasing appearance. When the one at Emporia, Kansas, was completed, William Allen White, with becoming civic modesty, wrote:

> This station is the best station on the Santa Fe railroad. It is not so elaborate as the station, offices, Harvey House and curio store at Albuquerque but as a station it is the best Santa Fe station of all.
>
> For a few months, or possibly a few years, Emporia can swell around with this distinction, but not for long. The Santa Fe is too progressive. Next year it will build a better station somewhere else, and the year after build a better station still. The people of the Middle West cannot move fast enough to keep up with the Santa Fe.

Enlargement of the shops at San Bernardino was the major change in housing of the Mechanical Department. The latest in equipment was acquired for repair centers all over the system. The main shops of the newly purchased Orient were converted and used primarily for the repair of refrigerator cars.

The growing complexities of business conduct for the nth time taxed the capacity of office space. More had to be provided everywhere but especially at Topeka and Amarillo. The general office quarters in Topeka had been enlarged in 1910 by construction of an imposing white brick building connecting with the old red brick structure. The latter was torn down and replaced with a new building which harmonized with the 1910 addition, so that to all outward appearances the whole was new. Formal opening of the new facilities took place on April 18, 1925. By incorporating the most advanced features of railroad office buildings and providing ample margin for expansion the Company met all its needs for many years.

Extension of lines in northwest Texas, western Kansas and Oklahoma, and eastern Colorado and New Mexico and the rapid development of the area necessitated many enlargements of the frame office building of the Western Lines in Amarillo.* The old structure was grossly inadequate and a definite firetrap. In 1928 work was begun on a replacement. A handsome fourteen-story Gothic building was erected for use beginning in 1930.

The heavy expenditures for all the diverse improvements seemed more than justified by the level of business maintained during the 'twenties. No other similar span approached this period. Below is a graph of the statistics for operating revenues.

The decline in passenger revenue has already been commented upon, but some postscripts are in order. The average length of trip per passenger more than doubled. In 1920 the figure was 139.83 miles and in 1929 it was 291.63. No better barometer of the influence of private automobiles and busses exists. The rival means of transportation first invaded the short-haul business. Passenger rates made a slight gain from 2.899 cents per mile in 1920 to 3.057 in 1929. The increase was inadequate to offet the loss in numbers, and the passenger revenue per train mile declined from $2.45 to $1.56. The many methods utilized by the Company to resist the trend were moderately effective but only in a negative way.

---

*The Western Lines of the Santa Fe comprised those west of Newton and Wellington to the Rio Grande River, Denver, and El Paso.

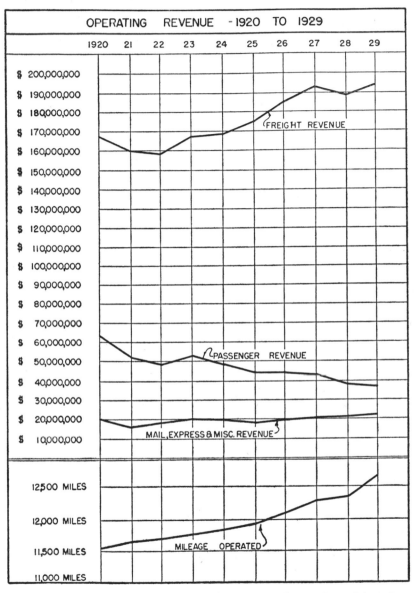

The best showing of the Santa Fe was in the realm of freight. Revenues forged ahead in the face of a reduction in rates and hauls. Gross earnings per ton mile eased from 1.316 cents to 1.234. The average distance sagged from 347 to 325. Various factors were

operative which affected the length of haul. A large volume of
tonnage which formerly moved by railroad was diverted to the
intercoastal water traffic through the Panama Canal. This business
had provided the maximum in distance and hence profitability.
The influence of trucks was not strong in the Santa Fe territory.
Like passenger cars, trucks initially preëmpted the short-haul business of the railroad, especially on LCL shipments.

The classification of freight tonnage disclosed the steady aging
of the economy of the Nation. Agricultural and animal products
yielded percentage points to manufacturing. Grains lagged far
behind citrus fruits and vegetables.* Absolute gains but relative
declines occurred in animals and their products. Major increases
were shown in certain minerals which far exceeded the loss in
bituminous coal. Copper ore and concentrates shipped in 1929
outweighed coal over one million tons. The gain in sulphur (brim-
stone) rose from a negligible amount to 1,759,800 tons. Forest products lagged, as did less-than-carload shipments. The movement of
manufactured items rose from 27 per cent to 30 per cent of the
total tonnage. Refined oils and automobiles made outstanding
advances. Most evident in a comparison of 1929 with 1920 was the
greater diversification in the tonnage. In 1920 the list of products
which moved in volume was restricted to staple items, but in 1929
considerable refinement had taken place, the list becoming widely
diversified.

Freight Development

Conditions were favorable for a heavy volume of freight tonnage during the 'twenties regardless of the policies and methods
of the Santa Fe. A significant fraction of the amount hauled, however, was the direct result of careful cultivation. Competition
among railroads was sharp, and a do-nothing attitude would have
been calamitous. Regulation had tended to equalize times as well
as charges between competing points and heightened the emphasis

---

*Special low rates on grains accorded in the spring of 1929 accounted for a greater
disparity in revenues from grains than in tonnage.

on advertising, courteous solicitation of shipments, minimization of damages, prompt handling of claims, agricultural and industrial development, and coöperation with shippers in countless other ways. The Santa Fe began to exercise extreme care in the selection of its contact men in freight solicitation. A combination of a pleasant personality and thorough knowledge of traffic was required. Initial shipments meant continued business if the clients' merchandising was undamaged. Shippers were advised on proper packaging. Engineers were counseled on correct handling of trains. Quick stops were to be avoided; slack in the train was to be eased out. The campaign was successful. Payments for loss and damage declined from 2.56 per cent of freight revenue in 1920 to .50 per cent in 1928; nor was there any change in the policy of recognizing valid claims.

The pre-war program of stimulating agricultural development was revived. "Squealers' Specials" carried fat hogs known as "safety razorbacks" over Kansas, Oklahoma, and Texas. Experts from Kansas State Agricultural College, representatives of the Department of Agriculture, and state officials made up the personnel. Lectures were given on various problems incidental to maximum production of pork. "Cow," "Sow," "Hen," and "Diversified" specials brought information about improved methods of agriculture. An agricultural newspaper edited by J. F. Jarrell, *The Earth,* was distributed to thousands. It kept its readers abreast of the latest techniques in farming. The Company installed improved loading facilities all over the system and offered faster shipment of livestock.

Equally effective as a traffic magnet was the industrial development sponsored by the Santa Fe. Industry, unlike agriculture, was obviously mobile to a certain extent. Often a company had no choice about its regional location because of the source of raw materials or some similar consideration. Within the region, however, a company might have a choice of locating on any of several railroads. The Santa Fe was determined to secure the traffic prizes. A carefully prepared report showing the precise advantages of a

Santa Fe location was frequently sufficient to draw the new business, providing rival lines did nothing or were less effective in their salesmanship. Sometimes the Santa Fe bought choice industrial sites in order to have them available to industries which might be in need of them. Vegetable sheds, elevators, and industrial buildings of all types were erected and leased or sold. The availability of tailor-made buildings offered at reasonable rentals (subject to I.C.C. review) lured many a ton mile. The Santa Fe coöperated in the establishment of stockyards, produce terminals and markets, and many other ventures intended to swell freight receipts. Three of these were outstanding: the Dallas Terminal; the Central Manufacturing District in Los Angeles; and the Chicago Produce Terminal.

The development of the Dallas Terminal unknowingly was begun in 1916 when the GC&SF moved from its passenger station to the new union station. The old building and tracks were no longer used. They covered a large area within a few blocks of the heart of the thriving business district. For a time city officials contemplated acquiring the land for conversion to a thoroughfare. Certain local business leaders led by Lloyd R. Whitson, an architect, believed that a jobbers' mart would be of greater benefit. The idea was laid before the Santa Fe and found ready acceptance. The Terminal Building Corporation of Dallas was organized in 1923 to carry out the project. Millions of dollars were expended. Four buildings approximately four square blocks were erected. They ranged in height from eight to nineteen stories and were designed for office space, general warehousing, and cold storage. Underground tracks enabled a fireless locomotive to pull freight cars where their contents could be unloaded directly on the elevators. The arrangement was superb for handling merchandise, and the location in the business district offered easy access for buyers. Space was readily rented, and today the buildings seem to house the entire list of large companies operating in Texas. The office building unit was taken over by the United States Government in October, 1942. Undoubtedly the volume of traffic added by the development has been enormous and has more than offset the disadvantages of the circuitous route of the Santa Fe with Dallas to and from the north.

The development in Los Angeles has been larger in scope than in Dallas. The Company not only endeavored to provide facilities for warehousing and display but sought location of the manufacturing enterprises. The Santa Fe and its subsidiaries have extensive holdings in and around Los Angeles on which have been established industries that contribute considerable tonnage, but the largest single development has been the Central Manufacturing District. The program was launched in 1923 on a strategic cauliflower patch along the Los Angeles River. Over three hundred acres of choice industrial land was the basis of the venture. An extensive network of tracks was laid to serve the area. A mammoth warehouse building became the hub of the enterprise. Sites were leased and the Los Angeles Union Stock Yards successfully promoted. By 1929 the buildings were valued at $15,000,000. In six years the area had become one of the major industrial districts of the city. A great produce market was completed. The Central Manufacturing District was such a success that the Santa Fe through a subsidiary bought the adjoining 1,135 acres of the Bandini Estate Company. Although the industrial development program in Los Angeles has already accomplished much, great expansion is possible, even probable.

The Chicago Produce Terminal was sponsored jointly with the Illinois Central. The construction of Wacker Drive had forced the razing of the old South Water Street market. After a new location was found for the latter, many of the old firms shifted. Not all moved together. Many elected to locate in the new market provided by the two railroads along the tracks of the Santa Fe. The first buildings were opened in 1925 and more space was added during the following years. By 1927 the Chicago Produce Terminal was reputed to be the second largest in the world.

In the middle 'twenties the *Santa Fe Magazine* launched a campaign among employees for the solicitation of business. Lists of names and accomplishments were published. A surprising amount of interest was manifested and some tonnage and passengers were attracted. The principal benefits had not been anticipated. A remarkable sense of unity was built up among employees and impetus was given to the public relations program of the Company.

The end of the 'twenties found the Santa Fe at its maximum in efficiency and strength. Equipment, buildings, and roadbed showed the result of heavy expenditures for maintenance and improvements. The personnel was well organized; management, sound. Net corporate income after taxes and interest had been ranging between forty and sixty millions, with the figure reaching $61,036,803 for 1929. Substantial amounts had been plowed back and a strong current position developed. The Company was prepared for fat or lean years, preferably the former.

PROGRESS DURING DEPRESSION

The next decade in railroading was colored by two major influences: the prolonged period of business prostration, with the attendant collapse of industry and agriculture; and the effective competition with other forms of transportation. Both occasioned readjustments, not in the form of submission but rather in the acceptance of a challenge. Depression was met with the administration of stimulants to the area by rate concessions to distressed farmers, while costs of service were pared to the minimum. Truck companies were met in their own province with trucks and by speeded freight service. Busses, private automobiles, and airplanes found the streamlined train a more worthy adversary than the old-style train. Moreover, the Santa Fe openly invaded the bus business with the acquisition of a vast network of lines. The Company, in effect, began to shift from the railroad business to the transportation business. Throughout the whole of the decade, doings in Washington affected the operating conditions of the Santa Fe as well as every other railroad.

Although graphs of traffic during the early 'thirties showed precipitous declines, the Company did not atrophy or remain static. Various moves indicated that officials had faith in the return of traffic. Samuel T. Bledsoe, who succeeded William B. Storey as president at the nadir, was a combined optimist and realist.* Some of the greatest improvements in locomotives and rolling stock took place in the financial twilight of the Bledsoe administration.

THE SHIFT TO DIESELS, STREAMLINING, AND AIR CONDITIONING

A reduction in the number of locomotives was inevitable. The spread between the number and the requirements widened. Old units were retired. Fewer trains, faster and more powerful replacements, made the total effective decline less than the change in numbers suggests. The following figures give an overall comparison of the fleet of the Santa Fe:

Date	Number	Total Tractive power	Average Tractive power
Jan. 1, 1930	1993	99,123,848	49,736
Dec. 31, 1939	1600	86,467,400	54,042

Undoubtedly the faster average at the later date minimized the difference in total tractive power. The diminution in the number affected nearly all types except the Mountain and Mikado engine.

---

*Samuel T. Bledsoe had long been identified with the Santa Fe. He was born in Clinton County, Kentucky, on May 12, 1868. He attended local public and private schools and later the Southern Normal and the Business College of Bowling Green, Kentucky. After teaching school in his home state from 1885 to 1887, he moved to Texas, where he read law under one of the leading barristers in Sherman and entered the University of Texas Law School, in 1888. The passing of two years and assiduous study brought admission to the bar. His shingle was hung successively in Ardmore, Guthrie, and Oklahoma City. There he grew in legal stature and became an outstanding authority on Indian land laws and on railroad matters. His initial association with the Santa Fe family came in 1895, when he was appointed local attorney for the GC&SF in Ardmore. For many years Bledsoe was a partner of James R. Cottingham. The firm acted as solicitor for the Company in Oklahoma. (Association with Cottingham must have been a good steppingstone, because another of Cottingham's partners, E. E. McInnis, also rose to hold the important post of general counsel of the Santa Fe.) Bledsoe progressively held the following positions: general attorney for the Company in Oklahoma City, assistant general solicitor, general counsel, and president after May 2, 1933. He was also chairman of the executive committee of the board and an official in several other companies. Bledsoe was a staunch proponent of good public relations and systematized Santa Fe efforts in this direction. His judicious administration lasted until March 8, 1939, when death intervened.

Mallets, Ten Wheel, and Balanced Compound Pacifics were eliminated. A slight gain was shown in Mountain locomotives. The
most significant change during the period was the introduction
of Diesel power. The Santa Fe added thirty-nine Diesel switch
engines and fifteen designed for road use on passenger trains.

The introduction of Diesels on the Santa Fe began in 1935
when a two-unit Diesel-electric was acquired and put on experimental runs. The results were impressive, and in May, 1936, a
new passenger train, the Super-Chief, began shuttle service between Chicago and Los Angeles. The scheduled time was 39
hours and 45 minutes, requiring an average speed of 57.3 miles
per hour including stops. Chicago and the Pacific were, in effect,
several hundred miles closer to each other. The new engine was
given the same public acclaim accorded streamliners on other railroads. From the initial runs numerous advantages, independent of
the traffic appeal, were apparent. The locomotive had faster ac-
celeration and was better on curves because of its lower center of
gravity. The distance traveled between servicings was much greater and the same engine could make the entire run. The eventual
consequence of the reduced need of servicing the growing fleet
of Diesels was to raise the allocation of overhead servicing expenses on the older types.

The historic death-defying run of the Coyote Special was surpassed daily by the performances of a fleet of streamliners acquired by the Company.* In May, 1937, the Super-Chief streaked
across the country to Chicago in 36 hours and 49 minutes at an
average of 63.5 miles per hour. The amazing speed of 87.3 was
maintained over one stretch of 202 miles.

The fifteen Diesels owned at the close of the 'thirties were of
proved quality. Their performances matched the greater efficiency
in the operating personnel and the improved conditions of the
roadbed.

---

*The Santa Fe bought its first streamlined steam locomotive in 1937.

Additions to locomotives in freight service continued the long-established progressive policy. Greater tractive power and speed seemed to be the main advances.

Diesel streamlined locomotives were complemented by a fleet of lightweight stainless-steel passenger cars. The new stock was approximately one-half the weight of standard coaches yet had adequate strength and immeasurably better riding quality. Interior decorations were as admirable as the exterior. The appointments of the Super-Chief, for example, blended the Navajo motif with modern requirements for comfort, and made clever use of photomurals.

Without belittling the merits of streamlining passenger trains, another development in cars was probably a more important achievement—air conditioning. Happily the two features were not mutually exclusive, all streamlined trains being air conditioned. Indeed, air conditioning was installed on much of the rolling stock before the era of racy lines. The lucky timing was fortuitous. The middle 'thirties broke all heat records in the history of several states traversed by the Santa Fe and by that time the installation was widespread. The project began in August, 1930, when mechanical equipment for cooling air was installed on a diner.* The gratifying results brought refinements and expansion. By 1933 more than one-third (twenty-three of fifty-nine) of the diners were equipped. Installation was extended to other types of cars the following year. The Company announced in 1935 that virtually all coaches and sleeping cars on important trains had manufactured weather. The benefits to the Santa Fe were greater than on most railroads primarily because of the hotter climates and, secondarily, because of the longer average passenger trip.

The use of motor coaches, which began on a large scale at the end of the preceding decade, was continued. At the end of 1939 a total of forty-four was in service.

---

*Between 1911 and 1926 the Santa Fe used an ineffective icing system for reducing temperatures.

A decline in the number of freight cars was largely offset by an increase in the tonnage capacity. On December 31, 1939, the Santa Fe had 75,381 freight cars in service with an average capacity of 43.65 tons for a total of 3,290,314 tons.

Fewer changes were made in shop facilities than in any other period in the Railway's history. Nevertheless, large expenditures were made to provide the best in repair equipment.

NEW STATIONS

Passenger and freight stations were replaced and enlarged. Some of the undertakings were of imposing proportions. A large bus and rail passenger terminal was built in San Francisco. The greatest development was in Los Angeles, where the Santa Fe united with the Southern Pacific and Union Pacific to build one of the finest stations in the country. The Spanish-mission style was well adapted to the requirements, and the result was an efficient structure blending perfectly with the traditions of early California. Final cost of the project was approximately $9,000,000. Fred Harvey was established, and the station opened May 7, 1939.

Santa Fe travelers destined for Chicago in the 1890's were much impressed with the station facilities. The Dearborn Station was considered one of the finest in the Nation. Fifty years later the station was the same, but the opinion of travelers was completely reversed. The corrective appeared to be dismantling and construction of a new building. Critics underestimated what could be done by remodeling, and the Dearborn Station has been completely rejuvenated, with startling results. On the inside, it is now one of the most attractive stations of the system.

A new home was provided for the general offices of the Gulf Lines in Galveston. The addition erected in 1913 was retained and integrated in the new structure. Work began early in 1931 and was completed the following year. The first floor was devoted to the passenger-station requirements of the railroads entering Galveston. Gulf Lines offices utilized the seven floors above. The new office raised the facilities of the GC&SF to a standard comparable to the quality of the major buildings in Amarillo and Topeka. In Los Angeles the Coast Lines were adequately, but not pretentiously, housed in a portion of the Kerchoff Building. Executive offices of the Santa Fe continued to be located in the Railway Exchange in Chicago facing Lake Michigan.

TRAFFIC IN THE 'THIRTIES

Viewed in perspective, the amount of betterment of locomotives, cars, shops, offices, and road was far less in the 'thirties than in the preceding decade. Nevertheless, technology had advanced so much that a dollar in new assets meant more power or efficiency than two dollars in old assets. These qualitative changes maintained the Santa Fe forward movement in spite of the light receipts. Freight revenue dropped 52 per cent from 1929 to 1933. Passenger revenue fell even more. Returns in 1934 were only one-third of the 1929 total and the latter was far off the showing in 1920. The record of the Santa Fe during the trying period is given below.

Decline in passenger miles was less pronounced than decline in revenue. Rates were subjected to heavy reductions in the first years of the depression. The average revenue per passenger mile had been 3.057 cents in 1929. Ten years later it was 1.77 cents. The correlation between the rate level and revenue was probably not perfect, and maintenance of rates would not necessarily have meant maintenance of revenue. Other forms of transportation had to be met. The amazing length of the average journey per passenger on the Santa Fe continued to stretch. In 1929 the figure was 292, and in 1939 it was 398. The latter distance was almost eight times the average on the Class I railroads of the Nation.

The factors affecting passenger traffic were also operative on freight, although in a less pronounced degree. From 1929 to 1939 average revenue per ton mile declined from 1.234 cents to 1.090 cents, while the haul increased from 325 miles to 377. Since freight revenue bulked much larger than passenger, the smaller relative changes in freight rates had a magnified effect on net operating revenue.

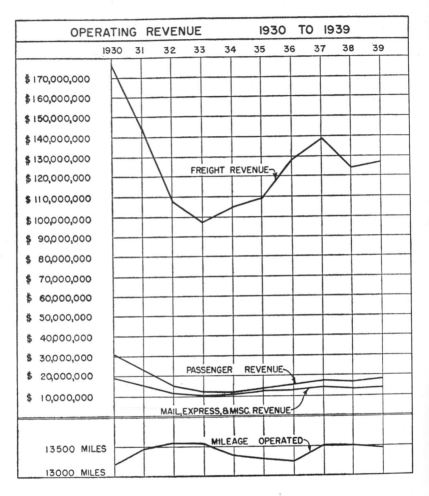

All major types of freight traffic declined during the fateful decade. Products of agriculture were curtailed by the series of droughts.* The same was true of traffic in animals and their deriva-

*While the period was generally dry, many floods spread devastation at scattered times and places. Damage in 1935 was heavy in Kansas. In October, 1932, a severe washout disrupted service on the Southern Pacific-Santa Fe line at Tehachapi Pass. The grape movement was at its peak, and the Company was unable to resume operations for two weeks. Loss in revenue was heavy. One locomotive disappeared in the flood waters and was finally located by means of a magnetic needle. Torrential downpours in rainless California early in March, 1938, caused major damages to lines, especially at Cajon Pass. Traffic was halted for eight days while repair crews and equipment from all over the system were rushed to the area and service was restored.

tives. Truck competition was especially severe in the movement of agricultural products. The greatest decline was in mineral volumes. Pipelines wrested the crude-oil flow. The disproportionate curtailment in heavy industries and building caused tonnage of ores, coal, stone, gravel and other materials to dwindle. In 1929 products of mines had accounted for 36 per cent of all tonnage, and in 1939 the percentage was less than 29. Manufactures were affected by the lack of urban, and, especially, rural purchasing power, but the showing was reasonably good. The percentage of total tonnage rose 5 per cent. LCL freight was siphoned off by trucking companies.

Various measures were taken to combat the plight of the Company. Remedial governmental action was sought through railroad organizations, with little relief. The best corrective for business doldrums and competition was believed to be progressive methods. Mention has already been made of the improved passenger equipment. In the face of a disastrous trend in railroad travel the Santa Fe acquired the largest fleet of streamliners owned by any company. Two Super-Chiefs, six Chiefs, two El Capitans, a Kansas Citian, a Chicagoan, a San Diegan, and two Golden Gates were worthy opponents of the most adverse forces. Economy meals on El Capitans and the Scout proved popular attractions. Registered nurses on the Scout freely rendered unexpected services. Faster and more comfortable accommodations enabled the Company to take maximum advantage of the gradual recovery of general business conditions.

BUS AND TRUCK LINES

The increased installation of motor coaches on branch lines met bus competition indirectly by reducing operating costs and increasing the Company's strength.

Notwithstanding the aggressiveness of the Santa Fe, the segment of public travel garnered by busses continued to grow. Officials recognized that busses were here to stay regardless of the Company. The rival was a strong competitor on short trips and had successfully invaded the realm of cross-country business. The Company faced the issue realistically and decided to begin bus operations, though planning to keep rail operations paramount. Whatever subsidy busses enjoyed as a result of alleged insufficient taxation it would then obtain. A more important reason for the invasion of the rival enterprise was to secure rather obvious economies of integrated operation. At the same time that bus interests were bought, the Santa Fe acquired an extensive system of truck lines and for similar reasons. Control over truck lines held forth promise of getting income one way or another and of maximizing profits of trucking and railroading by integrating service. There was a defensive aspect of the expansion. Rival railroads had blanketed Santa Fe territory with a cover of bus and truck lines.

In September, 1935, the controlling interest of the Southern Kansas Stage lines was acquired.* This company operated busses over most of the territory of the Railroad and conducted trucking in the Middle West. Subsequent to 1935 the Santa Fe created or bought subsidiaries which enlarged the scope of operations. It offered bus service connecting such points as Chicago, St. Louis, Denver, El Paso, Salt Lake City, Little Rock, Lincoln, San Diego, and San Francisco. Several of the motor-carrier companies were consolidated in 1937 into the Santa Fe Trail Transportation Company.

Vigorous expansion of bus operation followed the decision of the Santa Fe to become a motor carrier. Schedules of the ex-rivals were coördinated and common terminals were used at many points. None of the companies obtained by the Santa Fe had permits to handle intrastate business in California. A choice market loomed, and permission was sought to begin local service. This move was linked with a plan to establish bus-rail travel between Los Angeles and San Francisco. Prior to this time the Santa Fe had difficulty in competing for passenger traffic between the cities. Trains had to veer east of Barstow, thereby adding mileage and

---

*Only 65 per cent of the stock was initially purchased. An option to buy the remainder was exercised by 1939.

time. The proposed scheme was to run luxury busses between Los Angeles and Bakersfield, where a connection could be made with a new streamlined train to the Bay cities. The time schedule was comparable to that offered on the superior rail route of the Southern Pacific. Strong opposition came from the Southern Pacific and its satellites, the Greyhound and Pacific Electric Railway, and certain railroad brotherhoods. A spirited and costly struggle followed. Certificates were granted and the new service installed. It was unique in that rates by bus or rail were the same (a cent and a half per mile). Tickets were interchangeable. The system represented complete integration of the sort generally envisaged as the ultimate development for the Nation in rail-bus relations.

Equipment for the bus lines matched the Railway for progress. Air-conditioned busses were introduced in 1938. Streamlining appeared the next year. Busses purchased in 1940 had baggage compartments under the seats in the latest mode.

Truck operations in the 'thirties were confined to Kansas, Oklahoma, Nebraska, and Missouri with a short line into Arkansas. A large fleet of trucks was built up. Units acquired in 1939 had the cab over the engine to gain power and space. Additions during the following years were Diesel-powered and had corrugated stainless-steel trailers. Beginning in 1940 a coördinated system of handling freight was instituted. Heavy trains no longer stopped for LCL business at small towns between sizable cities. Trucks paralleled the track and collected shipments to be turned over to the railroads in quantities. The same trucks were used to pick up shipments at the terminals for delivery at intermediate points. This system offered many economies and stepped up the speed of freight trains by eliminating stops. Patrons in cities had faster service, and the schedule of the trucks was adjusted so that the merchants in the small towns also received goods more promptly.

In 1931 the Santa Fe introduced pickup and delivery service of freight by local truckers. This struck an effective blow at intercity motor carriers by providing door-to-door service.

Another means of coping with motor carriers was the inauguration of graduated LCL rates at certain points in the territory.[4] Reduction in delays and faster locomotives also enabled better operating results.

OPERATIONS DURING AND AFTER WORLD WAR II

A combination of modest business recovery and progressive methods stabilized the operating results of the Company during the last half of the 'thirties. The net income was by no means satisfactory, but the adverse trend had been stopped and considerable resistance developed against any future setback. Near the end of the decade the quickened pulse of industry began to turn the wheels of the Santa Fe faster as hostilities in Europe broke out.* The pump-priming scope of the early New Deal was dwarfed by the flood of purchasing power engendered by allied purchases and National Defense. By 1940 World War II was the dominant influence on the showing of the Santa Fe. The entry of the United States into the war late in 1941 brought record volumes of passengers and freight. Formerly the struggle was to get traffic; now the struggle was to handle traffic. Commendable as the early efforts

---

*In the midst of this pickup in traffic the death of President Bledsoe necessitated new leadership for the Santa Fe. Edward J. Engel had much in common with his predecessors. Each of them had been advanced to the presidency at a time when the affairs of the Company were in a state of flux and presented countless new problems. Ripley had the task of rehabilitating a convalescent; Storey had to make the post-war adjustment from government operation; Bledsoe had the monumental task of steaming through the depression; and Engel was responsible for a sizable segment of the Nation's waging of war. Like earlier presidents, Engel had a long background of experience. Unlike them, he had never worked for any firm other than the Santa Fe. His steady rise had followed a pattern familiar in railroading. The position of stenographer has long served as an apprenticeship to executive position in the industry. Engel began as a stenographer for the Santa Fe in 1899, when he was twenty-four years old. Engel was born in Havana, Ohio, July 28, 1874. He attended local schools and the business college at Sandusky. Shortly after joining his fortunes with the Santa Fe, he was transferred to the office of President Ripley. There he enjoyed the enviable privilege of executive training under the leadership of the Santa Fe's greatest. Promotions were rapid, and by 1910 Engel held the rank of assistant to the president. Election to a vice-presidency came in 1918 and to the executive vice-presidency in 1938. His long affiliation with the Company in important official capacities gave him an intimate knowledge of the business. Engel more than anyone else was in a position to exact the last unit of efficiency from the human and physical resources of the Company required by the exigencies of war. He retired from the presidency and the chairmanship of the Executive Committee of the Company on August 1, 1944, but remained a director until his death on May 30, 1947, at Pasadena, California.

had been, they seemed rather weak in comparison with the energy expended in carrying out the Civil War maxim of "Gettin' thar fustest with the mostest."

The extent of the impact of World War II on the Santa Fe is evident from the surge in revenue after 1940. The telltale record is on the following page.

Freight revenue in 1945 was almost four times the total in 1933. Passenger revenue increased ten times. The surge was difficult to handle because the period of gain was compressed into three or four years. Records established in World War I were dwarfed during the second conflict. Lower rates during World War II made the figures even more impressive. The number of freight and passenger miles rose to enormous proportions. Freight ton miles in 1945 were more than 37,000,000,000 and passenger miles were 6,400,000,000. Total operating revenue of $528,000,000 in 1944 was $232,000,000 more than the total earned by the Santa Fe from the day James Pratt bought the first ticket at Wakarusa, Kansas, on April 1, 1869, to the end of 1895. The increase in the volume of mail and express business incidental to the War almost kept pace with the swelling freight and passenger revenues. There was a gain of 150 per cent.

The number of miles each ton of freight was hauled increased between 1939 and 1949 from 377 to 5,503. The revenue per ton mile in 1949 was 1.393 cents, which was less than two-tenths of a cent above the record for 1929 and only three-tenths of a cent above that for 1939. The revenue per passenger mile in 1949 was 2.348 cents, and each passenger's average trip was 498 miles. In 1939 he had gone only 398 miles. Freight-rate increases averaging 17½ per cent were authorized near the end of 1947. Two small increases in 1949 added 7.9 per cent. The advance was a response to a request by all railroads. The pressure of mounting costs was more than most railroads had been able to bear, and the I.C.C. provided temporary relief. Passenger fares were increased at about the same time to 3½ cents per mile for first-class, 3 cents for intermediate, and 2½ cents for western coach fares. The basic 1½

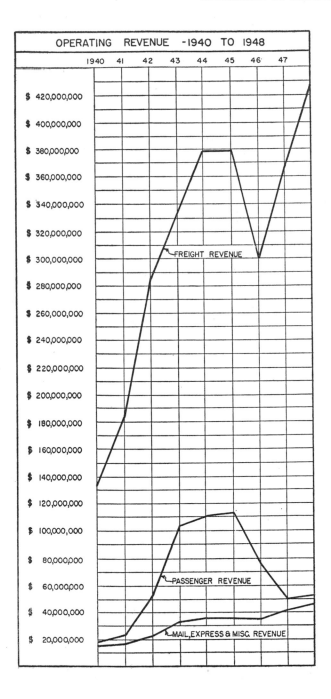

cents coach fare for transcontinental trips was not altered. The interim increase in rates for handling U. S. mail was granted December 23, 1947. The advance of 25 per cent was the first increase since 1928. A 10 per cent reduction in class freight rates was made on the portion of the Santa Fe east of the Rocky Mountains during 1947. The reduction was a part of the Interstate Commerce Commission order of 1945 calling for uniform freight classification and uniform class rates.

In 1947 the Department of Justice brought action against the railroads, alleging that unreasonable freight charges had been made during the War. The complaint called for refunds of two billion dollars. Successful action by the Department of Justice threatened the entire financial structure of the industry and the individual lines. Though Santa Fe officials regarded the suit as fantastic, they could not help being disturbed. Past experience with political moves has taught the Company some bitter lessons.

The tremendous expansibility of the Santa Fe was no less a revelation than the elasticity displayed by all of the railroads. No early-day problems of the struggling Company could compare with those posed by the war economy. Whether a solution to difficulties was found in 1875 was a concern only to the Santa Fe and to the limited number of employees and settlers whose fortunes were partly dependent on the Railroad. In 1940 and the succeeding years the functioning of a sizable and vital segment of the nation depended upon the Santa Fe's capacity to handle unprecedented volumes on short notice without corresponding increases in personnel and equipment. Although trucks, busses, airlines, and pipelines yielded a full measure of service, the greatest burden of the war transportation was thrust upon the railroads. Locomotives operated around the clock to rush troops and war materials to destinations. The raw fibers of battle were red-balled from field and mine to factories for processing. The Santa Fe never functioned more smoothly. Emergencies were conquered as quickly as they appeared. Not only were all demands met but officials on their own ititiative planned and executed countless schemes for furthering the war effort.*

Numerous parts of the Santa Fe machine could not be made larger during the war years. Critical shortages of metals and men as well as alterations in order of importance of use prevented the Company from taking advantage of the conventional means of handling traffic requirements. In the three years ending in 1942 only 117 locomotives were added, including 21 which were merely reinstated. Retirements were 78, so that the net gain was 39. The latter figure was not truly representative of the change, since the new locomotives were immeasurably superior to those retired. Included in the 117 were 86 Diesel units. Long before the United States became openly involved in war, the Santa Fe pioneered in freight locomotives by ordering a fleet of four-unit streamlined Diesels. Early in 1941 the first of these giants was delivered. A dozen more were added as rapidly as manufacturing permitted. The Diesel freighters were a boon to the Company. Any one of them could handle loads of a hundred heavy cars at the speed of a passenger train. The new equipment was assigned to runs between Argentine, Kansas, and Belen, New Mexico, and between Winslow, Arizona, and Bakersfield or San Bernardino, California. The extraordinary length of the runs is mute testimony of the savings in time.

The Santa Fe was unable to secure the number of locomotives desired during the war. The railroads in general could not con-

---

*No small portion of the credit for the wartime performance of the Company is due Fred G. Gurley, who moved up from executive vice-president to the presidency on August 1, 1944. Gurley in many ways operates like E. P. Ripley. Both served their executive apprenticeship on the Burlington and shifted at a high level to the Santa Fe. Both quickly became spokesmen for their industry as well as for the Company. Moreover, they came into leadership relatively young for railroad executives.

Fred Gurley was born near Sedalia, Missouri, February 20, 1889, and was brought up in the outskirts of Kansas City. He joined his brother on the Burlington in Wyoming in 1906, and worked up through the operating department to the post of general superintendent in 1925. Ralph Budd appointed Gurley assistant to the vice-president in charge of operations, and in due time the "to" came out of his title. Gurley's ability led the Santa Fe in 1939 to offer him the post of vice-president. He was a natural for the top post when the vacancy loomed. Although his interests are as broad as the operations of the Company, Gurley admits a strong bias in favor of locomotives, especially better ones. He spearheaded the Dieselization program, but he had enough perspective and courage to plan a gas turbine locomotive in the middle of the swing to Diesels.

vince the War Production Board of their need. After hostilities ended, deliveries improved. The decline in traffic enabled the Company to spread the use of freight locomotives over the system. At the end of 1946, 1,567 steam locomotives were in service. The Company operated 103 Diesel road locomotives, consisting of 374 units; 144 Diesel switch engines were in service. The total of 1,814 locomotives was only 158 more than at the end of 1943. Nearly all of the gain had been in Diesel equipment. At the beginning of 1947 none of the orders outstanding were for steam locomotives. With one exception contracts had been let for 11 Diesels. The most unusual locomotive on order was a gas turbine locomotive comparable in some respects to one placed in service by the Pennsylvania Railroad. The Santa Fe engine was unique in being the first in which oil rather than coal was utilized as the fuel for a gas turbine locomotive. On January 1, 1950, the Company had only 1,199 steam locomotives. Diesels were up to 444, consisting of 864 units, of which 627 were in road service.

Concern has been expressed over the policy of conversion to Diesel power, because of the alleged exhaustion of oil resources of the United States, coal being plentiful in comparison. Coal prices, however, have more than kept pace with the increase in the price of Diesel fuel. Almost as many influences are operating to raise the cost of coal as the cost of oil. The Company has no regrets and only pride over the partial shift to Diesel power. The capacity to handle wartime tonnages was in large measure attributable to the adoption of new locomotives.

The new equipment has made necessary major changes in repair facilities. Servicing of Diesels is entirely different from servicing steam locomotives. Even the roundhouse has been abandoned. Long training programs for mechanics have been necessary. Two heavy Diesel repair shops were soon established, one at Chicago and the other at Barstow. Regular running repairs and minor work are taken care of at Los Angeles, Cleburne, Bakersfield, Winslow, and Argentine. The Santa Fe still has many times more steam locomotives than Diesels. The "iron horses" of today are bigger, faster, and more efficient than ever. Passenger runs, which formerly were from 150 to 300 miles, exceeded 1500. Steam locomotive runs were also increased. Larger driving wheels contribute to greater performances. Other new features include techniques for enabling locomotives to go for a month instead of a trip between boiler washes, utilization of exhaust steam to heat steam water, improved roller bearings, larger tenders, and far superior lubrication systems.

Attempts to obtain passenger equipment to handle the throngs during World War II were mostly failures. Twenty-six cars were added in 1941 and forty-one in 1942. The great increase in travel during 1943 was handled with the addition of only one new car. Officials reëxamined equipment that had been retired and reinstated twenty-nine units, raising the total added through 1943 to ninety-seven. Offsetting this addition was the retirement of twenty-five passenger cars which were wrecked or which fell apart. Very little relief was afforded in 1944. Ten cars were retired and fifteen added. During the next two years additions were easier, but the pressure was off. One hundred and sixteen cars were added during 1945 and 1946, with seventeen retirements. The inclusion of ten diners among the early war additions eased the pressure and congestion in military service, but the difference was imperceptible because of the inadequacies that remained. The Santa Fe fortunately had the Harvey House to ease the burden of feeding passengers.

The wartime additions seemed nominal in comparison with the total number of units possessed by the Company. With equipment relatively a constant, the variable had to be more intensive utilization. Single sections of short trains were supplanted by multiple sections. The Santa Fe ran some of its trains in as many as seven sections, carrying up to 5,000 passengers. Rubber and gasoline shortages, larger paychecks, family separations, and business requirements accounted for record-breaking traffic. Astronomical numbers of military passenger miles were rolled up on regular trains as well as special troop trains. Swollen patronage necessarily occasioned delays, and certain schedules were slowed about 5 per cent.

The burden on the Santa Fe and other western railroads was especially great. The percentage increase in passenger volume was far greater for western railroads than eastern. The location of hostilities in the Pacific, the disproportionate number of camps in Texas and California, and industry expansion in the Southwest were responsible. The burden thrust on the Santa Fe was twice as much as for the majority of eastern roads. Although many lines ran far behind schedule, passenger officials jokingly contend that one story told on the Company is not true. A resident of a Kansas town is supposed to have noticed the Scout pulling into the station exactly on time. He remarked to an attendant that the Scout was on schedule for a change, only to hear the retort, "No, it is exactly twenty-four hours late." Employees did their bit and the public was tolerant. One way or another soldiers and civilians reached their destinations.

How many freight cars the Santa Fe would have bought during World War II if conditions permitted cannot be estimated. Certainly the number would be far more than were secured. Between 1940 and 1946 the Santa Fe added 22,700 boxcars. Three-fourths of these were acquired in 1940, 1941, and 1942. During the peak period of freight volume the Company was unable to secure new equipment. One-fourth of the additions were rebuilt cars which were part of the large volume of retired freight cars. The total retirements between 1940 and 1946 were 18,165, and almost 2,500 of the cars taken out of freight service were converted to Company use. Freight operations almost tripled from 1940 to 1944, advancing from 13 billion freight ton miles to over 37 billion freight ton miles. During the same period of time the Company had a net gain of only 6,000 boxcars, which amounted to less than an 8 per cent increase. Admittedly much unused capacity was evident on the Santa Fe at the start of the war, but no one had reason to suspect that the existing equipment could handle volume borne in subsequent years.

The car supply was enlarged by means of a thousand and one economies. Shippers coöperated by rapid loading and unloading. They were encouraged to order boxcars in advance, which enabled better allocation of equipment and more intensive use. The Company stepped up the rate for making repairs. Yard service was improved and valuable time saved. Better communications enabled the Company to reduce the amount of time that tenders were idle. Freight schedules were speeded up and trains lengthened.

Temporary shortages developed, especially during seasonal movements of crops, since the usual reservoir of idle capacity no longer existed. The Santa Fe encountered an unusual amount of difficulty as a result of the national pooling arrangement for boxcars. Throughout most of the war the Company had less than the number of its own cars on Santa Fe tracks. The shortage ranged from 7 to 28 per cent. Other railroads benefited at the expense of the Santa Fe. During July, when the Santa Fe would normally have a great excess of cars over the number owned, the figure did not rise above 2 per cent. Responsibility for these difficulties of the Company rests somewhere between the other railroads and the control system.

Material shortages following World War II did not permit replacement of boxcars as rapidly as desired. Slowness of deliveries from manufacturers caused the Santa Fe to undertake construction of part of its own needs. The persisting boxcar shortage, which continued after the War ended, was met in part by switching the use of generalized and specialized cars. Hoppers and slatted stock cars were used in grain shipments. Early in the war the Company had used lined boxcars for oil shipments. Like the wartime passengers, wartime freight was moved one way or another. Considering the magnitude of the task, a superlative job was done.

The labor force was increased during the war and its effort further expanded by overtime. This tended to compensate for the decline in quality through the movement of thousands of experienced employees into the armed forces and to other defense work.

The replacements were commonly inexperienced. The Company kept equipment rolling by putting the major shops on double shifts of eight hours each. One of the greatest facilitating influences was the modernized multichannel telegraph and telephone system which was installed on the eve of the rush. Whether the old system could have handled the war burden of train dispatching and other wire communications is doubtful.

Observers declared that the Santa Fe had stopped running separate freight trains and substituted a continuous two-way movement of boxcars with an occasional locomotive.

IMPROVED EFFICIENCY

The progress of the Santa Fe in operating efficiency has been measured in the selected statistics below. The numbers are unimpressive if read quickly but of tremendous significance if meditated upon.

	1946	1929	Index 1929 100 per cent
Car miles per car day (freight)	61.8	38.6	160
Net ton miles per freight-car day	1,103	550	200
Gross tons per train (freight)	2,363	1,975	120
Net tons per train (freight)	952	733	130
Gross ton miles per train hour (freight)	45,878	29,971	153
Net ton miles per train hour (freight)	18,486	11,208	165
Average speed of train-miles per hour (freight)	19.5	15.2	128
Gross ton miles (millions)	79,078	50,837	156
Average haul—revenue freight (miles)	533	325	164
Locomotive miles per locomotive day (freight)	111.2	73.2	152
Locomotive miles per locomotive day (passenger)	284.6	161.7	176
Passengers one mile (millions)	4,024	1,240	325
Passengers per train	143	51	280

Company officials calculated that their operating efficiency index rose 112 per cent during the period 1925-49. If 1929 methods had been used in 1949, expenses would have been $82,000,000 higher.

Centralized traffic control, popularly known as CTC, enabled the Santa Fe and other railroads to handle far more traffic than had been thought possible. CTC is the dispatcher's mechanical brain and is an intricate electrical machine which gives complete control of all switches and signals of an extended destination. Train orders are partially, if not wholly, eliminated, as is time lost by trains "in the hole." CTC enables single-track lines to operate up to 75 per cent of double-track capacity.

The movement of all trains within a distance up to a hundred miles is electrically recorded on the CTC board. Red, green, and amber lights give the exact location of all switches and their condition. The switches are controlled by the man at the board. CTC installation was made during the war in most of the congested areas on the Santa Fe system. Installation has continued; train service has been speeded and at the same time greater safety achieved.

Another wartime development was the use of extensive radio facilities in the major freight yards. The Santa Fe put the transmitters and receivers in the yard master's office and similar equipment on each switch engine. The yard master was able to keep in contact with all switching movements and speed up operations. The tremendous fleet operating in San Francisco Bay was radio-equipped, making possible continuous communication with shore installations in San Francisco and Richmond. Experiments were made with radio communications on freight trains with a view of providing radio control of all trains. Head-to-rear communications have been introduced and offer promise of expeditious operation and safety.

SANTA FE SKYWAY

The Company's policy of engaging in the transportation business rather than restricting itself to railroading was again evident in the operation of Santa Fe Skyway, Inc. This company was established in May of 1946 to round out the service afforded shippers. Air-freight service was offered over a far-reaching network of lines. Separate personnel manned Santa Fe Skyway. Within a few months over a hundred employees were engaged. Operations were restricted to those of a contract carrier, but applications were made for authority to act as a common carrier. The Santa Fe had high hopes for its subsidiary because of the opportunity for eventual integration of operations between the railroad and the airline. The economies possible were quite apparent and offered promises of enabling the Company to provide low rates and fast service on a profitable basis. The Civil Aeronautics Board viewed the venture with suspicion and refused to grant authority to act as a common carrier. The policy of the Government during the last twenty years of regulation has been to promote integration. The separation of air activities from other transportation companies, subject to the regulation of the Interstate Commerce Commission has prevented realization of full integration. Santa Fe Skyway, Inc., was discontinued late in 1947.

Truck and bus operations of Santa Fe subsidiaries matched the volume of the railroad. Bus service covered more than 12,000 miles. Ten million passengers were transported an average of eight miles. Common-carrier truck operations were conducted over 7,300 route miles and carried half a million tons of freight, a total of 71,500,000 ton miles. By 1949 service extended to 9,444 route miles over which 75,075,000 ton miles were recorded during the year.

The best explanation of the successful assumption of the heavy loads does not lie wholly in mechanical improvements and additions to personnel. The majority of the increased productivity of the Santa Fe stemmed from an amazing display of teamwork. Each member of the team worked with the maximum physical and mental vigor. Efforts were so skillfully coördinated that the total output was a revelation even to those responsible for the results.

POST-WAR PLANS

Preoccupation with wartime service between 1941 and 1945 led to the accumulation of a backlog of innovations. After the War the Company moved ahead with plans for utilizing improved methods and equipment. The use of streamlined trains was expanded. Early in 1948 daily service on two crack Chicago - Los Angeles trains, the Super-Chief and El Capitan, was begun. Much new equipment was necessary to make a change and the trains featured technical advances such as non-fogging windows, improved lighting and air conditioning, anti-slide wheel devices, and superior insulation. Radio installations in compartments on the Super-Chief were an added attraction. The streamlined train from Chicago to the Gulf, the Texas Chief, also began service and strengthened the competitive position of the Company in an area in which the Santa Fe had not been strong. Several changes were made in 1950. Outstanding among these was the re-introduction of off-train dining for passengers on the California Limited. A new streamlined train was authorized for service between Kansas City and Chicago.

Special service features were either begun or reëstablished. The courier-nurse service on some of the transcontinental trains was resumed. Registered nurses minister to the needs of all travelers, especially the infirm and mothers with children or children with mothers. Rail-auto service was reinstated which provided passengers with the use of an automobile at their destination at many cities. Travel credit cards were issued to permit charge accounts for railroad tickets. Rail accommodations and other traffic expenses were put on an installment basis under a "Traveloan Plan." Turret-type reservation desks in travel centers speeded reservations and information for passengers. A vigorous program has been launched to strengthen the competitive position of the Company not only in relation to other railroads and other means of transportation but also in relation to the good will and loyalty of the millions who "go Santa Fe."

Three trains of the Santa Fe deserve special comment. They were the Southwest Friendship Trains of November, 1947. Although their running times do not match those of the Nellie Bly and the Death Valley Scotty, their roles were of far greater significance. The Friendship Trains pulled 199 freight cars of food for the starving people of Europe. There were 106 cars of wheat, 60 of flour, 14 of canned goods, 7 of groceries, 3 of rice, 2 of hominy, 2 of oats, and 1 each of salt, sugar, soybeans, and corn. All of these were the gifts of people of Kansas, Texas, Oklahoma, Colorado, Arkansas, New Mexico, and Louisiana. The trains were given free billing and handled without charge by the train crews and other workers. The scheduling and operation were well done, but the trains were more significant as the generous gesture of the people of the area to their suffering neighbors. Early in 1949 the people of France sent a "Merci" train laden with "Thank you" gifts in appreciation of the "Friendship" supplies.

The history of operations from 1896 to date has mirrored the development of the Southwest. The Santa Fe has played an important part in the diverse enterprises which typify the area as it is today. Officials of the Company have conducted their business on the assumption that the fortunes of the Company and its hinterland were indissolubly linked. The broad gentlemen's agreement has rewarded both parties.

The period between 1896 and 1915 was one of steady accumulation of strength and improvement in services. The Company was able to assume the swollen volume of World War I. The high traffic level persisted throughout the 'twenties. Passenger revenues declined but were more than offset by increased freight tonnage and receipts. During this decade hundreds of millions of capital were spent in betterment of road and equipment. Although the number of locomotives declined, their speed and power raised the total working capacity. The depression forced contraction of many phases of the Santa Fe, but the showing was relatively good. Great technological advances were made in the equipment, and millions were expended to enable the realization of the potential speeds of the faster trains. Competition from other agencies of transportation was met by improved service and new operating economies. Because those rivals seemed to be assured a segment of transportation and because they were also complementary to rail service, the Santa Fe acquired an extensive truck and bus system. The eve of the second outbreak of world-wide conflict found the properties of the Company relatively unscathed by the adverse years. Santa Fe teamwork of lush days had been preserved. When the call came, the Santa Fe had been ready, and when the sound of the bugle faded, the Company was ready to meet the post-war needs of a booming nation.

XII

Confidently Clipping Coupons

"Capitalization of the Atchison, Topeka and Santa Fe Railway has often been referred to as a model of what a railroad capitalization should be."
Moody's *Manual of Railroads*.

CORPORATE REORGANIZATIONS, especially among railroads, have a spotty record of success. The primary obstacle has been the unwillingness of security-holders to recognize losses and the absolute refusal to compromise. Many a railroad has entered receivership because of overindebtedness and emerged after much squabbling with an equivalent in new bonds plus several millions in receiver's certificates. The first shudder of business usually found the company in straits for the identical reason that promoted the original collapse.

CONSERVATIVE FINANCING

The Santa Fe reorganization stands unique among those of its period. The work was done in a minimum of time while depressed conditions prevailed. This provided an excellent setting for properly scaling down the fixed charges. As Chapter XI points out, the Railway emerged with a model financial plan which showed every indication of proving successful. But the best capitalization is doomed to failure unless the management of a company is entrusted to competent men. The Santa Fe was fortunate in securing leaders of ability. The financial course of the Company was plotted with care. Risks were eliminated, avoided, or reduced. The flow of income was encouraged and expenditures were judiciously made. These methods lifted the Company to a position of financial eminence, far removed from the uncertainties of old.

The new administration disposed of hundreds of miles of lines which did not offer profit possibilities, besides taking other steps to solidify the fortunes of the Santa Fe. It reached a settlement with the Mexican government in the matter of the bond subsidy of the Sonora Railway. A total of $1,159,800 in 3 per cent bonds of the Interior Consolidated debt of the United States of Mexico was received in full payment. The extensive coal mines in Kansas, New Mexico, and Colorado which had been operated by subsidiaries were leased to outside operators. This move not only was profitable but brought an end to the public criticism which inevitably attended operation of coal mines by the Company. Land holdings of the Railway were put in order and small scattered parcels sold. Purchases were made on a cash basis and substantial discounts obtained. Year after year the independent auditors noted the absence of a floating debt as they recorded the accretion of resources.

A proper starting point for the financial affairs of the Railway is the statistical record prior to World War I. Below is a continuation of the tables presented in Chapter VI.

The gain in assets over capitalization is apparent. More than one hundred million dollars was retained out of earnings and plowed back into the business. This was almost half as much as the amount obtained through the sale of securities. Another noticeable feature of the record was the increase in the amount of bonds relative to stock. The ratio reached a peak in 1908 and then declined to more conservative proportions. The gain in income available for charges was substantial in the absolute sense but not in the relative. After 1900 the ratio of earnings to total invested capital remained relatively steady but some improvement was shown in 1916 and 1917. Between 1896 and 1917 the average rate of return was approximately 4.9 per cent. Since most of the financing was by bonds carrying set rates of 4 per cent, the amount earned on common was higher than the average return on the total invested capital (stocks, bonds, and surplus).

Early increases in indebtedness developed from the issuance of additional general-mortgage bonds for improvement. These were authorized in the original covenant. When the San Francisco and

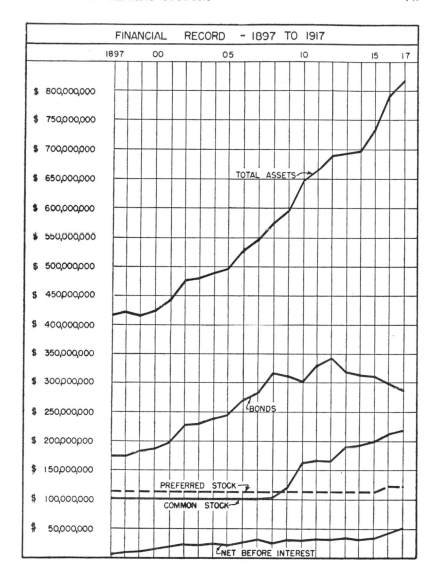

FINANCIAL   RECORD   - 1897 TO 1917

San Joaquin Valley Railway was purchased the Santa Fe assumed a 5 per cent first mortgage of $6,000,000.

The first major increase in the funded debt was in 1902. The contemplated purchase and construction of branch lines necessitated raising more money than the $3,000,000 a year limit on general-mortgage increases and the retention of earnings permitted. The Company also was in need of large additions to its equipment. A $30,000,000 issue of 4 per cent serial debentures was offered and readily sold. Repayment began on February 1, 1903, at the rate of $2,500,000 annually. The serial form enhanced marketability.

An issue of $10,000,000 in Eastern Oklahoma Division 4s of twenty-five year maturity was authorized in 1903 to cover new lines. Less than two-thirds of the authorization was sold at the outset, but later offerings were made.

Capital requirements continued to outrun the relief afforded by the sale of general-mortgage bonds. The situation was further complicated by the expiration in 1905 of the privilege of the annual increase of the issue as had been permitted under the original indenture. The Santa Fe had begun its program of double-tracking and grade reduction and planned to continue the addition of feeders. Other policies also called for large outlays. In December, 1904, the shareholders were notified of a meeting to approve a $50,000,000 issue of 4 per cent convertible debentures. Provision had to be made for increasing the common stock in the event of conversion. Consent followed, and in 1905 all stockholders were given the right to subscribe for the new issue up to 15 per cent of their holdings. An amount totaling more than $49,711,000 was finally sold.

The money raised by the convertible 4s of 1955 was quickly put to profitable use, and the passing of a single year brought new needs. At a special meeting of the stockholders held January 30, 1907, the authorized issue of common stock was raised $98,000,000 to total $250,000,000. Consent was secured to offer $30,000,000 in 5 per cent convertible bonds. The new bonds were of a short-term variety and were to come due in 1917. An offering of approximately $26,000,000 was received with mixed reaction by the stockholders. Chaotic market conditions made 1907 a poor year for the flotation of securities. About $16,000,000 had to be offered to outsiders. They subscribed readily.

The return of national and Santa Fe prosperity brought several changes in the debt structure between 1908 and 1910. An issue of $17,000,000 first-mortgage 4s was sold to finance the new transcontinental short line. The Company marketed $28,258,000 in convertible 4s of 1909 and $14,378,383 in convertible 4s of 1910. Simultaneously holders of the early issue of convertibles were induced by the high price of common to exchange their securities. During the year ending June 30, 1910, they exchanged approximately $44,000,000 worth.

Additional bonds of the convertible issue of 1910 due in 1960 were offered and provided the bulk of new funds during the operating year of 1910-11. The total of this type rose to $43,686,000.

The peak debt in the entire history of the Santa Fe came in 1912 when a 4½ series of first and refunding California-Arizona Lines of 1962 were sold. The new issue refunded a small amount of bonds and furnished new funds for the short line from central Arizona to California. The offering exceeded $18,000,000.

Conversion of bonds into stock continued, and the serial bonds of 1902 were steadily redeemed. The Chicago and St. Louis Railway first-mortgage 6s were paid on maturity in 1915. This extinguished the only high-yielding bond and the last carryover from the old Railroad Company. During the same year there was an issue of $3,000,000 in Rocky Mountain Division 4s.

Pre-war requirements were met by the cash sale of $5,545,000 in Transcontinental Short Line first-mortgage 4s and $10,000,000 in preferred stock. The discount on both transactions was slightly over $700,000. Throughout the whole of the period between 1896 and 1917 the Santa Fe was not forced to make concessions. The development of financial strength made the securities attractive.

Low rates of interest could be obtained. Ninety per cent of the bonds outstanding June 30, 1917, bore only 4 per cent. Those bonds which had emerged during the receivership were selling on a basis which indicated that their nominal rate was representative of the low risk. The improved record of the Company enhanced the value of common and caused a rapid reduction in the funded debt and fixed charges as a consequence of wholesale conversions. The debt in 1917 was $54,000,000 less than in 1912, and assets were $124,000,000 greater. The scale of retention of earnings is apparent in the fact that the increase in preferred and common stock was only $59,500,000.

Interest charges on the funded debt of the Santa Fe were covered by a wide margin except for the year and a half immediately following receivership. All of the fixed charges were covered from the beginning, but the contingent charges on the adjustment 4s were not entirely met. In the year ending June 30, 1897, the payment was 3 per cent. The full interest, however, was paid the following year. Coverage in later periods was excellent. Between 1896 and 1917 income available for all fixed and contingent charges was two and one-half times the requirements. The multiple was over four in the operating year 1916-17.

Dividends on preferred stock followed closely on the heels of the full-interest payment to holders of the adjustment bonds. A payment of 1 per cent was declared December 21, 1898, and paid the following month. Another distribution of 1¼ per cent raised the dividends for the fiscal year ending June 30, 1899, to 2¼ per cent. Improved results led to 4 per cent the following year and the full 5 per cent thereafter.

The last ones to share in the revival of Santa Fe fortunes were logically and properly the common stockholders. Not until June, 1901, were the first dividends declared—1½ per cent. Between 1902 and 1906 dividends were on a 4 per cent basis. The annual rate was raised to 5½ per cent for the two years ending June 30, 1907 and 1908. A reduction to 5 per cent followed for one year. The level was then raised to 6 per cent and maintained at that level until 1924. Dividends were covered by a wide margin and the difference reinvested in the enterprise.

The financial policy of the Santa Fe between 1896 and 1917 was characterized by conservatism. The directors were on guard at all times against any moves which might endanger the current or long-run position of the Company. This policy stemmed primarily from the relatively independent position which was maintained during the period of railroad consolidation. Fantastic mergers and amalgamations joined companies with more regard for promoters' gains at the moment than for profitable railroad operations. With a single exception, all of the financial tycoons of the period concentrated their efforts on lines other than the Santa Fe. In 1904 E. H. Harriman and some of his associates, including Otto H. Kahn, Henry Rogers, Henry Frick, William Rockefeller, and James Stillman announced the accumulation of $30,000,000 in par of Santa Fe stock. Representation was sought on the board and in 1905 Frick and Rogers were elected. Conflicting construction of the Santa Fe and Southern Pacific was the subject of compromise and other differences were dissolved, but the independence of the Santa Fe was relatively unaffected. In 1906 Harriman interests sold their holdings, but the Union Pacific through the Oregon Short Line bobbed up with $10,395,000 in preferred. Three years later this block was offered for sale. Rumors never ceased to circulate concerning a merger of the Santa Fe and the Pennsylvania. Apparently there was no basis in fact for the stories.

The board of directors was chosen without regard for any cliques and included reputable men of affairs. The House of Morgan was represented, yet the Road was decidedly not dominated by Morgan interests. The Santa Fe retained complete freedom from entangling alliances with other railroads and with investment houses. The stock of the Company was never a Wall Street football and the prestige of the Company was consistently high. Among the directors at the helm of the enterprise during the prewar period were Charles S. Gleed, Arthur T. Hadley, Walker D. Hines, Augustus Julliard, Ogden L. Mills, Victor Morawetz, Paul Morton, and Henry S. Pritchett. The others were of equal business stature and they guided the Santa Fe for the Santa Fe. The dominant figure throughout the period was Edward P. Ripley, the president. His sound judgment in affairs of business greatly eased the load on the directors. Ripley was a watchdog over the assets and earning power of his charge.

RIPLEY'S EPISTLES TO KANSAS

As state and federal regulations multiplied and began to tie the purse strings of the Company, Ripley was alert to attack legislation which he believed harmful. In 1906 he become involved in a bitter conflict with leading politicians of Kansas at a time when a two-cent passenger-rate bill was up before the Legislature. On August 2, 1906, he wrote the first of his famous "Epistles to Kansas." Ripley argued that the methods of the Road were forthright and that the Company made modest returns while spending much in Kansas. He was widely assailed. W. R. Stubbs was especially vitriolic and damned the Santa Fe for engaging in politics and giving free passes to government officials and editors. Ripley made no defense of the pass abuse and advocated abolition of the pernicious system. As to politics, on August 22 he wrote the newspapers:

> We have the same interest in good government as has any other citizen and the same right to display that interest. As the largest corporation in the State and the largest taxpayer, we have a vital interest in sane and conservative legislation and when (as has too often been the case) there is danger that the State will be swept off its feet by appeal to passion and prejudices made by designing demagogues, it becomes a duty to oppose those men by fair and legal means. In such cases and such cases only will the Santa Fe be found in politics.

Stubbs countered with a verbal blast on the same day. Among other things, he asserted:

> (1) That the common stock of the Santa Fe, aggregating upwards of one hundred million dollars, was practically all pure water and did not represent any value whatever. . . .
> (2) That the members of the Legislature are overwhelmed with free passes for themselves, their families and their friends, individual members using as much as 200,000 miles of free transportation during one session of the Legislature. . . .

The Topeka *Daily Capital* of September 3, 1906, carried one of a flood of letters which had descended upon the editor. Colonel Edward C. Little of Abilene in criticizing corporate participation in politics wrote:

What has the Atchison, Topeka and Santa Fe Railway done to put it on an equality with the men and women who have gone or go down into the valley of the shadow of death for the republic? Like the mule, the Santa Fe has no pride in ancestry and no hope for posterity. . . .

Ripley and Charles S. Gleed answered the critics with devastating force. Gleed concluded his letter with a quoted barb, "It beats hell what decent men will do to get offices."

Ripley's logic was hardly a match for the rabble-rousing of Stubbs, and the latter won the governorship. Kansas eventually gained two-cent fares on intrastate travel. This led to the anomalous situation of local rates being far below interstate fares. Kansans bound for Kansas City, Missouri, bought tickets to Kansas City, Kansas, at the lower rate and then paid for the remaining distance over the state line at the interstate rate. Other states pressed the same rate reduction. The Santa Fe protested, but several years passed before orders of the Director General, Supreme Court rulings, and the Transportation Act of 1920 gave relief.

President Ripley saw little in state regulation to commend it. He declared:

There is no more reason, as a matter of common sense and efficiency, why a state should regulate freight rates or passenger fares than there is that it should regulate the rates of postage.

The view of railway men who have met both forms of regulation is that supervision of the national government has been to a degree constructive and therefore helpful, while that of the states has been meddlesome, obstructive, expensive, and damaging.

Ripley was a staunch advocate of coöperation among railroads rather than enforced competition. He anticipated the shift in the attitude of the federal government by many years. Santa Fe presidents since Ripley have continued to battle against measures they believe deleterious to the Company's interest. Most of the controversies were directed against national legislation, because the province of state railroad commissions narrowed in World War I and never regained lost ground.

FEDERAL CONTROL

The assumption of operating control of the Santa Fe by the United States Railroad Administration tended to limit the lines of financial evolution during World War I. The Government put a ceiling and a basement on operating income by compensating the Company on a basis of 1915-17 earnings. Some latitude for variations remained in "Other Income." New financing was checked by the automatic curtailment of the extension of lines and major betterments. On the next page is a graphic representation of the years of federal control. Statistics for the years ending December 31, 1917 and 1920 are given for comparative purposes.*

The slight increase in the amount of common stock arose from conversion in bonds with a compensating reduction in the latter. In 1919 the Company arranged for an equipment trust issue of $7,356,000 to finance rolling stock ordered by the Government. The notes matured annually in equal amounts for a fifteen-year period. The rate of interest of 6 per cent reflected the inflationary influences which predominated at the time.

The marked rise in income available for charges in 1919 was attributable to nonoperating income. Large nonrecurring profits were realized in subsidiaries. These profits accrued over many years but were not given recognition in the books of account until 1919.

By far the most significant result of federal control of the Santa Fe was the excellent showing of Uncle Sam in relation to his results on other railroads. The loss from operations and guarantees on all lines in the United States to August 30, 1920, has been set at $1,641,867,000. Almost half of this staggering total was the excess of rentals over net railway operating income notwithstanding undermaintenance. In 1918 and 1919 the United States Railroad Administration showed railway operating income on the Santa Fe to be $86,231,956. The rental for the two-year period was $87,-500,398.06. Nor was this remarkable balance appreciably upset by

---

*The property of the Santa Fe was restored to private management March 1, 1920, and earnings were guaranteed until August 31, 1920.

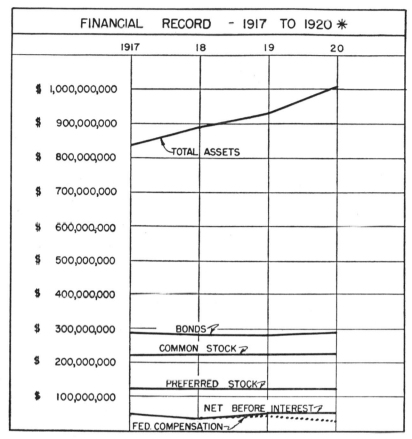

FINANCIAL   RECORD   ‑ 1917 TO 1920 ✳

*Includes various deferred assets and debits arising out of relations with the Government. In 1920 these contra-valuations amounted to $84,000,000.

the necessary adjusting payments for maintenance, depreciation, and other factors. The showing of the assets and personnel of the Company was one of the brightest spots of the Government's experience and gave further evidence of the fundamental soundness of the Santa Fe.

PROSPERITY AND DEPRESSION

While the financial history of the 'twenties was more prosaic in the annual reports than in the stock markets, many interesting changes took place in the structure of the Company. The assets

456 CONFIDENTLY CLIPPING COUPONS

and total invested capital grew, but the capitalization remained relatively the same. Millions in earnings were plowed into the business, so that the rather constant conservative ratio of funded debt to capitalization tended more and more to misrepresent the significant increase in strength. The amount invested in the business through surplus rose to $402,754,860 in 1929. This exceeded the combined total of common and preferred by $37,000,000. The ratio of funded debt to total invested capital was only 28.8 per cent and represented one of the most conservative financial structures among American railroads. The statistical record is reproduced below.

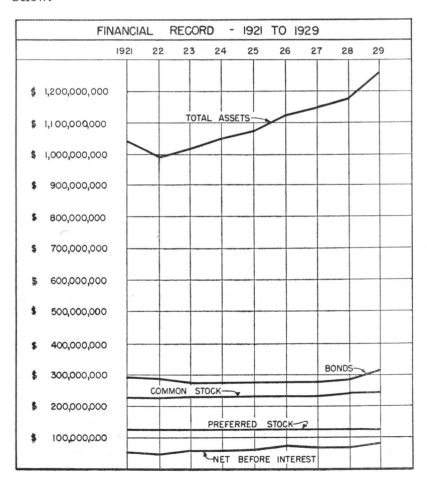

The total invested capital at the close of the last year (1929) was $1,080,132,161. The average return on invested capital was 5.65 per cent. The large element of surplus and the low rate paid on bonds enabled earnings of $22.28 per share of common.

The changes in the bond structure were few during the decade. The switch by holders of convertibles to common continued and was intensified in 1922. During the year 1923 the balance of $6,-375,200 of equipment trust notes was retired. Redemption before maturity was promoted by the excessive interest rate of 6 per cent.

During 1928 the amount of California-Arizona Lines First and Refunding 4½ per cent bonds was raised $14,691,881. The Eastern Oklahoma 4s were redeemed. This lowered the debt $9,603,000. The redemption was in effect a conversion, because stock rights were issued and $9,219,800 in common sold to acquire funds to extinguish the bonds.

In 1928-29 was issued a novel security which attracted much attention. Late in 1928 the Company secured approval for a new series of 4½ per cent convertible debenture bonds to mature in 1948. The unique feature lay in the excess of the market price of common over the par as bonds. The conversion ratio was one bond for six of common. The latter was above the conversion point. At the time, the financing seemed to be a deferred sale of stock to the shareholders, who received the rights to subscribe. The rapid decline in stock prices came before many of the $29,865,000 worth were converted.

Interest on outstanding indebtedness was covered by a wide factor of safety throughout the 'twenties. The range was from four to six times the requirements. The 5 per cent dividends on preferred were regularly paid. Common continued to receive $6 through 1924. The dividend rate was raised to $7 for two years; then a further increase was made to $10. These payments were earned more than twice.

Atchison common was subjected to the same speculative fever as any other security in the late 'twenties. In 1924 there were quotations as low as 97, and an all-time high came in 1929 when the price reached the unwarranted figure of $299. Not even the splendid earnings record of the Company justified the rise. Santa Fe stock was suspended in mid-air and a fall was inevitable.

What happened to the price of stock in the market was not nearly as significant to the long-run investors in the enterprise as it was to short-term speculators. Losses were sustained by both groups but in lesser amounts by the investors. The majority of them were to maintain their holdings during the trying decade of the 'thirties. Of greatest import to them was the sound conservative front presented by the Company as it faced the buffeting of stormy times.

The railroad industry endured multiplied reverses in the depression years. Heavy industries bore the brunt of industrial distress and when they shut down, the railroads lost their best customers. A majority of the railroads were unable to weather the storm, although some of these staved off receivership. Overwhelming losses were sustained by companies in the Western District (roughly the area west of Lake Michigan and the Illinois and the Mississippi rivers). Deficits were incurred every year from 1932 to 1939 inclusive. In the face of this discouraging showing, the Santa Fe performed creditably. Charges were covered every year. Moreover, the Company displayed considerable resiliency, rebounding with every evidence of business recovery. Business was by no means highly profitable and considerable belt-tightening was necessary; but the acid depression test was met squarely and conquered. Statistics for the 'thirties are presented in the graph below.

The outstanding fact indicated in the graph is the precipitous decline in the income available for charges. The effect is more evident in the figures for net corporate income. It sagged from $37,348,800 in 1930 to $3,698,671 in 1933. Expenses due to the very nature of railroading could not be pared at a rate corresponding to the loss in revenue.

For obvious reasons there was little change in the capitalization. The time was not propitious for expansion and the market was unreceptive to new securities. Both common and preferred stock

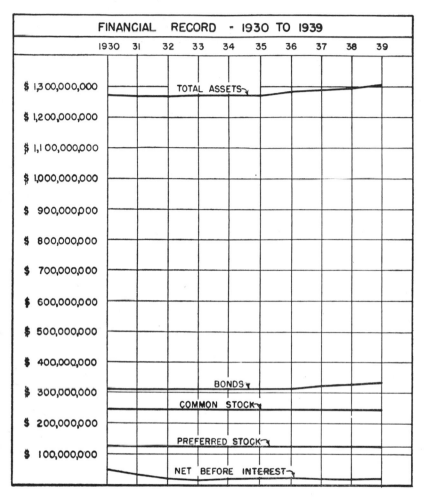

FINANCIAL   RECORD - 1930 TO 1939

| | 1930 | 31 | 32 | 33 | 34 | 35 | 36 | 37 | 38 | 39 |

$ 1,300,000,000 — TOTAL ASSETS

$ 1,200,000,000

$ 1,100,000,000

$ 1,000,000,000

$ 900,000,000

$ 800,000,000

$ 700,000,000

$ 600,000,000

$ 500,000,000

$ 400,000,000

$ 300,000,000 — BONDS

COMMON STOCK

$ 200,000,000

PREFERRED STOCK

$ 100,000,000

NET BEFORE INTEREST

remained the same. The funded debt diminished slightly until 1937. Late in 1936 the officials had made arrangements for a $20,-000,000 purchase of new equipment. The cost was met in part out of funds on hand in the treasury, and the balance was met out of the proceeds of the sale of $13,800,000 in equipment trust certificates. The usual staggered maturity over a fifteen-year period was provided. Full advantage was taken of the prevailing low money rates. The nominal rate of interest was 2¼ per cent, yet the certificates sold at a premium price of 100.353.

A second equipment trust was established in 1937 to enlarge the modernization program. A total of $3,900,000 in 2¼ per cent Series B certificates was sold. Another issue of $8,000,000 in Series C bearing 2½ per cent brought additional funds in 1939. The decision to modernize the fleet when current business was none too promising revealed prophetic judgment. The timing was perfect. The Company was ready in advance to meet the surge of traffic. No last-minute moves in 1940 or 1941 would have been adequate. Much of the commendable showing during World War II is attributable to decisions during the depression years.

Interest payments were met without fail through the lean years. The conservative funded debt with its low rates of interest enabled the Company to meet all obligations. Dividends on the noncumulative preferred were interrupted twice. The semi-annual payment of 2½ per cent was cut to 1½ per cent August 1, 1933. Part of the reduction was made up six months later when 3 3/10 per cent was paid. Regular dividends were met until August, 1938. Earnings had receded so much that the payment was skipped and only 1 per cent paid the following period. The old rate was restored August 1, 1939, and maintained.

Common stockholders enjoyed dividends in excess of earnings as redundant cash was drawn upon. Below is the record of earnings per share and dividends as well as the gyrations in the price of common:

Year	Range of Stock	Earned per Share	Paid per Share
1930	243—168	$12.86	$10.00
1931	204— 79	6.96	10.00
1932	94— 18	0.55	2.50
1933	80— 35	1.03 (d)	nil
1934	74— 45	0.33	2.00
1935	60— 36	1.38	2.00
1936	89— 59	1.56	2.00
1937	95— 33	0.60	2.00
1938	45— 22	0.83	nil
1939	43— 21	0.95	nil

The current position was maintained and the solidarity of the Company was not jeopardized. Current assets on December 31, 1933, were three times the current liabilities. The Company had $27,039,561 in cash and over $23,000,000 in marketable securities of the United States Government. Furthermore, the Santa Fe was even more strongly fortified at the end of 1938 than in 1933. Extreme care had been taken to safeguard the financial position.

FINANCING IN WORLD WAR II

The impact of World War II brought a flow of revenues which surpassed the boom years of the 'twenties. The same factors which had caused net profits to decline in excess of the slip in gross revenue, worked in reverse. Net corporate income increased three times as fast as gross revenue during the early years. The disposition of the profits was closely watched by outsiders to see how the experience of preceding years would affect the financial policy. Below is the record through 1948.

The precipitous drop in total assets from 1944 to 1945 was solely a bookkeeping adjustment, and in no way reflected a change in the scale of physical resources. A general order of the I.C.C. applicable to all railroads directed them to change the methods of handling reserves for accrued depreciation and accrued amortization of defense projects. Reserves had been on the liability side of the balance sheet as unadjusted credits and now depreciation became a deduction from the asset against which charge had been made. Current operations of the Santa Fe are, after allowance for the change in accounting, on the largest scale in history. The amount of common and preferred stock has remained unchanged, but surplus has been enlarged through the retention of earnings.

Part of the retained earnings have been used for debt retirement. More than $100,000,000 in funded debt has been extinguished since 1940. Debt reduction is not expected to continue, because the two large issues of the Company are non-callable and do not mature until 1995. Some purchases have been made in the open market. The balance of the indebtedness of the Company is

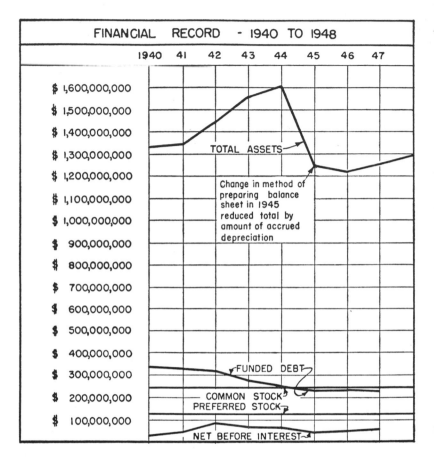

FINANCIAL   RECORD   - 1940 TO 1948

in equipment-trust certificates which will be extinguished within a relatively short number of years. The reduction in debt has given the Company a net worth-debt relationship matched by only one other railroad in the Nation. The financial position of the Company could scarcely be improved upon.

The statistical inconsistencies on income available for interest show the understatement that is characteristic of all railroad accounting. State and federal income taxes are deducted before computation of income available for interests, although interest is a business expense which is deductible for income-tax purposes. Interest coverage as reported in the railroad industry is consistently understated in companies which are making profits. The annual interest charge on the indebtedness of the Santa Fe is under $9,-000,000 a year, and the number of times which interest is earned as measured by the unduly conservative method of railroads is far in excess of the safety standards for high quality. A leading investment service computed 1946 interest coverage as 7.19. The correct figure was 9. Justification for railroad practice is found by its supporters in that "taxes have to be paid, if interest isn't."

Debt reduction was made steadily from 1940 through 1949. The low level in the operating ratio between 1942 and 1944 was attributable to the shortage of both materials and labor for maintenance, as well as to the rise in revenues. At the close of hostilities expenditures for maintenance were increased, and in 1945 the Company spent $237,000,000 for maintenance of way and structures and equipment. Only $89,000,000 had been spent in 1942. The unprecedented volume in 1945 accounts for the decline in income available for interest and arose out of the necessity for accelerated amortization of defense projects incidental to the end of the war. Maintenance expenditures in years immediately following 1945 were in excess of $110,000,000. The 1945-1947 total was $531,000,000.

According to the preceding chart the Santa Fe had $1,293,000,-000 in gross assets at the end of 1948. These were financed by a net investment of $1,177,000,000 from all classes of securities including corporate surplus. The ratio of debt to total invested capital was 19.8 per cent. This was the most conservative ratio among large railroads in the history of American finance.

In 1940 the San Francisco and San Joaquin Valley 5s were redeemed. This issue was in excess of $5,000,000. During the same year another equipment trust was organized to borrow $10,000,-000. The Series D certificates carried a rate of only 1¼ per cent. The call privilege on the 4½ per cent debentures of 1948 was exercised in 1941. The bonds were paid at 102, and $28,070,500 worth was retired. The usual reductions were made in the outstanding equipment issues. Much of the reduction in 1941 was offset by the fifth equipment series. The amount sought was $20,000,000. The trust was established for ten years and carried a nominal rate on the certificates of 1⅝ per cent. In spite of the low figure a premium was secured. The purchasing syndicate paid 100.434. The reoffering was made at prices intended to yield from 0.25 to 1.875 per cent from 1932 to 1951. No better evidence of the low market interest rates and the strength of the Company can be given.

No bonds were issued in 1942 and a total of $18,000,000 was redeemed or reacquired. The Rocky Mountain Division 4s of 1965 were called at 105. The Santa Fe, Prescott and Phoenix 5s amounting to $4,940,000 matured and were paid. Almost $5,000,000 in California-Arizona 4½s of 1962 was reacquired and held in the treasury. On December 31, 1942, the debt stood at $304,964,750. The highest rate of interest was 4½ per cent, and these bonds were called for redemption in 1943.

The Transcontinental Short Line 4s of 1958 were redeemed in 1944 and the convertible 4s of 1955 and 1960 in 1945. Funded debt at the close of the year consisted of $152,000,000 of General-Mortgage 4s due in 1995 and $51,000,000 of Adjustment-Mortgage 4s due during the same year. A development of interest to financial analysts was the return of the Adjustment Bonds to the status of an income issue with only contingent interest charges. Some of the issues which had been retired were junior to the Adjustment 4s and bore fixed interest charges, which had to be paid, yet payment could not be made until interest had been paid on the Adjustment issue. No comparable example existed in American finance. The interest rates on outstanding equipment trust certificates range from 1¼ per cent to 2½ percent. These rates were from 2 to 3 per cent under nominal yields of old. Secondly, the equipment issues were serial in form; that is, they matured in installments. Being of the usual short-term variety, shading the life of the equipment, they were tacit evidence of an overall plan of debt reduction. The eventual result in the absence of conflicting moves will be to reduce the total debt to $203,000,000. Wartime and postwar earnings and the range of stock are shown in the graph.

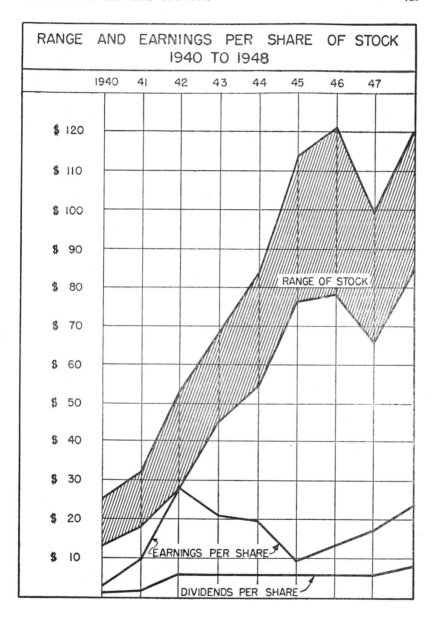

RANGE AND EARNINGS PER SHARE OF STOCK
1940 TO 1948

The amount distributed from the record earnings was stabilized at $6.00 per share of common plus extra dividends of $2 in 1948 and 1949. Between 1940 and 1949 the Company reinvested

$107.98 per share of common plus an unconsolidated amount. Demands for added working capital to finance military volumes, inflated costs of replacement of all kinds of equipment and facilities, and debt reduction necessitated the retention.

During 1949 the price of Santa Fe stock was lower than the amount that had been plowed back during the preceding nine years. Earnings seemed high, but the impression is misleading. The common-stock holders of the Santa Fe have reinvested through surplus an amount equal to 2½ times the outstanding stock. If earnings are to be related to common-stock investment to arrive at a per cent, a division of 3¼ should be used. The conservative dividend policy should enable the company to continue strong during leaner years. The reduction of debt and modernization of facilities will reduce the stress and strain to which the Company may be subjected.

Taxes Are Higher

A survey of the annual reports of the Santa Fe would be incomplete if it did not call attention to the striking increase in taxes paid by the Company into federal, state, and local coffers. No item of expense, not even those incidental to government regulation, has shown such a pronounced upward trend. Between 1869 and 1896 the Santa Fe paid a total of $10,940,708 in all taxes. The average Federal Income and Excess Profits tax accruals per month during the first six months of 1943 were $10,754,333. The latter represent only two of the many taxes levied against the Company and its service. If the Santa Fe of the early period had been of insignificant size the contrast would have been less astounding, but the Company had hundreds of millions of assets at work then. The portion of revenue going to governmental agencies grew so large that officials wondered whether any correlation existed between taxes and the cost of government services rendered to the railroads or ability-to-pay. Officials began to feel that the Santa Fe like other large corporations is an expedient medium for channelizing revenues or a branch of the Treasury. The following table should be considered in the light of the fact that earnings on invested capital in the Santa Fe were approximately 4.9 per cent between 1896 and 1920; slightly over 6 per cent during the 'twenties; 2⅓ per cent in the next decade; and about 4¾ per cent from 1940 to 1942 inclusive.

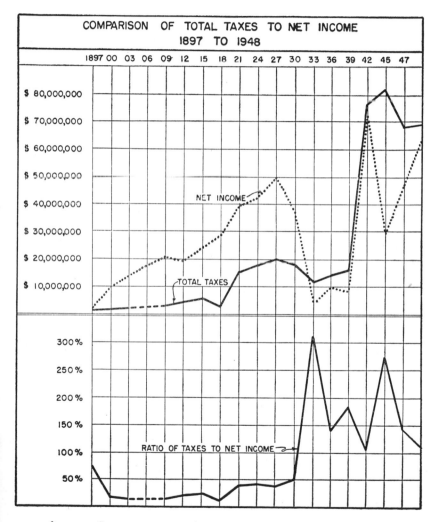

COMPARISON OF TOTAL TAXES TO NET INCOME
1897 TO 1948

Note:* Total taxes" does not include minor tax accruals.
Year ending June 30, 1897 to 1915

In early years the relative amount taken by government units was low. The only exception was in the lean years following receivership. Until 1930 taxes remained low, although officials thought the Company carried a heavy burden. After 1930 taxes were large whether the Company prospered or not. In 1933 the ratio of taxes to net corporate income was 308 per cent, in 1942 104 per cent, in 1945 277 per cent, in 1947 143 per cent, in 1948 110 per cent, and in 1949 123 per cent. Put in another way, the levy in 1942 was $31.42 per share of common stock, in 1945 $33.63 per share, in 1947 $28.05 per share, and in 1948 $28.47. The 1947 total of taxes took 15 cents of every dollar of operating revenue received by the Company. Perhaps an even better idea of the rise in taxes may be had by a study of the figures for 1918 and 1941. These war years are comparable, for net corporate income was substantially the same.

Year	Net Corporate Income	Taxes
1918	$28,348,433	$ 3,061,599
1941	30,236,581	27,626,429

Imposts had increased 902 per cent. Of greater concern to stockholders than what had taken place in the past was the likelihood of a projection of the trend. In 1943, for example, the ratio was more than double the previous year. The percentage of war profits which accrued to the Company was small, and a majority of normal profits was siphoned off into public treasuries.

Ownership of the Santa Fe

Material has not been assembled to present a current picture of the stockholders who are concerned with the ominous direction taken by taxation. The effects are far-reaching. In 1949 the Santa Fe had 62,144 stockholders, not to mention the greater number whose investment in insurance, investment trusts, and other organizations give an indirect interest. A survey made in 1926 gives some idea of the current spread of the financial stakes. A total of 60,943 stockholders resided in every state in the union, the District of Columbia, the Canal Zone, Hawaii, the Philippines, Puerto Rico, and thirty-nine foreign countries. Less than 5 per cent of the stock was held abroad, and this was largely repatriated during World War II. More than half of the individuals owning stock were women, 30,083 as compared with 25,939 men. In 1940 a similar condition existed, with 23,429 women owning 30 shares each, and 17,450 men owning 46 shares each. Fiduciaries, estates, insurance companies, educational and scientific institutions, hospitals, churches, and banks held 34 per cent of the stock in 1926. The largest single block was held by an educational institution which owned 26,100 shares or ¾ per cent of the total outstanding. The individual with the largest block was a woman who held 16,405 shares.

The bonds of the Santa Fe have never had as many primary holders, but the numbers indirectly dependent surpass estimate. Major holdings are by insurance companies, trusts, and various endowed organizations. The whole of one equipment series of $13,800,000 was purchased by a single insurance company. Every policyholder, therefore, became dependent in a limited degree on the fortunes of the Santa Fe.

SUBSIDIARIES AND SIMPLIFICATION

Ownership of securities of the Santa Fe has meant more than investment in an operating company. The Santa Fe is also a holding company of major proportions, having numerous subsidiaries on various levels. Since the ownership in subsidiaries has been complete, the motives for creation have been for purposes other than minimizing investment to maximize control over assets in the fashion of public utilities prior to 1935. Various reasons account for the multitude of subsidiaries: the strictures of after-acquired property clauses and other features of bond covenants; state laws requiring local incorporation of railroads; Interstate Commerce Commission regulations requiring separation of certain carrier and noncarrier activities; and other special qualifying considerations. At the beginning of 1940 the Santa Fe family included ninety-eight corporations. Twenty-four of these were inactive but wholly owned proprietary railroad companies. Their lines were leased and operated by the Atchison, Topeka and Santa Fe Railway. Steps were taken during the next two years to eliminate many of them in order to simplify the corporate structure. The application of depreciation accounting on roadway property other than track and the growing complexity of governmental reports and intercorporate taxation made a change imperative. Sixteen were dissolved during 1941 and 1942 and their assets taken over by the parent. Another fourteen transferred their assets in December, 1948, and were scheduled for dissolution in 1949.

The Gulf, Colorado and Santa Fe is the largest operating direct subsidiary of the Santa Fe proper. Second in size among the operating subsidiaries is the wholly owned Panhandle and Santa Fe Railway.

Two companies are jointly owned with other railroads but operated as separate business units. These are the Sunset Railway Company and the Central California Traction Company.

The motor carrier operations were for many years under Santa Fe affiliates, the Santa Fe Transportation Company of California, and the Santa Fe Transportation Company of Delaware. Authorizations of the extension of lines led officials to enter into a consolidation plan with independent companies. Certain physical properties and all business operating rights of the Santa Fe Trail Transportation Company were transferred in 1947 to the newly organized Transcontinental Bus System. This enterprise embraced the resources of the Continental Bus System, the Dixie Motor Coach Corporation, and the Santa Fe Trailway interest in the Southern Kansas Greyhound Lines. The Santa Fe received 39.1 per cent of the stock in the Transcontinental Bus System, plus $2,647,940 in par of fifteen-year 4 per cent Sinking Fund Debentures of the new company. The trucking operations of the Santa Fe Trail Transportation Company were not transferred, nor were the properties and rights of the Santa Fe Transportation Company in California which were used for the coördinated truck business and railroad services.

The noncarrier or nonrailroad operations of the Santa Fe are conducted by subsidiaries, the majority of which are owned by a holding company of the Santa Fe known as the Western Improvement Company. The scale of noncarrier operations is indicated by total consolidated assets of $104,781,319 at the close of 1949. The consolidated profit of all the subsidiaries in 1949 was $7,729,478. Profits from oil operations accounted for the showing. The leading noncarrier subsidiaries are the Central Manufacturing District Incorporated of Los Angeles, Chanslor-Canfield Midway Oil Company, the Cherokee and Pittsburg Coal and Mining Company, Coline Gasoline Corporation, Los Angeles Union Stockyards Company, Oil Development Company of Texas, the Oklahoma Land and Improvement Company, Santa Fe Land Improvement Company, Santa Fe Pacific Railroad Company, Santa Fe Trail Transportation Company, Santa Fe Transportation Company of California, the Union Passenger Depot Company of Galveston, Santa Fe Tie and Lumber Preserving Company, and Terminal Building Corporation of Texas. The Santa Fe Transportation Company of Delaware and the Santa Barbara Tie and Pole Company were dissolved late in 1947. Operations of Santa Fe Skyway, Inc., were discontinued in 1948.

The remainder of the complex corporate structure is made up of jointly owned allied companies. These are terminal and switching corporations, such as the Kansas City Terminal Railway Company, the Belt Railway of Chicago, the El Paso Union Passenger Depot, and the Denver Market and Produce Terminal, Inc.

While the trend is toward simplification of the financial structure, there are practical limits to which the process can be carried. A corporation with nearly one and one-half billion dollars in assets can never be reduced to the simplicity of a corner grocery even in the absence of the features peculiar to railroads which make for complexity.

Although the sketch of the financial evolution of the Santa Fe has emphasized the low returns made by the Company over the years, historical perspective reveals the Company as a leader in its industry. The Class I lines which have a comparable record can be counted without the use of a second hand. Years of adversity have touched lightly. Today the Company is in the best financial condition in its history, though its officials may well wonder whether Uncle Sam or the stockholders will get the future rewards.

XIII
Steel Trails to Santa Fe

The Santa Fe is the best thing that ever happened to Emporia. It is one of the best things that ever happened to Kansas. It is easily one of the best things that ever happened to this land. . . .
William Allen White in an expansive mood.

Holliday's Vision

THE LONGER THE PERIOD of incubation, the larger the bird. Perhaps this explains why the Santa Fe came to be the longest railroad in the Nation. Cyrus K. Holliday conceived the venture soon after arrival in Kansas in 1854. Almost five years elapsed before chartering, and nine more years before the first spade of dirt was lifted. When the enterprise finally was born, it grew rapidly and came to be all its sponsors had dreamed and more. Time has stamped Holliday as the most competent seer of his generation in Kansas, yet even his great insight into the future fell short of the actuality. Holliday, to be sure, predicted that the time would come when his project would touch Lake Michigan, the Gulf, Santa Fe, and the Pacific. He spoke, too, of great agricultural and industrial development. But all of his dreams seemed confined to a single-track railway with few branches, employing techniques not unlike those of his day. Holliday, however, envisaged most of what was to materialize in his long life span. Others had to predict the accomplishments of decades after 1900. No one assumed the role of prophet, but remarkable results came forth without advance notice. The only premonition grew from the association that came to exist in people's minds between the Santa Fe and periodic unveiling of something new, different, and better.

The history of the Santa Fe has been a cross section in the development of American business. The Company had its ups and downs, its good and its bad management; but, on the whole, the record is a story of enviable achievement of commendable ends.

The Santa Fe was built upon the assumption that the Great American Desert was a myth and that the West was capable of nurturing a flourishing economy. The Company was presumed to be an essential member of the combination necessary to effect the change. The idea of financing a railroad in an area where red men still wielded their tomahawks was not exactly magnetic in its attraction for investment capital. The West was new and could not finance the project. Hence, resort was made to eastern and foreign capitalists. The money was not secured readily and the extractive process was long and filled with disappointments. A sizable land grant helped a little, but an option to buy a smaller amount of well-located land was more significant at the outset. Early construction was boldly undertaken on a shoestring. The integrity of those in charge of construction was of the highest, and they built the best line which the limited resources and techniques permitted. Under A. A. Robinson, dollars were stretched to the limit of their elasticity.

DEVELOPMENT OF THE COMPANY

Though early financial operations were plagued by the lack of adequate working capital, strength came as traffic increased. By 1880 the Santa Fe had vindicated the judgment of its supporters. Late in the decade the Company became embroiled in competitive building which brought lines into being before their time. Other adverse factors conspired to exert a weakening influence. In the middle of the stream drivers were changed with disastrous consequences. The new officials attempted to conceal their troubles without success. The enterprise sank but was resuscitated by new leaders under Edward P. Ripley. From 1896 the Company moved steadily ahead in every phase. Finances were securely bound to conservative courses. New lines were acquired only when ample justification was present. Old lines were improved in every manner that careful research recommended. The equipment was raised to the most advanced technology. Millions of dollars were expended in betterments of a type not evident to outsiders. The greatest improvements were made at a time when the least progress seemed to be made. Streamlined service had to be preceded by years and millions. When the first of the great fleet was delivered the roadway and personnel were ready.

The labor relations of the Santa Fe have been above par. Difficulties have been few and the degree of loyalty and coöperation all that could be desired. The advent of the Government into the delicate relations has had its merits but it has also had its demerits. But the nationalizing influences have not entirely dimmed the spirit which distinguishes a Santa Fe man from all others.

As a result of acquisition of land grants and purchases, the Santa Fe from the first was in the real-estate business on a large scale. Disposal of agricultural land was pressed in order to establish settlers and enlarge the flow of traffic. Buyers were offered generous terms and aided in farming operations through diverse programs of the Company. The ultimate effect on earnings was all that could be desired. The net relations with the Government were somewhat different. The actual amount realized from the sale of the land amounted to much less than the ever growing rate discounts given to Uncle Sam. Final judgment on the equity of the entire transaction is difficult. The land aid was a powerful facilitating factor in enabling early financing, although not as important as is generally believed. The concessions and the balance went against the Company. Relief came in 1945, when land-grant rates were eliminated.

The long association of Fred Harvey with the Santa Fe is unique in the history of railroading. Other railroads have sublet meal service but none have had such an illustrious contractor. Meals by Fred Harvey have long been renowned the world over. Harvey Houses have played an important part in providing the good things in life for those who lived or visited in the empire of the Santa Fe. Fred Harvey and his service laid the basis for much of the folklore and romance of the taming of the West. More important today, Fred Harvey is one of the most powerful advertising media at the command of the Santa Fe.

THE EMPIRE TODAY

Ascertainment of the contribution which the Santa Fe has made to the development of its territory and the Nation has many imponderables. The problem is not unlike the allocation of costs and responsibility in cutting a tree. Did the man or the axe contribute more, and precisely how much more? Obviously a substitution could be made for either the man or the axe, but would the results have been equally good? If the tree were already cut, no substitution could be made for a repeat performance. In the case of the Santa Fe no controlled test can be made substituting other railroads headed by different men. Judgment on the Company has to be based on what has been done. What might have been done poses many "ifs."

An area rich in minerals and soil fertility with a moderate climate needs only transportation and people of skill and industry to make a prosperous economy. Advanced technology, sound currencies, and political stability facilitate development. In the course of time great commercial cities will develop and manufacturing will thrive. Regional specialization will emerge as surely as individual specialization. Standards of living will rise as improved methods enable more economical use of human and physical resources. But this is possible only if all of the fundamental factors are present. Each is essential to the whole framework.

The Middle West and the Southwest had few rivers suitable for navigation. Distances were great and canals impossible. The prairie schooner was at best a slow and costly mode of conveyance. Only railroads could transform a prairie trail into a thoroughfare to serve millions, not hundreds.

Those at the helm of the profit-seeking Santa Fe were fully cognizant of the inseparability of the fortunes of the Company and the economic development of the area. Consequently their land program called for the sale of family-sized farms rather than ranches where large-scale agriculture would have prevailed. Thousands of settlers were attracted. Whether they located on the land grant or beside it was relatively unimportant. The significant thing was that they came to the vicinity. The bases for commerce and industry followed. Towns were optimistically laid out. Some lived and some died. Among those that lived were the destined cities of today, populated by thousands who know not the why or whence of their metropolis. The vital meaning of transportation became lost on the minds of many because the system of business life became complicated. Actually the cities became progressively more dependent than ever as transportation led the way to economies of specialization; transportation is more important in our modern days than it was when the pioneers longed for things they could not produce. The whole mechanism of the Nation has been built upon a network over which goods flow swiftly and economically.

What gave farms their value was the accessibility to distant markets where produce could be sold for more than the cost of production. In 1945 the value of farm property in nine states served by the Santa Fe amounted to $16,505,669,000, or slightly more than one-third the total in the United States. The gross farm income in the nine states was also one-third. Gross receipts from farm marketings in 1947 were $9,915,000,000 as compared with a national total of $30,175,000,000. Not all of the farms in the nine states were served by the Santa Fe; other railroads shared in coverage. But the statistics represent in crude fashion the enormous changes wrought in the area since the origin of the Company. King Cotton, for example, moved his throne westward from the Black Belt into Texas, which produces from 20 to 30 per cent of the cotton of the Nation. California began to outdistance regions long devoted to the fiber. Oklahoma was another leader. Arizona and New Mexico cotton grew so luxuriantly that the pickers no longer had to stoop—so the story goes.

The span of Santa Fe existence saw Kansas lead the nation in the quality and quantity of wheat. The types and strains which gave the state its preëminent position were introduced by Mennonites who had been induced to migrate from Russia to the lands of the Santa Fe. Seven states traversed by the Santa Fe produced 458,851,000 bushels in 1945 out of a national yield of 1,155,715,000. The breadbasket of the Nation moved to the Middle West.

The corn acreage and yield were not as dominant in the Santa Fe states, but the area was more than self-supporting. Approximately one-fourth of all production in 1946 was centered there. Iowa, Louisiana, and Nebraska are not included in the estimate because of the limited mileage in those states.

Santa Fe states were heavy producers of sorghums, millet, rice, rye, barley, soybeans, hay, sugar beets, and other minor crops that nevertheless yielded much tonnage.

When T. J. Peter, the first builder of the Santa Fe, reasoned that a territory which would support so many buffaloes was a good place to build a railroad, his ideas were sound. The same fertility and sunshine that indirectly nourished millions of buffalo supported even larger numbers of domestic cattle. According to recent estimates of the Department of Agriculture there were 28,147,000 head of cattle in the nine Santa Fe states. This was over one-third the national total. Texas was the great breeding ground. Many of the states concentrated on feeders for shipment to corn areas for finishing.

The density of hog and sheep population per capita indicates that Santa Fe states are great exporters. Goat population had attained mammoth proportions in Texas, Arizona, and New Mexico. In 1940 Texas had 3,599,000 goats.

Probably no industry has thrived like the fruit and vegetable industry in the Santa Fe empire. California has been the salad and fruit bowl of the country. Figs, oranges, lemons, grapefruit, dates, carrots, beans, cabbage, lettuce, grapes, berries, apricots, prunes, and countless other good things of life are grown in profuse abundance far removed from the dining tables on which they will be served. The Santa Fe provides a direct route to Chicago, where a portion of the cargo may be shifted to other lines for movement eastward. Arizona and New Mexico enjoy a climate also conducive to the industry. More recently Texas has come to the fore in production of vegetables and citrus fruits. Although the Santa Fe does not originate much of the business in that state, a heavy tonnage is interchanged.

From the date of the first surveys of the route for the Santa Fe, glowing accounts were given of the mineral wealth ready for the taking. The predictions are being realized. In 1939 the nine major Santa Fe states accounted for $1,994,000,000 in mineral products or 47 per cent of the national output. The volume in 1939 in the nine states exceeded the total of the United States in 1910. The list of mineral products in the area covers a wide range. Partial listing is not representative, but the minerals include chromite, copper, nickel, salt, lead, tin, asbestos, sulphur, potash, and silver. Coal production is heavy, and oil extraction the greatest in the world. Over 80 per cent of the crude petroleum withdrawn in 1940 in the United States came from Illinois, Kansas, Oklahoma, Texas, and California. Although pipelines have cut into tonnage, the oil industry furnishes traffic in many forms.

Manufacturing runs into the billions of dollars in four Santa Fe states. Since it is relatively young, its output has not cornered the national volume. Large portions of the area will never become industrialized in the manner of the East, but will achieve great progress. Texas and California have made notable strides. Although operating revenues of the Santa Fe for many years did not keep pace with the rising Federal Reserve index of industrial activity, an improved relationship has recently been shown.

Another index of the position of the Santa Fe states in the national economy is the volume of wholesale trade. In 1939 over 26 per cent ($14,629,000,000) of the wholesale business was transacted in states that had contributed only a negligible per cent seventy-five years before.

THEY MADE EACH OTHER

What has been the part of the Santa Fe in these statistics? No precise figures can be given, but the billions of ton and passenger miles rolled up since 1869 have been a sizable fraction of what has come to pass in the Middle West and Southwest. There is scarcely a building, machine, animal, or person whose existence was not profoundly affected by the Company. The pattern of human and economic life is woven of many strands, and transportation seems to affect most of them. The fractions of influence yielded in other parts of the Nation and the world probably diminish with distance like waves in the concentric circles around a spot where a pebble disappears into a quiet pool.

Of no little importance has been the effect of the Company on the millions who have looked to it for a portion of their income in the form of wages, interest, or dividends. Other millions have seen the products shaped with their hands, purchased and put into use by the Railroad. Still more have traveled on the Plug or the Super-Chief for business and pleasure. Thousands of local governmental units have looked to the Santa Fe as a sure source of prompt payment of a portion of local levies. Indeed, the Company paid a portion of its taxes in one state a year in advance because the state treasury was devoid of funds.

An enterprise as deep-rooted as a railroad and as large as the Santa Fe performs so many services that the ramifications extend over every phase of the lives of millions. Today, the Santa Fe is the longest privately owned line in the world, operating over 13,000 miles. Its rank in assets is occasionally as high as third and not lower than fifth. Few railroads can match it in financial strength, the loyalty of its employees, and the good will of its clientele.

SIGNS AHEAD

The future of the Santa Fe is partly what Company officials make it, partly what governmental officials make it, and partly what the Middle West and Southwest make it. Most of the factors evident today are promising. Business should hold up for many of the same reasons that it did after World War I. There will be increased competition, but the Santa Fe should be able to make a creditable showing. Airlines will take over increasing amounts of the first-class passenger business. The Company is rather vulnerable in that its average distance per passenger is great. Streamlined trains, however, will demonstrate surprising retentive powers. Busses will command a share of passenger traffic, but the expansion of Santa Fe bus operations and integration with rail service may prevent marked weakness due to this cause. Inroads of automobiles will continue.

The development or lack of development of a sound national transportation policy among the rival forms will dominate developments in freight. The Santa Fe shares the risk of the industry. If the proper province of pipelines, airlines, waterways, motor carriers, and railroads is defined through rate and service regulations so that the various forms complement one another rather than compete, the outlook for railroads will be bright. Regardless of whether or not trucks and railroads are given spheres and are unified, the Santa Fe's long hauls render it relatively immune in a competitive struggle and certain of an equitable portion in any division. Even in the absence of conducive national policies the integration of rail and truck operations will continue.

Studies of the problems of the railroad industry call increasing attention to the need for an examination of labor practices. Obvious diseconomies are present, which beg for elimination. Several other developments affect the Santa Fe differently from other railroads. Deep water in the St. Lawrence has long been contemplated and may materialize. Its effects on eastern lines are apparent. On the whole, the Santa Fe would gain. The Company has little to fear from development of interior waterways except the payment of taxes. Scant likelihood exists that the Pecos or the Rattlesnake rivers will ever be made navigable.

The movement to equalize class rates on freight in the three territories into which the United States is divided might have effects on the Company through the relocation of industry. Class rates are lower in the South and appreciably less in the East. Con-

482 STEEL TRAILS TO SANTA FE

siderable pressure developed, political and otherwise, to make them uniform. In 1945 the Interstate Commerce Commission did order establishment of uniform class rates. Such equalization might give impetus to industry in the area served by the Santa Fe.

Regardless of what happens to the rates, within reasonable limits, the industrialization of the West will continue. The raw materials are there or are capable of being produced; the swelling population will provide labor, increasing portions of the final demand for the products, and the capital to finance production. The Santa Fe serves some of the most promising industrial areas in the world. Relatively speaking, the Southwest is still undeveloped.

In addition to all of the fundamental factors which promise great tonnage for the Company, there is the record of progressiveness in the Santa Fe which augurs well for the future. Line and equipment will be continually improved. Better methods of service will be discovered and put into practice. The Company of today will become a crudity and subject to the gibes of generations to come.

The signs which point to greater tonnage do not necessarily lead the way to greater profits. Rate adjustments are the inevitable accompaniments to signs of prosperity in the industry. In the past the Santa Fe has been able to net modest amounts in part because so many other lines were operating at a loss. The increased emphasis of the Government on business taxes rather than personal taxes will prove the major drag on income. The residual left for the stockholders will lag far behind operating revenues.

The extraordinarily low funded debt with its modest interest requirements will enable the Santa Fe to withstand tests much more severe than any encountered to date. The Company will have great power of resistance to adversity. Indeed for an organization born of adversity and strengthened on uncertainty, the future should hold no terrors.

Vestiges of the route to old Santa Fe may yet be seen where the feet of horses, oxen, mules, and men and the wheels of heavy-laden wagons laboriously etched the Trail. The inexorable passage of time is gradually erasing the last marks of the once great highway of commerce as "The old order changeth, yielding place to new." But are not steel trails to Santa Fe immeasurably better?

Appendix A

(Quotations from sections 1 and 2 are given on page 26.)

SECTION 3.—The said company are hereby authorized, and shall have the right-of-way upon, and may appropriate to its sole use and control, for the purposes contemplated herein, land, not exceeding one hundred feet in width, thru the entire length of said road, upon such route as may be determined; and, for the purposes of depots, side tracks, cuttings and embankments, for building engine houses and shops or wood and water stations, may take more land, earth or material, as may be necessary for the construction or completion, operation, preserving and maintaining said road.

SECTION 4.—All such lands, materials and privileges, belonging to this Territory, or state hereafter, are hereby granted to such railroad, for the purpose named in the previous section; and may construct such road on or across other railroads, common roads, rivers, or streams which it may intersect in sufficient manner not to materially impair its usefulness.

SECTION 5.—The capital stock of said corporation shall be one million and five hundred thousand dollars, which may be increased, from time to time, to any sum not exceeding the amount expended on account of said road, divided into shares of one hundred dollars each, which shall be deemed personal property, issued and transferred as may be ordered by the directors or laws of said company.

SECTION 6.—All the corporate powers of said company shall be vested in and exercised by a board of directors, and such officers and agents as they may appoint. The board of directors shall consist of thirteen persons, stockholders, three of whom, at least, shall be residents of Kansas, who shall be chosen annually, by the stockholders, each share having one vote by person or proxy, and continue in office until their successors are elected and qualified; vacancies in the board may be filled by a vote of two-thirds of the remaining directors.

SECTION 7.—The president and directors, for the time being, are hereby empowered or their officers or agents, to execute all the power herein granted for the purpose of surveying, locating, constructing and operating said railroad and branches and for transportation of persons, goods and merchandise, and authority of contract and management of the affairs, as may be necessary to carry into effect the intent of this act.

SECTION 8.—The said company shall have power to make, ordain and establish such by-laws, rules and regulations as may be deemed expedient for the objects and interests of the company: Provided, they be not inconsistent with the laws of the United States, or of this Territory. They shall have power to establish such rates for transportation and collect the same,

and matters and things respecting the use of said road, the transportation of persons or property as may be necessary.

SECTION 9.—It may be lawful for said railroad company, their agents or engineers for the purpose of exploring, surveying or locating said road, to enter upon any lands, doing no unnecessary damage, without the consent of the owner, and may acquire by release, donation or otherwise, any lands and may hold the same or convey to others, or use the same in any manner deemed for the interests of the said company.

SECTION 10.—If said company cannot obtain the right-of-way by purchase or otherwise, or if the owners refuse to agree upon terms, or where the owner is unknown, non-resident, idiot or under age, either party may make application to the district where the lands are situated, upon notice posted ten days in some public place, asking the appointment of commissioners to appraise the damage to lands required for the purpose of the road.

SECTION 11.—Upon such application being made to such judge, he shall appoint three disinterested persons to act as commissioners for the appraisal of all such damages, taking into consideration the advantages as well as any injury to the parties interested in such lands; said commissioners shall by public notice, appoint a time and place, and may adjourn, if necessary, for hearing the parties, and proceed to examine the lands, ascertain and determine the damage, if any, and under oath, impartially and justly to appraise the lands necessary for the use of said company and faithfully perform the duty to the best of their judgment and ability. They or a majority of them, shall make up and sign the award to the parties embracing a description of the lands and amount of damages to each, and make a return of their doings to the judge of the district court. The commissioners making such appraisal shall be entitled to pay for their services at the rate of three dollars per day and ordinary traveling expenses, which shall be paid by the said company.

SECTION 12.—If either party feel aggrieved by such appraisal or award, he may appeal within twenty days after such award is made known, by giving notice to that effect to the opposite party, otherwise both parties shall be bound by the award and the amount shall be paid, upon application of the persons entitled to receive the same. In case of the appeal, a bond shall be filed for the costs in the court, to be paid by the party who shall be entitled to pay the same, as determined by the court aforesaid.

SECTION 13.—In case of appeal of disagreement in regard to the damages, the railroad company may occupy, for the purpose of the construction of the road, by giving satisfactory security to the judge of said court for the ultimate payment of the damages so determined.

SECTION 14.—If any person shall carelessly, willfully or maliciously hinder, delay or obstruct the workmen, or the passage of trains, or shall place any obstruction on the tracks, or in any manner injure or destroy any tools, cars or other property of said railroad, or pertaining to it, or aid or abet any persons in the commission of such trespass, all such persons shall forfeit and pay said company, agents or servants, treble the damages, as shall be proved by any court, and shall be liable to indictment and imprisonment for a term not exceeding five years, in the discretion of the court who shall try the same.

SECTION 15.—Said corporation shall, within reasonable time after said road or branches are definitely located, cause a map and profile to be made of the route of said road, and file the same in the office of the Secretary of the Territory.

SECTION 16.—When fifty thousand dollars have been subscribed to the capital stock and ten percentum actually paid to the grantees herein named, and a certificate from the majority of them duly authenticated, filed in the office of the secretary of this Territory, they are authorized to organize the company and open books for further subscription, requiring payments or installments from time to time; and, in case of refusal or neglect on the part of stockholders to make payment as required, the shares of such delinquents may, after thirty days' public notice, be sold at auction, and the surplus, if any, deducting payments and interest, shall be paid to such stockholders.

SECTION 17.—When the citizens of any county or city of this Territory are desirous of subscribing to the stock of said company, the citizens of such city or county are authorized to purchase, subscribe or hold shares, not exceeding one hundred thousand dollars in amount, as shall be determined by the county court or common council making such subscription, in all respects as stock owned by individuals; and such railroad company may dispose of bonds, issued for such stock by said county or council, upon such terms as may be necessary.

SECTION 18.—Subscriptions to the stock of said company may be made in land, in the same manner as in cash, and said company are hereby authorized to hold, purchase and convey the same, as they may deem for their interest.

SECTION 19.—The company are hereby authorized to issue bonds upon their road, or hold and sell the same, in such amounts, upon such terms, above or below par, and at such rates of interest as may be determined, which shall be binding upon the parties interested; provided, however, that said bonds shall not be issued for a less sum than five hundred dollars.

SECTION 20.—This company shall have power to make such contracts and arrangements with other railroads which connect with or intersect the same, as may be mutually agreed upon by the parties, for leasing or running their road, or any part thereof, in connection with roads in other States; and shall be empowered to consolidate their property and stock with each other, such consolidation to take place whenever such companies shall respectively agree upon the terms and conditions; and shall have all the power, privileges and liabilities that they may hold by their separate charters, by filing a copy of such articles of consolidation in the office of the Secretary of this Territory.

Section 21.—This act to take effect and be in force from and after its passage.

A. Larzalere,
Speaker of the House of
Representatives.
C. W. Babcock,
President of the Council.

Approved February 11, 1859.
S. Medary,
Governor.

Appendix B

Copy of the Present Charter of

The Atchison, Topeka and Santa Fe Railway Company

Certificate of Incorporation

OF

THE ATCHISON, TOPEKA AND SANTA FE RAILWAY COMPANY

STATE OF KANSAS, ⎱ ss.
SHAWNEE COUNTY, ⎰

Whereas, The Atchison, Topeka and Santa Fe Railroad Company, a corporation created by an Act of the Territory of Kansas, entitled "An Act incorporating the Atchison and Topeka Railroad Company:" approved February 11, 1859, and existing under the laws of said Territory and of the State of Kansas, did, on the 15th day of October, 1889, execute its certain mortgage or deed of trust to the Union Trust Company of New York, as Trustee, to secure the bonds of said Atchison, Topeka and Santa Fe Railroad Company, issued under and pursuant to said mortgage or deed of trust, and in and by said mortgage or deed of trust, mortgaged and conveyed to said Union Trust Company of New York, as Trustee, all of its railroad constructed in the State of Kansas, running from Atchison on the Missouri River, through Topeka, to a point on the Western boundary of the State of Kansas, being four hundred and seventy and fifty eight hundredths (470.58) miles in length, together with all the appurtenances thereof, including telegraphs and telephones, and all franchises, rights, privileges and immunities, then or thereafter pertaining to said railroad, telegraphs, telephones and other property, or the appurtenances and appendages thereof; and all property, real and personal, of every name and nature whatsoever and wheresoever situated, including all shares of the capital stock and bonds of other corporations, whether then possessed or thereafter acquired by the said Atchison, Topeka and Santa Fe Railroad Company, for the purposes of the construction, equipment, maintenance or operation of the said railroad, telegraphs, telephones and other property, or for use in connection therewith, or with any or all of the same; together with all the revenues, income, profits, benefits and advantages of, or in any way growing out of, any or all of the said above-described property; and also certain stocks and bonds mentioned and described in said mortgage and then owned or thereafter to be acquired by said Atchison, Topeka and Santa Fe Railroad Company; and

Whereas, Thereafter, and on or about the 27th day of August, 1895, the Circuit Court of the United States for the District of Kansas, the same being a court of competent jurisdiction, made and entered a certain judgment or decree foreclosing said mortgage or deed of trust, which judgment or decree was entered in a certain consolidated cause pending in said Court, wherein the Union Trust Company of New York, the Trustee under said mortgage or deed of trust, was a complainant, and said Atchison, Topeka and Santa Fe Railroad Company was a defendant; and

Whereas, The said railroad, properties and franchises, on the tenth day of December, 1895, were duly sold in pursuance of the said judgment or decree of said Court to Edward King, Charles C. Beaman and Victor Morawetz, all of the city of New York, N.Y., and such sale having been duly confirmed by said Court, the said railroad, properties and franchises, in pursuance of said judgment or decree and the orders of said Court made thereon, were conveyed by deed, executed by John B. Johnson, Special Master in Chancery, appointed by said Court in said cause, to the said Edward King, Charles C. Beaman and Victor Morawetz, as joint tenants and not as tenants in common, who thereby acquired title to said railroad, properties and franchises under such sale; and the said purchasers and their associates, successors and assigns, under and by virtue of the laws of the State of Kansas in such case made and provided, did thereby have and acquire and become entitled thereafter to exercise and enjoy, all the rights, privileges, grants, franchises, immunities and advantages in and by said mortgage or deed of trust conveyed, which belonged to and were enjoyed by said Atchison, Topeka and Santa Fe Railroad Company, as far as the same relate and appertain to said railroad, described in and conveyed by said mortgage or deed of trust as above set forth; and

Whereas, The said Edward King, Charles C. Beaman and Victor Morawetz, the said purchasers, for the purpose of organizing a new corporation under and in pursuance of the laws of the State of Kansas, have associated with themselves the following named persons, viz.:

Edward P. Ripley, who is a citizen of the State of Illinois,
    residing at the City of Chicago.

Aldace F. Walker, who is a citizen of the State of Illinois,
    residing at the City of Chicago.

Benjamin P. Cheney, who is a citizen of the State of Massachusetts,
    residing at the City of Dover.

Edward N. Gibbs, who is a citizen of the State of New York,
    residing at the City of New York.

Charles S. Gleed, who is a citizen of the State of Kansas,
    residing at the City of Topeka.

R. Somers Hayes, who is a citizen of the State of New York,
    residing at the City of New York.

George G. Haven, who is a citizen of the State of New York,
    residing at the City of New York.

Cyrus K. Holliday, who is a citizen of the State of Kansas,
    residing at the City of Topeka.

Thomas A. Osborn, who is a citizen of the State of Kansas,
    residing at the City of Topeka.

William Rotch, who is a citizen of the State of Massachusetts,
    residing at the City of Boston.

Edward Wilder, who is a citizen of the State of Kansas,
    residing at the City of Topeka.

Whereas, The said purchasers and their said associates have organized
themselves and do hereby organize themselves as a new corporation as
hereinafter in this certificate set forth:

Now, Therefore, The undersigned, being the said purchasers, and their
associates, do hereby certify and state as follows:

First, The name of the corporation formed by the undersigned is The
Atchison, Topeka and Santa Fe Railway Company.

Second, The purposes for which such corporation is formed are as
follows:

To acquire, construct, own, maintain and operate a railway running
from the City of Atchison on the Missouri River, in the State of Kansas,
through Topeka to a point on the western boundary of the State of Kansas,
through the counties of Atchison, Jefferson, Shawnee, Osage, Lyon, Chase,
Marion, Harvey, Reno, Rice, Barton, Pawnee, Edwards, Ford, Gray,
Finney, Kearney and Hamilton, and a telegraph line in connection with
said railway, together with all the appurtenances thereof, the estimated
length of which railway is four hundred and seventy and fifty eight hundredths (470.58) miles; and also to acquire, own, use and enjoy the railroad and appurtenances, franchises, rights, privileges and immunities,
stocks and bonds, and all other properties acquired by said purchasers at
said sale as above recited.

Third. The place or places where the business of said corporation is to be transacted are in the City of Topeka, in the County of Shawnee, in the State of Kansas, and such other places and cities upon the line of said railway, or any of its branches, or leased, operated or controlled lines, as may from time to time be deemed desirable, and at such points or places where any business may be legally done by it in the exercise and enjoyment of its rights, powers and privileges.

Fourth. The term for which this corporation is to exist is nine hundred and ninety nine (999) years.

Fifth. The number of its directors shall be fifteen, and the names and residences of those who are appointed for the first year are as follows:

Names	Residences
Edward P. Ripley	Chicago, Ill.
Aldace F. Walker	Chicago, Ill.
Benjamin P. Cheney	Dover, Mass.
Edward N. Gibbs	New York, N.Y.
Charles S. Gleed	Topeka, Kans.
George G. Haven	New York, N.Y.
R. Somers Hayes	New York, N.Y.
Cyrus K. Holliday	Topeka, Kans.
Victor Morawetz	New York, N.Y.
Thomas A. Osborn	Topeka, Kans.
William Rotch	Boston, Mass.
Edward Wilder	Topeka, Kans.
Robert Fleming	London, Eng.
John Luden	Amsterdam, Holland
and Herman Kobbe	New York, N.Y.

Sixth. The amount of capital stock of such corporation shall be two hundred and thirty-three million, four hundred and eighty-six thousand ($233,486,000) dollars, and the same shall be divided into two million three hundred and thirty-four thousand eight hundred and sixty (2,334,860) shares of the par value of one hundred ($100) dollars each.

Of such capital stock one million, three hundred and fourteen thousand eight hundred and sixty (1,314,860) shares amounting in the aggregate to one hundred and thirty-one million, four hundred and eighty-six thousand ($131,486,000) dollars, shall be five per cent, non-cumulative preferred stock and

One million, twenty thousand (1,020,000) shares, amounting in the aggregate to one hundred and two million ($102,000,000) dollars shall be common stock.

The holders of the preferred stock shall be entitled to noncumulative dividends in each and every fiscal year beginning after the 30th day of June, 1896, at such rate, not exceeding five per centum per annum, as shall be declared by the Board of Directors of such corporation, in preference and priority to any payment in or for such fiscal year of any dividend on the common stock or on any other stock of said company, but only from undivided net profits when and as determined by the said Board; and in case of dissolution or liquidation of said corporation, the holders of the preferred stock shall be entitled to receive the par amount of their stock out of the assets of such corporation in priority to the common stock.

No mortgage, other than a mortgage to secure an issue of seventeen million dollars of Four Per Cent, Thirty-Year Prior Lien Gold Bonds and an issue of one hundred and sixty-five million four hundred and ninety thousand five hundred dollars of General Mortgage Four Per Cent One Hundred Year Gold Bonds, and another mortgage to secure an issue of not to exceed seventy-one million seven hundred and twenty-eight thousand dollars of Four Per Cent One Hundred Year Adjustment Bonds (bearing interest payable only out of surplus net earnings if earned), shall be executed by the corporation hereby formed, nor shall the amount of the Preferred Stock of said corporation be increased, unless the execution of such mortgage or such increase of the Preferred Stock shall have received the consent of the holders of a majority of the whole amount of the Preferred Stock which shall at the time be outstanding, given at a meeting of the stockholders called for that purpose and the consent of the holders of a majority of such part of the common stock as shall be represented at such meeting.

In Testimony Whereof, We have hereunto subscribed our names this 12th day of December, 1895.

References

Chapter I

1. *A Report on the Impracticability of Building a Railroad from the Mississippi River to the Pacific Ocean,* Dissenting Opinion of the Select Committee Appointed February 21, 1856.
2. An authentic and monumental account of the trials and tribulations of New Mexico may be found in Ralph Emerson Twitchell's *The Leading Facts of New Mexican History,* Cedar Rapids, Iowa, 1922.
3. No finer account of the Santa Fe Trail has ever been penned than that of Dr. Josiah Gregg. See his *Commerce of the Prairies,* New York, 1844, I, 23.
4. Francis Parkman, *The Oregon Trail,* Boston, 1896, p. 448.
5. Gregg, *op. cit.,* I, 110-11.
6. *Ibid.,* II, 160.
7. Twitchell, *op. cit.,* p. 133.
8. R. L. Duffus, *The Santa Fe Trail,* New York, 1930.
9. F. W. Giles, *Thirty Years in Topeka,* 1886, p. 268.

Chapter II

1. Charles P. Deatherage, *Early History of Greater Kansas City,* Kansas City, Missouri, 1927, p. 620.
2. 12 U.S. Statutes, p. 772.
3. *Congressional Globe,* 1st Session, 39th Congress, June 20, 1866, LXXII, 3278.
4. Letter of C. K. Holliday dated September 26, 1868. Published in the Topeka *State Record,* October 7, 1868.
5. *Ibid.*

Chapter III

1. F. W. Giles, *Thirty Years in Topeka,* pp. 307-08.
2. Wm. Hinckley, *The Early Days of the Santa Fe: Details of Interesting Events Truthfully and Accurately Recorded,* Topeka, n. d., pp. 30-31.
3. *Ibid.,* p. 23.
4. Letter of A. A. Robinson to W. B. Strong, Las Vegas, New Mexico, March 15, 1881.
5. Allan Kearney, "A Long Long Trail," *Santa Fe Magazine,* May, 1932, pp. 41-42. "Allan Kearney" was a *nom de plume* for Henry Allen Tice.
6. Letter of A. A. Robinson to W. B. Strong and Transmittal of Report of Wm. R. Morley on the Most Feasible Route West, November 28, 1878.
7. *Southwest Pacific Rail-Road Co.—Atlantic and Pacific Rail-Road Co.,* New York, 1867.
8. L. A. Ingersoll, *Century Annals of San Bernardino County 1769 to 1904,* p. 257.
9. Report of Fred T. Perris to J. N. Victor, March 23, 1884.
10. Letter of Braxton Bragg to Col. J. P. Fresenius, Galveston, August 14, 1874.
11. Letter of Norris L. Gage to A. A. Robinson, Topeka, Kansas, August 2, 1886.

Chapter IV

1. George L. Anderson, *General William J. Palmer: A Decade of Colorado Railroad Building 1870-1880,* Colorado College Publication, Colorado Springs, 1936, p. 69. Professor Anderson carefully separated the chaff from the wheat and has given a remarkably accurate account of the conflict. There are two other resumés upon which reliance has been justifiably placed. Glenn D. Bradley devoted three chapters of his book *The Story of the Santa Fe* to narration of hostilities. In spite of errors of detail, Bradley's work is substantially correct. J. M. Meade is responsible for the other authoritative record. He once compiled a detailed history of Santa Fe construction. His own role as a builder of the Santa Fe gave him first-hand knowledge of much of the subject matter. Meade's history was never polished for publication. The rough draft contained an excellent history of the D&RG War. Friends with legal training wrote the section dealing with the struggle.

2. *Ibid.*, pp. 83-84.
3. *Ibid.*, pp. 88-89.
4. J. M. Meade, *The D. & R. G. War with the Santa Fe,* unpublished and undated manuscript prepared about 1910. The late Joseph Weidel, Valuation Engineer of the Santa Fe and the leading authority on early history of the Company, was convinced that the manuscript was not written by Meade but that it was nevertheless the most accurate account of the War.
5. Anderson, *op. cit.*, p. 99.
6. *Ibid.*, pp. 102-03.
7. *Ibid.*, pp. 106-07.
8. Bradley, *op. cit.*, p. 189.
9. Meade, *op. cit.*
10. *The Valley Road—A History of the Traffic Association of California, the League of Progress, the North American Navigation Company, the Merchants' Shipping Association, and the San Francisco and San Joaquin Valley Railway,* San Francisco, 1896, p. 6.
11. *Ibid.*, p. 12.
12. Stuart Daggett, *Chapters on the History of the Southern Pacific,* New York, 1922, p. 328.
13. San Francisco *Call,* October 6, 1896.

Chapter V

1. Lt. Col. Richard I. Dodge, *The Plains of the Great West,* New York, 1877, p. 133.
2. S. R. Wood, *Locomotives of the Atchison, Topeka and Santa Fe System,* Boston, 1939, p. 9.
3. L. A. Ingersoll, *Century Annals of San Bernardino County 1769 to 1904,* p. 266.

Chapter VI

1. I. C. C. Valuation Reports, XXVII, 361.
2. *Commercial and Financial Chronicle,* December 20, 1873.
3. *Commercial and Financial Chronicle,* April 18, 1885.
4. I. C. C., *op. cit.*, p. 364.
5. *Commercial and Financial Chronicle,* December 16, 1893.

Chapter VII

1. C. Henry Smith, *The Story of the Mennonites,* Berne, Indiana, 1941, p. 287.
2. *Ibid.*, p. 402.

Chapter IX

1. *First Annual Report of the Bureau of Labor and Industrial Statistics,* Topeka, Kansas, January 1, 1886, p. 262.
2. *Eighth Annual Report of the Bureau of Labor and Industrial Statistics,* Topeka, Kansas, May 30, 1893.
3. Topeka *Journal,* June 14, 1904.
4. H. D. Wold, *The Railroad Labor Board,* Chicago, Illinois, 1927, p. 221.
5. *Ibid.*, p. 222.
6. Paul H. Douglas, *Real Wages in the United States 1890 to 1926,* New York, 1930, p. 325.

Chapter X

1. Lucile Anderson, "Railroad Transportation through Prescott—the Prescott and Arizona Central Railroad," *Arizona Historical Review,* July, 1936, p. 62.
2. *Arizona Weekly: Journal Miner,* June 17, 1891.
3. "The Texico-Coleman Cutoff," *Santa Fe Magazine,* August, 1909, p. 103. Quoted from a current but undated article in the St. Louis *Times.*
4. Letter of W. B. Storey to S. D. Myres, July 31, 1909.
5. A. E. Stilwell, *Cannibals of Finance,* Chicago, 1912.

Index